JAMES L. STEFFENSEN, ~~~~~~~~~~~~~~~.A. in the Final Honours School of English at Oxford. While there he directed and produced plays for the Experimental Theater Club and wrote sketches and lyrics for reviews at the Edinburgh Festival. He is a former William Morris Fellow in Playwrighting and David Sarnoff Fellow in Dramatic Arts at the Yale Drama School. GREAT SCENES FROM THE WORLD THEATER is one result of his work in workshop groups for young actors and playwrights.

GREAT SCENES FROM THE WORLD THEATER
VOLUME II

Edited by
James L. Steffensen, Jr.

Wesleyan University

 A BARD BOOK/PUBLISHED BY AVON BOOKS

AVON BOOKS
A division of
The Hearst Corporation
959 Eighth Avenue
New York, New York

Library of Congress Catalog Card Number: 65-2481
ISBN: 0-380-01033-X

First Printing (Bard Edition), September, 1972
Third Printing

BARD TRADEMARK REG. U.S. PAT. OFF. AND
FOREIGN COUNTRIES, REGISTERED TRADEMARK—
HECHO EN CHICAGO, U.S.A.

Printed in the U.S.A.

author's agent, Janet Roberts, c/o Ashley Famous Agency, Inc., 1301 Avenue of the Americas, New York, N. Y. 10019 (Bridget Aschenberg—foreign).
Reprinted by permission of Farrar, Straus, & Giroux.

From CANDIDA by George Bernard Shaw. Reprinted by permission of The Society of Authors, on behalf of the Bernard Shaw Estate.

From THE DANCE OF DEATH by August Strindberg, translated by Elizabeth Sprigge.

From A DAY BY THE SEA by N. C. Hunter. Application for permission to give stage performances of A DAY BY THE SEA, throughout the world, must be made to the publishers of the play ENGLISH THEATRE GUILD LTD., Ascot House, 52 Dean Street, London, W1V 6BJ, England.
Reprinted by permission of English Theatre Guild Ltd.

From ENTERTAINING MR. SLOANE by Joe Orton. Reprinted by permission of Grove Press, Inc. Copyright © 1964 by Joe Orton.

From GHOSTS by Henrik Ibsen, translated by Kai Jurgensen and Robert Schenkkan. Published by arrangement with the translators. All queries concerning performing rights should be addressed to Mr. Kai Jurgensen, Department of Dramatic Art, University of North Carolina, Chapel Hill, North Carolina.
Copyright © 1965 by Kai Jurgensen and Robert Schenkkan. Copyright © 1965 by Avon Book Division, The Hearst Corporation.

From A HATFUL OF RAIN by Michael V. Gazzo. Copyright © 1956 by Michael V. Gazzo. Reprinted by permission of Random House, Inc.
CAUTION: Professionals and amateurs are hereby warned that A HATFUL OF RAIN, being fully protected under the copyright laws of the United States of America, the British Empire, including the Dominion of Canada, and all other countries of the Copyright Union, is subject to royalty. All rights, including professional, amateur, motion pictures, recitation, public reading, radio and television broadcasting and the rights of translation in foreign languages are strictly reserved. Particular emphasis is laid upon the question of readings, permission for which must be secured from the author's agent in writing. All inquiries should be addressed to the author's agent, Audrey Wood, M.C.A. Artists Ltd., 598 Madison Avenue, New York, N. Y.

From HIPPOLYTUS by Euripides, translated by Kenneth Cavander. Copyright © 1962 by Kenneth Cavander. Application to publish or perform his version of this play should be made to Margaret Ramsay, Ltd., 14 Goodwin's Court, London W.C. 2, England. No publication or performance may take place unless a license has been obtained.
Reprinted by special arrangement with Kenneth Cavander.

From THE HOLE by N. F. Simpson. © 1958 by N. F. Simpson. CAUTION: Professionals and amateurs are hereby warned that THE HOLE, being fully protected under the copyright laws of the United States of America, the British Empire, including the Dominion of Canada, and all other countries of the Copyright Union, is subject to a royalty. All rights, including professional, amateur, motion pictures, recitation, public reading, radio and television broadcasting and rights of translation in foreign languages are strictly reserved. Amateurs may give stage production of this play upon payment of a royalty of Ten Dollars for each performance one week before the play is to be given to Samuel French, Inc., at 25 West 45th St., New York, N. Y. 10036, Or 7623 Sunset Blvd., Hollywood, Calif., or if in Canada to Samuel French (Canada) Ltd., at 27 Grenville St., Toronto, Ont.
Reprinted by permission of Samuel French, Inc.

From THE LARK by Jean Anouilh, translated by Christopher Fry. Copyright © 1955 by Christopher Fry. Reprinted by permission of Oxford University Press, Inc. All rights reserved.

From LOOK BACK IN ANGER by John Osborne. Reprinted by permission of S. G. Phillips, Inc. from LOOK BACK IN ANGER by John Osborne. Copyright © 1957 by S. G. Phillips, Inc.

From THE MELTING POT by David Thompson. Copyright © 1971 by David Thompson. Permission for publication, performance, recitation, motion pictures, radio and television broadcasting and rights of translation must be obtained from the author, David Thompson, 170 Cross St., Middletown, Connecticut.
Published by special arrangement with David Thompson.

From MORE STATELY MANSIONS by Eugene O'Neill. Reprinted by permission of Carlotta Monterey O'Neill and Yale University Press from MORE STATELY MANSIONS, by Eugene O'Neill, pp. 3-5. Copyright © 1964 by Carlotta Monterey O'Neill. All rights are strictly reserved.

From THE NIGHT OF THE IGUANA by Tennessee Williams. Tennessee Williams, THE NIGHT OF THE IGUANA. Copyright © 1961 by Two Rivers Enterprises, Inc.* Reprinted by permission of New Directions Publishing Corporation. *All Rights Reserved.

From OF MICE AND MEN by John Steinbeck. Copyright 1937, copyright © renewed 1965 by John Steinbeck. Reprinted by permission of The Viking Press, Inc.

From ORESTES by Euripides, translated by Kenneth Cavander. Copyright © 1971 by Kenneth Cavander. Application to publish or perform his version of this play should be made to Margaret Ramsay, Ltd., 14 Goodwin's Court, London W. C. 2, England. No publication or performance may take place unless a license has been obtained.
Published by special arrangement with Kenneth Cavander.

to the author's agents: Liebling-Wood, 551 Fifth Avenue, New York City.

Reprinted by permission of New Directions Publishing Company.

From THE SCHOOL FOR WIVES by Jean Baptiste Poquelin de Molière, translated by Richard Wilbur.

From THE SEAGULL by Anton Chekhov, translated by Elizaveta Fen. Reprinted by permission of Penguin Books Ltd.

From THE SHOW-OFF by George Kelly. Copyright, 1922 (As a One-Act Play), by George Edward Kelly; Copyright, 1924 (Three-Act Play Unpublished), by George Kelly; Copyright, 1924, by George Kelly; Copyright, 1949 (In Renewal), by George Edward Kelly; Copyright, 1951 (In Renewal), by George Kelly; Copyright, 1951, (In Renewal), by George Kelly.

CAUTION: Professionals and amateurs are hereby warned that THE SHOW-OFF, being fully protected under the copyright laws of the United States of America, the British Empire, including the Dominion of Canada, and all other countries of the Copyright Union, is subject to a royalty. All rights, including professional, amateur, motion pictures, recitation, public reading, radio and television broadcasting and the rights of translation in foreign languages are strictly reserved. Amateurs may give stage production of this play upon payment of royalty of Fifty Dollars for the first performance and Twenty-Five Dollars for each additional performance one week before the play is to be given to Samuel French, Inc., at 25 West 45th St., New York, N. Y. 10036, or 7623 Sunset Blvd., Hollywood, Calif., or if in Canada to Samuel French (Canada) Ltd., at 27 Grenville St., Toronto, Ont.

Reprinted by permission of Samuel French, Inc.

From THE SILVER CORD by Sidney Howard. Reprinted by permission of Charles Scribner's Sons from *The Silver Cord* by Sidney Howard. Copyright 1926, 1927 Sidney Howard; renewal copyright 1954, 1955 Leopoldine B. D. Howard.

From SWEET BIRD OF YOUTH by Tennessee Williams. Tennessee Williams, SWEET BIRD OF YOUTH. Copyright © 1959 by Two Rivers Enterprises, Inc. All Rights Reserved.

CAUTION: Professionals and amateurs are hereby warned that SWEET BIRD OF YOUTH, being fully protected under the copyright laws of the United States of America, the British Empire, including the Dominion of Canada, and all other countries of the Copyright Union, is subject to royalty. All rights, including professional, amateur, motion pictures, recitation, public reading, radio and television broadcasting and the rights of translation in foreign languages are strictly reserved. Particular emphasis is laid upon the question of readings, permission for which must be secured from the author's agent in writing. All inquiries should be addressed to the author's agent, Audrey Wood, M.C.A. Artists Ltd., 598 Madison Avenue, New York, N. Y.

Reprinted by permission of New Directions Publishing Corporation.

From THE THREE SISTERS by Anton Chekhov, translated by Elizaveta Fen. Reprinted by permission of Penguin Books Ltd.

From UNCLE VANIA by Anton Chekhov, translated by Elizaveta Fen. Reprinted by permission of Penguin Books Ltd.

From A VIEW FROM THE BRIDGE by Arthur Miller. Copyright 1955, © 1957 by Arthur Miller. Reprinted by permission of The Viking Press, Inc.

From WALKER, LONDON by Sir James M. Barrie.
CAUTION: Professionals and amateurs are hereby warned that WALKER, LONDON, being fully protected under the copyright laws of the United States of America, the British Empire, including the Dominion of Canada, and all other countries of the Copyright Union, is subject to a royalty. All rights, including professional, amateur, motion pictures, recitation, public reading, radio and television broadcasting and the rights of translation in foreign languages are strictly reserved. Amateurs may give stage production of this play upon payment of a royalty of 10 Dollars for each performance one week before the play is to be given to Samuel French, Inc., at 25 West 45th St., New York, N. Y. 10036, or 7623 Sunset Blvd., Hollywood, Calif., or if in Canada to Samuel French (Canada) Ltd., at 27 Grenville St., Toronto, Ont. Reprinted by permission of Samuel French, Inc.

From WHEN DID YOU LAST SEE MY MOTHER? by Christopher Hampton. Reprinted by permission of Grove Press, Inc. Copyright © 1967 by Christopher Hampton.

For
Los Comicos,
their parents
and mine.
First stages, and among the best.

CONTENTS

I do find that I am not able to conquer myself
as to going to plays . . .
                    Samuel Pepys
                    Diary, 2nd January, 1663-64

This second volume of *Great Scenes from the World
Theater,* like the first, is a book *for* actors, not *about*
acting. It is a workbook, a collection of over one hundred
scenes selected for their usefulness to actors and teachers
concerned with basic acting techniques. It is intended to
introduce actors to plays they have not come across before, to remind them of good scenes they may have
forgotten, to serve them as "sides" for rehearsals, to
challenge them as they practice their craft, and to provide
them with material for auditions. The new collection is a
response to requests that the well-used scenes in the first
volume be supplemented by more of the same—but most
of all it is evidence of the editor's inability to stay away
from plays.

Actors familiar with Volume I will recognize the general categories and chapter headings under which the scenes
have been arranged, and they will know that these ar-
rangements, as before, are open to reinterpretation and
adjustment. Only the individual actor and his coach can
finally decide which scene is appropriate when. However,
the categories parallel the progression of objectives fre-
quently followed in acting classes and the groupings will
suggest certain ways in which the scenes can be particularly useful. Thus the scenes in Chapter I, "Play It for
Truth," feature characters and situations likely to be
familiar to young actors. Memory, imagination, and playing "as if it were real" are emphasized in the scenes in
Chapter II, "Acting Means Believing," a chapter made up
of scenes of recollection in which actors are called upon
to use their emotional memories and, in some cases, to put
their imaginations to work to lend reality to situations of

fantasy. Concentration, communication, and communication between characters in conflict are demanded by the scenes in Chapter III. Actors will discover that the monologues and dialogues have been arranged in order of increasing complexity but that nearly all of the scenes emphasize subtext, the development of character through those progressions of feeling, thought, act, and word often called "beats" or "units and objectives."

Chapter IV, "Character Development in Two or More Scenes," has been expanded for this volume, as these exercises in characterization extending through entire plays have proved especially valuable. It should be noted, also, that Chapter V, "Advanced Scenes," ends with a set of five excerpts (for the same three characters) from Strindberg's double-length drama *The Dance of Death*.

The editor's relating of scenes to particular objectives or techniques is intended as a guide and need not, of course, be held to rigidly. Indeed, the actor, knowing well his own special requirements for a scene, is invited to ignore the chapter headings and to turn to the back of the book, where he will find the scenes listed according to the number of male and female characters involved, and broadly categorized as comedy, drama, and the like.

Those who know the first collection of *Great Scenes* will find a considerably broader range of material in this new set of scenes, for in the seven years since the first workbook was published, our theater and the demands it makes upon our actors have greatly expanded and diversified. The generation of playwrights which has followed Beckett and Brecht has required that a new (or perhaps quite old), highly presentational style be a part of every actor's repertoire. A recent succession of extraordinary productions—*The Bacchae* off-off Broadway; *'Tis Pity* at Yale; a revealing *Revenger's Tragedy* and an almost mod *Two Gentlemen* at Stratford-on-Avon; an elegant *Love's Labours Lost* and a superb *Beaux Stratagem* at the National Theatre in London; and most of all, perhaps, Peter Brook's *Midsummer*—has made clear the vigor and contemporaneity of plays once thought to have been relegated to the theatrical museums of classical acting companies. Even the young actor—or especially the young actor—can no longer be satisfied with perfecting only the techniques of modern realism, though these remain the foundation of his craft. Therefore, for this collection of scenes I have reached backward to a number of dramas from the Greek, Elizabethan, Jacobean, eighteenth and nineteenth century theaters, and forward to a selection of excerpts from new American and European plays. It is my hope that at least some of these scenes (the old included) will be new discoveries for the actors and directors using the book, that they will prove as viable, as demanding of exciting interpretation, to you as they have to me. I must confess, also, that in some cases I have included scenes that I hope will spark productions of plays that deserve to be better known than they now are.

In selecting scenes and beginning to rehearse them, actors may be helped by the introduction which precedes each of the excerpts in the book. These comments are intended to provide something of the story of each play, its setting, and the background of the scenes themselves. However, be warned: these introductions are not meant to substitute for a reading of the plays. This is a book of "sides," not plot outlines. When a scene has been selected, the actor should read the entire play from which it comes, for in no other way can he hope to understand the characters or situations in his scene. Those who wish to study other plays by authors whose scenes are included in this volume will find a listing of their major plays beginning on page 655.

No collection of this kind can ever fully satisfy its editor, and I am well aware of the many scenes that could or ought to be reprinted here but are not. Anyone introducing actors to the most stimulating plays of the contemporary theater must include on his list the plays of Pinter, Genet, Ionesco, and, of course, Stoppard's *Rosencrantz and Guildenstern*. Had selections from these been available for reprinting, I would certainly have included them. Beckett might well have been represented, and Brecht, if any actable American versions of his plays existed. However, few actors need to be introduced to these most famous moderns, and I am pleased that I have been able to reprint excerpts from some playwrights whose work, though not well known in America, merits recognition and performance.

To the playwrights, publishers, and agents who have generously allowed me to borrow from their plays, I am most grateful—in particular, to Kenneth Cavander for his translations of Euripides' *Orestes* made especially for this collection, and to Richard Wilbur for offering to allow me to reprint scenes from his exemplary translation of *School for Wives* almost as soon as it happened. I owe a special debt to the actors, directors, and colleagues who have been generous with their help and suggestions. To Wesleyan University I owe thanks for a sabbatical leave, a part of which was spent in rediscovering the British theater, and for research grants which helped to make this book possible. Without the labors of my research assistants, John Crigler, Glen MacLeod, and especially Keith Reierstad, the book would not have come about at all.

This collection of scenes can matter only when it is in the hands of an actor; its value, for me, increases with the signs of its hard use. To the actors and teachers who have given its predecessor a thorough workout, I give my thanks, and my hopes that this new volume will prove even more useful to them than the last.

James L. Steffensen, Jr.
Middletown, Connecticut
April, 1971

A Note to the Actors

It is never wise to cut or change a scene. However, in preparing scenes for class, it occasionally is useful or necessary to make minor adaptations, such as omitting the entrance of a maid or other character who appears for a line or two in a scene otherwise played by only two or three people. There are also times when students may wish to play without interruption two or three brief speeches or scenes which, together, form a monologue or scene of sufficient length for a classroom project. Such adaptations should never, of course, be performed publicly without the specific permission of the playwright or his authorized agent, and, even for classroom presentations, editing must be done with the greatest care not to destroy the author's meaning or the natural, dramatic flow of his scene.

With a very few exceptions (always noted in the text), the selections in the second volume of *Great Scenes from the World Theater* have been reprinted uncut, unedited, exactly as they were written and approved for publication by the playwrights. Where it seems that adaptations might be necessary or helpful in classroom work, the editor has marked these adaptations as follows:

§—§: lines which might be omitted to avoid the entrance of an extra character, or to allow two or three speeches to be spoken as a monologue.

[—]: a connecting or explanatory phrase necessary to bridge an omitted line or entrance, or to link two scenes.

Deletions in the printed texts are marked by three asterisks—***.

23

CHAPTER I

PLAY IT FOR TRUTH

from

THE TWO GENTLEMEN OF VERONA

by William Shakespeare

Act I, scene 2
JULIA, LUCETTA

Shakespeare's early—perhaps his first—comedy flashes across the stage with the grace and impetuousness of youth. Indeed, nearly all of its characters are young. Nearly all are in love—"overboots in love," as one describes himself—and for the first time. They are vulnerable in the freshness of their feelings, and quite resilient, and they are not always altogether certain who they are (a not unpredictable condition, say, for a young man who, having fallen overboots in love with Julia, discovers upon meeting Silvia that it is *she* he adores, while Julia's face is impossible to recall). They behave, as it were, suddenly, responding in rapture or despair. Their world is an exotic, romantic Italy that never was, the unreal landscape of first loves. Their drama is not deep. But they live—in the intensity of the pain, preposterousness, and delight of life newly discovered.

Julia is loved by Proteus. Later that will not be so, and Julia, wasting with love, will risk life and reputation to rush to Milan disguised as a boy simply to be near him. But for now she can afford to appear (and perhaps she is) uncertain of her feelings. Certainly when her waiting-woman attempts to promote Proteus' cause and then produces his love letter, Julia is required to seem uninterested and even rather annoyed. It is a game, with well-understood rules; and it is not a game, for Julia is surely at least a little afraid of the enormity of actually being in love and admitting it (to herself as well as to Lucetta). But the game goes too far, the letter is torn, Julia is suddenly struck with great compassion for the pieces, and she pets and kisses them in a way that neither she nor her suitor can manage in person. Julia, in fact, has not yet been kissed.

Verona. The garden of Julia's house.

Enter Julia and Lucetta.

Julia.

But say, Lucetta, now we are alone,
Wouldst thou then counsel me to fall in love?

Lucetta.

Ay, madam, so you stumble not unheedfully.

Julia.

Of all the fair resort of gentlemen
That every day with parle encounter me,
In thy opinion which is worthiest love?

Lucetta.

Please you repeat their names, I'll show my mind
According to my shallow simple skill.

Julia.

What think'st thou of the fair Sir Eglamour?

Lucetta.

As of a knight well-spoken, neat, and fine;
But, were I you, he never should be mine.

Julia.

What think'st thou of the rich Mercatio?

Lucetta.

Well of his wealth; but of himself, so so.

Julia.

What think'st thou of the gentle Proteus?

Lucetta.

Lord, Lord! to see what folly reigns in us!

Julia.

How now? What means this passion at his name?

Lucetta.

Pardon, dear madam. 'Tis a passing shame
That I, unworthy body as I am,
Should censure thus on lovely gentlemen.

Julia.

Why not on Proteus, as of all the rest?

Lucetta.

Then thus; of many good I think him best.

Julia.

Your reason?

Lucetta.

I have no other but a woman's reason: I think him so
because I think him so.

Julia.

And wouldst thou have me cast my love on him?

Lucetta.

Ay, if you thought your love not cast away.

Julia.

Why, he, of all the rest, hath never mov'd me.

Lucetta.

Yet he, of all the rest, I think best loves ye.

Julia.

His little speaking shows his love but small.

Lucetta.

Fire that's closest kept burns most of all.

Julia.

They do not love that do not show their love.

Lucetta.

O, they love least that let men know their love.

Julia.

I would I knew his mind.

Lucetta.

Peruse this paper, madam. (*Gives a letter.*)

Julia.

"To Julia." Say, from whom?

Lucetta.

That the contents will show.

Julia.

Say, say! Who gave it thee?

Lucetta.

Sir Valentine's page; and sent, I think, from Proteus.
He would have given it you; but I, being in the way,
Did in your name receive it. Pardon the fault, I pray.

Julia.

Now, by my modesty, a goodly broker!
Dare you presume to harbour wanton lines?
To whisper, and conspire against my youth?
Now trust me, 'tis an office of great worth
And you an officer fit for the place.
There, take the paper. See it be return'd,
Or else return no more into my sight.

Lucetta.

To plead for love deserves more fee than hate.

Julia.

Will ye be gone?

Lucetta.

That you may ruminate. (*Exit.*)

Julia.

And yet I would I had o'erlook'd the letter.
It were a shame to call her back again
And pray her to a fault for which I chid her.
What fool is she, that knows I am a maid
And would not force the letter to my view,
Since maids, in modesty, say "no" to that
Which they would have the profferer construe "ay"!
Fie, fie! how wayward is this foolish love,
That, like a testy babe, will scratch the nurse
And presently, all humbled, kiss the rod!
How churlishly I chid Lucetta hence
When willingly I would have had her here!
How angerly I taught my brow to frown
When inward joy enforc'd my heart to smile!
My penance is, to call Lucetta back
And ask remission for my folly past.
What ho! Lucetta!

　　　　　　　(*Enter Lucetta.*)

Lucetta.

　　　　　　　What would your ladyship?

Julia.

Is it near dinner time?

Lucetta.

　　　　　　　I would it were,
That you might kill your stomach on your meat
And not upon your maid.

Julia.

What is't that you took up so gingerly?

Lucetta.

Nothing.

Julia.

Why didst thou stoop then?

Lucetta.

To take a paper up that I let fall.

Julia.

And is that paper nothing?

Lucetta.

Nothing concerning me.

Julia.

Then let it lie, for those that it concerns.

Lucetta.

Madam, it will not lie where it concerns
Unless it have a false interpreter.

Julia.

Some love of yours hath writ to you in rhyme.

Lucetta.

That I might sing it, madam, to a tune.
Give me a note; your ladyship can set.

Julia.

As little by such toys as may be possible.
Best sing it to the tune of "Light o' love."

Lucetta.

It is too heavy for so light a tune.

Julia.

Heavy? Belike it hath some burden then?

Lucetta.

Ay! and melodious were it, would you sing it.

Julia.

And why not you?

Lucetta.

              I cannot reach so high.

Julia

Let's see your song.

         (Takes the letter.)

           How now, minion?

Lucetta.

Keep tune there still, so you will sing it out.
And yet methinks I do not like this tune.

Julia.

You do not?

Lucetta.

          No, madam. 'Tis too sharp.

Julia.

You, minion, are too saucy.

Lucetta.

Nay, now you are too flat
And mar the concord with too harsh a descant.

There wanteth but a mean to fill your song.
Julia.
The mean is drown'd with your unruly bass.
Lucetta.
Indeed I bid the base for Proteus.
Julia.
This babble shall not henceforth trouble me.
Here is a coil with protestation! (*Tears the letter.*)
Go, get you gone; and let the papers lie.
You would be fing'ring them to anger me.
Lucetta.
She makes it strange, but she would be best pleas'd
To be so ang'red with another letter. (*Exit.*)
Julia.
Nay, would I were so ang'red with the same!
O hateful hands, to tear such loving words!
Injurious wasps, to feed on such sweet honey
And kill the bees that yield it with your stings!
I'll kiss each several paper for amends.
Look, here is writ "kind Julia." Unkind Julia,
As in revenge of thy ingratitude,
I throw thy name against the bruising stones,
Trampling contemptuously on thy disdain.
And here is writ "love-wounded Proteus."
Poor wounded name! My bosom, as a bed,
Shall lodge thee till thy wound be throughly heal'd;
And thus I search it with a sovereign kiss.
But twice or thrice was "Proteus" written down.
Be calm, good wind, blow not a word away
Till I have found each letter in the letter,
Except mine own name. That some whirlwind bear
Unto a ragged, fearful, hanging rock
And throw it thence into the raging sea!
Lo, here in one line is his name twice writ:
"Poor forlorn Proteus, passionate Proteus,
To the sweet Julia." That I'll tear away;
And yet I will not, sith so prettily
He couples it to his complaining names.
Thus will I fold them one upon another.
Now kiss, embrace, contend, do what you will.

(*Enter Lucetta.*)

Lucetta.

Madam,
Dinner is ready, and your father stays.

Julia.

Well, let us go.

Lucetta.

What, shall these papers lie like telltales here?

Julia.

If you respect them, best to take them up.

Lucetta.

Nay, I was taken up for laying them down.
Yet here they shall not lie, for catching cold.

Julia.

I see you have a month's mind to them.

Lucetta.

Ay, madam, you may say what sights you see.
I see things too, although you judge I wink.

Julia.

Come, come! Will't please you go? (*Exeunt.*)

from

THE DANCE OF DEATH

by August Strindberg (translated by Elizabeth Sprigge)

Part II, Act I, scene 1
JUDITH, ALLAN

The second part of Strindberg's study of a hate-filled
marriage begins with a scene almost shocking in its contrast to the dark, tormented drama that has filled the stage
for half of a long evening. Instead of a shadowy chamber
in a stone tower, there is a white and gold drawing room
with tall French windows looking onto a terrace; instead
of sunset merging into night, there is morning sunshine;
instead of a middle-aged couple clawing at each other,
there is a girl in a summer dress and a cadet, very young,
who is discovering for the first time the delightful and
awful turmoil of love. Judith's rather cat-and-mouse flirting with Allan no doubt carries hints of the battle of the
sexes that totally occupies her parents, but the strength of
the scene—and its appeal to the audience—lies in the
honest sympathy (and honest humor) of its portraits of
young adults emerging, in something of a rush, from their
adolescence. (For introductory notes about the play, see
p. 597.

> *Allan is sitting at the writing-table, making calculations.*
> *Judith comes in through the French windows, wearing a*
> *short-skirted summer dress, her hair in a plait. In one*
> *hand she carries her hat, in the other a tennis-racquet. She*
> *stops in the entrance.*
> *Allan rises serious and courteous.*

Judith.

(*Seriously but amiably.*) Why don't you come and play
tennis?

34

Allan.

(*Shyly, fighting his emotion.*) I'm so busy . . .

Judith.

Didn't you see I left my bicycle *facing* the oak, not with its *back* to the oak?

Allan.

Yes, I did.

Judith.

Well, what does that mean?

Allan.

It means .. that you want me to come and play tennis . . . But my work . . . I have some problems to solve . . . and your father is a pretty strict master.

Judith.

Do you like him?

Allan.

Yes, I do. He takes such an interest in all his pupils.

Judith.

He takes an interest in everyone and everything. . . . Are you coming?

Allan.

You know very well I want to—but I mustn't.

Judith.

I'll ask Papa to give you leave.

Allan.

Don't do that. There'd only be a fuss.

Judith.

I can manage him, you know. What I want, he wants.

Allan.

That must be because you're so hard—yes!

Judith.

You ought to be too.

Allan.

I'm not of the wolf breed.

Judith.

Then you must be a sheep.

Allan.

Rather that.

Judith.

Tell me why you won't come and play tennis.

Allan.

You know why.

Judith.

Tell me all the same. The Lieutenant ...

Allan.

Yes, you don't care a pin about me, but you don't enjoy being with the Lieutenant unless I'm there too, so you can watch me being tortured.

Judith.

Am I so cruel? I didn't know that.

Allan.

You know it now.

Judith.

Then I'll have to reform, because I don't want to be cruel. I don't want to be bad—in your eyes.

Allan.

You're just saying that so as to get the upper hand of me. I'm your slave already, but you're not satisfied with that. The slave has to be tortured and thrown to the wild beasts.... You've already got the other one in your clutches, so what do you want with me then? Let me go my way and you go yours.

Judith.

Are you turning me out? (*Allan does not answer.*) All right, I'll go. Being cousins, we're bound to meet now and then, but I won't bother you. (*Allan sits at the table and goes on with his calculations. Judith, instead of going, gradually approaches him.*) Don't worry—I'm just going. I only wanted to see what the Quarantine Officer's quarters were like.... (*Looks round.*) White and gold! ... And a grand piano—a Bechstein! Ho! We're still in the fortress tower, although Papa's been pensioned off —the tower where Mamma has lived for twenty-five years.... And we're only there as a favour too. But your people are rich....

Allan.

(*Calmly.*) We aren't rich.

Judith.

So you say, but you're always very well turned out. Though, as a matter of fact, whatever you wear suits you.... Do you hear what I'm saying? (*Comes closer.*)

Allan.

(*Resigned.*) I hear.

Judith.

How can you hear while you're adding up, or whatever it is you're doing?

Allan.

I don't hear with my eyes.

Judith.

Your eyes . . . By the way, have you ever looked at them in a mirror?

Allan.

Get along with you!

Judith.

You despise me, don't you?

Allan.

My dear girl, I'm not thinking about you at all.

Judith.

(*Coming right up to the table.*) Archimedes doing his sums, while the soldier comes and cuts him down.

(*She stirs his papers with her racquet.*)

Allan.

Don't touch my papers!

Judith.

That's what Archimedes said too. . . . You're imagining things, you know. You think I can't live without you.

Allan.

Why can't you leave me in peace?

Judith.

Be polite, and I'll help you with your exam.

Allan.

You?

Judith.

Yes. I know the examiners.

Allan.

(*Severely.*) What of it?

Judith.

Don't you realise one has to be on good terms with one's instructors?

Allan.

You mean your father and the Lieutenant.

Judith.

And the Colonel.

Allan.

You mean that under your protection I shouldn't have to work.

Judith.

You are a bad translator.

Allan.

Of a bad original.

Judith.

You ought to be ashamed.

Allan.

I am—of your behaviour and my own. I'm ashamed of having listened to you. Why don't you go away?

Judith.

Because I know you value my company.... Yes, your way always leads under my window. You always have something that takes you to town by the same boat as me. You can't go out sailing without having me to man the foresail.

Allan.

(*Bashfully.*) That's not the way for a young girl to talk.

Judith.

Do you think I'm a child?

Allan.

Sometimes you're a good child and sometimes a wicked woman. You seem to have chosen me as your sheep.

Judith.

You are a sheep. That's why I'm going to protect you.

Allan.

(*Rising.*) The wolf makes a jolly bad shepherd.... You want to eat me—that's the truth of the matter. You want to pledge your pretty eyes so as to redeem my head for yourself.

Judith.

Oh, have you looked at my eyes? I didn't think you were as bold as that.

(*Allan gathers up his papers and starts to go out, right. Judith stands in front of the door.*)

Allan.

Get out of my way, or ...

Judith.

Or?

Allan.

If only you were a boy, I'd ... But you're just a girl.

Judith.

So what?

Allan.

If you had a spark of pride, you'd have gone—so you can consider yourself thrown out.

Judith.

I'll pay you out for this.

Allan.

I'm sure of that.

Judith.

(*As she goes, furiously.*) I'll—pay—you—out!

from
AS YOU LIKE IT
by William Shakespeare

Act IV, scene 1
ROSALIND, ORLANDO, (CELIA)

Take one romantic young man. Add a young lady (played by a boy), who masquerades as a boy and in that guise offers to act the part of the young lady—herself (himself?)—with whom the young man is in love. Somewhere amongst the changes, comedy is certain—and yet another meaning is discovered in that seemingly offhand title, *As You Like It.* With the arrival of actresses on the stage, one dimension of this compounded confusion was lost; but in its stead the audience was given a succession of lithe-limbed actresses, delightful in what the eighteenth century called "breeches parts." The comedy of the complexity of gender persisted, as did the truths of love—for *both* sexes—revealed by the character who was somehow masculine and feminine at the same time. And despite the complexities, with thier fascination for critics and performers, the play, like the young man, remained openly, simply romantic.

As You Like It is about love; its varied characters, set loose to pair off in the Forest of Arden, present the full range of the follies and delights to which couples are led by this confounding but necessary emotion. At the center is romantic love: Rosalind, with the insights and irony which her wit and disguises allow her; and Orlando, with his one-track romanticism which, though it may lead him to decorate good trees with bad verses, stands also as a reminder that eventually wit, like disguises, must be shed if true love is to become real.

The scene is the Forest of Arden, to which Rosalind and Orlando have come to escape the anger of the duke in whose court they met and, in an instant, fell in love.

40

Neither knew that the other had fled to the forest, and when they meet, Rosalind, disguised as a boy, does not reveal her identity to Orlando. Hearing him speak of his love for Rosalind, she does, however, offer to pretend to be his lady and to cure him of his lovesickness by enacting the true nature of women, "changeable, longing and liking, proud, fantastical, apish, shallow, inconstant, full of tears, full of smiles; for every passion something and for no passion truly anything." She does this in part because she longs to be wooed by Orlando, in part because her mischievous wit cannot resist the opportunity to tease him dreadfully, and in part because to be in love as deeply as she knows she is is to be vulnerable, and she needs to be more certain of him. Before the play is over, her love breaks through her pretense. But for now the disguise is well maintained. Orlando has agreed to meet her (him) for a session of the love-cure. He comes to the appointed place, but he is late.

Orlando.

Good day and happiness, dear Rosalind.

Rosalind.

***Why, how now, Orlando? Where have you been all this while? You a lover? And you serve me such another trick, never come in my sight more.

Orlando.

My fair Rosalind, I come within an hour of my promise.

Rosalind.

Break an hour's promise in love? He that will divide a minute into a thousand parts and break but a part of the thousand part of a minute in the affairs of love, it may be said of him that Cupid hath clapp'd him o' th' shoulder. But I'll warrant him heart-whole.

Orlando.

Pardon me, dear Rosalind.

Rosalind.

Nay. And you be so tardy, come no more in my sight; I had as lief be woo'd of a snail.

Orlando.

Of a snail?

Rosalind.

Ay, of a snail. For though he comes slowly, he carries his

house on his head—a better jointure, I think, than you make a woman. Besides, he brings his destiny with him.

Orlando.

What's that?

Rosalind.

Why, horns; which such as you are fain to be beholding to your wives for. But he comes armed in his fortune, and prevents the slander of his wife.

Orlando.

Virtue is no horn-maker, and my Rosalind is virtuous.

Rosalind.

And I am your Rosalind.

Celia.

It pleases him to call you so. But he hath a Rosalind of a better leer than you.

Rosalind.

Come, woo me, woo me; for now I am in a holiday humor and like enough to consent. What would you say to me now, and I were your very very Rosalind?

Orlando.

I would kiss before I spoke.

Rosalind.

Nay, you were better speak first; and when you were gravel'd for lack of matter, you might take occasion to kiss. Very good orators, when they are out, they will spit; and for lovers lacking—God warn us—matter, the cleanliest shift is to kiss.

Orlando.

How if the kiss be denied?

Rosalind.

Then she puts you to entreaty, and there begins new matter.

Orlando.

Who could be out, being before his beloved mistress?

Rosalind.

Marry, that should you if I were your mistress, or I should think my honesty ranker than my wit.

Orlando.

What of my suit?

Rosalind.

Not out of your apparel, and yet out of your suit. Am I not your Rosalind?

Orlando.

I take some joy to say you are, because I would be talking of her.

Rosalind.

Well, in her person, I say I will not have you.

Orlando.

Then, in mine own person, I die.

Rosalind.

No, faith, die by attorney. The poor world is almost six thousand years old, and in all this time there was not any man died in his own person, *videlicet*, in a love cause. Troilus had his brains dash'd out with a Grecian club, yet he did what he could to die before; and he is one of the patterns of love. Leander, he would have liv'd many a fair year though Hero had turn'd nun, if it had not been for a hot midsummer night; for, good youth, he went but forth to wash him in the Hellespont, and being taken with the cramp, was drown'd; and the foolish chroniclers of that age found it was 'Hero of Cestos.' But these are all lies. Men have died from time to time and worms have eaten them, but not for love.

Orlando.

I would not have my right Rosalind of this mind, for I protest her frown might kill me.

Rosalind.

By this hand, it will not kill a fly. But come. Now I will be your Rosalind in a more coming-on disposition; and ask me what you will, I will grant it.

Orlando.

Then love me, Rosalind.

Rosalind.

Yes, faith, will I—Fridays and Saturdays and all.

Orlando.

And wilt thou have me?

Rosalind.

Ay, and twenty such.

Orlando.

What sayest thou?

Rosalind.

Are you not good?

Orlando.

I hope so.

Rosalind.

Why then, can one desire too much of a good thing?
Come, sister, you shall be the priest and marry us. Give
me your hand, Orlando. What do you say, sister?

Orlando.

Pray thee, marry us.

Celia.

I cannot say the words.

Rosalind.

You must begin, 'Will you, Orlando . . .'

Celia.

Go to. Will you, Orlando, have to wife this Rosalind?

Orlando.

I will.

Rosalind.

Ay, but when?

Orlando.

Why, now. As fast as she can marry us.

Rosalind.

Then you must say, 'I take thee, Rosalind, for wife.'

Orlando.

I take thee, Rosalind, for wife.

Rosalind.

I might ask you for your commission, but I do take thee,
Orlando, for my husband. There's a girl goes before the
priest, and certainly a woman's thought runs before her
actions.

Orlando.

So do all thoughts; they are wing'd.

Rosalind.

Now tell me how long you would have her after you
have possess'd her?

Orlando.

For ever and a day.

Rosalind.

Say 'a day' without the 'ever.' No, no, Orlando. Men are
April when they woo, December when they wed; maids
are May when they are maids, but the sky changes when
they are wives. I will be more jealous of thee than a
Barbary cock-pigeon over his hen, more clamorous than
a parrot against rain, more new-fangled than an ape,
more giddy in my desires than a monkey. I will weep for

nothing, like Diana in the fountain, and I will do that when you are dispos'd to be merry. I will laugh like a hyena, and that when thou art inclin'd to sleep.

Orlando.

But will my Rosalind do so?

Rosalind.

By my life, she will do as I do.

Orlando.

O, but she is wise.

Rosalind.

Or else she could not have the wit to do this. The wiser, the waywarder. Make the doors upon a woman's wit, and it will be out at the casement; shut that, and 'twill out at the keyhole; stop that, 'twill fly with the smoke out at the chimney.

Orlando.

A man that had a wife with such a wit, he might say, 'Wit, whether wilt?'

Rosalind.

Nay, you might keep that check for it till you met your wive's wit going to your neighbor's bed.

Orlando.

And what wit could wit have to excuse that?

Rosalind.

Marry, to say she came to seek you there. You shall never take her without her answer unless you take her without her tongue. O, that woman that cannot make her fault her husband's occasion, let her never nurse her child herself, for she will breed it like a fool.

Orlando.

For these two hours, Rosalind, I will leave thee.

Rosalind.

Alas, dear love, I cannot lack thee two hours.

Orlando.

I must attend the Duke at dinner. By two o'clock I will be with thee again.

Rosalind.

Ay, go your ways, go your ways. I knew what you would prove; my friends told me as much, and I thought no less. That flattering tongue of yours won me. 'Tis but one cast away, and so come death. Two o'clock is your hour.

Orlando.

Ay, sweet Rosalind.

Rosalind.

By my troth, and in good earnest, and so God mend me, and by all pretty oaths that are not dangerous, if you break one jot of your promise or come one minute behind your hour, I will think you the most pathetical break-promise and the most hollow lover and the most unworthy of her you call Rosalind that may be chosen out of the gross band of the unfaithful. Therefore beware my censure and keep your promise.

Orlando.

With no less religion than if thou wert indeed my Rosalind. So adieu.

Rosalind.

Well, Time is the old justice that examines all such offenders, and let Time try. Adieu.

from

THE ROSE TATTOO

by Tennessee Williams

Two Scenes from Act I, scene 6, and Act III, scene 2
JACK, ROSA, (SERAFINA)

For Serafina, life is love. Her husband, a handsome truck
driver with the mark of love—a rose tattoo—on his torso,
was a man whose lovemaking no other man could match.
But Serafina's husband is dead, and her own life, she is
convinced, is over. By day she mourns for him, at night
she cries out for him in her dreams, and betweentimes she
furiously guards her daughter from encounters with the
passion she so needs herself.

But this Williams play is a comedy, its subjects are the
unexpected reawakening of Serafina and the awakening—
to love, of course—of her daughter, Rosa. The plot is
shaped to the patterns of frustration, but with Serafina
frustration tends to be as hilarious as it is intense, and the
story of Rosa's longing for something she has yet to
experience or fully understand is more gentle than anguished.

Rosa is young, just ready to graduate from high school;
her mother has seen to it that she is sexually naive. But
Rosa ia a woman, as Italian as Serafina and as emotionally volatile. At a high school party she has met Jack, a
sailor nearly as young as she though much more knowing.
No stereotype sailor, Jack is respectful of Rosa's innocence and rather frightened by her uninhibited delight in
him. For a week after the party, Rosa, forbidden to see
Jack, has moped and finally threatened to kill herself.
Now she has met him again, and late in the evening she
brings him home to meet her mother.

The scene is Serafina's house—the parlor and, behind,

the dining room in which Serafina has set up her dress-making shop. It is dark, but the house is not empty. In the dining room Serafina sits surrounded by the dress dummies; silent, unmoving, she waits, dour and wracked by her frustrations. There is the sound of a key in the lock. Jack opens the door and the parlor lights up faintly as he and Rosa enter.

Jack.

It's dark in here.

Rosa.

Yes, Mama's gone out!

Jack.

How do you know she's out?

Rosa.

The door was locked and all the shutters are closed! Put down those roses.

Jack.

Where shall I ...

Rosa.

Somewhere, anywhere!—Come here! (*He approaches her rather diffidently.*) I want to teach you a little Dago word. The word is "bacio."[1]

Jack.

What does this word mean?

Rosa.

This and this and this! (*She rains kisses upon him till he forcibly removes her face from him.*) Just think. A week ago Friday—I didn't know boys existed!—Did you know girls existed before the dance?

Jack.

Yes, I knew they existed ...

Rosa.

(*Holding him.*) Do you remember what you said to me on the dance floor? "Honey, you're dancing too close"?

Jack.

Well, it was—hot in the Gym and the—floor was crowded.

Rosa.

When my girl friend was teaching me how to dance, I asked her, "How do you know which way the boy's going to move?" And she said, "You've got to feel how he's

---

[1]"Kiss."

going to move with your body!" I said, "How do you
feel with your body?" And she said, "By pressing up
close!"—That's why I pressed up close! I didn't realize
that I was—Ha, ha! Now you're blushing! Don't go
away!—And a few minutes later you said to me, "Gee,
you're beautiful!" I said, "Excuse me," and ran to the
ladies' room. Do you know why? To look at myself in
the mirror! And I saw that I was! For the first time in
my life I was beautiful! You'd made me beautiful when
you *said* that I was!

Jack.

(*Humbly.*) You *are* beautiful, Rosa! So much, I . . .

Rosa.

You've changed, *too.* You've stopped laughing and jok-
ing. Why have you gotten so old and serious, Jack?

Jack.

Well, honey, you're sort of . . .

Rosa.

What am I "sort of"?

Jack.

(*Finding the right word.*) *Wild!*
            (*She laughs. He seizes the bandaged wrist.*)
I didn't know nothing like this was going to happen.

Rosa.

Oh, that, that's nothing! I'll take the handkerchief off and
you can forget it.

Jack.

How could you do a thing like that over me? I'm—
nothing!

Rosa.

Everybody is nothing until you love them!

Jack.

Give me that handkerchief. I want to show it to my
shipmates. I'll say, "This is the blood of a beautiful girl
who cut her wrist with a knife because she loved me!"

Rosa.

Don't be so pleased with yourself. It's mostly Mercuro-
chrome!

Serafina.

(*Violently, from the dark room adjoining.*) Stai zitta!—
Cretina!²

---

²Shut up!—Idiot!

(*Rosa and Jack draw abruptly apart.*)

Jack.

(*Fearfully.*) I knew somebody was here!

Rosa.

(*Sweetly and delicately.*) Mama? Are you in there, Mama?

Serafina.

No, no, no, I'm not, I'm dead and buried!

Rosa.

Yes, Mama's in there!

Jack.

Well, I—better go and—wait outside for a—while . . .

Rosa.

You stay right here!—Mama?—Jack is with me.—Are you dressed up nicely? (*There is no response.*) Why's it so dark in here?—Jack, open the shutters!—I want to introduce you to my mother . . .

Jack.

Hadn't I better go and . . .

Rosa.

No. Open the shutters!

SECOND SCENE

Serafina's pent-up emotions have burst out in suspicious anger with Jack. She has ordered him to go away and never to see Rosa again. But she relents: Rosa and Jack may spend one evening together if Jack will swear an oath to the Virgin Mary that he will respect the girl's innocence absolutely. Jack agrees, and he and Rosa leave the house.

It is early morning now. Jack and Rosa appear at the top of the stairs that lead over the embankment behind Serafina's house. They have been waiting a time behind the embankment, hoping to avoid the eyes of neighbors who would be certain to make gossip. Jack has kept his oath, though Rosa has done nothing to make it easy for him to do so.

(*It is just before daybreak of the next day. Rosa and Jack appear at the top of the embankment steps.*)

Rosa.

I thought they would never leave. (*She comes down the steps and out in front of the house, then calls back to him.*) Let's go down there.

(He obeys hesitatingly. Both are very grave. The scene is played as close as possible to the audience. She sits very straight. He stands behind her with his hands on her shoulders.)

Rosa.

(Leaning her head back against him.) This was the happiest day of my life, and this is the saddest night . . .
(He crouches in front of her.)

Serafina.

(From inside the house.) Aaaaaahhhhhhhh!

Jack.

(Springing up, startled.) What's that?

Rosa.

(Resentfully.) Oh! That's Mama dreaming about my father.

Jack.

I—feel like a—*heel!* I feel like a rotten heel!

Rosa.

Why?

Jack.

That promise I made your mother.

Rosa.

I hate her for it.

Jack.

Honey—Rosa, she—wanted to protect you.
(There is a long-drawn cry from the back of the house: "Ohhhh—Rosario!")

Rosa.

She wanted me not to have what she's dreaming about . . .

Jack.

Naw, naw, honey, she—wanted to—protect you . . .
(The cry from within is repeated softly.)

Rosa.

Listen to her making love in her sleep! Is that what she wants *me* to do, just—*dream* about it?

Jack.

(Humbly.) She knows that her Rosa *is* a rose. And wants her rose to have someone—better than *me* . . .

Rosa.

Better than—*you!* *(She speaks as if the possibility were too preposterous to think of.)*

Jack.

You see me through—rose-colored—glasses . . .

Rosa.

I see you with love!

Jack.

Yes, but your Mama sees me with—common sense . . .

      (Serafina cries out again.)

I got to be going!

      (She keeps a tight hold on him. A rooster crows.)

Honey, it's so late the roosters are crowing!

Rosa.

They're fools, they're fools, it's early!

Jack.

Honey, on the island I almost forgot my promise. Almost, but not quite. Do you understand, honey?

Rosa.

Forget the promise!

Jack.

I made it on my knees in front of Our Lady. I've got to leave now, honey.

Rosa.

(Clasping him fiercely.) You'd have to break my arms to!

Jack.

Rosa, Rosa! You want to drive me crazy?

Rosa.

I want you not to remember.

Jack.

You're a very young girl! Fifteen—fifteen is too young!

Rosa.

Caro, caro, carissimo![3]

Jack.

You got to save some of those feelings for when you're grown up!

Rosa.

Carissimo!

Jack.

Hold some of it back until you're grown!

Rosa.

I have been grown for two years!

Jack.

No, no, that ain't what I . . .

Rosa.

Grown enough to be married, and have a—baby!

[3]Dear, dear, dearest!

Jack.

(*Springing up.*) Oh, good—Lord! (*He circles around her, pounding his palm repeatedly with his fist and clamping his teeth together with a grimace. Suddenly he speaks.*) I got to be going!

Rosa.

You want me to scream? (*He groans and turns away from her to resume his desperate circle. Rosa is blocking the way with her body.*)—I know, I know! You don't want me! (*Jack groans through his gritting teeth.*) No, no, you don't want me . . .

Jack.

Now you listen to me! You almost got into trouble today on that island! You almost did, but not quite!—But it didn't quite happen and no harm is done and you can just—forget it . . .

Rosa.

It is the only thing in my life that I want to remember! —When are you going back to New Orleans?

Jack.

Tomorrow.

Rosa.

When does your—ship sail?

Jack.

Tomorrow.

Rosa.

Where to?

Jack.

Guatemala.

Serafina.

(*From the house.*) Aahh!

Rosa.

Is that a long trip?

Jack.

After Guatemala, Buenos Aires. After Buenos Aires, Rio. Then around the Straits of Magellan and back up the west coast of South America, putting in at three ports before we dock at San Francisco.

Rosa.

I don't think I will—ever see you again . . .

Jack.

The ship won't sink!

Rosa.

(*Faintly and forlornly.*) No, but—I think it could just happen once, and if it don't happen that time, it never can—later . . . (*A rooster crows. They face each other sadly and quietly.*) You don't need to be very old to understand how it works out. One time, one time, only once, it could be—God!—to remember.—Other times? Yes—they'd be something.—But only once, God—to remember . . . (*With a little sigh she crosses to pick up his white cap and hand it gravely to him.*)—I'm sorry to you it didn't—mean—that much . . .

Jack.

(*Taking the cap and hurling it to the ground.*) Look! Look at my knuckles! You see them scabs on my knuckles? You know how them scabs got there? They got there because I banged my knuckles that hard on the deck of the sailboat!

Rosa.

Because it—didn't quite happen?

(*Jack jerks his head up and down in grotesquely violent assent to her question. Rosa picks up his cap and returns it to him again.*)

—Because of the promise to Mama! I'll never forgive her . . . (*There is a pause.*) What time in the afternoon must you be on the boat?

Jack.

Why?

Rosa.

Just tell me what time.

Jack.

Five!—Why?

Rosa.

What will you be doing till five?

Jack.

Well, I could be a goddam liar and tell you I was going to—pick me a hatful of daisies in—Audubon Park.—Is that what you want me to tell you?

Rosa.

No, tell me the truth.

Jack.

All right. I'll tell you the truth. I'm going to check in at some flea-bag hotel on North Rampart Street. Then I'm going to get loaded! And then I'm going to get . . .

(He doesn't complete the sentence but she understands him. She places the hat more becomingly on his blond head.)

Rosa.

Do me a little favor. *(Her hand slides down to his cheek and then to his mouth.)* Before you get loaded and before you—before you—

Jack.

Huh?

Rosa.

Look in the waiting room at the Greyhound bus station, please. At twelve o'clock, noon!

Jack.

Why?

Rosa.

You might find me there, waiting for you . . .

Jack.

What—what good would that do?

Rosa.

I never been to a hotel but I know they have numbers on doors and sometimes—numbers are—lucky.—Aren't they?—Sometimes?—Lucky?

Jack.

You want to buy me a ten-year stretch in the brig?

Rosa.

I want you to give me that little gold ring on your ear to put on my finger.—I want to give you my heart to keep forever! And ever! And ever! *(Slowly and with a barely audible sigh she leans her face against him.)* Look for me! I will be there!

Jack.

(Breathlessly.) In all my life, I never felt nothing so sweet as the feel of your little warm body in my arms . . .

(He breaks away and runs toward the road. From the foot of the steps he glares fiercely back at her like a tiger through the bars of a cage. She clings to the two porch pillars, her body leaning way out.) . . . .

Rosa.

Look for me! I will be there!

(Jack runs away from the house. Rosa returns inside. Listlessly she removes her dress and falls on the couch in her slip, kicking off her shoes. Then she begins to cry, as one cries only once in a lifetime, and the scene dims out.)

from
THE PETRIFIED FOREST
by Robert E. Sherwood

Act I
GABBY, SQUIER

The Petrified Forest is best remembered now as the play
that brought to prominence an almost unknown young
actor called Humphrey Bogart and, in the movie version,
an actress called Bette Davis. But for the original audience—in 1935—Sherwood's play had the excitement of
good melodrama coupled with a philosophical message
that spoke directly to people who had seen economic
prosperity collapse into a depression, and technological
triumphs harnessed into war machines. The character who
made the strongest impression was not the gangster with
the two-days' growth of beard and two guns ready to
blaze, but the suicidal intellectual (played by Leslie
Howard) who has squandered his energy and spirit idling
on the Riviera with a rich wife. One day, discovering he
has nothing "worth living for—and dying for," he asks the
all-too-ready gunman to kill him, hoping that perhaps his
insurance money will enable a girl who has charmed him
with her wide-eyed belief in poetry and art to realize her
dream of going to Paris. In 1935 this character spoke
persuasively to people for whom "The Hollow Men"
seemed their own inevitable epitaph, and he did so conve-
niently in a compelling, if not altogether convincing, plot.
Sherwood himself credited the play's success to "two parts
of a highly improbable and sentimental romance," but
Brooks Atkinson called it "just the sort of play a liberal
with a sense of humor ought to write."

Sherwood's scenes still show the skillful craftsmanship
that made him for Atkinson the "greatest" American play-

wright of the realistic, actor-oriented theater of the 1930's. His directness in characterization demands a particular honesty in acting.

The scene excerpted here comes early in the play; the audience has met and begun to know the characters, but it still has much to learn. Gabrielle Maple—always called Gabby—is "young and pretty, with a certain amount of style about her. Her principal distinguishing feature is an odd look of resentment in her large, dark eyes." She has grown up in a little town along a highway in the desert of eastern Arizona. She speaks with the no-nonsense directness of westerners; but to the puzzlement of her local boy friend, she reads poetry (and likes it) and she paints pictures. When Alan Squier drifts into the gas station/lunchroom where Gabby works, she discovers he is a writer and is impressed and fascinated. Squier is a "thin, wan, vague man of about 35 . . . He is shabby and dusty but there is about him a sort of afterglow of elegance . . . Something about him . . . brings to mind the ugly word 'condemned' . . . He is diffident in manner, ultra-polite, and soft-spoken; his accent is that of an Anglicized American."

When Gabby and Squier have talked for a time, she shyly tells him about her pictures. "Are they any good?" he asks. "Hell, *no!*" she replies. But he asks to see them. When everyone else has left the lunchroom, she allows him to look at them. Coming over to the table where Squier sits, Gabby waits for him to react.

Gabby.

(*She is eager to know how Squier feels about her paintings, but she is trying desperately hard to be offhand about it.*) They're terrible, aren't they?

(*Squier is now examining the pictures with rapt attention.*)

Squier.

I—I don't know. Is—this a portrait of some one?

Gabby.

That's Paula, our Mexican cook. She's the only one knows I ever try to do that junk. It isn't much of a likeness.

Squier.

I'm sure it wasn't intended to be. (*He picks up another*

picture.) Certainly no critic could condemn you for being photographic.

Gabby.

This is the one I like best.

(*Squier looks at it.*)

I wanted to show how the storm clouds look when they roll down from the mountains.

Squier.

What made you paint in this strange manner?

Gabby.

It's—just the way I feel.

Squier.

You're a product of the ultimate French school, all right.

Gabby.

(*Pleased.*) You think so?

Squier.

These are somewhat in the Dufy manner—and yet—a lot less conventional.

Gabby.

But are they any *good?*

Squier.

I tell you, Gabrielle—I can't say. I'm tremendously impressed, and also bewildered.

Gabby.

I'll bet I could improve if I could get to France. You know, they've got some of the finest art schools in the world there. And they've got beautiful things to paint, too—flowers, and castles and rivers. But here in this desert—it's just the same thing over and over again.

Squier.

Don't you realize—there are probably thousands of artists in France to-day who are saying, "I'd find a really big theme for my canvas if I could only get out to Arizona."

Gabby.

I know. A lot of people come out here and go crazy about the desert. They say it's full of mystery, and it's haunted, and all that. Well—maybe it is. But there's something in me that makes me want something different.

Squier.

(*Looking at her.*) I know there's something in you. I wish I could figure out what it is.

Gabby.

Listen—you've been in France. What are they like there?

Squier.

Well—it's rather difficult to render a sweeping judgment.

Gabby.

I've always imagined they must all be like Villon—gay, reckless, poetic.

Squier.

No—I shouldn't call them any of those things. Especially, not reckless!

Gabby.

But they're always having a good time, aren't they?

Squier.

Not invariably.

Gabby.

Maybe I know them better than you do, because it's in my blood. Sometimes I can feel as though I were sparkling all over, and I don't care what happens—I want to go out and do something that's absolutely crazy—and marvelous. But then the American part of me speaks up and spoils everything. It makes me go to work and figure out a lot of dull accounts: so many pounds of coffee, so many frankfurters, so many rolls. . . .

Squier.

You keep the accounts correctly?

Gabby.

If I didn't, this place would be bankrupt.

Squier.

Then that's the French part of you. The sparkle must be 100% American. Would you like to marry a Frenchman?

Gabby.

I don't want to marry anybody. I want to always be free!

Squier.

How about that stalwart youth out there in the football jersey?

Gabby.

What makes you think I'd take any notice of him?

Squier.

Well—when I came in here . . .

Gabby.

Oh, sure. He was kissing me. That's nothing.

Squier.

Perhaps. But there's always the chance of development.

Gabby.

He's trying to make me. That's all he wants.

Squier.

Do you think he'll succeed?

Gabby.

I haven't decided yet. It would be experience, and that's what I need. Do you think I ought to give in?

Squier.

Don't ask me, Gabrielle. Let your French blood guide you. It's infallible, in matters like that.

Gabby.

But you ought to know *something*. You've seen a lot, and you've written a book, and you've been married . . .

Squier.

I don't know anything. You see—the trouble with me is, I belong to a vanishing race. I'm one of the intellectuals.

Gabby.

That means you've got brains. I can see you have.

Squier.

Yes—brains without purpose. Noise without sound. Shape without substance. Have you ever read "The Hollow Men"? (*She shakes her head.*) Don't. It's discouraging, because it's true. It refers to the intellectuals, who thought they'd conquered Nature. They dammed it up, and used its waters to irrigate the wastelands. They built streamlined monstrosities to penetrate its resistance. They wrapped it up in cellophane and sold it to drugstores. They were so certain they had it subdued. And now—do you realize what it is that is causing world chaos?

Gabby.

No.

Squier.

Well, I'm probably the only living person who can tell you. . . . It's nature hitting back. Not with the old weapons—floods, plagues, holocausts. We can neutralize them. She's fighting back with strange instruments called neuroses. She's deliberately afflicting mankind with the jitters. Nature is proving that she can't be beaten—not by the likes of us. She's taking the world away from the intellectuals and giving it back to the apes . . . Forgive me, Gabrielle . . . I can't tell you what a luxury it is to have someone to talk to. . . . But don't listen to me. I was born in 1901, the year Victoria died. I was just too late for the Great War—and too soon for the revolution. You're a war baby. You may be an entirely different species, for all I know. You can easily be one of Nature's own children, and therefore able to understand her, and laugh at her—or enjoy her—depending on how you feel. You're the only one who can say whether or not you should yield to the ardors of Number 42 out there. (*He finishes his glass of beer.*) That beer is excellent.

Gabby.

It's made in Phoenix. (*She is looking at him intently.*) You know—you talk like a goddam fool.

Squier.

I know it. (*He is taking out the last of his cigarettes.*)

Gabby.

No wonder your wife kicked you out. . . . And no wonder she fell for you in the first place.

   (*He pauses in the act of lighting a cigarette.*),

Squier.

That sounds alarmingly like a compliment.

Gabby.

It is a compliment. What did you say your name was?

Squier.

Alan Squier. I've been calling you Gabrielle, so you'd better . . .

Gabby.

Where are you going from here, Alan?

Squier.

That depends on where this road leads.

Gabby.

It leads to the petrified forest.

Squier.

What's that?

Gabby.

Oh—just a lot of dead old trees in the desert, that have turned to stone.

Squier.

The petrified forest! A suitable haven for me. Perhaps that's what I'm destined for—to make an interesting fossil for future study. Homo Semi-Americanus—a specimen of the in-between age.

Gabby.

I was just thinking—I'd like to go to France with you.

(*He looks at her, sharply—then looks sharply away.*)

Squier.

Oh, no, Gabrielle! I could never retrace my footsteps.

Gabby.

You mean you haven't enough money?

Squier.

Even that is an understatement.

Gabby.

I haven't enough, either—yet. But I can do this as well as you can. (*She gestures with her thumb.*)

Squier.

We'd reach a point, on the Atlantic Coast, where even that gesture would be unavailing.

Gabby.

You know, Alan—there's something about you that's very appealing.

Squier.

Appealing! Yes—that's been my downfall. It was that very quality which led me into the gigolo trade.

Gabby.

Why wouldn't you like to be a gigolo for me?

Squier.

For one very good reason: you couldn't afford it.

Gabby.

But I *will* be able to afford it.

Squier.

On your share of this property? (*He shakes his head.*)

Gabby.

Listen—I've got more than that coming to me. Do you know how much Gramp has got salted away in the bank in Santa Fé? Twenty-two thousand dollars! He had every cent of it in gold and silver in the safety vaults. Why— we didn't even know about it until the government passed a law against hoarding and they printed his name in the papers. It's in Liberty Bonds now, and it's all willed to me. I guess we could travel pretty far on that, couldn't we?

Squier.

Too far.

Gabby.

We could go to France, and you'd show me everything, all the cathedrals and the art—and explain everything.

And you wouldn't have to marry me, Alan. We'd just live in sin and have one hell of a time.

Squier.

That's a startling proposal, Gabrielle. I hadn't expected to receive anything like that in *this* desert.

Gabby.

We'd have to wait—maybe years. But I could have Boze fired and give you the job tending the gas station.

Squier.

You think you'd like to have me for a companion?

Gabby.

I know I would. And I don't make mistakes. You're no apeman, Alan—but you're lovable.

Squier.

Lovable! The next grade below appealing.

Gabby.

Wouldn't you like to be loved by me?

Squier.

(*Looking at her intently.*) Yes, Gabrielle . . . I should like to be loved by you.

Gabby.

You think I'm attractive?

Squier.

There are better words than that for what you are.

Gabby.

Then why don't we at least make a start at it? You haven't got anything else to do.

Squier.

(*Smiling.*) No—that's just it. You couldn't live very long with a man who had nothing else to do but worship you. That's a dull kind of love, Gabrielle. It's the kind of love that makes people old, too soon. (*He rises.*) But—I thank you for the suggestion. You've opened up a new channel of my imagination which will be pleasant to explore during my lonely wanderings. I'll think of the chimes of Bourges—and you—and sin.

Gabby.

You're going now?

Squier.

Yes. And I shall continue going until either I drop or that major artist emerges to announce his message to posterity.

Gabby.

(*Rising.*) Well—I can't stop you.

Squier.

No, Gabrielle, you can't. But you can do me one great favor, before I go.... Would you mind very much if I kissed you good-by?

> (*Gabby looks at him levelly.*)

Gabby.

No. I wouldn't mind.

Squier.

You'd understand that it would be nothing more . . .

Gabby.

I'd understand. It'd be just a kiss—that's all.

Squier.

That's absolutely all. (*He kisses her.*)

from

OF MICE AND MEN

by John Steinbeck

Act I, scene 1
GEORGE, LENNIE

Two plays vied for the New York Critics' Circle Award
for the best play of 1937–1938. *Our Town* was runner-up;
Of Mice and Men won. Steinbeck's play was chosen, the
critics said, "for its direct force and perception in handling
a theme genuinely rooted in American life; . . . for its
refusal to make the study of tragic loneliness and frustration either cheap or sensational; and finally for its simple,
intense, and steadily rising effect on the stage."

If Steinbeck's George and Lennie have not achieved the
phenomenal track record of Wilder's George and Emily, it
is perhaps because their play is rooted not simply in
American life but in American life of the Great Depression. In the 1930's the frustration of men who spent their
days wandering, eager to give their sweat to make other
men's land fruitful, was universally understood, and the
loneliness of men without families or homes could be
observed in every town.

Steinbeck's evocation of the mood of the ranchlands of
the southwest is still effective, as is his honest but sympathetic understanding of the dynamics of the unlikely
friendship of two men brought together by poverty and
loneliness. And, as always, the play's great strength is in
the truth of the portraits of its central characters: tough,
smart little George, and Lennie, the big man with a child's
brain, who tags after George like a puppy, but an overgrown puppy whose jaws crack bones when he means only
to play.

The play begins on a sandy, willow-shaded bank of the

Salinas River in central California. The stage is covered
with leaves, and in the last light of the setting sun the
feeling of the place is sheltered and quiet. There is the
distant sound of ranch dogs barking aimlessly and occasionally the call of a quail. Lennie and George have tossed
their blanket-rolls on the bank, drunk from the river, and
sat down to rest. They have work cards for jobs on a
ranch, but George has to remind Lennie that that is
where they are going. Lennie forgets things. George does
his best to drum it into Lennie that when they get to the
ranch he is not to say anything, not until they've been
hired.

There is an argument about a mouse. Lennie found it
and kept it to pet it—"just gently," with his thumb—but
his petting has killed it. George insists that Lennie throw it
away.

"The light is going fast, dropping into evening. A little
wind whirls into the clearing and blows leaves. A dog
howls in the distance."

George decides they won't go to the ranch until morning.

Lennie.

Why ain't we goin' on to the ranch to get some supper?
They got supper at the ranch.

George.

No reason at all. I just like it here. Tomorrow we'll be
goin' to work. I seen thrashing machines on the way
down; that means we'll be buckin' grain bags. Bustin' a
gut liftin' up them bags. Tonight I'm gonna lay right here
an' look up! Tonight there ain't a grain bag or a boss in
the world. Tonight, the drinks is on the . . . house. Nice
house we got here, Lennie.

Lennie.

(*Gets up on his knees and looks down at George,
plaintively.*) Ain't we gonna have no supper?

George.

Sure we are. You gather up some dead willow sticks. I
got three cans of beans in my bindle. I'll open 'em up
while you get a fire ready. We'll eat 'em cold.

Lennie.

(*Companionably.*) I like beans with ketchup.

George.

Well, we ain't got no ketchup. You go get the wood, and

don't you fool around none. Be dark before long. (*Lennie lumbers to his feet and disappears into the brush. George gets out the bean cans, opens two of them, suddenly turns his head and listens. A little sound of splashing comes from the direction that Lennie has taken. George looks after him; shakes his head. Lennie comes back carrying a few small willow sticks in his hand.*) All right, give me that mouse.

Lennie.

(*With elaborate pantomime of innocence.*) What, George? I ain't go no mouse.

George.

(*Holding out his hand.*) Come on! Give it to me! You ain't puttin' nothing over. (*Lennie hesitates, backs away, turns and looks as if he were going to run. Coldly.*) You gonna give me that mouse or do I have to take a sock at you?

Lennie.

Give you what, George?

George.

You know goddamn well, what! I want that mouse!

Lennie.

(*Almost in tears.*) I don't know why I can't keep it. It ain't nobody's mouse. I didn't steal it! I found it layin' right beside the road. (*George snaps his fingers sharply, and Lennie lays the mouse in his hand.*) I wasn't doin' nothing bad with it. Just stroking it. That ain't bad.

George.

(*Stands up and throws the mouse as far as he can into the brush, then he steps to the pool, and washes his hands.*) You crazy fool! Thought you could get away with it, didn't you? Don't you think I could see your feet was wet where you went in the water to get it? (*Lennie whimpers like a puppy.*) Blubbering like a baby. Jesus Christ, a big guy like you! (*Lennie tries to control himself, but his lips quiver and his face works with effort. George puts his hand on Lennie's shoulder for a moment.*) Aw, Lennie, I ain't takin' it away just for meanness. That mouse ain't fresh. Besides, you broke it pettin' it. You get a mouse that's fresh and I'll let you keep it a little while.

Lennie.

I don't know where there is no other mouse. I remember

a lady used to give 'em to me. Ever' one she got she used to give it to me, but that lady ain't here no more.

George.

Lady, huh! ... Give me them sticks there. ... Don't even remember who that lady was. That was your own Aunt Clara. She stopped givin' 'em to you. You always killed 'em.

Lennie.

(*Sadly and apologetically.*) They was so little. I'd pet 'em and pretty soon they bit my fingers and then I pinched their head a little bit and then they was dead ... because they was so little. I wish we'd get the rabbits pretty soon, George. They ain't so little.

George.

The hell with the rabbits! Come on, let's eat. (*The light has continued to go out of the scene so that when George lights the fire, it is the major light on the stage. George hands one of the open cans of beans to Lennie.*)

There's enough beans for four men.

Lennie.

(Sitting on *the other side of the fire, speaks patiently.*) I like 'em with ketchup.

George.

(*Explodes.*) Well, we ain't got any. Whatever we ain't got, that's what you want. God Almighty, if I was alone, I could live so easy. I could go get a job of work and no trouble. No mess ... and when the end of the month come, I could take my fifty bucks and go into town and get whatever I want. Why, I could stay in a cat-house all night. I could eat any place I want. Order any damn thing.

Lennie.

(*Plaintively, but softly.*) I didn't want no ketchup.

George.

(*Continuing violently.*) I could do that every damn month. Get a gallon of whiskey or set in a pool room and play cards or shoot pool. (*Lennie gets up to his knees and looks over the fire, with frightened face.*) And what have I got? (*Disgustedly.*) I got *you*. You can't keep a job and you lose me every job I get!

Lennie.

(*In terror.*) I don't mean nothing, George.

George.

Just keep me shovin' all over the country all the time. And that ain't the worst—you get in trouble. You do bad things and I got to get you out. It ain't bad people that raises hell. It's dumb ones. (*He shouts.*) You crazy son-of-a-bitch, you keep me in hot water all the time. (*Lennie is trying to stop George's flow of words with his hands. Sarcastically.*) You just wanta feel that girl's dress. Just wanta pet it like it was a mouse. Well, how the hell'd she know you just wanta feel her dress? How'd she know you'd just hold onto it like it was a mouse?

Lennie.

(*In panic.*) I didn't mean to, George!

George.

Sure you didn't mean to. You didn't mean for her to yell bloody hell, either. You didn't mean for us to hide in the irrigation ditch all day with guys out lookin' for us with guns. Alla time it's something you didn't mean. God damn it, I wish I could put you in a cage with a million mice and let them pet *you*. (*George's anger leaves him suddenly. For the first time he seems to see the expression of terror on Lennie's face. He looks down ashamedly at the fire, and maneuvers some beans onto the blade of his pocket-knife and puts them into his mouth.*)

Lennie.

(*After a pause.*) George! (*George purposely does not answer him.*) George?

George.

What do you want?

Lennie.

I was only foolin', George. I don't want no ketchup. I wouldn't eat no ketchup if it was right here beside me.

George.

(*With a sullenness of shame.*) If they was some here you could have it. And if I had a thousand bucks I'd buy ya a bunch of flowers.

Lennie.

I wouldn't eat no ketchup, George. I'd leave it all for you. You could cover your beans so deep with it, and I wouldn't touch none of it.

George.

(*Refusing to give in from his sullenness, refusing to look at Lennie.*) When I think of the swell time I could have without you, I go nuts. I never git no peace!

Lennie.

You want I should go away and leave you alone?

George.

Where the hell could you go?

Lennie.

Well, I could . . . I could go off in the hills there. Some place I could find a cave.

George.

Yeah, how'd ya eat? You ain't got sense enough to find nothing to eat.

Lennie.

I'd find things. I don't need no nice food with ketchup. I'd lay out in the sun and nobody would hurt me. And if I found a mouse—why, I could keep it. Wouldn't nobody take it away from me.

George.

(*At last he looks up.*) I been mean, ain't I?

Lennie.

(*Presses his triumph.*) If you don't want me, I can go right in them hills, and find a cave. I can go away any time.

George.

No. Look! I was just foolin' ya. 'Course I want you to stay with me. Trouble with mice is you always kill 'em. (*He pauses.*) Tell you what I'll do, Lennie. First chance I get I'll find you a pup. Maybe you wouldn't kill it. That would be better than mice. You could pet it harder.

Lennie.

(*Still avoiding being drawn in.*) If you don't want me, you only gotta say so. I'll go right up on them hills and live by myself. And I won't get no mice stole from me.

George.

I want you to stay with me. Jesus Christ, somebody'd shoot you for a coyote if you was by yourself. Stay with me. Your Aunt Clara wouldn't like your runnin' off by yourself, even if she is dead.

Lennie.

George?

George.

Huh?

Lennie.

(*Craftily.*) Tell me—like you done before.

George.

Tell you what?

Lennie.

About the rabbits.

George.

(*Near to anger again.*) You ain't gonna put nothing over on me.

Lennie.

(*Pleading.*) Come on, George . . . tell me! Please! Like you done before.

George.

You get a kick out of that, don't you? All right, I'll tell you. And then we'll lay out our beds and eat our dinner.

Lennie.

Go on, George. (*Unrolls his bed and lies on his side, supporting his head on one hand. George lays out his bed and sits crosslegged on it. George repeats the next speech rhythmically, as though he had said it many times before.*)

George.

Guys like us that work on ranches is the loneliest guys in the world. They ain't got no family. They don't belong no place. They come to a ranch and work up a stake and then they go in to town and blow their stake. And then the first thing you know they're poundin' their tail on some other ranch. They ain't got nothin' to look ahead to.

Lennie.

(*Delightedly.*) That's it, that's it! Now tell how it is with us.

George.

(*Still almost chanting.*) With us it ain't like that. We got a future. We got somebody to talk to that gives a damn about us. We don't have to sit in no barroom blowin' in our jack, just because we got no place else to go. If them other guys gets in jail, they can rot for all anybody gives a damn.

Lennie.

(*Who cannot restrain himself any longer. Bursts into speech.*) But not us! And why? Because . . . because I got you to look after me . . . and you got me to look

after you . . . and that's why! (*He laughs.*) Go on,
George!

George.

You got it by heart. You can do it yourself.

Lennie.

No, no. I forget some of the stuff. Tell about how it's
gonna be.

George.

Some other time.

Lennie.

No, tell how it's gonna be!

George.

Okay. Some day we're gonna get the jack together and
we're gonna have a little house, and a couple of acres
and a cow and some pigs and . . .

Lennie.

(*Shouting.*) And live off the fat of the land! And have
rabbits. Go on, George! Tell about what we're gonna
have in the garden. And about the rabbits in the cages.
Tell about the rain in the winter . . . and about the stove
and how thick the cream is on the milk, you can hardly
cut it. Tell about that, George!

George.

Why don't you do it yourself—you know all of it!

Lennie.

It ain't the same if I tell it. Go on now. How I get to
tend the rabbits.

George.

(*Resignedly.*) Well, we'll have a big vegetable patch and
a rabbit hutch and chickens. And when it rains in the
winter we'll just say to hell with goin' to work. We'll
build up a fire in the stove, and set around it and listen
to the rain comin' down on the roof—Nuts! (*Begins to
eat with his knife.*) I ain't got time for no more. (*He
falls to eating. Lennie imitates him, spilling a few beans
from his mouth with every bite. George, gesturing with
his knife.*) What you gonna say tomorrow when the boss
asks you questions?

Lennie.

(*Stops chewing in the middle of a bite, swallows painfully. His face contorts with thought.*) I . . . I ain't gonna
say a word.

George.

Good boy. That's fine. Say, maybe you're gittin' better. I bet I can let you tend the rabbits . . . specially if you remember as good as that!

Lennie.

(*Choking with pride.*) I can remember, by God!

George.

(*As though remembering something, points his knife at Lennie's chest.*) Lennie, I want you to look around here. Think you can remember this place? The ranch is 'bout a quarter mile up that way. Just follow the river and you can get here.

Lennie.

(*Looking around carefully.*) Sure, I can remember here. Didn't I remember 'bout not gonna say a word?

George.

'Course you did. Well, look, Lennie, if you just happen to get in trouble, I want you to come right here and hide in the brush.

Lennie.

(*Slowly.*) Hide in the brush.

George.

Hide in the brush until I come for you. Think you can remember that?

Lennie.

Sure I can, George. Hide in the brush till you come for me!

George.

But you ain't gonna get in no trouble. Because if you do I won't let you tend the rabbits.

Lennie.

I won't get in no trouble. I ain't gonna say a word.

George.

You got it. Anyways, I hope so. (*George stretches out on his blankets. The light dies slowly out of the fire until only the faces of the two men can be seen. George is still eating from his can of beans.*) It's gonna be nice sleeping here. Lookin' up . . . and the leaves . . . Don't build no more fire. We'll let her die. Jesus, you feel free when you ain't got a job—if you ain't hungry. (*They sit silently for a few moments. A night owl is heard far off. From across the river there comes the sound of a coyote howl*

*and on the heels of the howl all the dogs in the country
start to bark.*)

Lennie.

(*From almost complete darkness.*) George?

George.

What do you want?

Lennie.

Let's have different color rabbits, George.

George.

Sure. Red rabbits and blue rabbits and green rabbits.
Millions of 'em!

Lennie.

Furry ones, George. Like I seen at the fair in Sacramento.

George.

Sure. Furry ones.

Lennie.

'Cause I can jus' as well go away, George, and live in a
cave.

George.

(*Amiably.*) Aw, shut up.

Lennie.

(*After a long pause.*) George?

George.

What is it?

Lennie.

I'm shutting up, George. (*A coyote howls again.*)

from

A HATFUL OF RAIN

by Michael Gazzo

Act I, scene 2
CELIA, POLO

The play grew out of projects that Gazzo developed for the Actors Studio, and its strengths, as the Studio's Lee Strasberg has noted, are the "vividness of dialogue and a [close] relation between word, gesture, and behavior." Gazzo's concerns are the failure of communication between people in an "age of vacuum" and, when the gulf of inarticulateness can be bridged by love, the need to be responsible for what you love.

Three people—a young wife, her husband, and the husband's brother—share a tenement apartment of the lower East Side of New York. Johnny, the husband, is on drugs. His younger brother, Polo, knows Johnny's hang-up, and because he cannot bear the anguish he has seen Johnny suffer when he has tried to kick his habit, he has helped pay Johnny's pushers. Celia, Johnny's pregnant wife, knows only that her husband isn't really with her even when he is home, and often he is not home. But Polo is as attentive as Johnny is distant. He loves Celia, but accepts quite easily (most of the time) the fact that she is Johnny's, not his. Johnny has always been the one people chose. When they were children and their father had handed them over to relatives and then to an orphanage, Johnny was always being adopted, though he regularly ran back to the orphanage and Polo; no one picked Polo.

The father has returned—on a visit from Florida. He has made clear his love for Johnny but turned his back on Polo, because Polo has failed to produce the $2,500 he

75

had promised to help him start a business. The money has gone, in fact, to Johnny's pushers. And while Celia and Johnny entertained his father, Polo went out to get drunk.

The setting is the central room of the tenement apartment, the kitchen area partially partitioned off from the part of the room that serves as sitting room and as Johnny's and Celia's bedroom. Two doors lead from the kitchen to the hallway and Polo's bedroom. The apartment shows the work of a good housekeeper; the woodwork has been scraped down, stained, and varnished, and "there is everywhere the suggestion of a ceaseless effort to transform bedraggled rooms into rooms of comfort and taste." Pots with green plants line the shelves of the kitchen partition. "There is a sense of life."

It is about two o'clock in the morning. The lights are dim. In the darkness we see the city beyond—glowing. There is the sound of a dog barking in the distance. The door to Polo's room opens, and, in the lighted doorway, we see Polo standing in shorts. He moves to the sink shakily and begins throwing water down his throat. . . . The lights are flicked on.

Celia.

Don't do that, Polo! You'll give yourself a stomach cramp.

Polo.

I got no choice . . . stomach cramp or I'll die of thirst . . . Where's my pants . . . who robbed my pants? Hey Johnny, where did you put my pants?

Celia.

Johnny went out.

Polo.

You're mad at me too, huh?

Celia.

You ought to be ashamed of yourself. Your father was hurt . . . you almost took the door off the hinges slamming it.

Polo.

He was hurt, huh? His boy Johnny was here so he shouldn't feel so bad. Nobody said I was a bum, huh? All right, I never graduated high school . . . What's that make me, a bum?

Celia.

You're jealous . . .

Polo.

Why should I be jealous? It's always been the same. It's not only him . . . it's all my damn relatives. As long as I can remember, always laughing at me . . .

Celia.

You don't like your father very much, do you? Why didn't you lend your father the money? He said you promised . . . he said that—

Polo.

I know what he said—what I said . . . The money's gone. It flew south with the birds. I bet it on one of Ali Khan's horses—gone is gone, any kid knows that. Gone doesn't come back.

Celia.

I only asked a simple question, Polo.

Polo.

I'm glad you didn't ask a difficult one. I don't like my father, huh? He comes over to that nightly circus I work in, he tells me it's a joint. People don't come in there to drink, that's what he says—that's bright on his part. There's thirteen whores leaning on the bar and he tells me people don't come in there to drink.

Celia.

What's the matter with you, Polo? I've never seen you like this before.

Polo.

I'm drunk, that's all.

Celia.

I can see that you're drunk.

Polo.

Well, can't a guy drink just because he likes to drink? Do you have to have a reason to drink?

Celia.

You don't like Johnny any more, do you? Why does he have a heart like a snake?

Polo.

You're starting to sound like the 47th Precinct. Why? What? Who?

Celia.

Sometimes I get the feeling that you hate your brother . . .

Polo.

I'll tell you one thing, I used to hate him . . . When I was a kid . . . Johnny kept getting adopted, nobody ever adopted me. *And I wanted to get adopted.* They'd line us up, and he'd get picked—then he'd run away and come back to the home the old man put us in . . . and I used to think to myself . . . just let me get adopted once and I'll stay. I used to hate him every time he left—and every time he came back. He'd say the same goddamn thing . . . We gotta stick together, Polo . . . we're the only family we got.

Celia.

Johnny never told me that . . .

Polo.

Johnny never told you a lot of things. What I mean is . . . it's not a nice thing to say about the old man, is it?

Celia.

Polo, I want you to tell me what the matter is!

Polo.

Why don't you ask your husband Johnny what's the matter with him and leave me alone?

Celia.

Everybody wants to be left alone. We're getting to be a house full of Garbos.

Polo.

Just leave me alone . . .

Celia.

Just like Johnny. If I closed my eyes, I'd think you were Johnny.

Polo.

You ask the old man who I am, he'll tell you. I'm Polo, the no-good sonofabitch. He'll never forget anything. I threw a lemon at a passing car once . . . and hit the driver in the head. I set fire to a barn once . . . and I never graduated high school. No, I'm not Johnny, he's my brother and he's a sonofabitch. That sonofabitch is going to kill me.

(*Celia throws a glass of water in Polo's face.*)

Celia.

I'm sorry I did that.

Polo.

It's a sign of the times . . . a sign of the times. All the

king's men, and all the king's horses . . . Oh, what's the
difference. (*He goes into his room.*)

Celia.

Polo? Polo? Will you come out and talk to me.

Polo.

No!

Celia.

Polo, please, I'm lonely.

(*Polo comes out.*)

Celia.

There's some muffins from tonight's supper. Would you
like one?

Polo.

No.

Celia.

Well, I'm going to have one.

Polo.

I'll have one too. How's the job . . . ?

Celia.

Johnny got fired.

Polo.

I know Johnny got fired. I was asking about your job.

Celia.

Well, why didn't you come and tell me that, Polo?

Polo.

Honey, I'm not a personnel manager, I'm just a boarder.

Celia.

You're a bouncer in a cat house . . .

Polo.

Who said that?

Celia.

Your father . . .

Polo.

There must have been a full moon last night . . . boy,
they showed up last night, mean, ugly and out of their
minds . . . That slap-happy bouncer I work with, if he'd
just learn to try to talk these bums out of the place—
he's always grabbing somebody by the seat of their
pants, and we're off. You know that sonofabitchin
bouncer is six foot three and, as God is my witness,
honey, every time hell breaks loose I'm in there getting
the hell kicked out of me and that big bastard is up
against the wall cheering me on! Atta boy, Polo! Atta

boy! You got him going. Who have I got going? Who?
I'll be punchy before Christmas.

Celia.

You're too light to be a bouncer, Polo. Why don't you
quit?

Polo.

Quit? Where can I make a hundred and twenty-five
dollars a week? Where? Well, you can't beat it. You
come into the world poor and you go out owing
money. . . .

Celia.

You can say that again. . . .

Polo.

You come into the world poor, and . . .

Celia.

All right, smarty, forget it. . . . The Union Metal Company of America . . . that's where you should work, Polo.
At least there's a little excitement at your job . . . Do you
know that when I started working in the carpeted air-con-
ditioned desert I could take dictation at the rate of 120
words a minute? I could type 90 words . . . Today I was
sitting at my desk, pretending to be busy. I have papers
in all the drawers. I keep shuffling them from drawer to
drawer. I break pencils and sharpen them. Mr. Wagner
called me in his office today and I bustled in with my
steno pad and . . . you know what he called me in for?
He wanted to know. Was I happy? Was Union Metals
treating me right? I've been there five years come Ash
Wednesday . . . and every six months they call you in
and ask you the same thing. . . . Are you happy?

Polo.

Why don't you quit?

Celia.

Nobody ever quits Union Metals . . . and no one ever
gets fired. A bonus on Christmas, a turkey on Thanksgiv-
ing, long holiday weekends. They've insured Johnny and
I against sickness, and the plague, everything for the
employees . . . boat rides, picnics, sick leave, a triple-
savings interest, the vacations keep getting longer, we
have a doctor, a nurse, and a cafeteria, four coffee
breaks a day, if it gets too hot they send you home, and
if it rains it's perfectly all right if you're late . . . and it's
the dullest job in the whole world.

Polo.

Honey . . . you know what? You've got a real problem there.

Celia.

I don't know whether to laugh or cry. . . .

Polo.

Why?

Celia.

I got another raise today. . . .

Polo.

. Boy, I wish I didn't know right from wrong . . .

Celia.

What?

Polo.

Nothing. . . .

Celia.

Polo, I've been wanting to talk to you every night this week.

Polo.

We've been here every night this week . . . That's all we've done is talked.

Celia.

You're not listening to me, Polo. I've always liked you and Johnny thinks the world of you, but . . . but . . . I'm afraid you'll have to find a different place to live. . . . Maybe you could take a room somewhere in the neighborhood and still come over to dinner.

Polo.

I could, huh? And what about breakfast . . . ?

Celia.

You could come over for breakfast too . . . And I could do your shirts and everything but you'll have to find a different place to live.

Polo.

I can do my own shirts . . . Why do I have to move?

Celia.

I know how you feel about me and it's embarrassing.

Polo.

Love shouldn't be embarrassing.

Celia.

It's not really embarrassing, but I don't think the three of us can live together any more. I want you out of this

house tomorrow. Tomorrow night—after dinner, your
father gets his plane. I want you to leave.

Polo.

Why?

Celia.

Because I don't want to take any chances.

Polo.

What chances?

Celia.

Polo, let's not be children. You do know the difference
between right and wrong and so do I. Tomorrow . . . I
don't want you to go, but you have to. . . .

Polo.

Tomorrow, for crissakes, even Simon Legree gave Little
Eva two weeks' notice.

Celia.

I'm going to bed.

Polo.

Yeh, go to bed. You're tired. Lay your head down on the
pillow and close your eyes. If you want me to go, I'll go,
but tonight I'll be in the room next to yours . . . I'll say I
love you, but you won't be able to hear me because
you'll be asleep. Maybe I'll sing you a lullaby.

Celia.

Polo, why are you doing this? Why now? We've been
together so many nights and you've never been like
this. . . . Why?

Polo.

I'm drunk, that's the prize excuse for anything. I'm
drunk and I don't know what I'm saying or doing. I
could never say anything if I was sober . . . Celia?

Celia.

What?

Polo.

Look, you know how I feel about you. How do you feel
about me?

Celia.

I don't know.

Polo.

Let's feel and find out.

Celia.

Please . . . don't.

Polo.

Why didn't you slap me! I'll bet I could kiss you again and you wouldn't raise your hand.

Celia.

Why don't you? Go ahead, don't stop ... pick me up in your arms and carry me to your brother's bed; I'm going to have a baby, Polo, so I might be a little heavy.

Polo.

I'm sorry, but I love you. I didn't ask to. I didn't want to, but I do.

Celia.

Johnny ... please go to bed.

Polo.

I'm not Johnny, I'm Polo. . . .

CHAPTER II
ACTING MEANS BELIEVING

Scenes in which the actor exercises his memory, emotional memory, and imagination to act "as if it were real."

from

THE SILVER CORD

by Sidney Howard

Act II, scene 1
CHRISTINA

Christina Phelps is "tall, slender, grave, honest, shy, intelligent, most trusting, and, when need be, courageous." At a
time—1905—when it is not usual for a woman to seek a
career in science, she is both a doctor and a medical
researcher. She is open-minded, clear-sighted, and candid,
and though there is no questioning her charm and her
deep love for her new husband, a young architect, "she
has a scientist's detachment and curiosity, and these serve
oddly to emphasize a very individual womanliness which is
far removed from the accepted feminine." The speech
reprinted below focuses on this combination of qualities
which characterize Christina and make her a formidable
adversary for a mother-in-law whose strength is her old-
fashioned femininity, whose strategies are inevitably subtle
and oblique, and whose single purpose in life is to hold
onto her two sons. (For introductory notes about *The
Silver Cord*, see p. 296.)

Christina.
(*With a nod to Hester and speaking as she moves, leads
Hester back towards C, determined to take advantage of
the break and good-naturedly hoping to interest Mrs.
Phelps.*) Once last winter we had a big snowfall at
Heidelberg. I'd been all day in the laboratory, I remember, straining my eyes out at a scarlet-fever culture for
our bacteriology man.
    (*She is now at the back of the chair at the top of the
table C, standing with her hands on its back. She tips the*

87

*chair looking towards Mrs. Phelps and smiling. Hester is
on her R hand, above Robert. David still at the window.*)
Krause, his name was. They called him the "Demon of
the Neckar." The theory was that he used to walk along
the river bank, thinking up cruel things to say to his
students. I never knew such a terrifying man. . . .

(*She has advanced a step towards Mrs. Phelps, but,
getting no response, she returns to the chair, moves it to
a slight angle and sits on its L edge, putting her R arm
across its back, sitting in such a position that she may
turn easily to the L or the R as she speaks. David comes
down R to the R end of the settee.*)
Well, this day I'm talking about, I came out of Krause's
laboratory into the snow. Into Grimm's fairy-tales, as
Dave knows, because Dave's seen Heidelberg.

(*David sits at the R end of the settee.*)
Another bacteriologist, a dear boy from Marburg, came
with me. We looked at the snow and we wanted to coast.
(*She turns to Mrs. Phelps, speaking with a little laugh—
then she takes everybody in, turning from one to the
other naturally at the different points of her story.*) We
found a small boy with a very large sled and we rented
it, with the boy, who wouldn't trust us not to steal it.
We certainly coasted. We got so ardent, we took the
funicular up the Schlossberg and coasted down from
there. The lights came out along the Neckar and the
snow turned the colours, and colours snow can turn! And
still we coasted. . . . Presently we had an accident.

(*Robert's attention becomes more held.*)
A bob turned over in front of us with an old man in it.
We couldn't stop and so we just hit the bob and the old
man, and you know how that is when you're going fast!
. . . We picked ourselves up—or, rather, dug ourselves
out—and went to see if we'd hurt the old fellow, and it
was Krause himself! I don't mind telling you we stood
there petrified. But we needn't have worried. He smiled
the sweetest smile, and touched his cap and apologized
for his clumsiness. "My age hasn't improved my skill," he
said. . . . I could have kissed him. (*She turns directly to
Mrs. Phelps.*) I wasn't quite sure how he'd have taken
that, so, instead, I asked him to join us. He was delighted. We kept it up for another hour, we two students and
the great god Krause. "Jugend ist Trunkenheit ohne

Wein!" he said. I dare say he was quoting a poem. . . .
He couldn't have been a day under seventy. (*On a
deeper note and without action she finishes the story
—becoming introspective.*) Three days later he died of an
inoperable internal tumour. In his notes, they found an
observation he had written on his condition that very day
we coasted. Think of a man who could write observations on his approaching death and then go off to coast
afterwards! It's what life can be and should be. It's the
difference between life and self.

from

A HATFUL OF RAIN

by Michael Gazzo

Act I, scene 1
JOHNNY

Johnny Pope is homeless and alone. He is married to a
wife who loves him; she has turned their tenement flat
into a warm, living place, and she is pregnant with his
child. But Johnny stands separate from all this—not physically, but emotionally, in himself. He is hooked on drugs,
but deeper than this addiction is his psychological aliena-
tion, his fear of trusting love to those who might desert
him and his inability to communicate even with those who
are close to him. Though Johnny's involvement with drugs
is the sensational problem on the surface of the play,
Gazzo's real concern—and the level at which his play is
most valid—is understanding the barriers that stand between people. (For introductory notes about the play, see
p. 75.)

The background of Johnny's problems becomes clear
early in the play. Johnny's father has come from Florida
for a brief visit. Though he now makes much of his
concern for Johnny and his other son, Polo, he left them
as children to be cared for by grandparents, aunts and
uncles, and for a time an orphanage. This desertion—for
so it seemed to the boys—has left its mark on Johnny.
With memories awakened by his father's visit, and fearing
that if his wife finds out about his drug habit she too will
desert him, Johnny finds himself taking a train and a bus
to the town in which he lived when he was young and
there was a family that included him.

In the evening his wife asks where he has been, knowing that he has allowed her to think he was at work when
he in fact no longer has a job to go to, knowing that

90

something has come between them, and fearing that he is seeing another woman. Johnny refuses to talk about it at first. But when she brings up the other woman idea a second time, he interrupts her.

Johnny.

This morning you said that the marriage was a bust, that we were on the rocks . . . After you left . . . Did you ever feel like you were going crazy? Ever since I knew the old man was coming up . . . I just can't stop remembering things . . . like all night long I've been hearing that whistle . . . The old man used to whistle like that when he used to call us . . . I was supposed to come right home from school, but I played marbles. Maybe every half-hour he'd whistle . . . I'd be on my knees in the schoolyard, with my immie glove on—you take a woman's glove and you cut off the fingers . . . so your fingers are free and your knuckles don't bleed in the wintertime . . . and I just kept on playing and the whistle got madder and madder. It starts to get dark and I'd get worried but I wouldn't go home until I won all the marbles . . . and he'd be up on that porch whistling away. I'd cross myself at the door . . . and there was a grandmother I had who taught me to cross myself to protect myself from lightning . . . I'd open the door and go in . . . hold up the chamois bag of marbles and I'd say, hey, Pop, I won! Wham! Pow! . . . I'd wind up in the corner saying, Pop, I didn't hear you. I didn't hear you . . .

§Celia.

What did you do today? You didn't play marbles today, did you? You weren't home all day because I called here five times if I called once . . .§

Johnny.

I'm trying to tell you what I did today . . .

§Celia.

You're trying to avoid telling me what you did today.§

Johnny.

I took a train see . . . then I took a bus . . . I went to look at the house I was born in. It's only an hour away . . . but in fifteen years, I've never gone anywhere near that house . . . or that town! I had to go back . . . I can't explain the feeling, but I was ten years old when I left

there ... The way I looked around, they must have
thought I was crazy ... because I kept staring at the old
house—I was going to knock at the door and ask the
people if I could just look around ... and then I went to
that Saybrook school where I used to hear the old man
whistle ... and those orange fire escapes ... and ivy still
climbing up the walls. Then I took the bus and the train,
and I went to meet the old man's plane ... and we came
here.
§Celia.

You came here. Not home ... but here.§
Johnny.

I mean home.
§Celia.

You said here ...§
Johnny.

All right, here, not home. You know, I've lived in a lot
of places since I left that town. There was always a
table, some cups and some windows ... and somebody
was the boss, somebody to tell you what to do and what
not to do, always somebody to slap you down, pep you
up, or tell you to use will power ... there was always a
bed. What do I know about a home?

from

MORE STATELY MANSIONS

by Eugene O'Neill

Act I, scene 1
DEBORAH

The place is a log cabin facing a small lake near a
Massachusetts village on an afternoon in October 1832.
The cabin is tiny and clearly long abandoned. The mortar
between the stones of its chimney has crumbled and fallen
in spots, and here and there the moss stuffing between its
logs hangs in strips. But the weather-beaten wooden
bench, hand-hewn, that stands beside the door is sturdy
still. And in the wood that rises behind the cabin, the
autumn foliage is in full color, "purple and red and gold
mingled with the deep green of the conifers."

The autumn mood, the worn cabin, and the brilliance of
the colors form an appropriate setting for the woman who
has chosen this spot for a secret rendezvous. "Deborah
Harford is forty-five, but looks much younger. She is
small, not over five feet tall, with the slender immature
figure of a young girl. Her face is small, astonishingly
youthful, with only the first tracing of wrinkles about the
eyes and mouth. It is framed by a mass of wavy white
hair, which by contrast with the youthfulness of her face
gives her the appearance of a girl wearing a becoming wig
at a costume ball. Her nose is dainty and delicate above a
full-lipped mouth, too large and strong for her face,
showing big, even white teeth when she smiles. Her forehead is high . . . with sunken temples. Her eyes are so
large they look enormous, black, deep-set, beneath pro-
nounced brows that meet above her nose. Her hands are
small with thin, strong, tapering fingers, and she has tiny

93

feet. She is dressed with extreme care and good taste, entirely in white."

Though Deborah's imaginings—her game of pretending to be a lady of the court of eighteenth-century France— are romantic, her situation is not. The wife of a solid New England businessman, she is the mother of sons who have grown away from her, one into the dullness of account books and trade, the other into a marriage of which Deborah disapproves. She has come to the secluded cabin not to meet a lover but to talk to her son Simon, and to do so out of sight and hearing of his wife, whom Deborah detests, the daughter of an aristocratic officer turned alcoholic innkeeper and a plain Irish immigrant woman. Since Simon's wedding Deborah has removed herself from his life, but now she wishes to see him.

The scene begins O'Neill's intense late drama, left unrevised at his death but, edited and somewhat reduced in length, produced a few years ago in Sweden and then in New York. The play was intended to form part of an immense cycle, a family history spanning the years of American history. Only four of the plays were written, and only two survive—*More Stately Mansions* and the play that leads up to it, *A Touch of the Poet.*

As the curtain rises, Simon's wife appears by the corner of the cabin, looks furtively around the clearing, then slips into the cabin and locks herself in. Then Deborah steps into the clearing from the path.

Deborah.

(*Looks around the clearing—bitterly, forces a self-mocking smile.*)
What can you expect, Deborah? At your age, a woman must become resigned to wait upon every man's pleasure, even her son's.

(*She picks her way daintily through the grass toward the bench.*)
Age? You harp on age as though I were a withered old hag! I still have years before me.

(*She sits down.*)
And what will you do with these years, Deborah? Dream them away as you have all the other years since Simon deserted you? Dream yourself back until you become not the respectable, if a trifle mad, wife of the well known

merchant, but a noble adventuress of Louis' Court, and your little walled garden the garden of Versailles, your pathetic summer-house a Temple of Love the King has built as an assignation place where he keeps passionate trysts with you, his mistress, greedy for lust and power! Really, Deborah, I begin to believe that truly you must be a little mad! You had better take care! One day you may lose yourself so deeply in that romantic evil, you will not find your way back.

(With defiant bravado.)

Well, let that happen! I would welcome losing myself!

(She stops abruptly—exasperatedly.)

But how stupid! These insane interminable dialogues with self! I must find someone outside myself in whom I can confide, and so escape myself—someone strong and healthy and sane, who dares to love and live life greedily instead of reading and dreaming about it!

(Derisively.)

Ah, you are thinking of the Simon that was, *your* Simon— not the husband of that vulgar Irish biddy, who evidently has found such a comfortable haven in her arms! Yes. Why did I come? Perhaps he is not coming. Perhaps she would not permit him. Am I to sit all afternoon and wait upon his pleasure?

(Springing to her feet.)

I will go!

(Controlling herself—in a forced reasonable tone.)

Nonsense! He told the servant to tell me he would come. He would never break his word to me, not even for her.

(She sits down again.)

It is I who am early. I have only to be patient, keep my mind off bitter thoughts, while away the time—with any dream, no matter how absurd—shut my eyes and forget— not open them until he comes—

(She relaxes, her head back, her eyes shut. A pause. Then she dreams aloud.)

The Palace at Versailles—I wear a gown of crimson satin and gold, embroidered in pearls—Louis gives me his arm, while all the Court watches enviously—the men, old lovers that my ambition has used and discarded, or others who desire to be my lovers but dare not hope— the women who hate me for my wit and beauty, who envy me my greater knowledge of love and of men's hearts—I walk with the King in the gardens—he whispers tenderly: "My throne it is your heart, Beloved, and my fair kingdom your beauty." He kisses me on the lips—as I lead him into the little Temple of Love he built for me—

(*There is a sound from up the path at left-front, through the woods. Deborah starts quickly and opens her eyes as Simon Harford comes into the clearing.*

He is twenty-six but the poise of his bearing makes him appear much more mature. He is tall and loose-jointed with a wiry strength of limb. A long Yankee face, with Indian resemblances, swarthy, with a big straight nose, a wide sensitive mouth, a fine forehead, large ears, thick brown hair, light-brown eyes, set wide apart, their expression sharply observant and shrewd, but in their depths ruminating and contemplative. He speaks quietly, in a deep voice with a slight drawl.)

§Simon.

Mother!§

(*He strides toward her.*)

Deborah.

(*Rising—in a tone of arrogant pleasure.*)

You have been pleased to keep me waiting, Monsieur.

from

AFTER THE FALL

by Arthur Miller

Two Monologues from Act I
QUENTIN; MOTHER

Miller's drama of a man in search of meaning opens on an
empty, sharply raked stage. "As light dimly rises, the
persons in the play move in a random way up from behind
the high back platform." They are, with one exception,
memories. "Some . . . seem to recognize each other . . .
others move alone and in total separateness . . . In sibilant
whispers, some angry, some in appeal," they speak toward
the one who is not a memory, Quentin, a man in his
forties. He moves out of the group and walks to the front
of the stage. Behind him, movement ceases; these characters will exist only as Quentin calls them up or they persist
despite him in his thoughts. (For introductory notes about
After the Fall, see p. 412.)

(For introductory notes about *After the Fall*, see p. 412.)

   "Quentin addresses the Listener, who, if he could be
seen, would be sitting just beyond the edge of the stage
itself."

Quentin.
Hello! God, it's good to see you again! I'm very well. I
hope it wasn't too inconvenient on such short notice.
Fine, I just wanted to say hello, really. Thanks. (*He sits
on invitation. Slight pause.*) Actually, I called you on the
spur of the moment this morning; I have a bit of a
decision to make. You know—you mull around about
something for months and all of a sudden there it is and
you don't know what to do.
Ah . . .
(*He sets himself to begin, looks off.*)

97

(*Interrupted, he turns back to Listener, surprised.*)
I've quit the firm, didn't I write you about that? Really! I
was sure I'd written. Oh, about fourteen months ago: a
few weeks after Maggie died. (*Maggie stirs on the second platform.*) It just got to where I couldn't concentrate on a case any more; not the way I used to. I felt I
was merely in the service of my own success. It all lost
any point. Although I do wonder sometimes if I am
simply trying to destroy myself. . . . Well, I have walked
away from what passes for an important career. . . . Not
very much, I'm afraid; I still live in the hotel, see a few
people, read a good deal—(*Smiles.*)—stare out the window. I don't know why I'm smiling; maybe I feel that's
all over now, and I'll harness myself to something again.
Although I've had that feeling before and done nothing
about it, I—

   (*Again, interrupted, he looks surprised.*)
God, I wrote you about *that*, didn't I? Maybe I dream
these letters. Mother died. Oh, it's four—(*Airplane
sound is heard behind him*)—five months ago now. Yes,
quite suddenly; I was in Germany at the time and—it's
one of the things I wanted—(*Holga appears on upper
platform, looking about for him*)—to talk to you about.
I . . . met a woman there. (*He grins.*) I never thought it
could happen again, but we became quite close. In fact,
she's arriving tonight, for some conference at Columbia—
she's an archaeologist. I'm not sure, you see, if I want to
lose her, and yet it's outrageous to think of committing
myself again. . . . Well, yes, but look at my life. A life,
after all, is evidence, and I have two divorces in my
safe-deposit box. (*Turning to glance up at Holga.*) I tell
you frankly, I'm a little afraid. . . . Well, of who and
what I'm bringing to her. (*He sits again, leans forward.*)
You know, more and more I think that for many years I
looked at life like a case at law, a series of proofs. When
you're young you prove how brave you are, or smart;
then, what a good lover; then, a good father; finally, how
wise, or powerful or what-the-hell-ever. But underlying it
all, I see now, there was a presumption. That I was
moving on an upward path toward some elevation,
where—God knows what—I would be justified, or even
condemned—a verdict anyway. I think now that my
disaster really began when I looked up one day—and the

bench was empty. No judge in sight. And all that remained was the endless argument with oneself—this
pointless litigation of existence before an empty bench.
Which, of course, is another way of saying—despair.
And, of course, despair can be a way of life; but you
have to believe in it, pick it up, take it to heart, and
move on again. Instead, I seem to be hung up. (*Slight
pause.*) And the days and the months and now the years
are draining away. A couple of weeks ago I suddenly
became aware of a strange fact. With all this darkness,
the truth is that every morning when I awake, I'm full of
hope! With everything I know—I open my eyes, I'm like
a boy! For an instant there's some—unformed promise in
the air. I jump out of bed, I shave. I can't wait to finish
breakfast—and then, it seeps in my room, my life and its
pointlessness. And I thought—if I could corner that
hope, find what it consists of and either kill it for a lie,
or really make it mine . . .

SECOND MONOLOGUE

Among Quentin's memories are his father, who was
destroyed in the Wall Street crash of 1929 and did not
recover, and his mother, who never forgave her husband's
failure.

Trying to understand his reactions to his first sight of a
German concentration camp and to place this experience
in some context of human responsibility, Quentin asks
himself, "Why do I *know* something here?" He is startled
that the voice that speaks from his memory is his mother's.

The day of family catastrophe began in quite a different
mood. There was a wedding, there were children to be
dressed, and Quentin's mother fussed and chatted.

Mother.

(*To an invisible small boy.*) Not too much cake, darling,
there'll be a lot of food at this wedding.

§**Quentin.**

Mother! That's strange. And murder?§

Mother.

(*Getting down on her knees to tend the little boy.*) Yes,

garters, Quentin, and don't argue with me. . . . Because
it's my brother's wedding and your stockings are not to
hang over your shoes!
§**Quentin.**

(*He has started to laugh but it turns into.*) Why can't I
mourn her? And Holga wept in there, why can't I weep?
Why do I feel an understanding with this slaughterhouse?§

                (*Mother laughs. He turns to her.*)

Mother.

(*To the little boy.*) My brothers! Why must every wedding in this family be a catastrophe! . . . Because the girl
is pregnant, darling, and she's got no money, she's stupid,
and I tell you this one is going to end up with a
mustache! That's why, darling, when you grow up, I
hope you learn how to disappoint people. Especially
women.
§**Quentin.**

(*Watching her, sitting nearby.*) But what the hell has this
got to do with a concentration camp?§

Mother.

Will you stop playing with matches? (*Slaps an invisible
boy's hand.*) You'll pee in bed! Why don't you practice
your penmanship instead? You write like a monkey,
darling. And where is your father? If he went to sleep in
the Turkish bath again, I'll kill him! Like he forgot my
brother Herbert's wedding and goes to the Dempsey-
Tunney fight. And ends up in the men's room with the
door stuck, so by the time they get him out my brother's
married, there's a new champion, and it cost him a
hundred dollars to go to the men's room! (*She is laughing.*)

    (*Father with secretary has appeared on upper platform,
an invisible phone to his ear.*)

§**Father.**

Then cable Southampton.§

Mother.

But you mustn't laugh at him, he's a wonderful man.
§**Father.**

Sixty thousand tons. Sixty.§

                (*Father disappears.*)

Mother.

To this day he walks into a room you want to bow!

(*Warmly.*) Any restaurant—one look at him and the waiters start moving tables around. *Because,* dear, people know that this is a *man.* Even Doctor Strauss, at my wedding he came over to me, says, "Rose, I can see it looking at him, you've got a wonderful man," and he was always in love with me, Strauss.... Oh, sure, but he was only a penniless medical student then, my father wouldn't let him in the house. Who knew he'd end up so big in the gallstones? That poor boy! Used to bring me novels to read, poetry, philosophy, God knows what! One time we even sneaked off to hear Rachmaninoff together. (*She laughs sadly; and with wonder more than bitterness.*) That's why, you see, two weeks after we were married; sit down to dinner and Papa hands me a menu and asks me to read it to him. Couldn't *read*! I got so frightened I nearly ran away! ... Why? Because your grand-mother is such a fine, unselfish woman; two months in school and they put him into the shop! That's what some women are, my dear—and now he goes and buys her a new Packard every year. (*With a strange and deep fear.*) Please, darling, I want you to *draw* the letters, that scribbling is ugly, dear; and your posture, your speech, it can all be beautiful! Ask Miss Fisher, for years they kept my handwriting pinned up on the bulletin board; God, I'll never forget it, valedictorian of the class with a scholarship to Hunter in my hand . . . (*A blackness flows into her soul.*) And I came home, and Grandpa says, "You're getting married!" I was like—like with small wings, just getting ready to fly; I slept all year with the catalogue under my pillow. To learn, to learn every-thing! Oh, darling, the whole thing is such a mystery!

from

THE LARK

by Jean Anouilh (translated by Christopher Fry)

Two Monologues from Part I and Part II
JOAN

"Well, now; is everyone here? If so, let's have the trial and
be done with it. The sooner she is found guilty and
burned, the better for all concerned."

With these abrupt words, spoken by the Earl of Warwick, Anouilh begins his play of Joan of Arc. It is nothing
like a traditional history play. It takes place on an empty,
neutral stage with actors in plain clothes drifting on by
twos and threes. "The trial" is not simply the famous trial
before the churchmen, though that event has its place in
the play; Anouilh's trial is an examination of the meaning
of Joan: her career, her feelings, her significance, her
truth. But the meaning shifts with points of view. For
Warwick, Joan is "my grubby little witch lying on the
straw in the dungeon"; for Cauchon, the French bishop
who shares the stage with Warwick at the beginning of the
play, she is "the gentle and implacable warrior maid"; for
others, like the weakling Dauphin whom she led to
coronation, she is someone else still.

At the center, like a figure surrounded by distorting
mirrors, is Joan herself: plain, dressed in the man's cloth-
ing she wore when she lived among the soldiers, telling her
story. As she speaks, the people she mentions take life on
the stage, play their parts in brief, dramatic scenes—
attempting to persuade Joan to see herself as they do—
and then fade again into the neutral background.

The scenes reprinted here represent Joan at moments of
her greatest belief and greatest doubt. The first excerpt
begins Joan's story.

Warwick, demanding his quick trial and verdict, is interrupted by Cauchon, who insists that first they must play the whole story. Warwick reluctantly agrees. Cauchon turns to Joan, calls her name, and she looks up. "You may begin," he says.

Joan.

May I begin wherever I like?

§Cauchon.

Yes.§

Joan.

I like remembering the beginning: at home, in the fields, when I was still a little girl looking after the sheep, the first time I heard the Voices, that is what I like to remember. . . . It is after the evening Angelus. I am very small and my hair is still in pigtails. I am sitting in the field, thinking of nothing at all. God is good and keeps me safe and happy, close to my mother and my father and my brother, in the quiet countryside of Domremy, while the English soldiers are looting and burning villages up and down the land. My big sheep-dog is lying with his head in my lap; and suddenly I feel his body ripple and tremble, and a hand seems to have touched my shoulder, though I know no one has touched me, and the voice says—

§Someone in the Crowd.

Who is going to be the voice?

Joan.

I am, of course.§ I turned to look. A great light was filling the shadows behind me. The voice was gentle and grave. I had never heard it before, and all it said to me —was: "Be a good and sensible child, and go often to church." But I *was* good, and I *did* go to church often, and I showed I was sensible by running away to safety. That was all that happened the first time. And I didn't say anything about it when I got home; but after supper I went back. The moon was rising; it shone on the white sheep; and that was all the light there was. And then came the second time; the bells were ringing for the noonday Angelus. The light came again, in bright sunlight, but brighter than the sun, and that time I saw him.

§Cauchon.

You saw whom?§

Joan.

A man in a white robe, with two white wings reaching from the sky to the ground. He didn't tell me his name that day, but later on I found out that he was the blessed St. Michael.

§Warwick.

Is it absolutely necessary to have her telling these absurdities all over again?

Cauchon.

Absolutely necessary, my lord.

(*Warwick goes back to his corner in silence, and smells the rose he has in his hand.*) §

Joan.

(*In the deep voice of the Archangel.*)—Joan, go to the help of the King of France, and give him back his kingdom. (*She replies in her own voice.*) Oh sir, you haven't looked at me; I am only a young peasant girl, not a great captain who can lead an army.—You will go and search out Robert de Beaudricourt, the Governor of Vaucouleurs. He will give you a suit of clothes to dress you like a man, and he will take you to the Dauphin. St. Catherine and St. Margaret will protect you. (*She suddenly drops to the floor sobbing with fear.*)—Please, please pity me, holy sir! I'm a little girl; I'm happy here alone in the fields. I've never had to be responsible for anything, except my sheep. The Kingdom of France is far beyond anything I can do. If you will only look at me you will see I am small, and ignorant. The realm of France is too heavy, sir. But the King of France has famous Captains, as strong as you could need and they're used to doing these things. If they lose a battle they sleep as soundly as ever. They simply say the snow or the wind was against them; and they just cross all the dead men off their roll. But I should always remember I had killed them. Please have pity on me! . . . No such thing. No pity. He had gone already, and there I was, with France on my shoulders. Not to mention the work on the farm, and my father, who wasn't easy.

SECOND MONOLOGUE

The story progresses to Joan's imprisonment in Rouen, the long days of haranguing by bishops and canons determined to persuade Joan that her "voices" were false, and the confession, the denial of the miracles, that she agreed to sign to save herself from the fire.

In the prison she is visited by Charles, the king she helped to crown. He is pleased with himself: he has learned to act like a king. Since the coronation, he says, even his most imposing ministers call him "Sire." But the prison is damp, and the king hurries to leave.

Joan.

(*Murmuring.*) Goodbye, Sire. I am glad I got you that privilege at least.

(*The light changes again, as the Guard leads her to a three-legged stool; she is alone now in her cell.*)

Blessed St. Michael, blessed ladies Catherine and Margaret, are you never going to come again and speak to me? Why have you left me alone since the English captured me? You were there to see me safely to victory: but it's now, in the suffering time, that I need you most. I know it would be too simple, too easy, if God always held me by the hand: where would the merit be? I know He took my hand at the beginning because I was still too small to be alone, and later He thought I could make my own way. But I am not very big yet, God. It was very difficult to follow clearly everything the Bishop said to me. With the Canon it was easy: I could see where he was wrong, and where he was wicked, and I was ready to give him any answer which would make him furious. But the Bishop spoke so gently, and it often seemed to me he was right. Are you sure that you meant that, God? Did you mean me to feel so afraid of suffering, when the man said he would have no chance to strangle me before the flames could reach me? Are you sure that you want me to live? (*A pause. She seems to be waiting for an answer, her eyes on the sky.*) No word for me? I shall have to answer that question for myself, as well. (*A pause. She nods.*) Perhaps I am only proud and self-willed after all? Perhaps after all, I did imagine everything?

from
RICHARD II
by William Shakespeare

Three Monologues from Act III, scene 2; Act III, scene 3; and Act V, scene 5
RICHARD

Shakespeare's subject is the fall of a king and the discovery of the man within the regal image. At the outset, Richard is defined by his kingship; indeed, he seems never to have tried to see himself except as crown, throne, and a voice that commands life and death. But kingship does not maintain itself, royal symbols do not substitute for royal wisdom, and the princely voice loses its authority when the speaker commands no force beyond his power to speak. Unwise in his choice of counselors, irresponsible in the management of his lands and the noblemen who should be his strength, Richard loses his crown to a rebellious duke who, though born no king, has the sense and power to rule a kingdom.

Retold in so bare a way, this is the rather dismal story of the failure of a weak man. But Shakespeare is concerned with more than this. Paralleling the drama of Richard's descent into defeat and finally death is the progressive revelation of the man who remains as royalty is stripped from him. It is this drama—the characterization of Richard—that has kept the play on the stage and fascinated a long line of great actors.

Richard himself is a habitual and consummate actor, able in an instant to imagine himself in and out of a series of moving characterizations. If he cannot cope with a situation (the loss of his crown, for example), he can dramatize it superbly. But perhaps he does this too readily and too often; acting is no substitute for action. Similarly, though Richard lacks the command to rule, he commands words superbly. Poetry is his strength and weakness: no audience can resist the beauty of his speeches (he is his own keenest audience); and a critical event is for Richard inevitably the occasion for yet another outpouring of magnificent poetry—but words will not serve when deeds are called for. Contradictions, then, in the appeal of the character himself and in the double-edged responses Shakespeare requires of the audiences, become central to the play's effectiveness and to its demands on the actor.

Two of the speeches reprinted below reveal Richard at his poetic and theatrical best. The third is quite different.

On his return to the Welsh coast from an expedition in Ireland, Kind Richard learns that Henry Bolingbroke, whom Richard had exiled, has returned to the kingdom at the head of an army of rebels. Bolingbroke's announced purpose is to claim the titles and land that he would have inherited from his father if Richard had not interfered. The claims are just, the king's extravagance and irresponsibility are well-known, and many noblemen have given their support to Bolingbroke. Loyal forces have waited for Richard's return, but thinking that he will not come they have dispersed. As a series of messengers greet Richard with this and other disastrous news, he vacillates between despair and flights of hope. Then another messenger arrives with word that his three favorites, the men he had left to guard the kingdom in his absence, have been captured and put to death. In an effort to find some reason yet for hope, one of Richard's companions asks the messenger about the whereabouts of the troops of the loyal Duke of York. Before the man can answer, Richard interrupts.

King Richard.
No matter where. Of comfort no man speak.
Let's talk of graves, of worms, and epitaphs,
Make dust our paper, and with rainy eyes
Write sorrow on the bosom of the earth.
Let's choose executors and talk of wills.
And yet not so, for what can we bequeath
Save our deposed bodies to the ground?
Our lands, our lives, and all are Bullingbrooke's,
And nothing can we call our own but death

And that small model of the barren earth
Which serves as paste and cover to our bones.
For God's sake, let us sit upon the ground
And tell sad stories of the death of kings—
How some have been depos'd, some slain in war,
Some haunted by the ghosts they have depos'd,
Some poison'd by their wives, some sleeping kill'd,
All murther'd. For within the hollow crown
That rounds the mortal temples of a king
Keeps Death his court, and there the antic sits,
Scoffing his state and grinning at his pomp,
Allowing him a breath, a little scene,
To monarchize, be fear'd, and kill with looks,
Infusing him with self and vain conceit,
As if this flesh which walls about our life
Were brass impregnable, and humor'd thus
Comes at the last and with a little pin
Bores through his castle wall, and farewell king!
Cover your heads and mock not flesh and blood
With solemn reverence. Throw away respect,
Tradition, form, and ceremonious duty,
For you have but mistook me all this while.
I live with bread like you, feel want,
Taste grief, need friends. Subjected thus,
How can you say to me I am a king?

SECOND SPEECH

At Barkloughly Castle (Harlech) Bolingbroke and his army confront the defeated king. It is clear that Richard's kingdom is in Bolingbroke's hands and that the crown will soon follow. Yet when Richard shows himself on the walls of the castle, he has still the imposing appearance of majesty, and he speaks like a king, commanding Bolingbroke's ambassador to kneel before him and in thundering phrases warning him of the heavenly wrath that descends on those who dare attack a lawful king. A superb show—but Richard recognizes the great discrepancy between this appearance and the real situation, between the title he still bears and the powerless man he is. He submits to Bolingbroke's demands and sends the ambassador with a conciliatory greeting for the victor. As he awaits the return of the ambassador and word of what

Bolingbroke intends to do with him, he turns to one of his
remaining followers and speaks.

King Richard.

 What must the king do now? Must he submit?
The king shall do it. Must he be depos'd?
The king shall be contented. Must he lose
The name of king? A God's name, let it go!
I'll give my jewels for a set of beads,
My gorgeous palace for a hermitage,
My gay apparel for an almsman's gown,
My figur'd goblets for a dish of wood,
My scepter for a palmer's walking staff,
My subjects for a pair of carved saints,
And my large kingdom for a little grave,
A little little grave, an obscure grave.
Or I'll be buried in the king's highway,
Some way of common trade, where subjects' feet
May hourly trample on their sovereign's head;
For on my heart they tread now whilst I live,
And buried once, why not upon my head?
Aumerle, thou weep'st, my tender-hearted cousin.
We'll make foul weather with despised tears;
Our sighs and they shall lodge the summer corn
And make a dearth in this revolting land.
Or shall we play the wantons with our woes
And make some pretty match with shedding tears?
As thus—to drop them still upon one place
Till they have fretted us a pair of graves
Within the earth, and therein laid—there lies
Two kinsmen digg'd their graves with weeping eyes.
Would not this ill do well? Well, well, I see
I talk but idly, and you laugh at me.
Most mighty prince, my Lord Northumberland,
What says King Bullingbrooke? Will his majesty
Give Richard leave to live till Richard die?
You make a leg, and Bullingbrooke says aye.

THIRD SPEECH

 The crown is Bolingbroke's and Richard is a prisoner in
the Tower of London. Alone, lacking now even the title
and appearance of a king, he confronts himself. The scene

has been played in a variety of interpretations, some
presenting a hysterical Richard, nearly mad, others finding
in his lines a profound self-understanding. It seems clear,
however, that Richard has not only been brought to look
at himself without the accouterments of kingship but also
that he has moved beyond, perhaps seen through, his
facile poetry-making and playacting. When he speaks of
playing parts, it is with sharp awareness, and when he
reaches out for words and images, he grapples with them
with a kind of toughness, as though intent to force precise
meaning from them: "Yet I'll hammer it out."

King Richard.

  I have been studying how I may compare
This prison where I live unto the world.
And for because the world is populous
And here is not a creature but myself,
I cannot do it. Yet I'll hammer it out.
My brain I'll prove the female of my soul,
My soul the father, and these two beget
A generation of still-breeding thoughts,
And these same thoughts people this little world
In humors like the people of this world,
For no thought is contented. The better sort,
As thoughts of things divine, are intermix'd
With scruples, and do set the word itself
Against the word,
As thus: 'Come, little ones,' and then again,
'It is as hard to come as for a camel
To thread the postern of a small needle's eye.'
Thoughts tending to ambition, they do plot
Unlikely wonders—how these vain weak nails
May tear a passage through the flinty ribs
Of this hard world, my ragged prison walls,
And, for they cannot, die in their own pride.
Thoughts tending to content flatter themselves
That they are not the first of fortune's slaves,
Nor shall not be the last, like seely beggars
Who sitting in the stocks refuge their shame,
That many have and others must sit there.
And in this thought they find a kind of ease,
Bearing their own misfortunes on the back
Of such as have before endur'd the like.

Thus play I in one person many people,
And none contented. Sometimes am I king,
Then treasons make me wish myself a beggar,
And so I am. Then crushing penury
Persuades me I was better when a king.
Then am I king'd again. And by and by
Think that I am unking'd by Bullingbrooke,
And straight am nothing. But what ere I be,
Nor I nor any man that but man is
With nothing shall be pleas'd till he be eas'd
With being nothing. Music do I hear?

(The music plays.)

Ha, ha! Keep time. How sour sweet music is
When time is broke and no proportion kept!
So is it in the music of men's lives.
And here have I the daintiness of ear
To check time broke in a disorder'd string,
But for the concord of my state and time
Had not an ear to hear my true time broke.
I wasted time, and now doth time waste me;
For now hath time made me his numb'ring clock.
My thoughts are minutes, and with sighs they jar
Their watches on unto mine eyes, the outward watch,
Whereto my finger, like a dial's point,
Is pointing still, in cleansing them from tears.
Now, sir, the sound that tells what hour it is
Are clamorous groans which strike upon my heart,
Which is the bell. So sighs and tears and groans
Show minutes, times, and hours. But my time
Runs posting on in Bullingbrooke's proud joy,
While I stand fooling here, his Jack of the clock.
This music mads me. Let it sound no more,
For though it have help mad men to their wits,
In me it seems it will make wise men mad.
Yet blessing on his heart that gives it me!
For 'tis a sign of love, and love to Richard
Is a strange brooch in this all-hating world.

from

WHEN DID YOU LAST SEE MY MOTHER?

by Christopher Hampton

Three Monologues from Scene 4 and Scene 6
IAN

With *The Philanthropist*, news of Christopher Hampton, the youngest and among the best of Britain's new playwrights, reached Broadway. It was about time. Critics singled out Hampton for the superbly posed, near-epigrammatic style of his dialogue—a verbal elegance, too rarely heard in the contemporary theater, that glitters in its own right while never failing to enhance the honesty of his characterizations and the impact of his action.

When Did You Last See My Mother?, Hampton's first play, written while he was still an Oxford undergraduate, displays this same gift for finely shaped language, most notably in the speeches of the leading character, Ian, who is given to making set speeches and playing with words. But the author's style was little discussed when his play opened at London's Royal Court Theatre, for his most obvious strength was his truthful, no-compromise handling of a subject controversial but not infrequently treated on today's stage.

Ian is eighteen. Orphaned at sixteen and hard pressed for cash, he has finished school and is to go on to an Oxford scholarship. He is homosexual. For the summer he shares a small flat with a school friend, Jimmy, who has an affectionate sexual relationship with Ian but asserts his masculinity by chasing and bedding a series of girls. Much of the play concerns the breakup of the friendship, with Ian insisting and his friend denying that Jimmy is predominantly homosexual. A third major character is Jimmy's mother, Mrs. Evans, who pays three visits to the flat. She comes once for tea with Jimmy and Ian, and is given a dose of Ian's bitter wit and perhaps a sense of his loneliness. She returns after Jimmy has moved to the family house again to talk with Ian about Jimmy's angry restlessness, and she stays for Ian to make love to her. That is not the end of the play; having refused to settle for an easy romantic, self-pitying, or satiric treatment of his subject, Hampton will not resolve it with tea and sympathy. Mrs. Evans returns another time, to be rejected by Ian and told the truth about her son, and the play ends with a quiet conversation with Jimmy, who has come to tell Ian that his mother has been killed in a car crash. Mrs. Evans had just left Ian when the accident occurred. Jimmy does not know this; Ian does not tell him, but sends him away, knowing, however, that he will let him come back.

The excerpts reprinted here exemplify Ian's angry loneliness and the verbal virtuosity with which he copes with events. These are the qualities that appeal to the woman who in twenty years has never considered being unfaithful to her husband, and they make Hampton's play something much more than a shocker.

When Mrs. Evans first visits the flat, Jimmy asks Ian "to tell one of his stories"—a way to fill an awkward afternoon. When she returns, Ian is desperately alone and bored; sensing a sympathetic ear, he performs again.

It is a rainy afternoon. Mrs. Evans, "a still-attractive woman of about 40," is sitting on the battered sofa in the scruffy one-room flat. Ian stands. "He is not good-looking—he wears glasses, has a slight stoop, greasy, unmanageable hair. He does not look angry, but cool, sardonic, rather vicious." Mrs. Evans has asked about the argument that ended with Jimmy's leaving the flat. The answers are vague, and she changes the subject. "You're working again, now?" she asks.

Ian.

Yes, yes—with City and Guilds of London. Tying up parcels of examination papers for various schools. They call it 'collating'.

§Mrs. Evans.

That's a very grand name.§

Ian.

It's ... fascinating work. (*His voice reveals a deep gulf of misery and boredom.*) Fascinating.

§**Mrs. Evans.**

(*With quiet sympathy.*) I can imagine.§

Ian.

(*A sudden outburst.*) I'm sick of it. I'm there . . . clamped all day. And then in the evening I come home to this. From monotony to loneliness. (*Pause.*) Let me tell you about yesterday. Yesterday was an ordinary lousy day and yet somehow it was lived with a certain intensity. All day I worked thinking about the next tea-break, the next rest-period, and I passed the time working out how much I'd earned tying up one particular parcel, maybe if the foreman wasn't looking I could slow up and earn one and four just for wrapping up one small parcel, and that was my pleasure. (*Pause.*) And finally it came to knocking-off time, but I wasn't pleased because there were no more tea-breaks to look forward to, just hundreds of anonymous people making me sweat in the tube, and then the loneliness here that made me shiver. And I had toasted cheese and burnt the toast and my finger and I sat here by myself and watched the telly. And they had one of those retrospective programmes, you know, you probably saw it, looking back over the last year, one of those programmes about the racial problem. And it kind of brought things to a head. (*Pause.*) Did you see it? (*Mrs. Evans shakes her head.*) Well, it showed various bits of film—it showed the Ku Klux Klan, and an Apartheid supporter, and a man who keeps axe-handles in his restaurant to beat up Negroes, and a group of whites beating up blacks with chairs in a sports stadium in America. And I opened the window. And then they showed the worst thing of all. They showed a Negro policeman in the Congo beating a prisoner—another Negro—to death by hitting him on the head with a club. And I sat here and watched it; and the man who was being hit wasn't struggling, he was just sitting there, too, he just sat and bled and got beaten to death in my living-room. And I switched off. I switched him off because I didn't want him dying all over me. And I sat here thinking about it. And then I saw the flies.

I just looked up at the ceiling, see, and there were these

flies, hundreds of them, hundreds of little green ones that had come in through the open window. They were all up in one corner of the ceiling, hopping and crawling about. And I went on thinking for a bit and watched them. I'd never seen so many before. And then . . . all of a sudden I was angry. I was furious with these bloody little flies and . . . with everything, so I grabbed a pillow and . . . jumped up on the bed and lashed out at them and killed them and went on killing them till I couldn't see any more and my pillowcase was thick with green specks and remains and my knuckles were bruised where I smashed them against the wall and I was satisfied. For the first time in the day, because I'd done something different and achieved something I was . . . satisfied.

(*Long pause as Ian unwinds. Finally he speaks matter-of-factly.*)

So I went to bed.

§**Mrs. Evans.**

I . . . (*She looks distressed.*)§

Ian.

(*Smiling.*) Don't worry, I'm just playing my usual game.

§**Mrs. Evans.**

Which is?§

Ian.

Making people pity me. I'm very good at it.

SECOND MONOLOGUE

The conversation continues. Ian apologizes for the messiness of the flat. Mrs. Evans, afraid that he may not have enough to eat, offers to take him out for a meal. He refuses ."What are you going to do with your life?" she asks rather suddenly. "I don't know . . ." he replies, then adds with a smile, "Maybe I should go into advertising." (Note: For a monologue exercise of sufficient length, Ian's two major speeches can be run together, using some of the shorter speeches between as a bridge. The deletions are noted in the text below.)

Ian.

Yeah, I've got a great idea for a bad breath commercial. Great cathedral packed with people, little, persecuted man isolated in the cathedral, maybe between the choir stalls. The choir are bellowing out the 'Messiah,' vindictively, only it goes: (*He sings.*) "Alletosis, Alletosis, Alletosis.' And tears trickle down the little man's face. And he takes off his little hat and turns to the altar and looks at the Cross ... and there, clutched in ol' J.C.'s right hand, a tub of Fresho tablets . . . or whatever. And he walks up to the altar, a smile breaking through with the big backing, like at the end of a Biblical epic. It's great, you see—brings in the old religion. It'd go down big in the Home Counties, I tell you. (*He stops, broods a minute.*) Sorry, not very funny.

§Mrs. Evans.

I thought it was quite funny.§

Ian.

Yet another example of my bubbling, irrepressible wit. I'm such a bright little personality, you'd think it would turn my head. (*Pause.*) There's one thing that keeps me sane, though.

§Mrs. Evans.

What's that?§

Ian.

The grotesque and repeated failures of my love-life. To put it crudely, very few customers seem interested in the wares.

§Mrs. Evans.

Isn't a few sufficient?§

Ian.

Well, the point is, the customers that seem interested get a free sample if I approve of them. But they never come back for more. Consequently business is bad.

§Mrs. Evans.

How old are you?§

Ian.

[I'm] Eighteen; what's that got to do with it?

§Mrs. Evans.

Younger than Jimmy?

Ian.

Yeah, I suppose so.

Mrs. Evans.

Well, you can't expect to be an experienced ... man at eighteen, can you?

Ian.

Why not? (*Softly.*) Why not?§ (*Again brash.*) I know I'm ugly but even so ...

§**Mrs. Evans.**

Don't be stupid. You're not ugly. I think you're quite attractive.

Ian.

(*Smiles.*) You are nice. (*Pause.*) Even so, that doesn't mean a lot. I mean, I think you're attractive, but . . .

Mrs. Evans.

(*Uncertainly.*) Flattery will get you nowhere.

Ian.

I don't think it's trying to get me anywhere.

Mrs. Evans.

Ian, I think you're too . . . straightforward.

Ian.

You're so right; I prefer to say honest. I like to think honesty is my premier virtue. Hell, my only virtue.

Mrs. Evans.

(*Musing.*) I wonder why Jimmy left you.

Ian.

(*Caught off guard.*) What?

Mrs. Evans.

Why do you think? Really.

Ian.

I . . . told you. We had a great row.

Mrs. Evans.

I know but there must be something else. He's so miserable at home.

Ian.

He . . . it's a matter of pride. (*Pause.*) It wasn't the first argument we'd had you know. We were always having them. Anyway he's . . . quite welcome to come back. But I suspect we're just not compatible.

Mrs. Evans.

Sounds as if you were married.

Ian.

(*His self-control regained.*) Well, you started it—asking why he 'left' me.

Mrs. Evans.

I wish . . . I got on better with Jimmy.§

Ian.

My mother died when I was twelve. It was funny, we never got on too well. I was atrociously spoilt, a real little bleeder, and I was always having vicious arguments with her about something or other. But I missed her when she went into hospital. They took me to see her on the day she died because she'd been calling for me, and in a kind of delirium. I remember it was a beautiful day in June. She was in a private ward full of sun and flowers—she was quite beautiful, you know. My father was there too. He'd been there all night, he looked all in. They told me not to worry if my mother didn't recognize me. I sat by the bed and held her hand and said "Hello" or something, and she looked at me, and then she said, "I'm sorry". She said it two or three times and then I started crying and they took me away. I cried for ages. I couldn't get over her apologizing. There was a person who loved me more than anyone else ever has or ever will—and I didn't realize it until about ten minutes before she . . . snuffed it. On which note of turgid sentimentality . . .

§Mrs. Evans.

I find that very sad. I'm sorry.§

Ian.

(*Ghost of a smile.*) That story goes best with the big violin backing. It's always a success with the "Doctor Kildare" fans.

THIRD MONOLOGUE

Mrs. Evans is dead. Jimmy has come to the flat looking for . . . what?—a friend, consolation? For once, Ian finds it difficult to speak at all. But when Jimmy insists, he tries. The story he tells is one he told Mrs. Evans the day she came for tea. That is why he changes the ending now.

"Talk to me," Jimmy says, "Say anything. Just talk for a bit, so that I'll listen."

Ian.

(*Making an effort; after a moment's thought.*) Once, when I was in Paris I went to a lecture. On modern sculpture. (*Jimmy looks up in surprise.*) It wasn't a very good lecture and as you know, after a time she switched the lights off to show slides, and people started slipping out the swing-doors. And when my eyes got accustomed to the dark, you remember that I looked around and saw I was the only person left in the entire lecture hall. And I thought to myself, God, I can't go, because if I do, she'll be all alone and lecturing to herself. So I stayed. And about five minutes later she came to an end and switched the lights on and started packing up her things without even looking at the hall. I didn't even have to say anything as I thought I might. I just caught her eye as I was on the way out and smiled vaguely, that was all. And just on an impulse, I hung about a bit outside and watched her come out and she looked perfectly happy, and there was a man waiting for her in a car, her husband I expect, and she got in with him smiling and talking, and they drove off.

But when I thought about it afterwards, it seemed to me that it would have been much more . . . satisfying, er, aesthetically or whatever, if I'd left too and she'd been miserable. And so when I came to tell the story, that's the way I told it.

(Silence.)

§Jimmy.

And now?§

Ian.

Now, I don't want to tell the story that way any more.

(Silence.)

from

LOOK BACK IN ANGER

by John Osborne

Three Monologues from Act II, scene 1, and Act II, scene 2
JIMMY; COLONEL REDFERN

The angry young man was not born with Jimmy Porter,
but when Osborne's character flung himself onto the stage,
he was welcomed as the spokesman for a generation not
content to be silent in its disillusionment with the ruins of
a glorious but inhumane past and its frustration at the
hollowness of any attempt to construct a future. Jimmy
boiled with the bitter intensity of young men drawn from
the horizonless red brick and coal smoke of a once-
subservient lower middle class, educated at "white tile"
universities and dumped, vital and full of feeling, into a
society that had made them but made no place for them.
Most of all, Jimmy voiced the anger with an incandescent
articulateness—in tirades, comic routines, and parodies of
pop songs—that burst like fireworks in a rather tired
theater.

Jimmy belongs to the fifties, and reading Osborne's
stage directions, it is clear that Jimmy is neither as sympathetic nor as heroic as his first audiences took him to be.
His frustrations are, in part, of his own making, and the
demands he makes of the people who try to love him are
too great. But his vehemence, his wit, and his showman-
ship have lost none of their original impact. And in Jimmy
one can see the explosive theatricality of those characters
who would not (and did not long) remain locked behind
the invisible wall of an old realistic stage setting, the
characters who have moved out to entertain and harangue
audiences directly.

In Osborne's play Jimmy's audience is his wife Alison, his friend Cliff, and Helena, a rather imposing young lady who grew up with Alison and has come to visit her. Jimmy performs to get a reaction out of them, to drive them to respond. Alison refuses to give Jimmy that satisfaction. But Helena, who detests Jimmy and whom he detests as a representative of a snobbish, upper-class moralizing society, rises to the bait. And Jimmy, with this encouragement, is spurred on to grander (and more consciously shocking) harangues. (For introductory notes about the play, see p. 162.)

Jimmy is a tall, thin young man of about twenty-five. "He is a disconcerting mixture of sincerity and cheerful malice, of tenderness and free-booting cruelty; restless, importunate, full of pride, a combination which alienates the sensitive and insensitive alike. Blistering honesty, or apparent honesty, like his, makes few friends. To many he may seem sensitive to the point of vulgarity. To others, he is simply a loudmouth. To be as vehement as he is is to be almost non-committal."

The scene is Jimmy's attic flat in a Victorian house in a city in industrial Britain. It is evening, Alison is filling the teapot. Jimmy has been needling Helena, insisting that she has come to win Alison back to her family. Alison, recognizing one of Jimmy's onslaughts on the way, begins to panic. "Oh yes, we all know what you did for me!" she says, "I'd still be rotting away at home, if you hadn't ridden up on your charger and carried me off!"

The wild note in her voice reassures Jimmy. "His anger cools and hardens. His voice is quite calm when he speaks." (The excerpts printed below are two speeches which, in the play, are separated by a brief exchange of dialogue.)

Jimmy.

The funny thing is, you know, I really did have to ride up on a white charger—off white, really. Mummy locked her up in their eight bedroomed castle, didn't she. There is no limit to what the middle-aged mummy will do in the holy crusade against ruffians like me. Mummy and I took one quick look at each other, and, from then on, the age of chivalry was dead. I knew that, to protect her innocent young, she wouldn't hesitate to cheat, lie, bully and blackmail. Threatened with me, a young man without money, background or even looks, she'd bellow like a rhinoceros in labour—enough to make every male rhino for miles turn white, and pledge himself to celibacy. But even I under-estimated her strength. Mummy may look over-fed and a bit flabby on the outside, but don't let that well-bred guzzler fool you. Underneath all that, she's armour plated——

(*He clutches wildly for something to shock Helena with.*)

She's as rough as a night in a Bombay brothel, and as tough as a matelot's arms. She's probably in that bloody cistern, taking down every word we say. (*Kicks cistern.*) Can you 'ear me, mother. (*Sits on it, beats like bongo drums.*) Just about get her in there. Let me give you an example of this lady's tactics. You may have noticed that I happen to wear my hair rather long. Now, if my wife is honest, or concerned enough to explain, she could tell you that this is not due to any dark, unnatural instincts I possess, but because (a) I can usually think of better things than a haircut to spend two bob on, and (b) I prefer long hair. But that obvious, innocent explanation didn't appeal to Mummy at all. So she hires detectives to watch me, to see if she can't somehow get me into the *News of the World*. All so that I shan't carry off her daughter on that poor old charger of mine, all tricked out and caparisoned in discredited passions and ideals! The old grey mare that actually once led the charge against the old order—well, she certainly ain't what she used to be. It was all she could do to carry me, but your weight (*To Alison.*) was too much for her. She just dropped dead on the way.* * *

(*He crosses down to the armchair, and seats himself on the back of it. He addresses Helena's back.*)

Jimmy.

The last time she was in church was when she was married to me. I expect that surprises you, doesn't it? It was expediency, pure and simple. We were in a hurry, you see. (*The comedy of this strikes him at once, and he laughs.*) Yes, we were actually in a hurry! Lusting for the slaughter! Well, the local registrar was a particular pal of Daddy's, and we knew he'd spill the beans to the Colonel like a shot. So we had to seek out some local vicar who didn't know him quite so well. But it was no use. When my best man—a chap I'd met in the pub that morning—and I turned up, Mummy and Daddy were in the church already. They'd found out at the last moment, and had come to watch the execution carried out. How I remember looking down at them, full of beer for breakfast, and feeling a bit buzzed. Mummy was slumped over her pew in a heap—the noble, female rhino, pole-axed at last! And Daddy sat beside her, upright and unafraid, dreaming of his days among the Indian Princes, and unable to believe he'd left his horsewhip at home. Just the two of them in that empty church—them and me. (*Coming out of his remembrance suddenly.*) I'm not sure what happened after that. We must have been married, I suppose. I think I remember being sick in the vestry. (*To Alison.*) Was I?

SECOND MONOLOGUE

Helena does not shrink before Jimmy's performance; she attacks with equal vigor and some of his sharpness of wit. Jimmy's grin widens and he begins a new tack.

Jimmy.

I think you and I understand one another all right. But you haven't answered my question. I said: have you watched somebody die?

§Helena.

No, I haven't.§

Jimmy.

Anyone who's never watched somebody die is suffering from a pretty bad case of virginity.

(*His good humour of a moment ago deserts him, as he begins to remember.*)

For twelve months, I watched my father dying—when I was ten years old. He'd come back from the war in Spain, you see. And certain god-fearing gentlemen there had made such a mess of him, he didn't have long left to live. Everyone knew it—even I knew it.

(*He moves R.*)

But, you see, I was the only one who cared. (*Turns to the window.*) His family were embarrassed by the whole business. Embarrassed and irritated. (*Looking out.*) As for my mother, all she could think about was the fact that she had allied herself to a man who seemed to be on the wrong side in all things. My mother was all for being associated with minorities, provided they were the smart, fashionable ones.

(*He moves up C again.*)

We all of us waited for him to die. The family sent him a cheque every month, and hoped he'd get on with it quietly, without too much vulgar fuss. My mother looked after him without complaining, and that was about all. Perhaps she pitied him. I suppose she was capable of that. (*With a kind of appeal in his voice.*) But *I* was the only one who cared!

(*He moves L, behind the armchair.*)

Every time I sat on the edge of his bed, to listen to him talking or reading to me, I had to fight back my tears. At the end of twelve months, I was a veteran.

(*He leans forward on the back of the armchair.*)

All that that feverish failure of a man had to listen to him was a small, frightened boy. I spent hour upon hour in that tiny bedroom. He would talk to me for hours, pouring out all that was left of his life to one, lonely, bewildered little boy, who could barely understand half of what he said. All he could feel was the despair and the bitterness, the sweet, sickly smell of a dying man.

(*He moves around the chair.*)

You see, I learnt at an early age what it was to be angry—angry and helpless. And I can never forget it. (*Sits.*) I knew more about—love . . . betrayal . . . and death, when I was ten years old than you will probably ever know all your life.

THIRD MONOLOGUE

Colonel Redfern is Alison's father. When Helena persuades her to leave Jimmy, the Colonel comes to take her home. He is not the pompous officer Jimmy may have led one to think he is, though forty years of being a soldier sometimes conceals the essentially gentle, kindly man beneath. He is, however, the leftover of the Edwardian age that Jimmy has called him. His career was spent in India. Called home to England when India was granted independence, he is often slightly withdrawn and uneasy now that he finds himself in a world where his authority has lately become less and less unquestionable. He does not relish the present situation, though his wife would. Indeed, he says that he can rather admire Jimmy and understand that the latter has a certain amount of right on his side. While the Colonel waits for her to pack, Alison attempts to explain to him the intense loyalty Jimmy demands. Jimmy may have married her, she says, for revenge on the class that she and her family represent to him. Colonel Redfern is puzzled.

Colonel.

I am mystified. (*He rises, and crosses to the window R.*) Your husband has obviously taught you a great deal, whether you realise it or not. What any of it means, I don't know. I always believed that people married each other because they were in love. That always seemed a good enough reason to me. But apparently, that's too simple for young people nowadays. They have to talk about challenges and revenge. I just can't believe that love between men and women is really like that.

§Alison.

Only some men and women.§

Colonel.

But why you? My daughter. . . . No. Perhaps Jimmy is right. Perhaps I am a—what was it? an old plant left over from the Edwardian Wilderness. And I can't understand why the sun isn't shining any more. You can see what he means, can't you? It was March, 1914, when I left England, and, apart from leaves every ten years or so, I didn't see much of my own country until we all came back in '47. Oh, I knew things had changed, of course. People told you all the time the way it was going—going to the dogs, as the Blimps are supposed to say. But it seemed very unreal to me, out there. The England I remembered was the one I left in 1914, and I was happy to go on remembering it that way. Besides I had the Maharajah's army to command—that was my world, and I loved it, all of it. At the time, it looked like going on forever. When I think of it now, it seems like a dream. If only it could have gone on forever. Those long, cool evenings up in the hills, everything purple and golden. Your mother and I were so happy then. It seemed as though we had everything we could ever want. I think the last day the sun shone was when that dirty little train steamed out of that crowded, suffocating Indian station, and the battalion band playing for all it was worth. I knew in my heart it was all over then. Everything.

from

RIDERS TO THE SEA

by John M. Synge

MAURYA

Synge's magnificent one-act tragedy brings to the stage the
final episode of a lifelong struggle classic in its simplicity:
the battle of a woman, old now, and the power of nature,
represented by the sea. Husband and sons, one after the
other, have been taken from Maurya by this implacable
adversary. The action is minimal; only the loss of the
youngest son is dramatized, but in this single death all the
deaths are symbolized and re-experienced. Old Maurya,
remembering by the fire, speaks of the death of Patch
years ago and of the women who came to her, kneeling,
"crossing themselves and not saying a word." As she
pauses, the women enter, and after them the men bearing
the sail-covered body of the last of her men on a plank of
wood. Past and present are one, the struggle is unending,
and only the old woman's speech of resignation and recon-
ciliation makes bearable the implications of the action we
have seen.

The play is deceptively simple, its sparse details chosen
for their wider resonance. The speech has the realistic
accent of country Ireland, accurately reproduced, but it
takes on the rhythms of poetic tragedy.

The scene is the kitchen of a cottage on an island off
the west of Ireland. There are nets, oilskins, spinning
wheel, some new boards standing by the wall. Cathleen, a
girl of about twenty, is at the spinning wheel and Nora, a
young girl, sits at the chimney corner as old Maurya
comes in very slowly, without looking at the girls, and
goes over to her stool at the other side of the fire.
Cathleen speaks, but Maurya seems not to hear. Cathleen
tries again, and the old woman begins to talk, but not

really to the girls. (Note: Maurya's speeches may well be
played as a monologue, for in a sense she speaks only to
herself. However, the orchestration of the scene around
her is important, and it seems best to reprint it in its
entirety.)

Maurya.

(*With a weak voice.*) My heart's broken from this day.

§Cathleen.

(*As before.*) Did you see Bartley?§

Maurya.

I seen the fearfulest thing.

§Cathleen.

(*Leaves her wheel and looks out.*) God forgive you; he's
riding the mare now over the green head, and the gray
pony behind him.§

Maurya.

(*Starts, so that her shawl falls back from her head and
shows her white tossed hair. With a frightened voice.*)
The gray pony behind him.

§Cathleen.

(*Coming to the fire.*) What is it ails you at all?§

Maurya.

(*Speaking very slowly.*) I've seen the fearfulest thing any
person has seen, since the day Bride Dara seen the dead
man with the child in his arms.

§Cathleen and Nora.

Uah. (*They crouch down in front of the old woman at
the fire.*)

Nora.

Tell us what it is you seen.§

Maurya.

I went down to the spring well, and I stood there saying
a prayer to myself. Then Bartley came along, and he
riding on the red mare with the gray pony behind him.
(*She puts up her hands, as if to hide something from her
eyes.*) The Son of God spare us, Nora!

§Cathleen.

What is it you seen?§

Maurya.

I seen Michael himself.

§Cathleen.

(*Speaking softly.*) You did not, mother; it wasn't Michael

you seen, for his body is after being found in the far north, and he's got a clean burial by the grace of God.§

Maurya.

(*A little defiantly.*) I'm after seeing him this day, and he riding and galloping. Bartley came first on the red mare; and I tried to say "God speed you," but something choked the words in my throat. He went by quickly; and "the blessing of God on you," says he, and I could say nothing. I looked up then, and I crying, at the gray pony, and there was Michael upon it—with fine clothes on him, and new shoes on his feet.

§Cathleen.

(*Begins to keen.*) It's destroyed we are from this day. It's destroyed, surely.

Nora.

Didn't the young priest say the Almighty God wouldn't leave her destitute with no son living?§

Maurya.

(*In a low voice, but clearly.*) It's little the like of him knows of the sea. . . . Bartley will be lost now, and let you call in Eamon and make me a good coffin out of the white boards, for I won't live after them. I've had a husband, and a husband's father, and six sons in this house—six fine men, though it was a hard birth I had with every one of them and they coming to the world— and some of them were found and some of them were not found, but they're gone now the lot of them. . . . There were Stephen, and Shawn, were lost in the great wind, and found after in the Bay of Gregory of the Golden Mouth, and carried up the two of them on the one plank, and in by that door. (*She pauses for a moment, the girls start as if they heard something through the door that is half open behind them.*)

§Nora.

(*In a whisper.*) Did you hear that, Cathleen? Did you hear a noise in the north-east?

Cathleen.

(*In a whisper.*) There's some one after crying out by the seashore.§

Maurya.

(*Continues without hearing anything.*) There was Sheamus and his father, and his own father again, were lost in a dark night, and not a stick or sign was seen of them when the sun went up. There was Patch after was drowned out of a curragh that turned over. I was sitting here with Bartley, and he a baby, lying on my two knees, and I seen two women, and three women, and four women coming in, and they crossing themselves, and not saying a word. I looked out then, and there were men coming after them, and they holding a thing in the half of a red sail, and water dripping out of it—it was a dry day, Nora—and leaving a track to the door. (*She pauses again with her hand stretched out towards the door. It opens softly and old women begin to come in, crossing themselves on the threshold, and kneeling down in front of the stage with red petticoats over their heads.*)

Maurya.

(*Half in a dream, to Cathleen.*) Is it Patch, or Michael, or what is it at all?

§Cathleen.

Michael is after being found in the far north, and when he is found there how could he be here in this place?§

Maurya.

There does be a power of young men floating round in the sea, and what way would they know if it was Michael they had, or another man like him, for when a man is nine days in the sea, and the wind blowing, it's hard set his own mother would be to say what man was it.

§Cathleen.

It's Michael, God spare him, for they're after sending us a bit of his clothes from the far north.§ (*She reaches out and hands Maurya the clothes that belonged to Michael. Maurya stands up slowly and takes them in her hands. Nora looks out.*)

§Nora.

They're carrying a thing among them and there's water dripping out of it and leaving a track by the big stones.

Cathleen.

(*In a whisper to the women who have come in.*) Is it Bartley it is?

One of the Women.

It is surely, God rest his soul.

(*Two younger women come in and pull out the table. Then men carry in the body of Bartley, laid on a plank, with a bit of sail over it, and lay it on the table.*)

Cathleen.

(*To the women, as they are doing so.*) What way was he drowned?

One of the Women.

The gray pony knocked him into the sea, and he was washed out where there is a great surf on the white rocks.§

(*Maurya has gone over and knelt down at the head of the table. The women are keening softly and swaying themselves with a slow movement. Cathleen and Nora kneel at the other end of the table. The men kneel near the door.*)

Maurya.

(*Raising her head and speaking as if she did not see the people around her.*) They're all gone now, and there isn't anything more the sea can do to me. . . . I'll have no call now to be up crying and praying when the wind breaks from the south, and you can hear the surf is in the east, and the surf is in the west, making a great stir with the two noises, and they hitting one on the other. I'll have no call now to be going down and getting Holy Water in the dark nights after Samhain, and I won't care what way the sea is when the other women will be keening. (*To Nora.*) Give me the Holy Water, Nora, there's a small sup still on the dresser.

(*Nora gives it to her.*)

Maurya.

(*Drops Michael's clothes across Bartley's feet, and sprinkles the Holy Water over him.*) It isn't that I haven't prayed for you, Bartley, to the Almighty God. It isn't that I haven't said prayers in the dark night till you wouldn't know what I'd be saying; but it's a great rest I'll have now, and it's time surely. It's a great rest I'll have now, and great sleeping in the long nights after Samhain, if it's only a bit of wet flour we do have to eat, and maybe a fish that would be stinking. (*She kneels down again, crossing herself, and saying prayers under her breath.*)

§Cathleen.

(*To an old man.*) Maybe yourself and Eamon would make a coffin when the sun rises. We have fine white boards herself bought, God help her, thinking Michael would be found, and I have a new cake you can eat while you'll be working.

The Old Man.

(*Looking at the boards.*) Are there nails with them?

Cathleen.

There are not, Colum; we didn't think of the nails.

Another Man.

It's a great wonder she wouldn't think of the nails, and all the coffins she's seen made already.

Cathleen.

It's getting old she is, and broken.

(*Maurya stands up again very slowly and spreads out the pieces of Michael's clothes beside the body, sprinkling them with the last of the Holy Water.*)

Nora.

(*In a whisper to Cathleen.*) She's quiet now and easy; but the day Michael was drowned you could hear her crying out from this to the spring well. It's fonder she was of Michael, and would any one have thought that?

Cathleen.

(*Slowly and clearly.*) An old woman will be soon tired with anything she will do, and isn't it nine days herself is after crying and keening, and making great sorrow in the house?§

Maurya.

(*Puts the empty cup mouth downwards on the table, and lays her hands together on Bartley's feet.*) They're all together this time, and the end is come. May the Almighty God have mercy on Bartley's soul, and on Michael's soul, and on the souls of Sheamus and Patch, and Stephen and Shawn; (*Bending her head.*) and may He have mercy on my soul, Nora, and on the soul of every one is left living in the world. (*She pauses, and the keen rises a little more loudly from the women, then sinks away.*)

Maurya.

(*Continuing.*) Michael has a clean burial in the far north, by the grace of the Almighty God. Bartley will have a fine coffin out of the white boards, and a deep grave surely. What more can we want than that? No man at all can be living for ever, and we must be satisfied.

(*She kneels down again and the curtain falls slowly.*)

from

THE BOYS IN THE BAND

by Mart Crowley

Act I
MICHAEL, DONALD

Insight into character, an ironic, deadly accurate ear for
dialogue, and the ability to build sharply theatrical scenes
in the context of a realistic play marked Mart Crowley as
a more than promising new playwright when *Boys in the
Band* opened in 1968. No doubt Crowley's subject—a
frank treatment of homosexuality—stimulated the play's
initial success at the box office; but it was Crowley's skill
as a dramatist—his talent for the theatrically heightened
psychological realism that has typified the best Broadway
theater in the years since World War II—that kept his
comedy-drama running for two years in New York and
over a year in London. This is actor-oriented drama;
Crowley demands (and received from his original cast)
the finely tuned ensemble playing that also grew up in
New York in the 1950's and 1960's, performances by
groups of actors who together can in an instant shift the
mood of play and audience from broad comedy to pathos
and pessimism.

The Boys in the Band is about a birthday party and the
men who come to join this somewhat ironic celebration of
someone's getting older. Most of the play is written in
scenes for four, five, or more people—excellent scenes for
actors' projects when it is possible to collect so large a
group together for rehearsals. The play begins, however,
with an extended scene for two men, from which the
excerpt below is taken.

Michael, the host for the party, is getting dressed, and
worrying about his receding hairline, when Donald turns

133

up early, his analyst having canceled an appointment at the last minute. Michael is thirty and smartly groomed; Donald is two years younger, with "wholesome American good looks." Neither of them is much in the mood for a party.

The scene is Michael's smartly done up duplex apartment in Manhattan's East Fifties—a living room and, on a higher level, a bedroom with a doorway leading to the bathroom. Michael stands in the bedroom, pulling on a sweater. Donald has just walked into the bathroom, having decided to take a shower; when he appears, he is wearing Michael's robe.

Michael.

What are you so depressed about? I mean, other than the usual *everything.*

(*A beat.*)

Donald.

(*Reluctantly.*) I really don't want to get into it.

Michael.

Well, if you're not going to tell me, how can we have a conversation *in depth*—a warm, rewarding, meaningful friendship?

Donald.

Up yours!

Michael.

(*Southern accent.*) Why, Cap'n Butler, how you talk!

(*Pause. Donald appears in the doorway holding a glass of water and a small bottle of pills. Michael looks up.*)

Donald.

It's just that today I finally realized that I was *raised* to be a failure. I was *groomed* for it.

(*A beat.*)

Michael.

You know, there was a time when you could have said that to me and I wouldn't have known what the hell you were talking about.

Donald.

(*Takes some pills.*) Naturally, it all goes back to Evelyn and Walt.

Michael.

Naturally. When doesn't it go back to Mom and Pop. Unfortunately, we all had an Evelyn and a Walt. The crumbs! Don't you love that word—crumb? Oh, I love it! It's a real Barbara Stanwyck word. (*A la Stanwyck's frozen-lipped Brooklyn accent.*) "Cau'll me a keab, you kr-rumm."

Donald.

Well, I see all vestiges of sanity for this evening are now officially shot to hell.

Michael.

Oh, Donald, you're so serious tonight! You're fun-starved, baby, and I'm eating for two!

(*Sings.*)

"Forget your troubles, c'mon get happy! You better chase all your blues away. Shout, 'Hallelujah!' c'mon get happy . . ."

(*Sees Donald isn't buying it.*)—what's more boring than a queen doing a Judy Garland imitation?

Donald.

A queen doing a Bette Davis imitation.

Michael.

Meanwhile—back at the Evelyn and Walt Syndrome.

Donald.

America's Square Peg and America's Round Hole.

Michael.

Christ, how sick analysts must get of hearing how mommy and daddy made their darlin' into a fairy.

Donald.

It's beyond just that now. Today I finally began to see how some of the other pieces of the puzzle relate to them.—Like why I never finished anything I started in my life . . . my neurotic compulsion to not succeed. I've realized it was always when I failed that Evelyn loved me the most—because it displeased Walt, who wanted perfection. And when I fell short of the mark she was only too happy to make up for it with her love. So I began to identify failing with winning my mother's love. And I began to fail on purpose to get it. I didn't finish Cornell—I couldn't keep a job in this town. I simply retreated to a room over a garage and scrubbing floors in order to keep alive. Failure is the only thing with which I feel at home. Because it is what I was taught at home.

Michael.

Killer whales is what they are. Killer whales. How many whales could a killer whale kill . . .

Donald.

A lot, especially if they get them when they were babies.

(*Pause, Michael suddenly tears off his sweater, throws it in the air, letting it land where it may, whips out another, pulls it on as he starts down the stairs for the living room. Donald follows.*)

Hey! Where're you going?

Michael.

To make drinks! I think we need about thirty-seven!

Donald.

Where'd you get *that* sweater?

Michael.

This clever little shop on the right bank called Hermes.

Donald.

I work my ass off for forty-five lousy dollars a week *scrubbing* floors and you waltz around throwing cashmere sweaters on them.

Michael.

The one on the floor in the bedroom is vicuña.

Donald.

I *beg* your pardon.

Michael.

You could get a job doing something else. Nobody holds a gun to your head to be a charwoman. That is, how you say, your neurosis.

Donald.

Gee, and I thought it's why I was born.

Michael.

Besides, just because I *wear* expensive clothes doesn't necessarily mean they're paid for.

Donald.

That is, how you say, *your* neurosis.

Michael.

I'm a spoiled brat, so what do I know about being mature. The only thing mature means to me is *Victor* Mature, who was in all those pictures with Betty Grable.
(*Sings à la Grable.*)
"I can't begin to tell you, how much you mean to me ..." Betty sang that in 1945. '45?—'43. No, '43 was "Coney Island," which was remade in '50 as "Wabash Avenue." Yes, "Dolly Sisters" was in '45.

Donald.

How did I manage to miss these momentous events in

the American cinema. I can understand people having an affinity for the stage—but movies are such garbage, who can take them seriously.

Michael.

Well, I'm sorry if your sense of art is offended. Odd as it may seem, there wasn't any Shubert Theatre in Hot Coffee, Mississippi!

Donald.

However—thanks to the silver screen, your neurosis has got style. It takes a certain flair to squander one's unemployment check at Pavillion.

Michael.

What's so snappy about being head over heels in debt. The only thing smart about it is the ingenious ways I dodge the bill collectors.

Donald.

Yeah. Come to think of it, you're the type that gives faggots a bad name.

Michael.

And you, Donald, *you* are a credit to the homosexual. A reliable, hard-working, floor-scrubbing, bill-paying fag who don't owe nothin' to nobody.

Donald.

I am a model fairy.

   (*Michael has taken some ribbon and paper and begun to wrap Harold's birthday gift.*)

Michael.

You think it's just nifty how I've always flitted from Beverly Hills to Rome to Acapulco to Amsterdam, picking up a lot of one-night stands and a lot of custom-made duds along the trail, but I'm here to tell you that the only place in all those miles—the only place I've ever been *happy*—was on the goddamn plane.

   (*Puffs up the bow on the package, continues.*)

Bored with Scandinavia, try Greece. Fed up with dark meat, try light. Hate tequila, what about slivovitz. Tired of boys, what about girls—or how about boys and girls mixed and in what combination? And if you're sick of people, what about poppers? Or pot or pills or the hard stuff. And can you think of anything else the bad baby would like to indulge his spoiled-rotten, stupid, empty, boring, selfish, self-centered self in? Is that what you think has style, Donald? Huh? Is that what you think

you've missed out on—my hysterical escapes from coun-
try to country, party to party, bar to bar, bed to bed,
hangover to hangover, and all of it, hand to mouth!
                    (*A beat.*)
Run, charge, run, buy, borrow, make, spend, run, squan-
der, beg, run, run, run, waste, waste, *waste!*
                    (*A beat.*)
And why? And why?
Donald.
Why, Michael? Why?
Michael.
I really don't want to get into it.
Donald.
Then how can we have a conversation in depth?
Michael.
Oh, you know it all by heart anyway. Same song, second
verse. Because my Evelyn refused to let me grow up. She
was determined to keep me a child forever and she did
one helluva job of it. And my Walt stood by and let her
do it.

                    (*A beat.*)
What you see before you is a thirty-year-old infant. And
it was all done in the name of love—what *she* labeled
love and probably sincerely believed to be love, when
what she was really doing was feeding her own need—
satisfying her own loneliness.
                    (*A beat.*)
She made me into a girl-friend dash lover.
                    (*A beat.*)
We went to all those goddamn cornball movies together.
I picked out her clothes for her and told her what to
wear and she'd take me to the beauty parlor with her
and we'd both get our hair bleached and a permanent
and a manicure.
                    (*A beat.*)
And Walt let this happen.
                    (*A beat.*)
And she convinced me that I was a sickly child who
couldn't run and play and sweat and get knocked around
—oh, no! I was frail and pale and, to hear her tell it,
practically female. I can't tell you the thousands of times
she said to me, "I declare, Michael, you should have
been a girl." And I guess I should have—I was frail and

pale and bleached and curled and bedded down with
hot-water bottles and my dolls and my paper dolls, and
my doll clothes and my doll houses!

(*Quick beat.*)

And Walt bought them for me!

(*Beat. With increasing speed.*)

And she nursed me and put Vicks salve on my chest and
cold cream on my face and told me what beautiful eyes I
had and what pretty lips I had. She bathed me in the
same tub with her until I grew too big for the two of us
to fit. She made me sleep in the same bed with her until I
was fourteen years old—until I finally flatly refused to
spend one more night there. She didn't want to prepare
me for life or how to be out in the world on my own or
I might have left her. But I left anyway. This goddamn
cripple finally wrenched free and limped away. And here
I am—unequipped, undisciplined, untrained, unprepared
and unable to live!

(*A beat.*)

And do you know until this day she still says, "I don't
care if you're seventy years old, you'll always be my
baby." And can I tell you how that drives me mad! Will
that bitch never understand that what I'll always *be* is
her son—but that I haven't been her baby for twenty-five
years!

(*A beat.*)

And don't get me wrong. I know it's easy to cop out and
blame Evelyn and Walt and say it was *their* fault. That
we were simply the helpless put-upon victims. But in the
end, we are responsible for ourselves. And I guess—I'm
not sure—but I want to believe it—that in their own
pathetic, *dangerous* way, they just loved us too much.

(*A beat.*)

Finis. Applause.

(*Donald hesitates, walks over to Michael, puts his arms
around him and holds him. It is a totally warm and
caring gesture.*)

There's nothing quite as good as feeling sorry for yourself, is there?

Donald.

Nothing.

Michael.

(*A la Bette Davis.*) I adore cheap sentiment.

from
THE HOLE
by N. F. Simpson

CEREBRO, ENDO, SOMA

There is no explaining N. F. Simpson's one-act play; or
rather, there are any number of explanations, little indica-
tion that one is more likely than another, and that is
probably the point—perhaps. The author of such re-
vealingly titled plays as *A Resounding Tinkle* (see p.
145) and *The One-Way Pendulum,* Simpson has a peculiar sensitivity to and very little patience with our charac-
teristically human habit of trying to make "sense" of
everything we run into, even when (as usually) that sense
has everything to do with us and nothing to do with it,
whatever it is. That is probably what *The Hole* is about.

The setting is an ordinary street—shop fronts, sidewalk,
and, most important, a hole, the sort that happens when
dig they must. Various people pass by, peer into the hole,
remark on what's down there, and go on their ways. Some
are quite ordinary, a pair of housewives, for example. The
three in this scene are given no descriptions beyond their
names. The actors may want to know that there is actually a fourth character in the scene; the Visionary he is
called, and though he has talked amiably enough with
Endo, he has now transferred his attention to his newspaper. Endo has given up on him and stands looking down
into the hole.

(*Cerebro enters down R, looking at the Visionary. He
takes up a position R of Endo, leans on the pole and
looks down into the hole.*)
Cerebro.
(*Nodding towards the Visionary but looking at Endo.*)
140

We ought to be able to work something out if we put our minds to it. He must be waiting for *something*.

Endo.

He says he's queueing for dark glasses.

> (*Cerebro looks questioningly at Endo.*)

For the radiance. In case he gets blinded.

Cerebro.

(*Looking across at the Visionary and then down into the hole.*) Perhaps your eyesight's better than mine. Can *you* make out any radiance?

Endo.

They haven't unveiled the window, yet. Or so he says.

Cerebro.

(*In mock comprehension.*) Ah. (*He glances quickly at the Visionary, then dismisses him and looks intently down into the hole.*)

> (*Endo looks intently down into the hole.*)

There may be others in the shadows down there—but you can distinctly make out two people.

Endo.

They're playing some game.

> (*There is a pause.*)

Cerebro.

They're playing dominoes down there.

> (*There is a pause.*)

Endo.

In boxing gloves?

Cerebro.

They're playing dominoes. You can see the double six. There. In his left hand.

> (*There is a pause.*)

Endo.

(*Pointing.*) Over there. Look. Coming out of the corner.

> (*There is a pause.*)

Cerebro.

He looks rather keyed up.

Endo.

I wonder if that could be the Battling Bombardier? Because if that's the Battling Bombardier, the other one must be Spider. (*He pauses.*) Wait till he comes into the light. Yes. It is. It's Spider and the Battling Bombardier.

Cerebro.

Splendid! That's the boxing gloves accounted for.
(*There is a pause.*)

Endo.

But not the shuttlecock.

Cerebro.

We'll come to that.
(*There is a pause.*)

Endo.

You can always recognize the Battler . . .

Cerebro.

Snap!

Endo.

Snap! You could always recognize the Battling Bombardier even if you'd never seen him before because he's the only boxer who carries his own dartboard around with him.

Cerebro.

If the other one's Spider, he's just coming out of his corner.
(*Cerebro and Endo look down with intensified interest.*)

Endo.

They'll probably limber up now with a brisk five minutes of Happy Families.
(*Soma enters down L and stands L of the hole.*)

Soma.

Keep your eye on Spider. He's the one to watch down there.
(*There is a pause.*)

Cerebro.

Is he the one with the domino poised?

Soma.

That's only a blind. The domino's a blind. (*He pauses.*) Any minute now he's going right in. (*He pauses.*) The domino doesn't mean a thing. He's just waving that about for a blind. It's the seven of clubs—that's what you've got to keep your eye on.
(*There is a pause.*)

Cerebro.

He seems to be threatening him with it, or something.

Soma.

I tell you it's a blind. It doesn't mean a thing. I've seen him do that for sometimes five minutes at a stretch. He'll

come out brandishing a double six and he'll go on until
he's got the other fellow practically mesmerized—in fact
he is mesmerized more often than not the way Spider
does it—and then whoosh! He's on him with Mr. Rake
the Gardener. It never fails.

Endo.

Snap!

Cerebro.

He seems to be biding his time at the moment.

Soma.

Snap! (*To Cerebro.*) He knows what he's doing. (*He
transfers his attention to Endo, as to a kindred spirit.*)
What do you think of him?

Endo.

He certainly seems to know what he's doing.

Soma.

Spider knows what he's doing, believe me. Once he's got
his eye in I've known him trump every bishop from
love-all to double twenty and not a pawn out of breath.
He'd clear five foot six inches with as clean a backhand
drive as you'd be likely to see in a lifetime of snooker.
I've known people who claim to have seen him hold his
opponent off with the ace of diamonds just long enough
to re-load his dice, and then perhaps he'd huff him two
or three times just for the hell of it, and then you'd see
it. Then you'd see the real *coup de grace*—packed,
sealed, addressed, delivered. First of all he'd come out
behind his two rooks. He always did that—he always
covered himself with his rooks—and he'd come out very
slowly, very unconcerned as if it didn't matter today or
tomorrow and then—you wouldn't see what happened
next except that suddenly the other fellow wasn't there.
Then you'd look again and he'd be picking himself up
out of baulk with Mrs. Grain the Grocer's Wife.

(*Soma draws back and watches while both Endo and
Cerebro become absorbed in what they can see in the
hole. He looks suspiciously and with dislike towards the
Visionary from time to time also.*)

Cerebro.

Lead with your left!

(*Endo looks sharply at Cerebro, then down, then back
to Cerebro.*)

Endo.

Lead with his what? He's in check.

from

A RESOUNDING TINKLE

by N. F. Simpson

MIDDIE, BRO

N. F. Simpson shares Ionesco's amazement at the persistence with which we human creatures attempt to cram the disorder of our lives into neat logical boxes. These boxes—set ideas, habits of mind, syntax, labels, words themselves—are not real, of course, but we regularly act as though they were, and when experience contradicts the boxes, we flatly—if absurdly—insist that the boxes are the more real and true. Once, perhaps, the boxes were constructed to fit experience; now, as Simpson shows us, we have reversed the process. A pigeonhole in the midst of chaos is very reassuring, and attaching a name to something, even a name that doesn't fit, seems very like taming it.

Simpson does not lecture. He simply allows his characters to live their logic all the way; the result is madness, very funny and rather unnerving. Bro Paradock and his wife Middie (that is, the Paradocks) are as ordinary as can be: middle class, middle-aged, suburban, British. Everything about them, and about their play, is matter-of-fact, and if the comedy is to work, that is how it needs to be acted—realistically and plainly. Bro insists that they live in a bungalow (one story), while Middie is equally certain that the house is a "semi-detached" (two or three stories). This is a subject of contention between them, but not really awkward: each follows his conviction, and Bro has never been upstairs (for him, of course, there *isn't* an upstairs). Later in the play Bro and Middie speak of "having a good read" as most of us would speak of having a good meal, and they carefully balance their diet—some verse, some critical essay with a bit of a bite to it, and a dash or two of dictionary. In the scene reprinted here, the beginning of the one-act version of the play (there is also a full-length version), the Paradocks face a problem: they've been sent an elephant larger than the one they ordered. Why they have an animal each year (it's usually an elephant) is never discussed—they do; doesn't everyone? The problem is simply the size of the beast, and what to call it.

The scene is the Paradocks' living room, early evening. There are the usual sofa, coffee-table, chairs. A door at the back leads to a small entrance hall with a hatstand with hats and coats on it. A fire burns in the fireplace and through the window on the back wall one can see that it is still light outside.

Bro and Middie have just come in. A shopping basket full of books is on the coffee-table. Both Bro and Middie are staring out of the window into the garden.

Middie.
It'll have to stay out.
Bro.
(*Turning away from the window.*) What are the measurements?
Middie.
(*Contuining to stare through the window.*) You don't need measurements. A thing that size in a semi!
Bro.
(*Moving to the sideboard.*) I thought we were living in a bungalow. (*He picks up two small adjustable spanners from the sideboard.*)
Middie.
People think you're trying to go one better than everybody else.
Bro.
What are these doing here? When did we order adjustable spanners?
Middie.
(*Without turning.*) They were samples.
Bro.
What do they think we want with two?
Middie.
(*Turning away from the window and beginning to put*

books from the shopping basket onto the bookshelf.)
One of them is probably for loosening things.

Bro.

You can do that with any spanner.

Middie.

(*With a handful of small identical books.*) I've brought in some more of these in case Uncle Ted comes. I expect he'll ask for critical essays with his coffee.

Bro.

(*After a pause.*) There's no difference between them. You can use either of them for tightening and you can use either of them for loosening.

(*Middie puts the last book on the shelf, picks up the basket and moves to the door.*)

Middie.

One is probably bigger than the other or something.

(*Middie exits up C to L, leaving the door open.*)

Bro.

They're *adjustable*, Middie. (*He puts the spanners on the sideboard, goes to the armchair RC, picks up a newspaper, sits and reads.*)

Middie.

(*Off.*) Or smaller or something.

Bro.

The plain fact is that we don't need adjustable spanners and are never likely to. (*He pauses.*) It would be interesting to know what would have happened if *I'd* answered the door and let them foist adjustable spanners on to us.

Middie.

(*Off.*) We don't have to use them if we don't like them.

Bro.

(*After a pause.*) We shall have them unloading a complete tool-kit on us before we know where we are.

Middie.

(*Off.*) They won't be round again.

Bro.

I hope you're right—that's all I can say.

Middie.

(*Off.*) I wish it were.

(*Middie enters up C from L, and as though attracted compulsively towards it, crosses to the window R.*)

I wish that were all you could say. Except that then we'd

have you saying it all day long, I suppose, like a mentally deficient parakeet. (*She looks steadily through the window.*)

Bro.

What a typical woman's remark. A parakeet saying the same thing over and over again wouldn't necessarily be mentally deficient. If that's all it's been taught how can it say anything different?

Middie.

Look at it.

Bro.

It may be educationally subnormal—but that's another matter.

Middie.

Look at its great ears flapping about.

Bro.

(*After a pause.*) It's only once a year for goodness sake.

Middie.

Surely they know by now what size we always have.

Bro.

Perhaps they've sent us the wrong one.

Middie.

(*Crossing above the armchair to the sofa.*) It's big enough for a hotel. (*She picks up a magazine from the coffee-table and sits on the sofa.*) If you had a hotel or a private school or something you wouldn't need a thing that size. (*She looks through the magazine.*)

Bro.

I suppose not.

Middie.

And supposing it goes berserk in the night? I'm not getting up to it.

Bro.

Why should it go beserk any more than a smaller one?

Middie.

We shall have old Mrs. Stencil round again if it does—threatening us with the R.S.P.C.A.

Bro.

You should have been in when they came with it, then you could have queried the measurements.

Middie.

I can't think what we're going to call it. We can't call it Mr. Trench again.

Bro.

The only time we've not called it Mr. Trench was three years ago when we had to make do with a giraffe.

Middie.

And look at the fuss we had before they'd take it in part exchange.

Bro.

Of course they made a fuss. There was something wrong with it.

(*Middie puts the magazine on the coffee-table, then picks up her rug-making materials and works on the rug. She does this intermittently throughout the evening.*)

Middie.

Imagine calling a clumsy great thing that size Mr. Trench.

Bro.

Why not?

Middie.

We can't go on year after year calling it Mr. Trench.

Bro.

You talk as if it were the same animal every time.

Middie.

You can hear the neighbours, can't you? They'll think we never launch out.

Bro.

I know what you want to call it.

Middie.

It looks all the time as if we're hard up for a name to give the animal.

Bro.

You want to call it Oedipus Rex, don't you?

Middie.

It's better than Mr. Trench year after year. At least it sounds as if we knew what was going on in the world.

Bro.

(*Contemptuously.*) Oedipus Rex! (*He wags a finger archly through the window.*) Ah, ah! Only the *edible* blooms, remember, Oedipus.

Middie.

If you say it in that tone of voice—of course it sounds ridiculous.

Bro.

Oedipus! Not all your weight on that glass, eh?

Middie.

Anything would sound ridiculous if you said it like that.

Bro.

It isn't Mr. Trench we want a change from.

Middie.

The only thing to do is ring up the Zoo. Tell them to come and collect it.

Bro.

And be without an elephant at all?

Middie.

Tell them to come and collect it and the sooner the better. I'd rather not have one.

Bro.

That's only your point of view.

Middie.

We did without one the year we had a giraffe instead.

Bro.

I know we did without one the year we had a giraffe instead. And look at the trouble we had getting it changed. I don't want that all over again.

Middie.

It's the R.S.P.C.A. I'm worried about.

Bro.

They haven't been round yet. In any case you wouldn't get the Zoo at this time. They'll be closed.

Middie.

I don't know why they couldn't send us what we asked for in the first place.

Bro.

Is it any use trying to get hold of Eddie on the phone?

Middie.

Yes. Ring Eddie up. Or Nora. Nora'd be sure to know what to do. They used to keep pigeons and things. They had a room full of nothing else but different kinds of birds when they were all living at number eighty-nine, and white mice and things.

Bro.

It'll have to stay outside tonight.

Middie.

I'm not having it in the kitchen, if that's what you're leading up to.

Bro.

If it starts straying all over the place during the night we shall have the R.S.P.C.A. making a lot of difficulties.

Middie.

Not if we get it changed first thing. Get on to Nora.

Bro.

If we're getting it changed first thing in the morning, where's the sense in thinking up a name like Oedipus Rex for it now?

Middie.

Because I'm not calling it Mr. Trench six years running. You can if you like. I'm not.

Bro.

I didn't want to call it Mr. Trench the year it was a giraffe. That was your idea. It was your idea it would make a pleasant change to give the name to a giraffe instead of an elephant. Now you complain about calling it Mr. Trench six years running.

Middie.

I think we'd be better off without it.

Bro.

How would we?

Middie.

I do really. I think we'd be better off without. We've done nothing except bicker ever since they came with it.

Bro.

We weren't in when they came with it.

Middie.

That's the whole point.

(*Both relapse into silence. Bro reads his paper. After a few moments he looks up.*)

Bro.

If we're going to change the name at all, I can't see what you've got against "Hodge" for that matter.

Middie.

"Hodge" is all right for a monkey.

Bro.

We'll go through some names and see what we can agree on. "Hodge."

Middie.

"Hodge" for a monkey. "Gush" for an elephant.

Bro.

"Admiral Benbow."

Middie.

"Hiram B. Larkspur."

Bro.

"Playboy."

Middie.

"Killed-with-kindness Corcoran."

Bro.

"New-wine-into-old-bottles Backhouse."

Middie.

" 'Tis-pity-she's-a-whore Hignett."

Bro.

"Lucifer."

Middie.

"Stonehenge."

Bro.

"Haunch."

                        (There is a pause.)

Middie. }
Bro. }

(Almost simultaneously.) "Splinter."

Bro.

Thank goodness we can agree on something.

Copies of this play, in individual paper covered acting editions, are available from Samuel French, Inc., 25 W. 45th St., New York, N. Y. or 7623 Sunset Blvd., Hollywood, Calif., or in Canada Samuel French (Canada) Ltd., 26 Grenville St., Toronto, Canada.

from
THE SHOW-OFF
by George Kelly

Act II
AUBREY, GILL, (AMY)

Aubrey Piper is the show-off of the title, the walking (strutting), talking (incessantly), never-say-die epitome of a persistent and generally loathed American type—a firm believer in the great success dream, with a carnation in his buttonhole, a cliché on his lips, and if he can't make it, he'll fake it. Aubrey is nonstop bluff. When he descends on a family, intent on marrying their daughter, he drives the girl's father from the house with his chatter, antagonizes her mother and sister, sponges on her brother-in-law, all but ruins her brother's opportunity to earn a fortune—and he gets the girl. Moreover, before the play is done we begin, despite ourselves it seems, to feel a certain affection for Aubrey. This change of attitude in his audience is the triumph of George Kelly's play; while never softening Aubrey's brashness, the playwright leads us to smile at and even to pity him. When Aubrey's biggest bluff proves to be precisely what is needed to overwhelm the heads of a mammoth corporation who are as full of wind and as sententious as he, we can groan with his mother-in-law and at the same time not regret that what he inevitably is can be of use somewhere. (For family reactions to Aubrey, see p. 399; and for the closest thing to his comeuppance, see p. 231.)

Heywood Broun called the play "the best comedy which has yet been written by an American." Certainly it is as American as any comedy ever produced. Its setting, its speech, its characters and their concerns (marriage, death, paying the bills) are compellingly authentic. Any doubts

153

about the play's power to hold the stage after nearly half a century (it was first produced in 1924) were dispelled by a recent APA production that won a new national audience for Aubrey.

The scene reprinted below shows Aubrey maintaining his confidence at a difficult time. Having borrowed a friend's car, he has smashed into a streetcar, another automobile, and a policeman, whose arm he has broken. He does not have a valid driver's license. Not surprisingly his wife, Amy, is worried. Aubrey reassures her, "It'd only be a fine for reckless driving, even if they could prove it *was* reckless driving; and *I* can prove it was the copper's fault."

They are interrupted by the doorbell. Amy's father is in the hospital, having collapsed at his work, and one of his friends has come by the house with the things he left at the factory.

The setting is the central room in Amy's parents' house. There is a dining table in the center and a clutter of easy chairs, sofa, whatnot stands, and lamps. A doorway up right leads to the entrance hall, a doorway up left opens onto the cellar stairs, and side doors lead to other parts of the house. Amy is alone in the room as Aubrey leads in Mr. Gill. Aubrey's forehead is decorated with adhesive tape and he is without his usual toupé, but he has a long cigar and, on the way to the door, he stopped to transfer his carnation from his overcoat to his jacket. (Note: The portion of the scene that includes Amy can be cut and the remainder of the scene, along with its opening lines, played by two men alone.)

Gill.

(*At the front-door.*) Good evenin'.

Aubrey.

Good evening, sir.

Gill.

Is this where Mr. Fisher lives?

Aubrey.

This is Mr. Fisher's residence, yes, sir. What can I do for you?

Gill.

Why, I got some things of his here that the boss ast me to leave.

Aubrey.

Oh, just step inside for a minute. Getting a little colder I think. (*The front-door closes.*)

Gill.

Well, we can look for it any time, now.

Aubrey.

Will you just step in this way, please? (*Aubrey enters from the hallway.*) There's a gentleman here, Amy, with some things belonging to your Father. Just come right in. (*Aubrey comes forward a few steps at the left; and Gill enters.*)

Gill.

Good evenin'.

Amy.

Good evening.

Aubrey.

This is my wife, Mrs. Piper.

Gill.

(*Nodding.*) How do you do. (*Amy nods.*)

Aubrey.

Mrs. Piper is Mr. Fisher's daughter. The rest of the folks have gone down to the hospital.

Gill.

I see. (*Turning to Amy.*) Have you *heard* anything from the hospital yet?

Amy.

Not yet, no.

Aubrey.

We didn't know anything about it at all, till fifteen minutes ago.

Gill.

It's too bad.

Aubrey.

Those hospitals won't tell you anything.

Amy.

Do you work with my Father?

Gill.

No, ma'am, I'm a twister on the second floor. But, one of the machinist's-helpers that works with your Father knows I live out this way, so he ast me to stop by with these things on me way home. (*He crosses towards Amy, with a hat and overcoat, and a more or less discolored lunch-box.*)

Amy.

(*Taking the things.*) Thanks ever so much.

Gill.

There's just the overcoat and hat, and his lunch-box.

Amy.

Thanks.

Gill.

McMahon sez if he comes across anything else he'll let me know.

Amy.

(*Crossing to the sofa with the things.*) No, I don't imagine there's anything else.

Gill.

If there is, I'll bring it up.

Amy.

Well, that's very nice of you; I'm ever so much obliged to you. (*She comes back towards Gill.*)

Aubrey.

Who is this McMahon?

Gill.

He's one of the machinist's-helpers down there.

Aubrey.

I see.

Amy.

Were you there when my Father was taken sick?

Gill.

No, ma'am, I wasn't. I don't think there was anybody there, to tell you the truth. McMahon sez he was talkin' to him at a quarter of three, and he sez when he came back from the annex at three o'clock, he found Mr. Fisher layin' in front of number five.

Aubrey.

(*With a suggestion of professionalism.*) Very likely a little touch of Angina Pectoria. (*Gill looks at him.*)

Gill.

The doctor down there sez he thought it was a stroke.

Aubrey.

Same thing.

Amy.

Won't you sit down, Mr.—a—

Gill.

No, thank you, ma'am, I can't stay; I've got to get along

out home. (*There's a rapping out at the right. They all look in the direction of the kitchen.*)

Amy.

Oh, I guess it's Mrs. Harbison—I'll go. (*She goes out at the right.*)

Aubrey.

(*Crossing above Gill towards the right.*) Don't stand out there talking now, Amy, with nothing around you. (*Surveying himself in the buffet-mirror at the right.*) Do you live up this way, Governor?

Gill.

No, sir, I live out Richmond way.

Aubrey.

I see.

Gill.

I take number thirty-two over Allegheny Avenue.

Aubrey.

(*Turning and moving over towards the center-table.*) Too bad my car's laid up, I could run you out there.

Gill.

Oh, that's all right; the trolley takes me right to the door.

Aubrey.

I had to turn it in Thursday to have the valves ground.

Amy.

(*Appearing in the kitchen-door.*) I'm wanted on the telephone, Aubrey; I'll be right in. Will you excuse me for a minute?

Gill.

That's all right, ma'am; I'm goin' right along meself.

Aubrey.

Very likely some word from the Hospital.

Gill.

I hope it ain't any bad news.

Aubrey.

Well, you've got to be prepared for most anything, Governor, when a man gets up around the old three-score mark.

Gill.

That's true, a lot of them push off about that age.

Aubrey.

Especially when a man's worked hard all his life.

Gill.

Yes, I guess Mr. Fisher's worked pretty hard.

Aubrey.

Not an excuse in the world for it, either.—I've said to him a thousand times if I've said to him once, "Well, Pop, when are you going to take the big rest?" "Oh," he'd say, "I'll have lots of time to rest when I'm through." "All right," I'd say, "go ahead; only let me tell you, Pop, you're going to be through ahead of schedule if you don't take it soon."

Gill.

Well, I guess it comes pretty hard on a man that's been active all his life to quit all of a sudden.

Aubrey.

Well, he wouldn't have to quit exactly.—I mean, he's a handy man; he could putter around the house. There are lots of little things here and there that I'm not any too well satisfied with. (*He glances around the room.*)

Gill.

Is Mr. Fisher's wife livin'?

Aubrey.

Yes, she's here with us too.

Gill.

Well, that makes it nice.

Aubrey.

Well, it's a pretty big house here; so when I married last June, I said, "Come ahead, the more the merrier." (*He laughs a little.*)

Gill.

'Tis a pretty big house this.

Aubrey.

Yes, they don't make them like this anymore, Governor. Put up by the McNeil people out here in Jenkintown.

Gill.

Oh, yes.

Aubrey.

They just put up the twenty of them—kind of sample houses—ten on that side and ten on this. Of course, these on this side have the southern exposure,—so a man's got to do quite a bit of wire-pulling to get hold of one of these.

Gill.

You've got to do some wire-pullin' to get hold of *any* kind of a house these days.

Aubrey.

Well, I have a friend here in town that's very close to the city architect, and he was able to fix it for me.

Gill.

(*Glancing toward the window, at the left.*) It's a nice street.

Aubrey.

Nice in summer.

Gill.

I was surprised when I saw it, because when I ast a taxicab-driver down here where it was, he said he never heard of it.

Aubrey.

(*Looking at him keenly.*) Never heard of Cresson Street?

Gill.

He said not.

Aubrey.

(*With pitying amusement.*) He must be an awful straw-ride.

Gill.

I had to ast a police officer.

Aubrey.

Well, I'll tell you, Governor,—I don't suppose they have many *calls* for taxicabs out this way. You see, most everybody in through here has his own *car*.

Gill.

I see.

Aubrey.

Some of them have a half dozen, for that matter. (*He laughs, a bit consequentially.*)

Gill.

(*Starting for the parlor-doors.*) There certainly is plenty of them knockin' around.

Aubrey.

All over the ice. (*Aubrey indicates the hall-door.*) This way, Governor.

Gill.

(*Turning towards the hall-door.*) Oh, excuse me.

Aubrey.

(*Moving towards the hall-door.*) Those doors go into the parlor.

Gill.

I see. (*He turns at the hall-door.*) A fellow was tellin' me over here in the cigar store that there was quite a smashup about a half hour ago down here at Broad and Erie Avenue.

Aubrey.

That so?

Gill.

He sez there was some *nut* down there runnin' into everything in sight. He sez he even ran into the traffic-cop; and broke his arm. Can you imagine what they'll *do* to that guy, knockin' the traffic-cop down!

Aubrey.

What was the matter with him, was he stewed?

Gill.

No,—the fellow in the cigar store sez he was just a *nut*. He sez they didn't know where he got hold of this car; he sez it didn't belong to him. I guess he picked it up somewhere. They took it away from him and pinched him. (*Starting to go out.*) So I guess he won't be runnin' into anything else for a while.

Aubrey.

(*Following him out.*) Traffic's in pretty bad shape in this town right now.

Gill.

Certainly is. Why, a man's not safe walkin' along the sidewalk, these days. I hope your wife'll hear some good news.

Aubrey.

Well, while there's life there's hope, you know.

Gill.

That's right. No use lookin' on the dark side of things. (*Amy enters from the right, with a wide-eyed, wan expression and comes slowly down to the center-table.*)

Aubrey.

Where do you get your car, Governor?

Gill.

Why, I can get one right at the corner here, and transfer.

Aubrey.

Oh, that's right, so you can. Well, we're ever so much obliged to you.

Gill.

Don't mention it.

Aubrey.

Good-night, sir.

Gill.

Good-night. (*The door closes.*)

Aubrey.

(*Coming in from the hall-door.*) When did *you* come in, Amy? (*He stops to look at himself in the mantelpiece-mirror.*)

from
LOOK BACK IN ANGER
by John Osborne

Act III, scene 2
ALISON, HELENA

The revolution came on May 8, 1956: *Look Back in Anger*
opened at London's Royal Court Theatre, and by the
following morning John Osborne was recognized as England's most exciting playwright in thirty years, the Royal
Court itself was established as the place for playwrights in
London, and the way was open for the new generation of
writers—Pinter, Arden, Wesker, Hampton, and the rest—
who have changed the shape of English-speaking drama.
Directed by Tony Richardson with a cast that included
Kenneth Haigh, Mary Ure, and Alan Bates, *Look Back*
was greeted with cheers and some bellows of annoyance.
But the play, like its bitterly intense hero, roared over the
opposition and revitalized a theater too long dependent for
excitement on the realism of New York and the experiments of Paris.

Osborne was an actor before he became known as a
writer; his strengths are an ear finely tuned for dialogue
and a sure sense for tight dramatic situations—a combination that produces scenes that all but play themselves. His
approach in this play is essentially realistic, but the realistic dialogue regularly bursts into rhetorical brilliance that
reflects his having grown up in a theatrical tradition of
poet-playwrights and actors born (or so it seems) with a
sense of style.

The play concerns the breakup and the re-establishment
of an awkward marriage. Alison Porter is the daughter of
the blandly selfish Edwardian establishment. Her husband,
Jimmy, is a bitter representative of the generation that

162

detests the inequities of a crumbling past but has found no secure footing or hope in the future. Jimmy loves Alison, but he seems to have married her primarily for the triumph of stealing her from her parents and her friends, who disapproved of him and whom he hates. Jimmy demands a special sort of loyalty, a total commitment to him, his ways, and his friends, and a complete break with everything else. The marriage is marked by brief moments of gentle, childlike romance, violent lovemaking, and endless, tense days in which Jimmy hurls savage verbal attacks at Alison, pouring out anger and vicious humor in an effort to draw from her a sharp response, which she refuses to give. When a school friend of Alison comes to stay, Jimmy doubles his attacks, and Alison allows the friend to persuade her to go home to her family. The friend, however, is an adequate adversary for Jimmy and stays on as his mistress. (Monologues for Jimmy are reprinted starting on p. 120.)

The scene is a one-room flat at the top of a Victorian house in a large provincial city in Britain. The sloping ceiling presses down upon the room. There is some rather old furniture, a double bed against the back wall, a gas stove for cooking, some shelves with books. Small windows, high up, open toward the world outside; a larger window looks onto the landing.

It is Sunday evening. Jimmy has spent the day reading and exploding over the Sunday papers with his friend Cliff, who has a room in the house and was the buffer that kept Jimmy's and Alison's marriage going as long as it did. Cliff has gone to his room, and Jimmy, in his softer mood, has announced that he can almost believe that Helena loves him. There is a knock on the door and Alison walks in. Jimmy leaves abruptly, and soon from Cliff's room comes the wailing sound of Jimmy's jazz trumpet.

Alison is tall, dark, slim. She has a striking beauty, but normally has an air of "well-bred malaise" and a "surprising reservation in her eyes." Now, however, she seems simply a bit disheveled and clearly ill. She was pregnant when she left Jimmy; she has lost the baby and any possibility of having another. Helena, in contrast to Alison, has an impressive air of authority, though "when she allows her rather judicial expression of alertness to soften, she is very attractive." Pouring a cup of tea, she turns to Alison, who is seated in the armchair. Alison bends down and picks up Jimmy's pipe. She scoops up a little pile of ashes from the floor and drops it in the ashtray on the arm of the chair.

Alison.

He still smokes this foul old stuff. I used to hate it at first, but you get used to it.

Helena.

Yes.

Alison.

I went to the pictures last week, and some old man was smoking it in front, a few rows away. I actually got up, and sat right behind him.

Helena.

(*Coming down with cup of tea.*) Here, have this. It usually seems to help.

Alison.

(*Taking it.*) Thanks.

Helena.

Are you sure you feel all right now?

Alison.

(*Nods.*) It was just—oh, everything. It's my own fault—entirely. I must be mad, coming here like this. I'm sorry, Helena.

Helena.

Why should you be sorry—you of all people?

Alison.

Because it was unfair and cruel of me to come back. I'm afraid a sense of timing is one of the things I seem to have learnt from Jimmy. But it's something that can be in very bad taste. (*Sips her tea.*) So many times, I've just managed to stop myself coming here—right at the last moment. Even today, when I went to the booking office at St. Pancras, it was like a charade, and I never believed that I'd let myself walk on to that train. And when I was on it, I got into a panic. I felt like a criminal. I told myself I'd turn round at the other end, and come straight back. I couldn't even believe that this place existed any more. But once I got here, there was nothing I could do. I had to convince myself that everything I remembered about this place had really happened to me once.

(*She lowers her cup, and her foot plays with the newspapers on the floor.*)
How many times in these past few months I've thought of the evenings we used to spend here in this room. Suspended and rather remote. You make a good cup of tea.

Helena.

(*Sitting L of table.*) Something Jimmy taught *me*.

Alison.

(*Covering her face.*) Oh, why am I here! You must all wish me a thousand miles away!

Helena.

I don't wish anything of the kind. You've more right to be here than I.

Alison.

Oh, Helena, don't bring out the book of rules—

Helena.

You are his wife, aren't you? Whatever I have done, I've never been able to forget that fact. You have all the rights—

Alison.

Helena—even I gave up believing in the divine rights of marriage long ago. Even before I met Jimmy. They've got something different now—constitutional monarchy. You are where you are by consent. And if you start trying any strong arm stuff, you're out. And I'm out.

Helena.

Is that something you learnt from him?

Alison.

Don't make me feel like a blackmailer or something, please! I've done something foolish, and rather vulgar in coming here tonight. I regret it, and I detest myself for doing it. But I did not come here in order to gain anything. Whatever it was—hysteria or just macabre curiosity, I'd certainly no intention of making any kind of breach between you and Jimmy. You must believe that.

Helena.

Oh, I believe it all right. That's why everything seems more wrong and terrible than ever. You didn't even reproach me. You should have been outraged, but you weren't. (*She leans back, as if she wanted to draw back from herself.*) I feel so—*ashamed*.

Alison.

You talk as though he were something you'd swindled me out of—

Helena.

(*Fiercely.*) And you talk as if he were a book or something you pass around to anyone who happens to want it for five minutes. What's the matter with you? You sound as though you were quoting *him* all the time. I thought you told me once you couldn't bring yourself to believe in him.

Alison.

I don't think I ever believed in your way either.

Helena.

At least, I still believe in right and wrong! Not even the months in this madhouse have stopped me doing that. Even though everything I have done is wrong, at least I have known it was wrong.

Alison.

You loved him, didn't you? That's what you wrote, and told me.

Helena.

And it was true.

Alison.

It was pretty difficult to believe at the time. I couldn't understand it.

Helena.

I could hardly believe it myself.

Alison.

Afterwards, it wasn't quite so difficult. You used to say some pretty harsh things about him. Not that I was sorry to hear them—they were rather comforting then. But you even shocked me sometimes.

Helena.

I suppose I was a little over-emphatic. There doesn't seem much point in trying to explain everything, does there?

Alison.

Not really.

Helena.

Do you know—I have discovered what is wrong with Jimmy? It's very simple really. He was born out of his time.

Alison.

Yes, I know.

Helena.

There's no place for people like that any longer—in sex, or politics, or anything. That's why he's so futile. Sometimes, when I listen to him, I feel he thinks he's still in the middle of the French Revolution. And that's where he ought to be, of course. He doesn't know where he is, or where he's going. He'll never do anything, and he'll never amount to anything.

Alison.

I suppose he's what you'd call an Eminent Victorian. Slightly comic—in a way. . . . We seem to have had this conversation before.

Helena.

Yes, I remember everything you said about him. It horrified me. I couldn't believe that you could have married someone like that. Alison—it's all over between Jimmy and me. I can see it now. I've got to get out. No—listen to me. When I saw you standing there tonight, I knew that it was all utterly wrong. That I didn't believe in any of this, and not Jimmy or anyone could make me believe otherwise. (*Rising.*) How could I have ever thought I could get away with it! He wants one world and I want another, and lying in that bed won't ever change it! I believe in good and evil, and I don't have to apologise for that. It's quite a modern, scientific belief now, so they tell me. And, by everything I have ever believed in, or wanted, what I have been doing is wrong and evil.

Alison.

Helena—you're not going to leave him?

Helena.

Yes, I am. (*Before Alison can interrupt, she goes on.*) Oh, I'm not stepping aside to let you come back. You can do what you like. Frankly, I think you'd be a fool—but that's your own business. I think I've given you enough advice.

Alison.

But he—he'll have no one.

Helena.

Oh, my dear, he'll find somebody. He'll probably hold court here like one of the Renaissance popes. Oh, I know

I'm throwing the book of rules at you, as you call it, but, believe me, you're never going to be happy without it. I tried throwing it away all these months, but I know now it just doesn't work. When you came in at that door, ill and tired and hurt, it was all over for me. You see—I didn't know about the baby. It was such a shock. It's like a judgment on us.

Alison.

You saw me, and I had to tell you what had happened. I lost the child. It's a simple fact. There is no judgment, there's no blame—

Helena.

Maybe not. But I feel it just the same.

Alison.

But don't you see? It isn't logical!

Helena.

No, it isn't. (*Calmly.*) But I know it's right.
                    (*The trumpet gets louder.*)

Alison.

Helena, (*Going to her.*) you mustn't leave him. He needs you, I know he needs you—

Helena.

Do you think so?

Alison.

Maybe you're not the right one for him—we're neither of us right—

Helena.

(*Moving upstage.*) Oh, why doesn't he stop that damned noise!

Alison.

He wants something quite different from us. What it is exactly I don't know—a kind of cross between a mother and a Greek courtesan, a henchwoman, a mixture of Cleopatra and Boswell. But give him a little longer—

Helena.

(*Wrenching the door open.*) Please! Will you stop that! I can't think!

(*There is a slight pause, and the trumpet goes on. She puts her hands to her head.*)

Jimmy, for God's sake!

(*It stops.*)

Jimmy, I want to speak to you.

Jimmy.

(*Off.*) Is your friend still with you?

Helena.

Oh, don't be an idiot, and come in here!

(*She moves down L.*)

Alison.

(*Rising.*) He doesn't want to see me.

Helena.

Stay where you are, and don't be silly. I'm sorry. It won't be very pleasant, but I've made up my mind to go, and I've got to tell him now.

from

THE CONSCIOUS LOVERS

by Sir Richard Steele

Act II, scene 3
ISABELLA, INDIANA

Steel's eighteenth-century comedy is based on a play of
Terence, but anyone who comes to *The Conscious Lovers*
expecting the frank and sometimes slapstick sexuality of
the original will be disappointed; for this is the famous
example of those curious combinations of farce and sentiment that came to the English stage with the reaction
against the bawdry and coldness (or was it realism?) of
Restoration comedy. Steele's hero, Bevil Junior, loves Indiana, the orphan daughter of a British merchant, whom
he has discovered and saved from the fate worse than
death in that dangerously un-English city Toulon, and
whom he has brought home to London along with her
maiden aunt. Bevil Junior's father, who has only a nasty
suspicion of the girl's existence, has chosen another young
lady, Lucinda, the daughter of his friend Mr. Sealand, as
the bride for his son. This is a problem, and it is compounded by the fact that Bevil Junior's greatest friend,
Mr. Myrtle, adores the chosen bride. As it happens, Indiana is the half–sister of Lucinda; she is the long-lost daughter of Sealand (on the way to join her father in India, she,
her mother, and her aunt were captured by pirates and
presumably killed). In an old comedy, overcoming such
obstacles to the lovers' happiness was easy enough: the
young generation outwitted or overwhelmed the old. But
this is sentimental drama, that moralizing stuff, written
under the influence of the "Lugubrious Muse," which
Goldsmith and Sheridan had so much fun exploding some
years later. Young Bevil will do nothing to contradict or

170

upset his parent (nor, indeed, anything that might suggest
to his friend Myrtle that Indiana is in some way more
attractive than Lucinda). He and Lucinda agree to pretend to look forward to their marriage, while hoping desperately that something will prevent it. In the meantime his
relations with Indiana—and his intentions—are absolutely
pure, though her aunt refuses to believe this, perhaps because
she has a Restoration imagination—the result, no doubt, of
her experiences in Toulon. For all of this, many of Steele's
scenes are effective and ring with humorous truth—indeed,
Indiana is about as direct and open as an ingénue can be.
And before one dismisses Steele's morality too quickly, it is
as well to remember that the resolutions of the mainstream
comedies of today regularly are contrived to meet the requirements of sentimental morality. Indiana is a predecessor
of our own comic heroines.

In the rooms in London which Bevil Junior has
provided for her, Indiana, with her ever attendant aunt,
awaits a visit from her benefactor. He has provided her
with every comfort, comes to visit her regularly, and his
interest in her seems more than casual, but he has never
once spoken to her of love. The reason for this is simple
enough: as Bevil Junior explains to his father's old servant, "My tender obligations to my father have laid so
inviolable a restraint upon my conduct that till I have his
consent to speak I am determined, upon that subject, to
be dumb forever." Indiana, of course, knows nothing of
this, and she is somewhat puzzled, though her faith in
Bevil's honor is absolute. Aunt Isabella, however, is certain that the young man's seemingly disinterested generosi-
ty is a subterfuge, the mask for a carefully planned seduction. She has a duty, she feels, to speak her mind.

As the scene begins, the two ladies are discovered in
intense conversation.

Isabella.

Yes, I say 'tis artifice, dear child: I say to thee again and
again, 'tis all skill and management.
Indiana.

Will you persuade me there can be an ill design in
supporting me in the condition of a woman of quality—
attended, dressed, and lodged like one—in my appearance
abroad and my furniture at home, every way in the most

sumptuous manner—and he that does it has an artifice, a design in it?

Isabella.

Yes, yes.

Indiana.

And all this without so much as explaining to me that all about me comes from him!

Isabella.

Ay, ay, the more for that. That keeps the title to all you have the more in him.

Indiana.

The more in him! He scorns the thought—

Isabella.

Then he—he—he—

Indiana.

Well, be not so eager. If he is an ill man, let us look into his strategems. Here is another of them. (*Showing a letter.*) Here's two hundred and fifty pound in bank notes, with these words: 'To pay for the set of dressing-plate which will be brought home to-morrow.' Why, dear aunt, now here's another piece of skill for you, which I own I cannot comprehend, and it is with a bleeding heart I hear you say anything to the disadvantage of Mr. Bevil. When he is present I look upon him as one to whom I owe my life and the support of it—then, again, as the man who loves me with sincerity and honor. When his eyes are cast another way and I dare survey him, my heart is painfully divided between shame and love. Oh! could I tell you—

Isabella.

Ah! you need not; I imagine all this for you.

Indiana.

This is my state of mind in his presence, and when he is absent, you are ever dinning my ears with notions of the arts of men—that his hidden bounty, his respectful conduct, his careful provision for me, after his preserving me from utmost misery, are certain signs he means nothing but to make I know not what of me.

Isabella.

Oh! You have a sweet opinion of him, truly.

Indiana.

I have, when I am with him, ten thousand things, besides my sex's natural decency and shame, to suppress my heart, that yearns to thank, to praise, to say it loves him. I say, thus it is with me while I see him; and in his absence I am entertained with nothing but your endeavors to tear this amiable image from my heart and in its stead to place a base dissembler, an artful invader of my happiness, my innocence, my honor.

Isabella.

Ah, poor soul! has not his plot taken? don't you die for him? has not the way he has taken been the most proper with you? Oh! ho! He has sense, and has judged the thing right.

Indiana.

Go on, then, since nothing can answer you; say what you will of him. Heigh! ho!

Isabella.

Heigh! ho! indeed. It is better to say so, as you are now, than as many others are. There are, among the destroyers of women, the gentle, the generous, the mild, the affable, the humble, who all, soon after their success in their designs, turn to the contrary of those characters. I will own to you, Mr. Bevil carries his hypocrisy the best of any man living, but still he is a man, and therefore a hypocrite. They have usurped an exemption from shame for any baseness, any cruelty towards us. They embrace without love; they make vows without conscience of obligation; they are partners, nay, seducers to the crime wherein they pretend to be less guilty.

Indiana.

(*Aside.*) That's truly observed.—But what's all this to Bevil?

Isabella.

This it is to Bevil and all mankind. Trust not those who will think the worse of you for your confidence in them— serpents who lie in wait for doves. Won't you be on your guard against those who would betray you? Won't you doubt those who would contemn you for believing 'em? Take it from me, fair and natural dealing is to invite injuries; 'tis bleating to escape wolves who would devour you! Such is the world—(*Aside.*) and such (since the behavior of one man to myself) have I believed all the rest of the sex.

Indiana.

I will not doubt the truth of Bevil; I will not doubt it. He has not spoke it by an organ that is given to lying; his eyes are all that have ever told me that he was mine. I know his virtue, I know his filial piety, and ought to trust his management with a father to whom he has uncommon obligations. What have I to be concerned for? my lesson is very short. If he takes me forever, my purpose of life is only to please him. If he leaves me (which heaven avert), I know he'll do it nobly, and I shall have nothing to do but to learn to die, after worse than death has happened to me.

Isabella.

Ay, do! persist in your credulity! Flatter yourself that a man of his figure and fortune will make himself the jest of the town, and marry a handsome beggar for love.

Indiana.

The town! I must tell you, madam, the fools that laugh at Mr. Bevil will but make themselves more ridiculous. His actions are the result of thinking, and he has sense enough to make even virtue fashionable.

Isabella.

O' my conscience, he has turned her head!—Come, come, if he were the honest fool you take him for, why has he kept you here these three weeks without sending you to Bristol in search of your father, your family, and your relations?

Indiana.

I am convinced he still designs it, and that nothing keeps him here but the necessity of not coming to a breach with his father in regard to the match he has proposed him. Beside, has he not writ to Bristol? and has not he advice that my father has not been heard of there almost these twenty years?

Isabella.

All sham—mere evasion; he is afraid if he should carry you thither, your honest relations may take you out of his hands and so blow up all his wicked hopes at once.

Indiana.

Wicked hopes! did I ever give him any such?

Isabella.

Has he ever given you any honest ones? Can you say, in your conscience, he has never once offered to marry you?

Indiana.

No; but by his behavior I am convinced he will offer it

the moment 'tis in his power, or consistent with his honor, to make such a promise good to me.

Isabella.

His honor!

Indiana.

I will rely upon it; therefore desire you will not make my life uneasy by these ungrateful jealousies of one to whom I am, and wish to be, obliged, for from his integrity alone I have resolved to hope for happiness.

Isabella.

Nay, I have done my duty; if you won't see, at your peril be it!

Indiana.

Let it be.—This is his hour of visiting me.

Isabella.

(*Apart.*) Oh, to be sure, keep up your form; don't see him in a bed-chamber! This is pure prudence, when she is liable, wherever he meets her, to be conveyed where'er he pleases.

Indiana.

All the rest of my life is but waiting till he comes. I live only when I'm with him. (*Exit.*)

Isabella.

Well, go thy ways, thou wilful innocent! I once had almost as much love for a man who poorly left me to marry an estate—and I am now, against my will, what they call an old maid—but I will not let the peevishness of that condition grow upon me; only keep up the suspicion of it, to prevent this creature's being any other than a virgin, except upon proper terms. (*Exit.*)

(*Re-enter Indiana, speaking to a Servant.*)

Indiana.

Desire Mr. Bevil to walk in.—Design! impossible! A base, designing mind could never think of what he hourly puts in practice. And yet, since the late rumor of his marriage, he seems more reserved than formerly; he sends in, too, before he sees me, to know if I am at leisure—such new respect may cover coldness in the heart. It certainly makes me thoughtful. I'll know the worst at once; I'll lay such fair occasions in his way that it shall be impossible to avoid an explanation, for these doubts are insupportable.—But see, he comes and clears them all.

from

SHE STOOPS TO CONQUER

by Oliver Goldsmith

Act II, scene 1
HASTINGS, MISS NEVILLE, MARLOW, MISS HARD-
CASTLE

Two young men from London in search of a night's
lodging arrive at what they believe is an inn but in fact is
a gentleman's country house. The gentleman, as it happens, is the parent of the girl to whom one of the young
men, Mr. Marlow, has been betrothed by his father and
whom he has been sent to meet and woo. The other young
man, Mr. Hastings, learns the truth about the "inn" when
he runs into the young lady, Miss Neville, whom *he* has
come to snatch away from the country and from her too
zealous aunt and uncle, the parents of Marlow's intended.
They decide, however, to let Marlow go on thinking that
he is staying in hired lodgings, and Marlow's would-be
fiancée, Miss Hardcastle, agrees to cooperate in this
deception. For Marlow has a problem: although he is
altogether at ease and something of a rake among the
low women who frequent London's taverns and theaters,
the very sight of a proper young lady sends him into
speechless, quivering panic. If he is ever to get to know
Miss Hardcastle, much less propose to her, he must somehow be led to treat her as something other than a lady. So
Hastings and the girls decide to let Marlow believe that
Miss Hardcastle is a servant at the inn. The strategy works
splendidly: Marlow does not recognize his intended when
she is dressed in workaday clothes, and though his offhand
treatment of the girl's father (who he thinks is the
innkeeper) leads to complications, both couples are happily united by the end of the play.

176

The scene reprinted below comes early in Goldsmith's eighteenth-century comedy and demonstrates the necessity of Miss Hardcastle's masquerade. Marlow and Hastings have just arrived at the "inn," have bellowed an order for supper at a rather dumbfounded Mr. Hardcastle, and Marlow has demanded to see their rooms. Mr. Hastings, left alone, has barely time to muse on the excessive friendliness of the innkeeper when he catches sight of Miss Neville.

Hastings.

   * * *Ha! what do I see? Miss Neville, by all that's happy!

                       (*Enter Miss Neville.*)

Miss Neville.

   My dear Hastings! To what unexpected good fortune, to what accident, am I to ascribe this happy meeting?

Hastings.

   Rather let me ask the same question, as I could never have hoped to meet my dearest Constance at an inn.

Miss Neville.

   An inn! sure you mistake! My aunt, my guardian, lives here. What could induce you to think this house an inn?

Hastings.

   My friend, Mr. Marlow, with whom I came down, and I, have been sent here as to an inn, I assure you. A young fellow, whom we accidentally met at a house hard by, directed us hither.

Miss Neville.

   Certainly it must be one of my hopeful cousin's tricks, of whom you have heard me talk so often; ha! ha! ha! ha!

Hastings.

   He whom your aunt intends for you? He of whom I have such just apprehensions?

Miss Neville.

   You have nothing to fear from him, I assure you. You'd adore him if you knew how heartily he despises me. My aunt knows it too, and has undertaken to court me for him, and actually begins to think she has made a conquest.

Hastings.

   Thou dear dissembler! You must know, my Constance, I have just seized this happy opportunity of my friend's visit here to get admittance into the family. The horses that carried us down are now fatigued with their journey, but they'll soon be refreshed; and then, if my dearest girl will trust in her faithful Hastings, we shall soon be landed in France, where even among slaves the laws of marriage are respected.

Miss Neville.

I have often told you that, though ready to obey you, I yet should leave my little fortune behind with reluctance. The greatest part of it was left me by my uncle, the India director, and chiefly consists in jewels. I have been for some time persuading my aunt to let me wear them. I fancy I'm very near succeeding. The instant they are put into my possession, you shall find me ready to make them and myself yours.

Hastings.

Perish the baubles! Your person is all I desire. In the meantime, my friend Marlow must not be let into his mistake. I know the strange reserve of his temper is such that, if abruptly informed of it, he would instantly quit the house before our plan was ripe for execution.

Miss Neville.

But how shall we keep him in the deception? Miss Hardcastle is just returned from walking; what if we still continue to deceive him?—This, this way— (*They confer.*)

(*Enter Marlow.*)

Marlow.

The assiduities of these good people tease me beyond bearing. My host seems to think it ill manners to leave me alone, and so he claps not only himself but his old-fashioned wife on my back. They talk of coming to sup with us too; and then, I suppose, we are to run the gauntlet through all the rest of the family.—What have we got here?

Hastings.

My dear Charles! Let me congratulate you!—The most fortunate accident!—Who do you think is just alighted?

Marlow.

Cannot guess.

Hastings.

Our mistresses, boy, Miss Hardcastle and Miss Neville. Give me leave to introduce Miss Constance Neville to your acquaintance. Happening to dine in the neighborhood, they called, on their return to take fresh horses, here. Miss Hardcastle has just stepped into the next room, and will be back in an instant. Wasn't it lucky? eh!

Marlow.

(*Aside.*) I have just been mortified enough of all conscience, and here comes something to complete my embarrassment.

Hastings.

Well! but wasn't it the most fortunate thing in the world?

Marlow.

Oh! yes. Very fortunate—a most joyful encounter—But our dresses, George, you know, are in disorder—What if we should postpone the happiness till to-morrow?—to-morrow at her own house—It will be every bit as convenient—and rather more respectful—To-morrow let it be. (*Offering to go.*)

Hastings.

By no means, sir. Your ceremony will displease her. The disorder of your dress will show the ardor of your impatience. Besides, she knows you are in the house, and will permit you to see her.

Marlow.

O! the devil! how shall I support it? Hem! hem! Hastings, you must not go. You are to assist me, you know. I shall be confoundedly ridiculous. Yet, hang it, I'll take courage! Hem!

Hastings.

Pshaw, man! it's but the first plunge, and all's over! She's but a woman, you know.

Marlow.

And of all women, she that I dread most to encounter!
    (*Enter Miss Hardcastle, as returned from walking, a bonnet, etc.*)

Hastings.

(*Introducing them.*) Miss Hardcastle, Mr. Marlow; I'm proud of bringing two persons of such merit together, that only want to know, to esteem each other.

Miss Hardcastle.

(*Aside.*) Now for meeting my modest gentleman with a demure face, and quite in his own manner. (*After a pause, in which he appears very uneasy and disconcerted.*) I'm glad of your safe arrival, sir—I'm told you had some accidents by the way.

Marlow.

Only a few, madam. Yes, we had some. Yes, madam, a good many accidents, but should be sorry—madam—or rather glad of any accidents—that are so agreeably concluded. Hem!

Hastings.

(*To him.*) You never spoke better in your whole life. Keep it up, and I'll insure you the victory.

Miss Hardcastle.

I'm afraid you flatter, sir. You that have seen so much of the finest company can find little entertainment in an obscure corner of the country.

Marlow.

(*Gathering courage.*) I have lived, indeed, in the world, madam; but I have kept very little company. I have been but an observer upon life, madam, while others were enjoying it.

Miss Neville.

But that, I am told, is the way to enjoy it at last.

Hastings.

(*To him.*) Cicero never spoke better. Once more, and you are confirmed in assurance forever.

Marlow.

(*To him.*) Hem! stand by me then, and when I'm down, throw in a word or two to set me up again.

Miss Hardcastle.

An observer, like you, upon life, were, I fear, disagreeably employed, since you must have had much more to censure than to approve.

Marlow.

Pardon me, madam. I was always willing to be amused. The folly of most people is rather an object of mirth than uneasiness.

Hastings.

(*To him.*) Bravo, bravo. Never spoke so well in your whole life. Well, Miss Hardcastle, I see that you and Mr. Marlow are going to be very good company. I believe our being here will but embarrass the interview.

Marlow.

Not in the least, Mr. Hastings. We like your company of all things. (*To him.*) Zounds, George, sure you won't go? How can you leave us?

Hastings.

Our presence will but spoil conversation, so we'll retire to the next room. (*To him.*) You don't consider, man, that we are to manage a little *tête-à-tête* of our own.

(*Exeunt Hastings with Miss Neville.*)

Miss Hardcastle.

(*After a pause.*) But you have not been wholly an observer, I presume, sir. The ladies, I should hope, have employed some part of your addresses.

Marlow.

(*Relapsing into timidity.*) Pardon me, madam, I—I—I—as yet have studied—only—to—deserve them.

Miss Hardcastle.

And that, some say, is the very worst way to obtain them.

Marlow.

Perhaps so, madam. But I love to converse only with the more grave and sensible part of the sex.—But I'm afraid I grow tiresome.

Miss Hardcastle.

Not at all, sir; there is nothing I like so much as grave conversation myself; I could hear it forever. Indeed I have often been surprised how a man of *sentiment* could ever admire those light, airy pleasures, where nothing reaches the heart.

Marlow.

It's—a disease—of the mind, madam. In the variety of tastes there must be some who, wanting a relish—for—um—a—um—

Miss Hardcastle.

I understand you, sir. There must be some who, wanting a relish for refined pleasures, pretend to despise what they are incapable of tasting.

Marlow.

My meaning, madam, but infinitely better expressed. And I can't help observing—a—

Miss Hardcastle.

(*Aside.*) Who could ever suppose this fellow impudent upon some occasions! (*To him.*) You were going to observe, sir,—

Marlow.

I was observing, madam—I protest, madam, I forget what I was going to observe.

Miss Hardcastle.

(*Aside.*) I vow and so do I. (*To him.*) You were observing, sir, that in this age of hypocrisy—something about hypocrisy, sir.

Marlow.

Yes, madam. In this age of hypocrisy there are few who upon strict enquiry do not—a—a—a—

Miss Hardcastle.

I understand you perfectly, sir.

Marlow.

(*Aside.*) Egad! and that's more than I do myself.

Miss Hardcastle.

You mean that in this hypocritical age there are few who do not condemn in public what they practise in private; and think they pay every debt to virtue when they praise it.

Marlow.

True, madam; those who have most virtue in their mouths have least of it in their bosoms. But I'm sure I tire you, madam.

Miss Hardcastle.

Not in the least, sir; there's something so agreeable and spirited in your manner, such life and force—pray, sir, go on.

Marlow.

Yes, madam, I was saying—that there are some occasions—when a total want of courage, madam, destroys all the—and puts us—upon—a—a—a—

Miss Hardcastle.

I agree with you entirely; a want of courage upon some occasions assumes the appearance of ignorance, and betrays us when we most want to excel. I beg you'll proceed.

Marlow.

Yes, madam. Morally speaking, madam—But I see Miss Neville expecting us in the next room. I would not intrude for the world.

Miss Hardcastle.

I protest, sir, I never was more agreeably entertained in all my life. Pray go on.

Marlow.

Yes, madam. I was— But she beckons us to join her. Madam, shall I do myself the honor to attend you?

Miss Hardcastle.

Well, then, I'll follow

Marlow.

(*Aside.*) This pretty smooth dialogue has done for me. (*Exit.*)

(*Miss Hardcastle sola.*)

Miss Hardcastle.

Ha! ha! ha! Was there ever such a sober, sentimental interview? I'm certain he scarce looked in my face the whole time. Yet the fellow, but for his unaccountable bashfulness, is pretty well, too. He has good sense, but then so buried in his fears, that it fatigues one more than ignorance. If I could teach him a little confidence, it would be doing somebody that I know of a piece of service. But who is that somebody?—that, faith, is a question I can scarce answer. (*Exit.*)

THE SHOW-OFF

Chapter III

Concentration, Communication, Conflict, and Characterization

Twelve monologues and twenty-one scenes in which the actor "gets into character," relates to his fellow players, and finds the "beats" or "units and objectives" which carry him through the scene and play.

from

SWEET BIRD OF YOUTH

by Tennessee Williams

Four Monologues from Act I, scene 1; Act I, scene 2; Act
II, scene 1; and Act III, scene 1
PRINCESS; CHANCE; BOSS FINLEY

To the Royal Palms, a grand if aging hotel in a town
called St. Cloud somewhere along the Gulf Coast, comes a
big white Cadillac with trumpet horns bearing Andrea del
Lago, a grand if aging film star, and her companion,
Chance Wayne, a handsome, not-quite-young man. Miss
del Lago is traveling under an assumed name, Princess
Kosmonopolis, for she is on the run—from the disaster of
an attempted comeback, a film (her first in some time)
that she is certain served only to expose her as old and
ridiculous. Chance is running, too—from time that will
rob him of his definition of himself, sexual attractiveness.
But for him their arrival in St. Cloud is a returning: he
was born here, grew up here, here discovered his dream of
youthful love in an idyllic though thoroughly passionate
affair with a young girl, Heavenly, whom Chance now
intends to take away with him. Chance's returning is far
from auspicious. He is clearly del Lago's hired companion
(she found him working as a beachboy/masseur in Florida). He is greeted by threats from the son and cohorts of
Heavenly's father, a tough and highly successful political
boss. And he finds that Heavenly is, in a sense, dead—that
is, she is sexually dead as the result of an operation made
necessary by a venereal infection acquired from Chance
during his last visit. Boss Finley's men threaten Chance
with similar surgery.

Despite the violence of its story and the harshness of its

187

detail, Williams frames the play and develops its scenes with a lyrical theatricalism, and he paints his characters with strong, ironic comedy. Del Lago is a spectacular portrait, (perhaps as broadly lined as Williams has drawn.) Chance Wayne in the innocence of his imagination (whatever his body has done) and the fan-magazine naiveté of his plans is funny at the same time that he is rather sad. As the figure of love destroyed by hate he is pathetic. And both he and del Lago, preyed on by time that kills all beauty, have a tragic dimension, or so Williams works to persuade us at the end of his play. Neither is an inherently attractive character, yet each calls strongly on the sympathies of the audience, and both require skillful playing.

Three of the four excerpts below are set in del Lago's room in the Royal Palms Hotel. "The principal set-piece is a great double bed ... In a sort of Moorish corner backed by shuttered windows is a wicker tabouret and two wicker stools, over which is suspended a Moorish lamp on a brass chain. The windows are floor length and they open out onto a gallery. There is also a practical door frame, opening onto a corridor: the walls are only suggested." This setting is surrounded by a wide sweep of cyclorama, an expanse of tropical sky against which can be projected stylized projections of sea and of royal palm trees. In the background are heard "soft, urgent cries of birds."

It is morning, Easter Sunday. Chance is already up, still wearing only the trousers of white silk pajamas, when del Lago struggles awake out of a nightmare and seeing him cries, "Who are you? Help!" Chance gives her the oxygen she uses to stop her "attacks of panic" and explains to her how they have come to be in this place. When he begins to remind her of other things—her real name, for example—she orders him to stop; she is, she says, determined to forget, to will herself not to remember. Hauled out of bed, she sways dizzily for a moment, clutching the bed, then crosses to the window to see for herself where they are. As she squints into the noon's brilliance, Chance asks her, "Well, what do you see? Give me your description of the view, Princess." (Note: editorial marks indicate how the scene can be played as a monologue for the Princess, with pauses indicating Chance's lines. However, it may well play more easily as the dialogue it is. If this is done, the actor should know that Chance in the hope of black-mailing the Princess has turned on a tape recorder and is trying to get her to talk openly about the narcotics she uses.)

Princess.

(*Faces the audience.*) I see a palm garden.

§Chance.

And a four-lane highway just past it.§

Princess.

(*Squinting and shielding her eyes.*) Yes, I see that and a strip of beach with some bathers and then, an infinite stretch of nothing but water and . . . (*She cries out softly and turns away from the window.*)

§Chance.

What? . . .§

Princess.

Oh God, I remember the thing I wanted not to. The goddam end of my life! (*She draws a deep shuddering breath.*)

§Chance.

(*Running to her aid.*) What's the matter?§

Princess.

Help me back to bed. Oh God, no wonder I didn't want to remember, I was no fool!

(*He assists her to the bed. There is an unmistakable sympathy in his manner, however shallow.*)

§Chance.

Oxygen?§

Princess.

(*Draws another deep shuddering breath.*) §No! § Where's the stuff? Did you leave it in the car?

§Chance.

Oh, the stuff? Under the mattress. (*Moving to the other side of the bed, he pulls out a small pouch.*)§

Princess.

A stupid place to put it.

§Chance.

(*Sits at the foot of the bed.*) What's wrong with under the mattress?§

Princess.

(*Sits up on the edge of the bed.*) There's such a thing as chambermaids in the world, they make up beds, they come across lumps in a mattress.

§**Chance.**

This isn't pot. What is it?§

Princess.

Wouldn't that be pretty? A year in jail in one of those model prisons for distinguished addicts. What is it? Don't you know what it is, you beautiful, stupid young man? It's hashish, Moroccan, the finest.

§**Chance.**

Oh, hash! How'd you get it through customs when you came back for your come-back?§

Princess.

I didn't get it through customs. The ship's doctor gave me injections while this stuff was winging over the ocean to a shifty young gentleman who thought he could black-mail me for it. (*She puts on her slippers with a vigorous gesture.*)

§**Chance.**

Couldn't he?

Princess.

Of course not. I called his bluff.

Chance.

You took injections coming over?

Princess.

With my neuritis? I had to.§ Come on give it to me.

§**Chance.**

Don't you want it packed right?§

Princess.

You talk too much. You ask too many questions. I need something quick. (*She rises.*)

§**Chance.**

I'm a new hand at this.

Princess.

I'm sure, or you wouldn't discuss it in a hotel room. . . .§

(*She turns to the audience, and intermittently changes the focus of her attention.*)

For years they all told me that it was ridiculous of me to feel that I couldn't go back to the screen or the stage as a middle-aged woman. They told me I was an artist, not just a star whose career depended on youth. But I knew in my heart that the legend of Alexandra del Lago couldn't be separated from an appearance of youth. . . .

There's no more valuable knowledge than knowing the right time to go. I knew it. I went at the right time to go. RETIRED! Where to? To what? To that dead planet the moon. . . .

There's nowhere else to retire to when you retire from an art because, believe it or not, I really was once an artist. So I retired to the moon, but the atmosphere of the moon doesn't have any oxygen in it. I began to feel breathless, in that withered, withering country, of time coming after time not meant to come after, and so I discovered . . . Haven't you fixed it yet?

(*Chance rises and goes to her with a cigarette he has been preparing.*)

Discovered this!*

And other practices like it, to put to sleep the tiger that raged in my nerves. . . . Why the unsatisfied tiger? In the nerves jungle? Why is anything, anywhere, unsatisfied, and raging? . . .

Ask somebody's good doctor. But don't believe his answer because it isn't . . . the answer . . . if I had just been old but you see, I wasn't old. . . .

I just wasn't young, not young, young. I just wasn't young anymore. . .

SECOND MONOLOGUE

Del Lago has easily squelched Chance's rather fumbling attempt at blackmail and he has turned instead to trying to persuade her to underwrite a plan that means much more to him: she is to produce a movie in which he and Heavenly will star. When he mentions that he was born in St. Cloud, she asks him to tell her his life story. "Let's make it an audition, a sort of screen test," she says, "and if you can hold my attention with your life story, I'll know you have talent . . ."

Chance is standing by the open shutters, looking out. "He's in his late twenties and his face looks slightly older than that; you might describe it as a 'ravaged young face' and yet it is still exceptionally good-looking. His body shows no decline, yet it's the kind of body that white silk pajamas are, or ought to be, made for." He is dressed now, however, in dark slacks, white shirt, and loafers.

Chance.

—I was born in this town. I was born in St. Cloud.* * * (*Moving out on the forestage.*) Here is the town I was born in, and lived in till ten years ago, in St. Cloud. I was a twelve-pound baby, normal and healthy, but with some kind of quantity "X" in my blood, a wish or a need to be different. . . . The kids that I grew up with are mostly still here what they call "settled down," gone into business, married and bringing up children, the little crowd I was in with, that I used to be the star of, was the snobset, the ones with the big names and money. I didn't have either . . . (*The Princess utters a soft laugh in her dimmed-out area.*) What I had was . . . [beauty.] (*The Princess half turns, brush poised in a faint, dusty beam of light.*)

§Princess.

BEAUTY! Say it! Say it! What you had was beauty! I had it! I say it, with pride, no matter how sad, being gone, now.§

Chance.

Yes, well . . . the others . . . (*The Princess resumes brushing hair and the sudden cold beam of light on her goes out again.*) . . . are all now members of the young social set here. The girls are young matrons, bridge-players, and the boys belong to the Junior Chamber of Commerce and some of them, clubs in New Orleans such as Rex and Comus and ride on the Mardi Gras floats. Wonderful? No boring . . . I wanted, expected, intended to get, something better . . . Yes, and I did, I got it. I did things that fat-headed gang never dreamed of. Hell when they were still freshmen at Tulane or LSU or Ole Miss, I sang in the chorus of the biggest show in New York, in "Oklahoma," and had pictures in LIFE in a cowboy outfit, tossin' a ten-gallon hat in the air! YIP . . . EEEEEE! Ha-ha. . . . And at the same time pursued my other vocation. . . .

Maybe the only one I was truly meant for, love-making . . . slept in the social register of New York!

Millionaires' widows and wives and debutante daughters
of such famous names as Vanderbrook and Masters and
Halloway and Connaught, names mentioned daily in
columns, whose credit cards are their faces. . . . And . . .
§**Princess.**

What did they pay you?§

Chance.

I gave people more than I took. Middle-aged people I
gave back a feeling of youth. Lonely girls? Understanding, appreciation! An absolutely convincing show of
affection. Sad people, lost people? Something light and
uplifting! Eccentrics? Tolerance, even odd things they
long for. . . .

But always just at the point when I might get something back that would solve my own need, which was
great, to rise to their level, the memory of my girl would
pull me back home to her . . . and when I came home
for those visits, man oh man how that town buzzed with
excitement. I'm telling you, it would blaze with it, and
then that thing in Korea came along. I was about to be
sucked into the Army so I went into the Navy, because a
sailor's uniform suited me better, the uniform was all
that suited me, though. . . .

§**Princess.**

Ah-ha!§

Chance.

(*Mocking her.*) Ah-ha. I wasn't able to stand the goddam routine, discipline. . . .

I kept thinking, this stops everything. I was twenty-
three, that was the peak of my youth and I knew my
youth wouldn't last long. By the time I got out, Christ
knows, I might be nearly thirty! Who would remember
Chance Wayne? In a life like mine, you just can't stop,
you know, can't take time out between steps, you've got
to keep going right on up from one thing to the other,
once you drop out, it leaves you and goes on without you
and you're washed up.

§**Princess.**

I don't think I know what you're talking about.§

Chance.

I'm talking about the parade. THE parade! The parade!

the boys that go places that's the parade I'm talking about, not a parade of swabbies on a wet deck. And so I ran my comb through my hair one morning and noticed that eight or ten hairs had come out, a warning signal of a future baldness. My hair was still thick. But would it be five years from now, or even three? When the war would be over, that scared me, that speculation. I started to have bad dreams. Nightmares and cold sweats at night, and I had palpitations, and on my leaves I got drunk and woke up in strange places with faces on the next pillow I had never seen before. My eyes had a wild look in them in the mirror. . . . I got the idea I wouldn't live through the war, that I wouldn't come back, that all the excitement and glory of being Chance Wayne would go up in smoke at the moment of contact between my brain and a bit of hot steel that happened to be in the air at the same time and place that my head was . . . that thought didn't comfort me any. Imagine a whole lifetime of dreams and ambitions and hopes dissolving away in one instant, being blacked out like some arithmetic problem washed off a blackboard by a wet sponge, just by some little accident like a bullet, not even aimed at you but just shot off in space, and so I cracked up, my nerves did. I got a medical discharge out of the service and I came home in civvies, then it was when I noticed how different it was, the town and the people in it. Polite? Yes, but not cordial. No headlines in the papers, just an item that measured one inch at the bottom of page five saying that Chance Wayne, the son of Mrs. Emily Wayne of North Front Street had received an honorable discharge from the Navy as the result of illness and was home to recover . . . that was when Heavenly became more important to me than anything else. . . .

§Princess.

Is Heavenly a girl's name?§

Chance.

Heavenly is the name of my girl in St. Cloud.

§Princess.

Is Heavenly why we stopped here?

Chance.

What other reason for stopping here can you think of?

Princess.

So . . . I'm being used. Why not? Even a dead race horse is used to make glue. Is she pretty?§

Chance.

(*Handing Princess a snapshot.*) This is a flashlight photo I took of her, nude, one night on Diamond Key, which is a little sandbar about half a mile off shore which is under water at high tide. This was taken with the tide coming in. The water is just beginning to lap over her body like it desired her like I did and still do and will always, always. (*Chance takes back the snapshot.*) Heavenly was her name. You can see that it fits her. This was her at fifteen.

§**Princess.**

Did you have her that early?§

Chance.

I was just two years older, we had each other that early.

§**Princess.**

Sheer luck!§

Chance.

Princess, the great difference between people in this world is not between the rich and the poor or the good and the evil, the biggest of all differences in this world is between the ones that had or have pleasure in love and those that haven't and hadn't any pleasure in love, but just watched it with envy, sick envy. The spectators and the performers. I don't mean just ordinary pleasure or the kind you can buy, I mean great pleasure, and nothing that's happened to me or to Heavenly since can cancel out the many long nights without sleep when we gave each other such pleasure in love as very few people can look back on in their lives . . .

§**Princess.**

No question, go on with your story.§

Chance.

Each time I came back to St. Cloud I had her love to come back to. . . .

§**Princess.**

Something permanent in a world of change?§

Chance.

Yes, after each disappointment, each failure at something, I'd come back to her like going to a hospital. . . .

§**Princess.**

She put cool bandages on your wounds? Why didn't you marry this Heavenly little physician?§

Chance.

Didn't I tell you that Heavenly is the daughter of Boss Finley, the biggest political wheel in this part of the country? Well, if I didn't I made a serious omission.

§**Princess.**

He disapproved?§

Chance.

He figured his daughter rated someone a hundred, a thousand percent better than me, Chance Wayne. . . . The last time I came back here, she phoned me from the drugstore and told me to swim out to Diamond Key, that she would meet me there. I waited a long time, till almost sunset, and the tide started coming in before I heard the put-put of an outboard motor boat coming out to the sandbar. The sun was behind her, I squinted. She had on a silky wet tank suit and fans of water and mist made rainbows about her . . . she stood up in the boat as if she was water-skiing, shouting things at me an' circling around the sandbar, around and around it!

§**Princess.**

She didn't come to the sandbar?

Chance.

No,§ just circled around it, shouting things at me. I'd swim toward the boat, I would just about reach it and she'd race it away, throwing up misty rainbows, disappearing in rainbows and then circled back and shouting things at me again. . . .

§**Princess.**

What things?§

Chance.

Things like, "Chance go away," "Don't come back to St. Cloud." "Chance, you're a liar." "Chance, I'm sick of your lies!" "My father's right about you!" "Chance, you're no good any more." "Chance, stay away from St. Cloud." The last time around the sandbar she shouted nothing, just waved good-by and turned the boat back to shore.

THIRD MONOLOGUE

Boss Finley's place is a "white frame house of Victorian Gothic design, suggested by a door frame at the right and a single white column." The terrace, where he stands talking to his daughter Heavenly, is furnished with Victorian wicker painted bone white. The Boss is angry; Heavenly has refused to attend a political rally with him, and he needs her there, needs her presence, her apparently unspoiled beauty, as proof against the rumors about her operation which have been spread by the opposition. When he shouts at her about the scandal she has caused, she replies that he could have saved her if he had allowed her to marry Chance when he was young. "You married for love," she tells him, and "you broke Mama's heart" by taking a mistress before she died. The Boss denies this, though it is true. "Mama was just a front for you," Heavenly says. "What a terrible, terrible thing for my baby to say," he answers and takes her in his arms.

Boss.

Tomorrow, tomorrow morning, when the big after-Easter sales commence in the stores—I'm gonna send you in town with a motorcycle escort, straight to the Maison Blanche. When you arrive at the store, I want you to go directly up to the office of Mr. Harvey C. Petrie and tell him to give you unlimited credit there. Then go down and outfit yourself as if you was—buyin' a trousseau to marry the Prince of Monaco. ... Purchase a full wardrobe, includin' furs. Keep 'em in storage until winter. Gown? Three, four, five, the most lavish. Slippers? Hell, pairs and pairs of 'em. Not one hat—but a dozen. I made a pile of dough on a deal involvin' the sale of rights to oil under water here lately, and baby, I want you to buy a piece of jewelry. Now about that, you better tell Harvey to call me. Or better still, maybe Miss Lucy had better help you select it. She's wise as a backhouse rat when it comes to a stone,—that's for sure. ... Now where'd I buy that clip that I give your mama? D'you remember the clip I bought your mama?

last thing I give your mama before she died . . . I
knowed she was dyin' when I bought her that clip, and I
bought that clip for fifteen thousand dollars mainly to
make her think she was going to get well. . . . When I
pinned it on her on the nightgown she was wearing, that
poor thing started crying. She said, for God's sake, Boss,
what does a dying woman want with such a big diamond? I said to her, honey, look at the price tag on it.
What does the price tag say? See them five figures, that
one and that five and them three aughts on there? Now,
honey, make sense, I told her. If you was dying, if there
was any chance of it, would I invest fifteen grand in a
diamond clip to pin on the neck of a shroud? Ha, haha.
That made the old lady laugh. And she sat up as bright
as a little bird in that bed with the diamond clip on,
receiving callers all day, and laughing and chatting with
them, with that diamond clip on inside and she died
before midnight, with that diamond clip on her. And not
till the very last minute did she believe that the diamonds
wasn't a proof that she wasn't dying. (*He moves to
terrace, takes off robe and starts to put on tuxedo coat.*)
§Heavenly.
Did you bury her with it?§
Boss.
Bury her with it? Hell, no. I took it back to the jewelry
store in the morning.

FOURTH MONOLOGUE

Determined to force del Lago to commit herself to
producing a film in which he will star, Chance places a
telephone call to her old friend, Sally Powers, a Hollywood columnist. Del Lago will tell Miss Powers about the
plans for the film, he says, and about him; after that, she
will have to go through with the deal. For del Lago,
however, the call has a very different significance. From
Sally, if she dares to speak to her, she can learn what the
reactions have been to her comeback movie—learn, that
is, whether she is still a star or whether her career is
finished.

As Chance calls the number, del Lago moves out onto
the forestage, out of the realistic scene in which Chance

has a part. Light in the surrounding areas dims until nothing is clear behind her except the projection of the hotel palm garden.

Princess.

Why did I give him the number? Well, why not, after all, I'd have to know sooner or later . . . I started to call several times, picked up the phone, put it down again. Well, let him do it for me. Something's happened. I'm breathing freely and deeply as if the panic was over. Maybe it's over. He's doing the dreadful thing for me, asking the answer for me. He doesn't exist for me now except as somebody making this awful call for me, asking the answer for me. The light's on me. He's almost invisible now. What does that mean? Does it mean that I still wasn't ready to be washed up, counted out?

§**Chance.**

All right, call Chasen's. Try to reach her at Chasen's.§

Princess.

Well, one thing's sure. It's only this call I care for. I seem to be standing in light with everything else dimmed out. He's in the dimmed out background as if he'd never left the obscurity he was born in. I've taken the light again as a crown on my head to which I am suited by something in the cells of my blood and body from the time of my birth. It's mine, I was born to own it, as he was born to make this phone call for me to Sally Powers, dear faithful custodian of my outlived legend. (*Phone rings in distance.*) The legend that I've outlived. . . . Monsters don't die early; they hang on long. Awfully long. Their vanity's infinite, almost as infinite as their disgust with themselves. . . . (*Phone rings louder: it brings the stage light back up on the hotel bedroom. She turns to Chance and the play returns to a more realistic level.*) The phone's still ringing.

§**Chance.**

They gave me another number. . . .§

Princess.

If she isn't there, give my name and ask them where I can reach her.* * *

§**Chance.**

Is that you, Miss Powers? This is Chance Wayne talking

... I'm calling for the Princess Kosmonopolis, she wants
to speak to you. She'll come to the phone in a minute. ...§

Princess.

I can't. ... Say I've ...

§Chance.

(*Stretching phone cord.*) This is as far as I can stretch
the cord, Princess, you've got to meet it halfway.§

   (*Princess hesitates; then advances to the extended
                     phone.*)

Princess.

(*In a low, strident whisper.*) Sally? Sally? Is it really
you, Sally? Yes, it's me, Alexandra. It's what's left of
me, Sally. Oh, yes, I was there, but I only stayed a few
minutes. Soon as they started laughing in the wrong
places, I fled up the aisle and into the street screaming
Taxi—and never stopped running till now. No, I've
talked to nobody, heard nothing, read nothing . . . just
wanted—dark . . . What? You're just being kind.

§Chance.

(*As if to himself.*) Tell her that you've discovered a pair
of new stars. Two of them.§

Princess.

One moment, Sally, I'm—breathless!

§Chance.

(*Gripping her arm.*) And lay it on thick. Tell her to
break it tomorrow in her column, in all of her columns,
and in her radio talks . . . that you've discovered a pair
of young people who are the stars of tomorrow!§

Princess.

(*To Chance.*) Go into the bathroom. Stick your head
under cold water. ... Sally ... Do you really think so?
You're not just being nice, Sally, because of old times—
Grown, did you say? My talent? In what way, Sally?
More depth? More what, did you say? More power!—
well, Sally, God bless you, dear Sally.

§Chance.

Cut the chatter. Talk about me and *HEAVENLY!*§

Princess.

No, of course I didn't read the reviews. I told you I flew,
I flew. I flew as fast as I could. Oh. Oh? Oh . . .
How very sweet of you, Sally. I don't even care if you're

not altogether sincere in that statement, Sally. I think
you know what the past fifteen years have been like,
because I do have the—"out-crying heart of an—artist."
Excuse me, Sally, I'm crying, and I don't have any
Kleenex. Excuse me, Sally, I'm crying. . . .

§Chance.

(*Hissing behind her.*) Hey. Talk about me! (*She kicks
Chance's leg.*)§

Princess.

What's that, Sally? Do you really believe so? Who? For
what part? Oh, my God! . . . Oxygen, oxygen, quick!

§Chance.

(*Seizing her by the hair and hissing.*) Me! Me!—You
bitch!§

Princess.

Sally? I'm too overwhelmed. Can I call you back later?
Sally, I'll call back later. . . . (*She drops phone in a daze
of rapture.*) My picture has broken box-office records. In
New York and L.A.!

§Chance.

Call her back, get her on the phone.§

Princess.

Broken box-office records. The greatest comeback in the
history of the industry, that's what she calls it. . . .

§Chance.

You didn't mention me to her.§

Princess.

(*To herself.*) I can't appear, not yet. I'll need a week in
a clinic, then a week or ten days at the Morning Star
Ranch at Vegas. I'd better get Ackermann down there
for a series of shots before I go on to the Coast. . . .

§Chance.

(*At phone.*) Come back here, call her again.§

Princess.

I'll leave the car in New Orleans and go on by plane to,
to, to—Tucson. I'd better get Strauss working on publicity for me. I'd better be sure my tracks are covered up
well these last few weeks in—hell!—

§Chance.

Here. Here, get her back on this phone.§

Princess.

Do what?

§**Chance.**

Talk about me and talk about Heavenly to her.§

Princess.

Talk about a beach-boy I picked up for pleasure, distraction from panic? Now? When the nightmare is over? Involve my name, which is Alexandra del Lago with the record of a— You've just been using me. Using me. When I needed you downstairs you shouted, "Get her a wheel chair!" Well, I didn't need a wheel chair, I came up alone, as always, I climbed back alone up the beanstalk to the ogre's country where I live, now, alone. Chance, you've gone past something you couldn't afford to go past; your time, your youth, you've passed it. It's all you had, and you've had it.

from

THE THREE SISTERS

by Anton Chekhov (translated by Elizaveta Fen)

Act III
IRENA

Irena is the youngest of the three sisters who, with the death
of their father find themselves stranded in the dreary
backwater of a country town, geographically far from the
centers of the culture they have been educated to enjoy
and need, financially unable to escape or to maintain the
aristocratic life they had been born to. The play traces
their progress from making do, made possible by hope,
through disappointment to resignation. The sisters' only
brother marries an ambitious, domineering peasant woman and settles pudgily into the unimaginative life of a
minor country official. The brigade of soldiers, literally the
last outpost of urbanity in the town, is assigned elsewhere
and marches away. And two of the sisters face a future of
spinsterhood and the mundane jobs in which their education can earn them a living, or marriage to the kind but
rather foolish men who are available to ask them.

The orchestration of Chekhov's plays has fascinated
critics and directors—the duets, the trios, and the arias
that sound out for brief, intense moments, then fade again
into the ensemble that is the play. Irena's cry of hopelessness, reprinted below, is such a solo passage.

It is after three in the morning, but no one in the house
is asleep. A fire rages through a section of the town and
everyone has been busy finding room for the homeless and
searching out old clothes and bedding for those whose
possessions have been destroyed. For a moment Irena and
Masha, exhausted, come to rest in the bedroom which

203

Irena shares with the third sister, Olga. Masha, the only married sister, has just sent away her little schoolmaster husband; she is furious with her own boredom and with the extravagance of her brother, who has mortgaged the house (which belongs to the four of them) to pay his gambling debts. The schoolmaster scuttles away docilely and after a moment Irena speaks. Of the sisters she is the prettiest; she has been the most aspiring, the one who most intensely believed the words that summed up the hopes of them all, "to go to Moscow . . .!"

Irena.

The truth is that Andrey is getting to be shallow-minded. He's ageing and since he's been living with that woman he's lost all the inspiration he used to have! Not long ago he was working for a professorship, and yet yesterday he boasted of having at last been elected a member of the County Council. Fancy him a member, with Protopopov as chairman! They say the whole town's laughing at him, he's the only one who doesn't know anything or see anything. And now, you see, everyone's at the fire, while he's just sitting in his room, not taking the slightest notice of it. Just playing his violin. (*Agitated.*) Oh, how dreadful it is, how dreadful, how dreadful! I can't bear it any longer, I can't, I really can't! . . .

(*Enter Olga. She starts arranging things on her bedside table.*)

Irena.

(*Sobs loudly.*) You must turn me out of here! Turn me out; I can't stand it any more!

§Olga.

(*Alarmed.*) What is it? What is it, darling?§

Irena.

(*Sobbing.*) Where. . . . Where has it all gone to? Where is it? Oh, God! I've forgotten. . . . I've forgotten everything . . . there's nothing but a muddle in my head. . . . I don't remember what the Italian for "window" is, or for "ceiling". . . . Every day I'm forgetting more and more, and life's slipping by, and it will never, never come back. . . . We shall never go to Moscow. . . . I can see that we shall never go. . . .

§Olga.

Don't, my dear, don't. . . .§

Irena.

(*Trying to control herself.*) Oh, I'm so miserable! . . . I can't work, I won't work! I've had enough of it, enough! . . . First I worked on the telegraph, now I'm in the County Council office, and I hate and despise everything they give me to do there. . . . I'm twenty-three years old, I've been working all this time, and I feel as if my brain's dried up. I know I've got thinner and uglier and older, and I find no kind of satisfaction in anything, none at all. And the time's passing . . . and I feel as if I'm moving away from any hope of a genuine, fine life, I'm moving further and further away and sinking into a kind of abyss. I feel in despair, and I don't know why I'm still alive, why I haven't killed myself. . . .

§Olga.

Don't cry, my dear child, don't cry. . . . It hurts me.§

Irena.

I'm not crying any more. That's enough of it. Look, I'm not crying now. Enough of it, enough! . . .

from
THE SILVER CORD
by Sidney Howard

Act I
MRS. PHELPS, (CHRISTINA)

Mrs. Phelps has a single definition of herself: she is a
Mother, and for her that is more than enough. When one
of her two sons comes home with a bride—a charming,
intelligent woman, and as determined and strong as the
mother herself—Mrs. Phelps is not simply jealous, she
feels her very being threatened. Ultimately she forces a
head-on confrontation and an absolute choice: wife or
mother. Before that, however, she attempts to win over
her daughter-in-law to persuade her to acknowledge the
primacy of a mother's claims on the love of her children.
Mrs. Phelps is ruthless, but she is neither foolish nor
unsubtle. The speech reprinted below, an except from Mrs.
Phelps's first private conversation with her son's new wife,
is carefully calculated, and it works: for the moment the
rival is won to Mrs. Phelps's side. (For introductory notes
about *The Silver Cord*, see p. 296.)

It is afternoon and the two women are seated in Mrs.
Phelps's living room. The latter is "pretty, distinguished,
stoutish, soft, disarming, and . . . possesses . . . a real gift
for looking years younger than her age, which is well past
fifty. She boasts a reasonable amount of conventional
culture, no great amount of intellect, a superabundant
vitality, perfect health, and a prattling spirit." She has
discovered that her son and his wife, Christina, plan to
live in New York, in part because Christina will have an
opportunity there to continue her medical research career.
Mrs. Phelps is determined that the move to New York

will not be made; as a first step, she wishes simply to win her daughter-in-law's sympathy. Christina has asked Mrs. Phelps to try to understand her need to carry on her medical experiments, work which Mrs. Phelps finds rather shocking. Mrs. Phelps agrees to try, and she continues:

Mrs. Phelps.

Now you must try to understand me.... Look at me. What do you see? Simply—David's mother. I can't say of you that you're simply David's wife, because, clearly, you're many things beside that. But I am simply his mother.... In my day, we considered a girl immensely courageous and independent who taught in a school or gave music lessons. Nowadays, girls sell real estate and become scientists and think nothing of it. Give us our due, Christina. We weren't entirely bustles and smelling-salts, we girls who did not go into the world. We made a great profession, which I fear may be in some danger of vanishing from the face of the earth. We made a profession of motherhood.

(*Christina is about to protest. Mrs. Phelps stops her.*)
Your father died of his investigations of a dangerous disease. You called that splendid of him, didn't you? Would you say less of us who gave our lives to being mothers? Mothers of sons, particularly. Listen to me, Christina. For twenty-four years, since my husband died, I've given all my life, all my strength, to Dave and Rob. They've been my life and my job. Where do I stand, now? Rob is marrying. Dave is married already. This is the end of my life and my job.... Oh, I'm not asking for credit or praise. I'm asking for something more substantial. I'm asking you, my dear, dear Christina, not to take all my boy's heart. Leave me, I beg you, a little, little part of it. I've earned that much. I'm not sure I couldn't say that you owe me that much—as David's mother. I believe I've deserved it. Don't you think I have?

from

THE NIGHT OF THE IGUANA

by Tennessee Williams

Act I
SHANNON

An unfrocked parson turned haphazard tourist guide leads
a party of females from a Texas Bible college to a "rather
rustic and very Bohemian hotel," the Costa Verde, which
"sits on a jungle-covered hilltop overlooking the . . .
'morning beach' of Puerto Barrio in Mexico" and is run
by a rather nymphomanical widow who has an eye for the
parson-guide. This comic and almost too provocative situation begins one of the better (and more serious) of
Tennessee Williams' later plays. The female tourists are
not long in the play, but they help to establish the character of Shannon, the guide who is lost in himself. (For
other introductory notes, see p. 335.)

Shannon is about thirty-five, "black Irish," sweating
through his crumpled white linen suit, and wild-eyed. "His
nervous state is terribly apparent; he is a young man who
has cracked up before and is going to crack up again—
perhaps repeatedly." The "roommate" he mentions in the
scene below is not simply a girl but a private specter, the
"spook" he carries with him; and what in part has driven
him from his church to the jungle is a compulsion to make
love to young girls and to detest himself and them afterward.

At the start of the play, Shannon is certain of only one
thing: he will not leave the Costa Verde, whatever the
female tourists may demand. While they remain in the
tour bus, insisting that the tour follow its announced
schedule, he sprawls in a hammock on the veranda of the

hotel and Maxine, the owner, rubs his forehead with ice.
The bus driver climbs the hill to the hotel to urge Shannon
to come back to the bus. "There's this kid that's crying on
the back seat all the time," the driver says, "and that's
what's rucked up the deal. Hell, I don't know if you did or
you didn't, but they all think that you did 'cause the kid
keeps crying." After the driver has been sent down the hill
to talk to the ladies, Maxine turns to Shannon, still in the
hammock, and asks with a chuckle, "Ha, so you took the
young chick and the old hens are squawking about it,
Shannon?"

Shannon.

The kid asked for it, no kidding, but she's seventeen—
less, a month less'n seventeen. So it's serious, it's very
serious, because the kid is not just emotionally precocious, she's a musical prodigy, too.

§Maxine.

What's that got to do with it?§

Shannon.

Here's what it's got to do with it, she's traveling under
the wing, the military escort, of this, this—butch vocal
teacher who organizes little community sings in the bus.
Ah, God! I'm surprised they're not singing now, they
must've already suffocated. Or they'd be singing some
morale-boosting number like "She's a Jolly Good Fellow" or "Pop Goes the Weasel."—Oh, God. . . . (*Maxine
chuckles up and down the scale.*) And each night after
supper, after the complaints about the supper and the
check-up on the checks by the math instructor, and the
vomiting of the supper by several ladies, who have in-
spected the kitchen—then the kid, the canary, will give a
vocal recital. She opens her mouth and out flies Carrie
Jacobs Bond or Ethelbert Nevin. I mean after a day of
one indescribable torment after another, such as three
blowouts, and a leaking radiator in Tierra Caliente. . . .
(*He sits up slowly in the hammock as these recollections
gather force.*) And an evening climb up sierras, through
torrents of rain, around hairpin turns over gorges and
chasms measureless to man, and with a Thermos-jug
under the driver's seat which the Baptist College ladies
think is filled with icewater but which I know is filled

with iced tequila—I mean after such a day has finally come to a close, the musical prodigy, Miss Charlotte Goodall, right after supper, before there's a chance to escape, will give a heartbreaking and earsplitting rendition of Carrie Jacobs Bond's "End of a Perfect Day"— with absolutely no humor. . . .

§Maxine.

Hah!§

Shannon.

Yeah, "Hah!" Last night—no, night before last, the bus burned out its brake linings in Chilpancingo. This town has a hotel . . . this hotel has a piano, which hasn't been tuned since they shot Maximilian. This Texas songbird opens her mouth and out flies "I Love You Truly," and it flies straight at *me*, with *gestures*, all right at *me*, till her chaperone, this Diesel-driven vocal instructor of hers, slams the piano lid down and hauls her out of the mess hall. But as she's hauled out Miss Bird-Girl opens her mouth and out flies, "Larry, Larry, I love you, I love you truly!" That night, when I went to my room, I found that I had a roommate.

from

THE SEAGULL

by Anton Chekhov (translated by Elizaveta Fen)

Two Monologues from Act II and Act IV
TRIGORIN; NINA

The drama that simultaneously began the theatrical successes of Chekhov and of the Moscow Art Theatre is in every sense an actors' play—for actors, about actors, and almost too rich with challenges to the actor to exercise his perceptivity and technique. The ambiguity of characters— intensely serious, pathetically trapped by life and themselves, yet inevitably inclined to self-dramatization and undeniably comic—is not easily caught and performed; yet it must be if the extraordinary insight of Chekhov's realism is to reach the stage. In the excerpts below two characters consider themselves, and the contradictions, just below the surface, are even greater than usual: how much is true recollection, how much a romantic revision of the facts, how much melodrama to move the hearer (or the character himself)?

For any playwright but Chekhov, Trigorin would almost certainly be a villain. The disillusioned lover of an aging actress who keeps him on a tight leash, self-centered, a writer for whom people are simply subjects to be used and, if necessary, manipulated to enliven the plot of a story, Trigorin accepts without much thought the adoration of a stagestruck girl for whom he is the romantic epitome of the artist. He uses her, destroys her, and forgets her—his story, after all, is finished. Yet Trigorin, brought tamely to heel by the histrionics of his actress, is a comic figure and rather pathetic.

In the scene reprinted here Trigorin comes face to face

with himself as he exists in the imagination of the young girl, Nina. "What a wonderful world you live in!" she says, "How I envy you—if only you knew! . . . How different people's destinies are! Some just drag out their obscure, tedious existences, all very much like one another, and all unhappy. And there are others—like you, for instance, one in a million—who are given an interesting life, a life that is radiant and full of significance. You are fortunate!"

For him, of course, *she* is the wonder—youth—and he cannot resist painting for her his own quite different portrait of himself.

Trigorin.

I? (*Shrugs his shoulders.*) Hm! You talk about fame and happiness, and this radiant and interesting life, but to me all these fine words of yours—you must forgive me—are just like so many delicious sweets which I never eat. You are very young and very kind.

§Nina.

Your life is beautiful.§

Trigorin.

[My life?] But what is there beautiful about it? (*Looking at his watch.*) I must go and do some writing presently. Forgive me, I haven't much time to spare. . . . (*Laughs.*) You've stepped on my favourite corn, as the saying goes, and here I am getting excited and a little bit angry, too. All the same, let's talk. Let's talk about my radiant and beautiful life. Well, where shall we begin? (*After a moment's thought.*) You know what it is to have a *fixed idea,* for instance when a man keeps on thinking about the same thing day and night, about . . . let us say, the moon. Well, I, too, have a kind of moon of my own. I'm obsessed day and night by one thought: I must write, I must write, I just must. . . . For some reason, as soon as I've finished one novel, I feel I must start writing another, then another, then another. . . . I write in a rush, without stopping, and can't do anything else. What is there radiant or beautiful in that, I ask you? Oh, it's a fatuous life! Here I am with you, I'm quite worked up, and yet not for a single moment do I forget that there's an unfinished novel waiting for me. I look over there and I see a cloud shaped like a grand piano. . . . At once I think I must put it into some story or other—the fact that a cloud looking like a grand piano has floated by. There's the scent of heliotrope in the air. I make a mental note: "sickly scent . . . flower—the colour of a widow's dress . . . mention when describing a summer evening." . . . I snatch at every word and sentence I utter, and every word you utter, too, and hurriedly lock them up in my literary pantry—in case they might come in useful! When I finish a piece of work, I dash off to the theatre, or go off on a fishing trip, and that's the time when I ought to relax and forget myself—but no! Something that feels like a heavy cast-iron ball begins to revolve in my brain—a new subject for a novel! So immediately I drag myself back to my desk again, and I have to push on with my writing once more, to keep on writing and writing. . . . And it's like that always, always . . . and I can't get any rest away from myself. I feel as though I'm devouring my own life, that for the sake of the honey I give to all and sundry I'm despoiling my best flowers of their pollen, that I'm plucking the flowers themselves and trampling on their roots. Am I out of my mind? Do you think my relatives and friends treat me like a sane person? "What are you jotting down now? What surprises have you in store for us?" It's the same thing over and over again, until I begin to imagine that this attentiveness on the part of my friends, all this praise and admiration, is just a sham, that they are trying to deceive me just as if I were insane. Sometimes I feel afraid of them stealing up on me from behind, seizing me and carrying me off, like Poprishchin,[1] to a lunatic asylum. As for the years when I was starting—my younger, better years—in those days my writing used to be one continuous torment. A minor writer, especially if he hasn't had much luck, sees himself as clumsy, awkward, and unwanted. He gets nervous and overwrought, and feels irresistibly drawn towards people connected with literature, or art, but then he just wanders among them unrecognized and unnoticed, unable to look them straight and courageously in

[1] The principal character in the story *The Diary of a Madman*, by N. V. Gogol.

the eye, like a passionate gambler who hasn't any money. I could not see my readers, but for some reason I always imagined them as unfriendly and sceptical. I was afraid of the public, it terrified me, and whenever a new play of mine was produced, I always felt that the dark-haired people in the audience were hostile to it, and the fair-haired ones coldly indifferent. Oh, how dreadful it all was! What a torment!

§Nina.

But even so, don't you have moments of happiness and exaltation—moments when you feel inspired, when your creative work is actually in progress?§

Trigorin.

Yes, while I'm writing I enjoy it. I enjoy reading proofs, too, but . . . as soon as the thing comes out in print I can no longer bear it. I immediately see that it's not what I intended, that it's a mistake, that it oughtn't to have been written at all, and I feel angry and depressed. . . . (*Laughing.*) And then the public reads it and says: "Yes, it's charming, so cleverly done. . . . Charming, but a far cry from Tolstoy." . . . Or "A very fine piece of work, but Turgenev's *Fathers and Children* is a better book." And so it will go on till my dying day—everything will be charming and clever—and nothing more. And when I die, my friends as they pass by my grave, will say: "Here lies Trigorin. He was a good writer, but not as good as Turgenev."

SECOND MONOLOGUE

Nina runs away to Moscow to become an actress and to be with Trigorin. When she has borne his child, been disillusioned and finally deserted by him, she continues the acting career she dreamed of in the country. Brought to the provinces for an acting engagement, she comes one night to the estate where she met Trigorin and where she was loved by Trepliov, the son of the successful, middle-aged actress whom Trigorin has never really left. Trepliov still loves Nina and she, oppressed with memories and the intensity of his love, attempts to tell him what happened in Moscow and who she has become. When she compares herself to a seagull, she is recalling a time when Trigorin

seeing a seagull that had been shot by Trepliov finds in it
"a subject for a short story: a young girl, like you, has
lived all her life beside a lake; she loves the lake like a
seagull, and is as free and happy as a seagull. But a man
comes by chance, sees her, and having nothing better to
do, destroys her like that seagull there."

Nina's performance—and it is a performance, at least
in part—is an extraordinary amalgam of hysteria, truth,
romanticizing, genuine anguish, and perhaps a sample of
Nina's not very skillful acting. It is, I would add, as
difficult as anything Chekhov ever asked of an actor.

Trepliov, working in the drawing room he has converted
into a study, has heard a noise outside, discovered Nina,
and brought her in. Why has she not come before, he
asks, and tells her that he has tried to see her, waiting like
a beggar under her window.

Nina.

I was afraid that you might hate me. Every night I
dream that you look at me and don't recognize me. If
only you knew! Ever since I came I've been walking
round here . . . beside the lake. I've been near this house
many times, but I dared not come in. Let us sit down.
(*They sit down.*)
Let us sit and talk, talk. . . . It's nice here, warm and
comfortable. . . . Do you hear the wind? There's a passage in Turgenev: "Fortunate is he who on such a night
has a roof over him, who has a warm corner of his
own." I am a seagull. . . . No, that's not it. (*Rubs her
forehead.*) What was I saying? Yes. . . . Turgenev. . . .
"And Heaven help the homeless wayfarers". . . . Never
mind. . . . (*Sobs.*)
§**Trepliov.**
Nina, you're crying again! . . . Nina!§
. **Nina.**
Never mind, it does me good. . . . I haven't cried for two
years. Yesterday, late in the evening I came into the
garden to see whether our stage was still there. And it is
still standing! I began to cry for the first time in two
years, and it lifted the weight from my heart, and I felt
more at ease. You see, I'm not crying now. (*Takes his
hand.*) And so you've become a writer. . . . You are a

writer and I'm an actress. We've been drawn into the
whirlpool, too. I used to live here joyously, like a child—
I used to wake up in the morning and burst into song. I
loved you and dreamed of fame. . . . And now? Tomorrow morning early I have to go to Yelietz in a third-class
carriage . . . with the peasants; and at Yelietz, upstart
business men will pester me with their attentions. Life is
coarse! * * *

Nina.

Why did you say you kissed the ground where I walked?
Someone ought to kill me. (*Droops over the table.*) I am
so tired. Oh, I wish I could rest . . . just rest! (*Raising
her head.*) I'm a seagull . . . No, that's not it. I'm an
actress. Oh, well! (*She hears Arkadina and Trigorin
laughing off-stage, listens, then runs to the door at left
and looks through the keyhole.*) So he is here, too! . . .
(*Returning to Trepliov.*) Oh, well! . . . Never mind. . . .
Yes. . . . He didn't believe in the theater, he was always
laughing at my dreams, and so gradually I ceased to
believe, too, and lost heart. . . . And then I was so preoc-
cupied with love and jealousy, and a constant fear for
my baby. . . . I became petty and common, when I acted
I did it stupidly. . . . I didn't know what to do with my
hands or how to stand on the stage, I couldn't control
my voice. . . . But you can't imagine what it feels like—
when you know that you are acting abominably. I'm a
seagull. No, that's not it again. . . . Do you remember
you shot a seagull? A man came along by chance, saw it
and destroyed it, just to pass the time. . . . A subject for a
short story. . . . That's not it. (*Rubs her forehead.*) What
was I talking about? . . . Yes, about the stage. I'm not
like that now: . . . Now I am a real actress. I act with
intense enjoyment, with enthusiasm; on the stage I am
intoxicated and I feel that I am beautiful. But now, while
I'm living here, I go for walks a lot. . . . I keep walking
and thinking . . . thinking and feeling that I am growing
stronger in spirit with every day that passes. . . . I think I
now know, Kostia, that what matters in our work—
whether you act on the stage or write stories—what
really matters is not fame, or glamour, not the things I
used to dream about—but knowing how to endure
things. How to bear one's cross and have faith. I have

faith now and I'm not suffering quite so much, and when
I think of my vocation I'm not afraid of life.* * *

Nina.

(*Listening.*) Sh-sh! . . . I'm going now. Good-bye. When
I become a great actress, come and see me act. Promise?
and now.·... (*Presses his hand.*) It's late. I can hardly
stand up.... I'm so tired and hungry....

§Trepliov.

Do stay, I'll give you some supper.§

Nina.

No, no. . . .Don't see me off, I'll go by myself. . . . My
horses are not far off.... So she brought him with her?
Oh, well, it doesn't matter.... When you see Trigorin
don't tell him anything. . . . I love him. I love him even
more than before. A subject for a short story.... Yes, I
love him, I love him passionately, I love him desperately!
How nice it all used to be, Kostia! Do you remember?
How tranquil, warm, and joyous, and pure our life was,
what feelings we had—like tender, exquisite flowers....
Do you remember? . . . (*Recites.*) "The men, the lions,
the eagles, the partridges, the antlered deer, the geese,
the spiders, the silent fishes of the deep, starfishes and
creatures unseen to the eye—in short all living things, all
living things, all living things, having completed their
mournful cycle, have been snuffed out. For thousands of
years the earth has borne no living creature, and this
poor moon now lights its lamp in vain. The cranes no
longer wake up in the meadows with a cry, the May
beetles are no longer heard humming in the groves of
lime trees." . . .

from

THE LONDON MERCHANT

by George Lillo (edited by J. L. Steffensen)

Act IV, scene 18
MILLWOOD

For a century or more Lillo's eighteenth-century tragedy,
the story of an almost good young man dragged into
immorality and crime by a villainous woman, was regularly performed at Drury Lane and Covent Garden on ap-
prentices' holidays, it having been decided by the city's
merchants (who sponsored many of the performances)
that the play was an instructive example for their youthful
employees. Today it is not easy to take the play seriously,
but Lillo's intention was to create a tragedy of common
men and, despite his predilection for hyperbole and moralizing sentiment, his drama contains the seeds of modern
serious drama that entered the theater with Ibsen and
crystallized in plays such as Arthur Miller's *Death of a
Salesman.* Moreover, it includes one extraordinary, surprisingly contemporary character—Millwood, a prototype
of the modern, independent (indeed, liberated) woman.

For much of the play Millwood is simply the beautiful
but ruthless temptress who seduces an apprentice in order
to persuade him to rob his master's cash box. But later,
when she has led him to kill his beneficent old uncle and
the forces of justice close in on her as well as on the
young murderer, she confronts her moralizing captors
with an angry self-defense. Suddenly her character breaks
out of the framework of the neatly moral play. She speaks
in bitter condemnation of the inequities of society's treatment of woman and of the hypocrisy of men. And one
almost hears the voices of characters such as Ibsen's Mrs.

218

Alving (see p. 285). It is a remarkable outburst, and one wonders how the theaters' complacent merchant-sponsors accounted for it. For today's actress it requires acting on a large scale coupled with the belief of realism.

The scene is Millwood's house. Confronted by his master and officers of the law, the apprentice, George Barnwell, has confessed his crimes, repented, and been taken to prison. Millwood, however, refuses to confess, though Barnwell's master, Mr. Thorowgood, has indisputable proof of her guilt. Cornered, she goes to another room where she claims there is evidence that will show her innocence. She returns with a pistol, but is quickly disarmed by Barnwell's friend, the good apprentice, Trueman. "Here thy power of doing mischief ends," Trueman exclaims, "deceitful, cruel, bloody woman!"

Millwood turns on him, angered as much by the final word of his shout of triumph as by the fact of her capture.

Millwood.

Fool, Hypocrite, Villain,—Man! thou can'st not call me that.

§Trueman.

To call thee Woman, were to wrong the Sex, thou devil!§

Millwood.

[Call me Devil?] That imaginary Being is an Emblem of thy cursed Sex collected. A Mirrour, wherein each particular Man may see his own likeness, and that of all Mankind.

§Thorowgood.

Think not by aggravating the Faults of others to extenuate thy own, of which the Abuse of such uncommon Perfections of Mind and Body is not the least.§

Millwood.

[My Perfections!] If such I had, well may I curse your barbarous Sex, who robb'd me of 'em, e'er I knew their Worth, then left me, too late, to count their Value by their Loss. Another and another Spoiler came, and all my Gain was Poverty and Reproach. My Soul disdain'd, and yet disdains Dependence and Contempt. Riches, no Matter by what Means obtain'd, I saw secur'd the worst of Men from both; I found it therefore necessary to be rich; and,

to that End, I summon'd all my Arts. You call 'em
wicked, be it so, they were such as my Conversation with
your Sex had furnish'd me withal.
§**Thorowgood.**
Sure none but the worst of Men convers'd with thee.§
Millwood.

Men of all Degrees and all Professions I have known, yet
found no Difference, but in their several capacities; all
were alike wicked to the utmost of their Power. In
Pride, Contention, Avarice, Cruelty, and Revenge, the
Reverend Priesthood were my unerring Guides. From
Suburb-Magistrates, who live by ruin'd Reputations, as
the unhospitable Natives of *Cornwall* do by Ship-wrecks,
I learn'd, that to charge my innocent Neighbours with
my Crimes, was to merit their Protection; for to skreen
the Guilty, is the less scandalous, when many are suspect-
ed, and Detraction, like Darkness and Death, blackens
all Objects, and levels all Distinction. Such are your
venal Magistrates, who favour none but such as, by their
Office, they are sworn to punish: With them, not to be
guilty, is the worst of Crimes; and large Fees privately
paid, is every needful Virtue.
§**Thorowgood.**
Your Practice has sufficiently discover'd your Contempt
of Laws, both human and divine; no wonder then that
you shou'd hate the Officers of both.§
Millwood.

I hate you all; I know you, and expect no Mercy; nay, I
ask for none; I have done nothing that I am sorry for; I
follow'd my Inclinations, and that the best of you does
every Day. All Actions seem alike natural and indifferent
to Man and Beast, who devour, or are devour'd, as they
meet with others weaker or stronger than themselves.
§**Thorowgood.**
What Pity it is, a Mind so comprehensive, daring and
inquisitive, shou'd be a Stranger to Religion's sweet and
powerful Charms.§
Millwood.

I am not Fool enough to be an Atheist, tho' I have
known enough of Mens Hypocrisy to make a thousand
simple Women so. Whatever Religion is in it self, as
practis'd by Mankind, it has caus'd the Evils you say it

was design'd to cure. War, Plague, and Famine, has not destroy'd so many of the human Race, as this pretended Piety has done; and with such barbarous Cruelty, as if the only Way to honour Heaven, were to turn the present World into Hell.

§Thorowgood.

Truth is Truth, tho' from an Enemy, and spoke in Malice. You bloody, blind, and superstitious Bigots, how will you answer this?§

Millwood.

What are your Laws, of which you make your Boast, but the Fool's Wisdom, and the Coward's Valour; the Instrument and Skreen of all your Villanies, by which you punish in others what you act your selves, or wou'd have acted, had you been in their Circumstances. The Judge who condemns the poor Man for being a Thief, had been a Thief himself had he been poor. Thus you go on deceiving, and being deceiv'd, harrassing, plaguing, and destroying one another; but Women are your universal Prey.

> Women, by whom you are, the Source of Joy,
> With cruel Arts you labour to destroy:
> A thousand Ways our Ruin you pursue,
> Yet blame in us those Arts, first taught by you.
> O—may, from hence, each violated Maid,
> By flatt'ring, faithless, barb'rous Man betray'd;
> When robb'd of Innocence, and Virgin Fame,
> From your Destruction raise a nobler Name;
> To right their Sex's Wrongs devote their Mind,
> And future Millwoods prove to plague Mankind.

from

MARAT/SADE (full title: The Persecution and Assass-
ination of Jean-Paul Marat as Performed by the Inmates
of the Asylum of Charenton Under the Direction of the
Marquis de Sade)

by Peter Weiss (English version by Geoffrey Skelton,
verse adaptation by Adrian Mitchell)

Two Monologues from Scenes 10 and 29, and Scene 20
CORDAY; SADE

The scene is the bathhouse of a mental asylum, Charenton, in 1808. The subject is the killing of Marat in 1793.
The characters are lunatics who present the play of Marat
as imagined and directed by the Marquis de Sade, whose
views about the event, the meaning of Marat's life, and the
nature of mankind differ radically from those of Marat
himself. The audience within the play (Weiss's play, not
Sade's) is an official of the asylum, his family, and guests,
whose views are not those of Sade or Marat or necessarily
of us, the "real" audience, who, in our own era, look at
1808 looking from its various viewpoints at 1793—look
and ask, as the play forces us to do, what *is* the reality of
this event, the murder; or indeed what is reality in the
theater itself?

It is perhaps extraordinary, given the complexity of any
attempt to explain Weiss's play, that onstage *Marat/Sade*
connects with the audience directly and with great power.
For Peter Brook and the Royal Shakespeare Company the
play provided an opportunity for one of the most exciting
productions of the contemporary theater. Its demands for
total ensemble acting make it a particular challenge and
inspiration to actors' workshops. But individual performers, too, will find themselves challenged by the play in

special and instructive ways. The requirement, for example, to act the lunatic acting a part sets up some unique problems. Sunk deep in his private imagination, can the lunatic fully become his character, or will there be some separation, at times an obvious one? On the other hand, already out of touch with reality may not the lunatic find it easier to live his part with utter belief, especially when his character's feelings closely parallel his own? Moreover, the actor is always playing two parts, the lunatic and his character, and must make clear to the audience their separateness and, when it happens, their coalescence.

The gulf between lunatic and character is perhaps most sharply evident in Corday, an inmate afflicted with something like sleeping sickness, who must struggle simply to retain consciousness, much less to play her part. Her lines come out haltingly, not always in the logical word groups, yet at times the intensity of her battle to get on with her speech must merge with the intensity of Charlotte Corday, the murderess of Marat.

The speeches reprinted here are taken from two widely separated scenes, but together they seem to form a useful exercise.

Corday's first experience of Paris, where she is to commit her murder, is summed up in a wild song and pantomime of the reign of the guillotine. There is the raucous procession of the tumbrels to the place of execution; then, while the crowd continues its stamping, Corday speaks.

Corday.

   (*In front of the arena, turned to the public. Behind her the stamping continues.*)
What kind of town is this
The sun can hardly pierce the haze
not a haze made out of rain and fog
but steaming thick and hot
like the mist in a slaughterhouse
Why are they howling
What are they dragging through the streets
They carry stakes but what's impaled on those stakes
Why do they hop what are they dancing for
Why are they racked with laughter
Why do the children scream

What are those heaps they fight over
those heaps with eyes and mouths
What kind of town is this
hacked buttocks lying in the street
What are all these faces
(*Behind her the dance of death takes place.*
*The Four Singers join the dancers. The cart is turned
into a place of execution. Two Patients represent the
guillotine. The execution is prepared in gruesome detail.*
Corday sits slumped at the foremost edge of the arena.)
Soon these faces will close around me
These eyes and mouths will call me to join them * * *

[The play has wound its way to the murder scene. In
silence Corday is pushed to the center of the stage. Two
nursing sisters of the asylum stand at her side holding her
firmly. The inmate playing Duperret, Corday's lover,
stands behind her, supporting her back.]

Corday.
(*Her eyes still closed, speaking softly, nervously.*)
Now I know what it is like
when the head is cut off the body
Oh this moment
hands tied behind the back
feet bound together
neck bared
hair cut off
knees on the boards
the head already laid
in the metal slot
looking down into the dripping basket
The sound of the blade rising
and from its slanting edge
the blood still drops
and then the downward slide
to split us in two
                    (*Pause.*)
They say
that the head
held high in the executioner's hand
still lives

that the eyes still see
that the tongue still writhes
and down below the arms and legs still shudder* * *
[Duperret speaks briefly, begging Corday to waken from
this nightmare, and, discovering the dagger she has hidden
in her bosom, he asks her to throw it away.]

Corday.
 (*Pushes his hand away.*)
 We should all carry weapons nowadays
 in self-defence
§Duperret.
 (*Beseechingly.*)
 No one will attack you Charlotte
 Charlotte throw the dagger away
 go away
 go back to Caen§
Corday.
 (*Drawing herself up and pushing the Sisters' hands
 away.*)
 In my room in Caen
 on the table under the open window
 lies open The Book of Judith
 Dressed in her legendary beauty
 she entered the tent of the enemy
 and with a single blow
 slew him
§Duperret.
 Charlotte
 what are you planning§
Corday.
 (*Forlorn again.*)
 Look at this city
 Its prisons are crowded
 with our friends
 I was among them just now
 in my sleep
 They all stand huddled together there
 and hear through the windows
 the guards talking about executions
 Now they talk of people as gardeners talk of leaves for
  burning

Their names are crossed off the top of a list
and as the list grows shorter
more names are added at the bottom
I stood with them
and we waited
for our own names to be called

§**Duperret.**
Charlotte
let us leave together
this very evening§

Corday.
(*As if she has not heard him.*)
What kind of town is this
What sort of streets are these
Who invented this
who profits by it
I saw peddlers
at every corner
they're selling little guillotines
with tiny sharp blades
and dolls filled with red liquid
which spurts from the neck
when the sentence is carried out
What kind of children are these
who can play
with this toy so efficiently
and who is judging
who is judging

SECOND MONOLOGUE

The Marquis de Sade writes the play of Marat, but he does not agree with the beliefs of Marat. Where the revolutionary calls for the action and hope of men banded together, the Marquis articulates the perceptions of the alienated individual who has looked deep into himself and found only cruelty and despair. Sade's view of himself and of the hopelessness of Marat's cause are made clear in a speech, reprinted below, punctuated by the crack of a whip.

In Peter Brook's production, the sensuality of the beating was emphasized. The stage direction calling for a

whip was ignored. Instead, Corday bent over Sade and
with flicks of her head drew the long strands of her hair
across his back. Sade reacted as though he had been
struck by an actual whip.

Sade.
 Marat
 Today they need you because you are going to suffer for
  them
 They need you and they honour the urn which holds
  your ashes
 Tomorrow they will come back and smash that urn
 and they will ask
 Marat who was Marat
 Marat
 Now I will tell you
 what I think of this revolution
 which I helped to make
  (*It has become very quiet in the background.*)
 When I lay in the Bastille
 my ideas were already formed
 I sweated them out
 under the blows of my own whip
 out of hatred for myself
 and the limitations of my mind
 In prison I created in my mind
 monstrous representatives of a dying class
 who could only exercise their power
 in spectacularly staged orgies
 I recorded the mechanics of their atrocities
 in the minutest detail
 and brought out everything wicked and brutal
 that lay inside me
 In a criminal society
 I dug the criminal out of myself
 so I could understand him and so understand
 the times we live in
 My imaginary giants committed
 desecrations and tortures
 I committed them myself
 and like them allowed myself to be bound and beaten

And even now I should like to take
this beauty here

(*Pointing to Corday, who is brought forward.*)
who stands there so expectantly
and let her beat me
while I talk to you about the Revolution

(*The Sisters place Corday in the arena. Sade hands her
a many-stranded whip. He tears off his shirt and offers
his back to Corday. He stands facing the audience. Corday stands behind him. The Patients advance slowly from
the background. The ladies on Coulmier's dais stand up
expectantly.*)
At first I saw in the revolution a chance
for a tremendous outburst of revenge
an orgy greater than all my dreams

(*Corday slowly raises the whip and lashes him. Sade
cowers.*)
But then I saw
when I sat in the courtroom myself

            (*Whiplash. Sade gasps.*)
not as I had been before the accused
but as a judge
I couldn't bring myself
to deliver the prisoners to the hangman

            (*Whiplash.*)
I did all I could to release them or let them escape
I saw I wasn't capable of murder

        (*Whiplash. Sade groans asthmatically.*)
although murder
was the final proof of my existence
and now

            (*Whiplash. He gasps and groans.*)
the very thought of it
horrifies me
In September when I saw
the official sacking of the Carmelite Convent
I had to bend over in the courtyard
and vomit

        (*Corday stops, herself breathing heavily.*)
as I saw my own prophecies coming true

    (*He falls down on his knees. Corday stands before
him.*)

and women running by
holding in their dripping hands
the severed genitals of men
 (Corday flogs him again. He groans and falls forward.)
And then in the next few months
     (Hindered by his asthma.)
as the tumbrels ran regularly to the scaffolds
and the blade dropped and was winched up and dropped
again
    (Whiplash.)
all the meaning drained out of this revenge
It had become mechanical
 *(Another blow. He crumples. Corday stands very
erect.)*
It was inhuman it was dull
and curiously technocratic
    (Whiplash.)
And now Marat
   (Whiplash. Sade breathes heavily.)
now I see where
this revolution is leading
 *(Corday stands breathlessly, holding the whip over
Sade. The two Sisters move forward and pull her back.
She does not resist, dragging the whip behind her. Sade
continues, lying on his knees.)*
To the withering of the individual man
and a slow merging into uniformity
to the death of choice
to self denial
to deadly weakness
in a state
which has no contact with individuals
but which is impregnable
So I turn away
I am one of those who has to be defeated
and from this defeat I want to seize
all I can get with my own strength
I step out of my place
and watch what happens
without joining in
observing
noting down my observations

and all around me
stillness

        (Pauses, breathing heavily.)

And when I vanish
I want all trace of my existence
to be wiped out

   (He takes his shirt and returns to his chair, slowly dressing.)

from
THE SHOW-OFF
by George Kelly

Act III
CLARA, AUBREY

Clara Hyland is less than happy with her brother-in-law.
Having smashed up a borrowed car while driving without
a license (he struck, among other objects, a streetcar and
a policeman), he has been fined $1,000 and persuaded
Clara's husband to foot the bill. Clara did not want
Aubrey Piper as her brother-in-law in the first place: he
talks too much, he's a braggart, an egotist, and he's the
furthest thing from a success. A clerk in the freight office
at the Pennsylvania Railroad, Aubrey tells everyone that
he has eighty men working under him. And just now,
when a friend of Clara's late father came to call at her
mother's house, Aubrey—along with other prevarications—
allowed the man to think that the house was his and that
his mother-in-law was the guest of his charity. (For introductory notes about *The Show-off*, see p. 153.)

Aubrey caught a glimpse of Clara listening in on his
conversation with his father-in-law's friend, and when he
has shown the man out of the sitting room, he glides
rapidly toward a doorway himself. Clara, however, is
faster. Popping in through another door and taking a
quick look to make certain that no one else can hear
them, she calls out.

Clara.
Come here, Aubrey, I want to talk to you. (*He turns
towards her, with an attempt at nonchalance.*) What do
you mean by telling people that this is your house?

231

Aubrey.

I didn't tell anybody it was my house.

Clara.

You *must* have told this man, or he wouldn't have said so.

Aubrey.

What do you think I am, a liar?

Clara.

Yes, I do; one of the best I know.

Aubrey.

Well, ask Amy what I said to him, she was here when I was talking to him.

Clara.

(*Before he has finished speaking.*) I don't have to ask anybody anything!—you were lying to him here to-day, right in front of me.

Aubrey.

(*With a shade of challenge in his manner.*) What'd I say?

Clara.

That you'd fixed the automobile thing up.

Aubrey.

It's fixed up, isn't it?

Clara.

You didn't fix it up. (*There is a slight pause, during which Aubrey, his dignity considerably outraged, moves forward and crosses in front of her to the front of the center-table, where he stops. Clara moves down at the right of the Morris-chair to a point near him.*) You'd have gone to jail for six months only for Frank Hyland. And telling this man that you tried to pursuade Pop to stop working.

Aubrey.

(*Over his left shoulder.*) So I did.

Clara.

When?

Aubrey.

I didn't say it to him. But I told Amy he ought to stop. And I think he'd be right here to-day if he'd taken my advice.

Clara.

He wouldn't be right here to-day if he'd stopped expecting *you* to keep him. (*He moves further over to the right; and she follows him.*) And now, listen to me, Aubrey; I want to talk seriously to you. You've made a lot of trouble for us since you've been in this family; and I want you to stop it. There's no reason my husband, because he happens to have a few dollars, should be going around paying *your* bills.

Aubrey.

(*Half-turning to her.*) What do you want me to do?

Clara.

I want you to stop telling *lies;* for that's about all everything you do amounts to. Trying to make people believe your something that you're not;—when if you'd just stop your talking and your showing-off, you *might* be the thing that you're trying to make them believe you are. (*She glances toward the kitchen-door, and then speaks to him again, in a slightly lower tone.*) Your wife's going to have a child one of these days, Aubrey, and you want to pull yourself together and try to be sensible, like the man of a family *should* be. You're smart enough;—there's no reason why a fellow like you should be living in two rooms over a barber shop. I should think you'd have more respect for your wife. (*She turns and moves a few steps up towards the kitchen-door.*)

Aubrey.

A man doesn't stand much chance of getting ahead, Clara, when the boss has got a grudge against him.

Clara.

(*Turning sharply to her right, and moving to the upper right-hand corner of the center-table.*) Well, stop your silly talk, and get rid of that carnation, and the boss might get rid of his grudge. (*She glances toward the kitchen-door again, leans across the table towards him, and lowers her voice.*) But, what I wanted to tell you was this, Aubrey,—I've asked Mom to let you and Amy come in here; and she sez she wouldn't mind it only that she knows that the first thing she'd *hear* is that you'd told someone that you'd taken *her* in. And, you see, that's exactly what you've done already,—to this man that brought the watch. If I told Mom that there'd be war.

Aubrey.

Are you going to tell her?

Clara.

(*With authoritative levelness.*) I'm going to put that up to you. And the very first time I hear that you've told anybody that this is *your* house,—I'll see to it that you'll get a house that *will* be your own. (*Aubrey smiles, a bit smugly, and looks at her out of the sides of his eyes.*)

Aubrey.

I guess your Mother'ud have something to say about that, Clara.

Clara.

(*With a measured evenness.*) Well, the only thing that needs to worry you, is what *I'll* have to say about it. (*Aubrey's smugness begins to fade—into a questioning narrowness.*) This is my house—Pop left it to me; so that Mom'ud always have a roof over her. For he knew how long she'd have it if Amy ever got round her. And if Amy ever got hold of it, he knew what she'd do if it ever came to a choice between you and Mom. •

Aubrey.

What are you doing, kidding me? (*Clara holds his eyes steadily for a fraction of a second.*)

Clara.

I'm giving you a tip;—see that you keep it to yourself. (*Aubrey withdraws his eyes slowly and looks straight out, weighing this new bit of intelligence carefully in his mind.*) Be wise, now, Aubrey—you've got a chance to sit *in* here and live like a human being; and if you throw it way, you'll have nobody to blame but yourself. (*There is a sound at the front-door of a newspaper being thrown into the vestibule, and a man's voice says,* "Paper!" *Then the front-door is heard to close.*) Open that door there, Mom'll be wondering what it's doing shut. (*She crosses up to the hall-door and goes out for the newspaper. Aubrey stands for a second thinking; and then Amy opens the kitchen-door and comes in. She glances about the room.*)

from

A VIEW FROM THE BRIDGE

by Arthur Miller

Act I
BEATRICE, CATHERINE

In this second, longer version of the play Miller combines
the bold lines and passionate drive of a classical tragedy
with the details of the naturalistic theater of the twentieth
century. The scene reprinted here is one of those smaller
moments which make effective the stark shape of this
drama of a man who could not bear to see the girl he
adopted as a child grow up and learn to love another man.

When Catherine was a baby, her mother died and her
aunt's husband, Eddie Carbone, a longshoreman, took her
into their home as a daughter. Now Catherine has finished
high school and a year of secretarial school; she has a job,
and she has begun to fall in love with Rodolpho, a young
Italian—cousin of Eddie's wife—who has entered the
country illegally and is being sheltered by Eddie. Eddie
strongly objects to this friendship, for reasons that are clear
enough to the audience but not to Beatrice, Eddie's wife,
nor to Catherine, nor to Eddie himself. Eventually the
feelings he cannot, or dare not, explain lead to violence and
death, but for a time they simply make life in the crowded
tenement apartment edgy and uncomfortable. Beatrice is
the first to sense the truth. She cannot get through to
Eddie; he cannot hear her. She tries to make things clear to
Catherine, but it is difficult for Catherine to begin to know
what Bea is talking about; Eddie is like a father, she loves
him. When Eddie attempts to persuade Catherine that Rodolpho does not love her but simply wants to use her in
order to be able to claim American citizenship, Catherine

refuses to believe him, but she is shaken and confused, and Bea tries again to get her to understand.

The scene is the living room-dining room of the tenement flat in Red Hook, the Brooklyn waterfront. There is a rocker down front; a round dining table center, with chairs. Beatrice is in the room when Catherine rushes in, sobbing. Eddie follows. "Why don't you straighten her out?" he shouts at Bea, "The guy is no good!"

Beatrice.

(*Suddenly, with open fright and fury.*) You going to leave her alone? Or you gonna drive me crazy? (*He turns, striving to retain his dignity, but nevertheless in guilt walks out of the house, into the street and away. Catherine starts into a bedroom.*) Listen, Catherine. (*Catherine halts, turns to her sheepishly.*) What are you going to do with yourself?

Catherine.

I don't know.

Beatrice.

Don't tell me you don't know; you're not a baby any more, what are you going to do with yourself?

Catherine.

He won't listen to me.

Beatrice.

I don't understand this. He's not your father, Catherine. I don't understand what's going on here.

Catherine.

(*As one who herself is trying to rationalize a buried impulse.*) What am I going to do, just kick him in the face with it?

Beatrice.

Look, honey, you wanna get married, or don't you wanna get married? What are you worried about, Katie?

Catherine.

(*Quietly, trembling.*) I don't know B. It just seems wrong if he's against it so much.

Beatrice.

(*Never losing her aroused alarm.*) Sit down, honey, I want to tell you something. Here, sit down. Was there ever any fella he liked for you? There wasn't, was there?

Catherine.

But he says Rodolpho's just after his papers.

Beatrice.

Look, he'll say anything. What does he care what he says? If it was a prince came here for you it would be no different. You know that, don't you?

Catherine.

Yeah, I guess.

Beatrice.

So what does that mean?

Catherine.

(*Slowly turns her head to Beatrice.*) What?

Beatrice.

It means you gotta be your own self more. You still think you're a little girl, honey. But nobody else can make up your mind for you any more, you understand? You gotta give him to understand that he can't give you orders no more.

Catherine.

Yeah, but how am I going to do that? He thinks I'm a baby.

Beatrice.

Because *you* think you're a baby. I told you fifty times already, you can't act the way you act. You still walk around in front of him in your slip—

Catherine.

Well I forgot.

Beatrice.

Well you can't do it. Or like you sit on the edge of the bathtub talkin' to him when he's shavin' in his underwear.

Catherine.

When'd I do that?

Beatrice.

I seen you in there this morning.

Catherine

Oh . . . well, I wanted to tell him something and I—

Beatrice.

I know, honey. But if you act like a baby and he be treatin' you like a baby. Like when he comes home sometimes you throw yourself at him like when you was twelve years old.

Catherine.
Well I like to see him and I'm happy so I—
Beatrice.
Look, I'm not tellin' you what to do honey, but—
Catherine.
No, you could tell me, B.! Gee, I'm all mixed up. See, I—
He looks so sad now and it hurts me.
Beatrice.
Well look Katie, if it's goin' to hurt you so much you're
gonna end up an old maid here.
Catherine.
No!
Beatrice.
I'm tellin' you, I'm not makin' a joke. I tried to tell you
a couple of times in the last year or so. That's why I was
so happy you were going to go out and get work, you
wouldn't be here so much, you'd be a little more inde-
pendent. I mean it. It's wonderful for a whole family to
love each other, but you're a grown woman and you're in
the same house with a grown man. So you'll act different
now, heh?
Catherine.
Yeah, I will. I'll remember.
Beatrice.
Because it ain't only up to him, Katie, you understand? I
told him the same thing already.
Catherine.
(*Quickly.*) What?
Beatrice.
That he should let you go. But, you see, if only I tell
him, he thinks I'm bawlin' him out, or maybe I'm
jealous or somethin', you know?
Catherine.
(*Astonished.*) He said you was jealous?
Beatrice.
No, I'm just sayin' maybe that's what he thinks. (*She
reaches over to Catherine's hand; with a strained smile.*)
You think I'm jealous of you, honey?
Catherine.
No! It's the first I thought of it.
Beatrice.
(*With a quiet sad laugh.*) Well you should have thought

of it before . . . but I'm not. We'll be all right. Just give
him to understand; you don't have to fight, you're just—
You're a woman, that's all, and you got a nice boy, and
now the time came when you said good-by. All right?

Catherine.

(*Strangely moved at the prospect.*) All right. . . . If I can.

Beatrice.

Honey . . . you gotta.

(*Catherine, sensing now an imperious demand, turns
with some fear, with a discovery, to Beatrice. She is at
the edge of tears, as though a familiar world had shattered.*)

Catherine.

Okay.

from

A DAY BY THE SEA

by N. C. Hunter

Act II, scene 2
MATTY, DOCTOR

Doctor Farley has fought a not remarkably successful battle
against gin, and seeing he was not likely to win and knowing the damage he might someday do a patient, he has
retired from his practice and come to live in a seaside house
in England as the companion caretaker of a very old man.
Matty—Miss Mathieson—is a warm, cheerful Scot who
takes care of other people's children. She has come to the
house on the cliffs with the family whose children she has
fed and scolded and loved for the last seven years. Now
the youngest is to go to school, Matty's services are no
longer needed and she is to go to live with her sister.
(For introductory notes about *A Day by the Sea*, see p.
383.)

Matty regularly scolds the doctor as she would the children. She lectures him about the gin, condemns him for
wasting his life, does her best to cover up for him, and
clearly feels a great affection for him.

On the day before she is to leave the house, there is a
picnic on the beach. Late in the afternoon the others rush
to watch one of the guests attempt to rescue the children's
kite, which has swooped down and is stuck halfway up the
cliff. The doctor, who has been to the pub and is in an
expansive mood, starts to follow the group but Matty stops
him.

Matty.

(*To stop him.*) Doctor!

Doctor.

Hmm?

Matty.

May I speak to you?

Doctor.

What—now?

Matty.

There won't be another chance.

Doctor.

(*Rather reluctantly.*) Oh, very well. Speak on. You have our ear.

Matty.

Please—don't joke.

Doctor.

(*Looking at her.*) My dear girl—what is it? You're trembling.

Matty.

(*In distress, turning away.*) Don't laugh—that's all.

Doctor.

Of course not! Come and sit down.

Matty.

No, I'd prefer to stand. We've no time. (*Jerkily.*) Doctor, it may not be very long before your employment here is ended.

Doctor.

Well—yes. That is so.

Matty.

I believe you are quite alone in the world. I think I heard you say you have no relations living.

Doctor.

True.

Matty.

So—you'd have nowhere to go from here.

Doctor.

Oh, as to that, a nomad existence suits me. I'm an independent old cuss.

Matty.

(*With an effort.*) Doctor, would you not consider letting me make a home for you?

Doctor.

(*Embarrassed.*) Oh, my dear girl—

Matty.

(*Eagerly.*) I'd not interfere with you! You could come and go as you liked. If you wanted to drink, if it gave you any pleasure, I'd not try to stop you by lecturing or nagging. As long as I could look after you, make a home where you were comfortable—

Doctor.

Matty, please! I beg you! . . . My dear girl, you're not thinking what you're saying. It's out of the question! Why —consider our ages!

Matty.

I'm thirty-five.

Doctor.

Exactly. I'm fifty-six—twenty-one years older! You're a fine young woman, and you should be thinking of a man who could offer you some sort of future, a young fellow with energy and prospects—

Matty.

Do you think there are many young fellows with energy and prospects who want to marry a penniless governess of thirty-five—?

Doctor.

When I say young—

Matty.

I've never had a proposal of marriage in my life—not one. Of course I'm not pretty, but uglier women than I get married, plenty of them. Maybe I've not the right way of speaking to men. My sister always says I'm too solemn, too serious, and I daresay she's right, but am I never to be married because I've no great sense of humour? (*Near tears.*) And what have I to joke about, will you tell me?

Doctor.

(*Comforting her.*) Now, now, Matty . . .

Matty.

Some women have only to lift their eyes and take a pick of a dozen. (*Indicating R.*) Look at her! How many men has she had, and young too! It's not fair! (*Weeps.*) It's not fair!

Doctor.

Hush!

Matty.

(*Mastering herself.*) I'm sorry . . . I'm sorry. . . . I just

thought, before it was too late, I might as well offer to live
for someone who'd not be too particular, perhaps.

Doctor.

(*Shocked.*) Not too particular! This is simply unheard of!
What can I say?

Matty.

You don't need to say anything. I'm not so dense I can't
understand.

Doctor.

Could I let you throw yourself away on a waster, a drunkard? Look at me! A nice sort of bridegroom I'd make for
any woman!

Matty.

(*An outburst.*) What do I care that you're poor or a
drunkard? You're kind, gentle, understanding. And you'd
be someone that belonged to me at last! (*In tears.*) You'd
be mine! . . . If you knew how tired I am of loving other
people's children, and losing them, and starting again, and
never a soul that's mine to keep! (*She weeps.*)

Doctor.

(*Taking her arm.*) Come, now. Let's sit down and talk
this over calmly.

(*They sit side by side on breakwater.*)

There. Now, let me say, first of all, that I don't see in
your situation any need for such desperate remedies as
you suggest. Because a young woman has reached the
age of thirty-five, that is no reason why she should throw
herself away on an old fool who can be no help or
comfort to her—

Matty.

Why do you speak of yourself like that?

Doctor.

Because it's true. I've had my life: marriage, a career, a
child—I've had it all. In what's to come, I'm not particularly interested, and to live with a man who's uninterested in life would be dreadful, depressing. . . . But
at thirty-five, good Heavens, there's hope! A chance meeting, a letter, some trivial little incident may suddenly transform your whole life! (*Earnestly.*) And I believe it will!
Yes, I have a strong conviction that your star is in the
ascendant!

Matty.

(*Dully.*) You're very kind.

Doctor.

Your day will come—I'm certain of it. (*Looks out to sea.*) Look at the sea now. Splendid, eh? What colours! Emerald and blue and violet—the tender, delicate shades of evening. (*He pats her hand.*) Don't cry. . . . You know, there's a certain sort of tree that only flowers every twelve years—or ten perhaps—I forget which. And so it is with certain lives; for years they are grey and monotonous and then, one day, unexpectedly, they blossom out in happiness. . . . Don't cry.

(*They sit in silence. This is broken by shouts
and laughter off R.*)

Yes, he's rescued the kite. . . . (*A laugh.*) How absurd! You can see he's quite delighted with himself. (*Shouting ironically.*) Oh, very clever, very daring! (*A laugh.*) What extraordinary little things will suddenly please people! (*Shouting.*) Hurrah! Bravissimo! Encore!

from
WALKER, LONDON
by Sir James M. Barrie

Act I
SARAH, MRS. GOLIGHTLY

Barrie's first play is worth discovering if only for the delight
of uncovering the existence of a whole clan of Golightlys
who had to do with a moony river more than half a century before Truman Capote's Holly breakfasted (or didn't)
at Tiffany's. But the play has other attractions. There is also
comedy—in the vein of jokes told at slightly raucous
Victorian tea parties. There is a barber masquerading as a
gentleman, an intellectual young lady (Bell Golightly) concerned about the treatment of women as sex objects, a
hero of the cricket pitch, a medical student longing to
dissect real patients, and the singularly determined young
person from London, known only as Sarah, who makes her
first, memorable appearance in the scene reprinted below.

The producer, however, may be discouraged by such
stage directions as "Bell punts out of sight." Barrie *does*
mean that Miss Golightly stands up in a flat-bottomed
boat and pushes herself across a stretch of water with
the aid of a very long pole. His play, first presented in
1892, takes place on a houseboat on the Thames—the
Golightly summer retreat—and his staging requirements
are rather demanding.

Sarah's moment requires no difficult special effects,
however. It is morning, and while the residents and guests
of the houseboat await breakfast, Mrs. Golightly sits on
deck with her knitting. Sarah enters along the riverbank.
She looks sharply into the houseboat windows, then jumps

245

to see who is on deck. Mrs. Golightly looks up and sees her.

Sarah.

Good morning, ma'am. (*Starts.*)

Mrs. Golightly.

(*Wondering.*) Good morning, who are you?

Sarah.

I'm from London.

Mrs. Golightly.

Yes?

Sarah.

And outspoken. You don't happen to have a villain on board?

Mrs. Golightly.

Gracious, no!

Sarah.

I've tracked him from London to this neighbourhood.

Mrs. Golightly.

Who is he?

Sarah.

Jasper Phipps by name, barber by trade, deceiver by nature.

Mrs. Golightly.

What has he done?

Sarah.

Didn't turn up.

Mrs. Golightly.

Where?

Sarah.

At the church door.

Mrs. Golightly.

You were to be married to him?

Sarah.

I was, yesterday, and I waited an hour. Then this letter is handed to me. He is a scholar, is Jasper. (*Hands Mrs. Golightly a letter.*)

Mrs. Golightly.

'My dearest Sarah. You will be surprised at my not turning up to marry you, and I feel I owe you an apology.' (*Looks up.*) I should think he did! 'First, my love, it is a startler to a man to wake up on his marriage morning and remember that in an hour he will be tied for life.

Second, through shaving so many gents, I feel that I want to have a burst as one myself. Sarah, it can only be done with the honeymoon money. Third, my sweet, I know a swell I am like in appearance, and I am going to pass for him, but he is a bachelor so it wouldn't be proper to take you with me. Fourth, it would be more difficult for you than for me to look like a swell. Fifth, there is not enough money for two at any rate. Everything considered, dear Sarah, I have decided to have the honeymoon before the marriage, and to have it by myself. Then, my girl, when my week's leave is up, I will come back and marry you. Fear not; I am staunch, and don't follow me. Your affectionate Jasper. P.S.—I love you! I love you! I love you!' The scoundrel!

Sarah.

Nothing of the kind.

Mrs. Golightly.

You said he was a villain yourself!

Sarah.

I won't let others miscall him.

Mrs. Golightly.

You are well rid of him.

Sarah.

I ain't. I tell you I'll find him yet.

Mrs. Golightly.

And then what will you do?

Sarah.

Be revenged! Marry him!

(*Exit along bank.*)

Mrs. Golightly.

Well, well, well!

Copies of this play, in individual paper covered acting editions, are available from Samuel French, Inc., 25 W. 45th St., New York, N. Y. or 7623 Sunset Blvd., Hollywood, Calif. or in Canada Samuel French (Canada) Ltd., 26 Grenville St., Toronto, Canada.

from

THE APPLE CART

by George Bernard Shaw

An Interlude
ORINTHIA, MAGNUS

Shaw's comedy is a speculation about what might happen if
Britain's monarch should decide in some future era to
demand full use of those powers which he, a constitutional
monarch, still retains. That situation, however, has not
much to do with the scene reprinted below, for the scene
is taken from an "interlude" that occurs midway through
the play; it is something of a holiday from politics for king
and audience alike. For Magnus it is also a holiday from
Amanda, his queen, a rather dumpy lady though, as it
turns out, thoroughly regal. And for Shaw it is a romp, less
in the kingdom of futuristic Britain than in the realm of
the comedy of manners. When Sir Noel Coward played
King Magnus to the Orinthia of Miss Margaret Leighton,
the stage was swash with beige draperies, and the "settee"
called for by Shaw was a very elegant, very velvet chaise
longue. It *is* that sort of scene.

The place is Orinthia's boudoir at "half-past fifteen."
Orinthia "is at her writing-table scribbling notes. She is
romantically beautiful, and beautifully dressed. As the table
is against the wall near a corner, with the other wall at her
left, her back alone is visible from the middle of the room.
The door is near the corner diagonally opposite. There is
a large settee in the middle of the room."

Magnus enters and waits on the threshold. He is "a
tallish, studious looking gentleman of 45 or thereabouts."

Orinthia.
(*Crossly, without looking round.*) Who is that?

248

Magnus.

His Majesty the King.

Orinthia.

I dont want to see him.

Magnus.

How soon will you be disengaged?

Orinthia.

I didnt say I was engaged. Tell the king I dont want to see him.

Magnus.

He awaits your pleasure. (*He comes in and seats himself on the settee.*)

Orinthia.

Go away. (*A pause.*) I wont speak to you. (*Another pause.*) If my private rooms are to be broken into at any moment because they are in the palace, and the king is not a gentleman, I must take a house outside. I am writing to the agents about one now.

Magnus.

What is our quarrel today, belovéd?

Orinthia.

Ask your conscience.

Magnus.

I have none when you are concerned. You must tell me.

(*She takes a book from the table and rises; then sweeps superbly forward to the settee and flings the book into his hands.*)

Orinthia.

There!

Magnus.

What is this?

Orinthia.

Page 16. Look at it.

Magnus.

(*Looking at the title on the back of the book.*) "Songs of our Great Great Grandparents". What page did you say?

Orinthia.

(*Between her teeth.*) Six-teen.

Magnus.

(*Opening the book and finding the page, his eye lighting up with recognition as he looks at it.*) Ah! The Pilgrim of Love!

Orinthia.

Read the first three words—if you dare.

Magnus.

(*Smiling as he caresses the phrase.*) "Orinthia, my beloved".

Orinthia.

The name you pretended to invent specially for me, the only woman in the world for you. Picked up out of the rubbish basket in a secondhand bookseller's! And I thought you were a poet!

Magnus.

Well, one poet may consecrate a name for another. Orinthia is a name full of magic for me. It could not be that if I had invented it myself. I heard it at a concert of ancient music when I was a child; and I have treasured it ever since.

Orinthia.

You always have a pretty excuse. You are the King of liars and humbugs. You cannot understand how a falsehood like that wounds me.

Magnus.

(*Remorsefully, stretching out his arms towards her.*) Beloved: I am sorry.

Orinthia.

Put your hands in your pockets: they shall not touch me ever again.

Magnus.

(*Obeying.*) Dont pretend to be hurt unless you really are, dearest. It wrings my heart.

Orinthia.

Since when have you set up a heart? Did you buy that, too, secondhand?

Magnus.

I have something in me that winces when you are hurt— or pretend to be.

Orinthia.

(*Contemptuously.*) Yes: I have only to squeal, and you will take me up and pet me as you would a puppy run over by a car. (*Sitting down beside him, but beyond arm's length.*) That is what you give me when my heart demands love. I had rather you kicked me.

Magnus.

I should like to kick you sometimes, when you are especially aggravating. But I shouldnt do it well. I should be afraid of hurting you all the time.

Orinthia.

I believe you would sign my death warrant without turning a hair.

Magnus.

That is true, in a way. It is wonderful how subtle your mind is, as far as it goes.

Orinthia.

It does not go as far as yours, I suppose.

Magnus.

I dont know. Our minds go together half way. Whether it is that your mind stops there or else that the road forks, and you take the high road and I take the low road, I cannot say; but somehow after a certain point we lose one another.

Orinthia.

And then you go back to your Amandas and Lysistratas: creatures whose idea of romance is a minister in love with a department, and whose bedside books are blue books.

Magnus.

They are not always thinking of some man or other. That is a rather desirable extension of their interests, in my opinion. If Lysistrata had a lover I should not be interested in him in the least; and she would bore me to distraction if she could talk of nothing else. But I am very much interested in her department. Her devotion to it gives us a topic of endless interest.

Orinthia.

Well, go to her: I am not detaining you. But dont tell her that I have nothing to talk about but men; for that is a lie; and you know it.

Magnus.

It is, as you say, a lie; and I know it. But I did not say it.

Orinthia.

You implied it. You meant it. When those ridiculous political women are with us you talk to them all the time, and never say a word to me.

Magnus.

Nor you to me. We cannot talk to one another in public:

we have nothing to say that could be said before other
people. Yet we find enough to say to one another when
we are alone together. Would you change that if you
could?

Orinthia.

You are as slippery as an eel; but you shall not slip
through my fingers. Why do you surround yourself with
political bores and frumps and dowdy busybodies who
cant talk: they can only debate about their dull departments and their fads and their election chances. (*Rising
impatiently.*) Who could talk to such people? If it were
not for the nonentities of wives and husbands they drag
about with them, there would be nobody to talk to at
all. And even they can talk of nothing but the servants
and the baby. (*Suddenly returning to her seat.*) Listen
to me, Magnus. Why can you not be a real king?

Magnus.

In what way, belovédest?

Orinthia.

Send all these stupid people packing. Make them do their
drudgeries in their departments without bothering you
about it, as you make your servants here sweep the floors
and dust the furniture. Live a really noble and beautiful
life—a kingly life—with me. What you need to make you
a real king is a real queen.

Magnus.

But I have got one.

Orinthia.

Oh, you are blind. You are worse than blind: you have
low tastes. Heaven is offering you a rose; and you cling
to a cabbage.

Magnus.

(*Laughing.*) That is a very apt metaphor, belovéd. But
what wise man, if you force him to choose between doing
without roses and doing without cabbages, would not
secure the cabbages? Besides, all these old married cabbages were once roses; and, though young things like you
dont remember that, their husbands do. They dont notice
the change. Besides, you should know better than anyone
else that when a man gets tired of his wife and leaves her
it is never because she has lost her good looks. The new
love is often older and uglier than the old.

Orinthia.

Why should I know that better than anyone else?

Magnus.

Why, because you have been married twice; and both your husbands have run away from you to much plainer and stupider women. When I begged your present husband to come back to court for a while for the sake of appearances he said no man could call his soul his own in the same house with you. And yet that man was utterly infatuated with your beauty when he married you. Your first husband actually forced a good wife to divorce him so that he might marry you; but before two years were out he went back to her and died in her arms, poor chap.

Orinthia.

Shall I tell you why these men could not live with me? It was because I am a thoroughbred, and they are only hacks. They had nothing against me: I was perfectly faithful to them. I kept their homes beautifully: I fed them better than they had ever been fed in their lives. But because I was higher than they were, and greater, they could not stand the strain of trying to live up to me. So I let them go their way, poor wretches, back to their cabbages. Look at the old creature Ignatius is living with now! She gives you his real measure.

Magnus.

An excellent woman. Ignatius is quite happy with her. I never saw a man so changed.

Orinthia.

Just what he is fit for. Commonplace. Bourgeoise. She trots through the streets shopping. (*Rising.*) I tread the plains of Heaven. Common women cannot come where I am; and common men find themselves out and slink away.

Magnus.

It must be magnificent to have the consciousness of a goddess without ever doing a thing to justify it.

from

TIMON OF ATHENS

by William Shakespeare

Act IV, scene 3
TIMON, APEMANTUS

Timon is Shakespeare's ultimate misanthrope. The first acts
of his drama retell the traditional story of the fall of a
too-easily fortunate man: in his prosperity Timon is
generous to all; indeed, so generous that he wastes away
his riches. When he has lost all his property and calls
for help on the friends who enjoyed his bounty, they
answer with feeble excuses, slip away, and give nothing.
The final acts detail Timon's bitter disillusionment: dark,
splendid variations—tirades often—on the theme of man's
vileness and ingratitude. In his hermit's cave, shunning all
human contact, Timon rehearses his anguished contempt
for all mankind and desires only that final loss a man can
suffer, death.

Critics have disagreed extremely about the play's strength
as a tragedy, but all have been moved by the powerful
poetry and profound impact of those scenes in which
Timon roars out the bitterness of his soul, scenes that call
for a Timon with the stature of a Lear.

In Timon's years of good fortune, one man, the cynical
Apemantus, warned him about his hypocritical friends.
And later, curious to observe Timon now that he has had
forced upon him the truth about humankind, Apemantus
seeks out his friend in the woods near his cave. There have
already been other visitors: soldiers marching on Athens
under the leadership of Alcibiades, a general who has been
unjustly exiled from the city. Timon shares with Alcibiades
some of a treasure of gold he has discovered while digging

for roots to eat: Timon will not spend these riches himself,
but he is willing to see them used to destroy the Athenians
who falsely befriended and then deserted him. As the
soldiers march off, Timon's curses in their ears, Apemantus
appears.

Timon.

That nature, being sick of man's unkindness,
Should yet be hungry! Common mother, thou *(Digs.)*
Whose womb unmeasurable and infinite breast
Teems and feeds all; whose selfsame mettle
Whereof thy proud child, arrogant man, is puffed
Engenders the black toad and adder blue,
The gilded newt and eyeless venomed worm,
With all th' abhorrèd births below crisp heaven
Whereon Hyperion's quick'ning fire doth shine—
Yield him who all thy human sons doth hate,
From forth thy plenteous bosom, one poor root!
Ensear thy fertile and conceptious womb;
Let it no more bring out ingrateful man!
Go great with tigers, dragons, wolves, and bears;
Teem with new monsters whom thy upward face
Hath to the marbled mansion all above
Never presented!—O, a root! Dear thanks!—
Dry up thy marrows, vines, and plough-torn leas,
Whereof ingrateful man with liquorish drafts
And morsels unctuous greases his pure mind,
That from it all consideration slips—
                    (Enter Apemantus.)
More man? Plague, plague!

Apemantus.

I was directed hither. Men report
Thou dost affect my manners and dost use them.

Timon.

'Tis then because thou dost not keep a dog,
Whom I would imitate. Consumption catch thee!

Apemantus.

This is in thee a nature but infected,
A poor unmanly melancholy sprung
From change of fortune. Why this spade? this place?
This slave-like habit and these looks of care?
Thy flatterers yet wear silk, drink wine, lie soft,

Hug their diseased perfumes, and have forgot
That ever Timon was. Shame not these woods
By putting on the cunning of a carper.
Be thou a flattterer now and seek to thrive
By that which has undone thee; hinge thy knee
And let his very breath whom thou'lt observe
Blow off thy cap; praise his most vicious strain
And call it excellent. Thou wast told thus;
Thou gav'st thine ears, like tapsters that bade welcome,
To knave and all approachers. 'Tis most just
That thou turn rascal; hadst thou wealth again,
Rascals should have't. Do not assume my likeness.

Timon.

Were I like thee, I'd throw away myself.

Apemantus.

Thou hast cast away thyself, being like thyself;
A madman so long, now a fool. What, think'st
That the bleak air, thy boisterous chamberlain,
Will put thy shirt on warm? Will these mossed trees,
That have outlived the eagle, page thy heels
And skip when thou point'st out? Will the cold brook,
Candied with ice, caudle thy morning taste
To cure thy o'er-night surfeit? Call the creatures
Whose naked natures live in all the spite
Of wreakful heaven, whose bare unhousèd trunks,
To the conflicting elements exposed,
Answer mere nature; bid them flatter thee.
O, thou shalt find—

Timon.

A fool of thee. Depart.

Apemantus.

I love thee better now than e'er I did.

Timon.

I hate thee worse.

Apemantus.

Why?

Timon.

Thou flatter'st misery.

Apemantus.

I flatter not, but say thou art a caitiff.

Timon.

Why dost thou seek me out?

Apemantus.

To vex thee.

Timon.

Always a villain's office or a fool's.
Dost please thyself in't?

Apemantus.

Ay.

Timon.

What, a knave too?

Apemantus.

If thou didst put this sour cold habit on
To castigate thy pride, 'twere well; but thou
Dost it enforcedly. Thou'dst courtier be again
Wert thou not beggar. Willing misery
Outlives incertain pomp, is crowned before;
The one is filling still, never complete,
The other at high wish; best state, contentless,
Hath a distracted and most wretched being,
Worse than the worst, content.
Thou shouldst desire to die, being miserable.

Timon.

Not by his breath that is more miserable.
Thou art a slave whom Fortune's tender arm
With favor never clasped, but bred a dog.
Hadst thou, like us from our first swath, proceeded
The sweet degrees that this brief world affords
To such as may the passive drugs of it
Freely command, thou wouldst have plunged thyself
In general riot, melted down thy youth
In different beds of lust, and never learned
The icy precepts of respect, but followed
The sug'red game before thee. But myself,
Who had the world as my confectionary,
The mouths, the tongues, the eyes, and hearts of men
At duty, more than I could frame employment;
That numberless upon me stuck, as leaves
Do on the oak, have, with one winter's brush,
Fell from their boughs and left me open, bare
For every storm that blows—I to bear this,
That never knew but better, is some burden.
Thy nature did commence in sufferance; time
Hath made thee hard in't. Why shouldst thou hate men?

They never flattered thee. What hast thou given?
If thou wilt curse, thy father, that poor rag,
Must be thy subject, who in spite put stuff
To some she-beggar and compounded thee
Poor rogue hereditary. Hence; be gone!
If thou hadst not been born the worst of men,
Thou hadst been a knave and flatterer.

Apemantus.

Art thou proud yet?

Timon.
Ay, that I am not thee.

Apemantus.

I, that I was

No prodigal.

Timon.

I, that I am one now.
Were all the wealth I have shut up in thee,
I'd give thee leave to hang it. Get thee gone.
That the whole life of Athens were in this!
Thus would I eat it. (*Gnaws a root.*)

Apemantus.

Here! I will mend thy feast.
(*Offers him food.*)

Timon.
First mend my company; take away thyself.

Apemantus.
So I shall mend mine own, by th' lack of thine.

Timon.
'Tis not well mended so; it is but botched.
If not, I would it were.

Apemantus.
What wouldst thou have to Athens?

Timon.
Thee thither in a whirlwind. If thou wilt,
Tell them there I have gold. Look, so I have.

Apemantus.
Here is no use for gold.

Timon.

The best and truest;
For here it sleeps, and does no hirèd harm.

Apemantus.
Where liest a-nights, Timon?

Timon.

Under that's above me.

Where feed'st thou a-days, Apemantus?

Apemantus.

Where my stomach finds meat; or rather, where I eat it.

Timon.

Would poison were obedient and knew my mind!

Apemantus.

Where wouldst thou send it?

Timon.

To sauce thy dishes.

Apemantus.

The middle of humanity thou never knewest, but the extremity of both ends. When thou wast in thy gilt and thy perfume, they mocked thee for too much curiosity; in thy rags thou know'st none, but art despised for the contrary. There's a medlar for thee; eat it.

Timon.

On what I hate I feed not.

Apemantus.

Dost hate a medlar?

Timon.

Ay, though it look like thee.

Apemantus.

An thou'dst hated meddlers sooner, thou shouldst have loved thyself better now. What man didst thou ever know unthrift that was beloved after his means?

Timon.

Who, without those means thou talk'st of, didst thou ever know beloved?

Apemantus.

Myself.

Timon.

I understand thee. Thou hadst some means to keep a dog.

Apemantus.

What things in the world canst thou nearest compare to thy flatterers?

Timon.

Women nearest; but men—men are the things themselves. What wouldst thou do with the world, Apemantus, if it lay in thy power?

Apemantus.

Give it the beasts, to be rid of the men.

Timon.

Wouldst thou have thyself fall in the confusion of
men, and remain a beast with the beasts?

Apemantus.

Ay, Timon.

Timon.

A beastly ambition, which the gods grant thee t' attain
to! If thou wert the lion, the fox would beguile thee;
if thou wert the lamb, the fox would eat thee; if thou
wert the fox, the lion would suspect thee when per-
adventure thou wert accused by the ass; if thou wert
the ass, thy dullness would torment thee, and still thou
livedst but as a breakfast to the wolf. If thou wert the
wolf thy greediness would afflict thee, and oft thou
shouldst hazard thy life for thy dinner. Wert thou the
unicorn, pride and wrath would confound thee and make
thine own self the conquest of thy fury; wert thou a
bear, thou wouldst be killed by the horse; wert thou a
horse, thou wouldst be seized by the leopard; wert thou
a leopard, thou wert germane to the lion, and the spots
of thy kindred were jurors on thy life: all thy safety were
remotion, and thy defense absence. What beast couldst
thou be that were not subject to a beast? And what a
beast art thou already, that seest not thy loss in transformation!

Apemantus.

If thou couldst please me with speaking to me, thou
mightst have hit upon it here. The commonweatlh of
Athens is become a forest of beasts.

Timon.

How has the ass broke the wall, that thou art out of the
city?

Apemantus.

Yonder comes a poet and a painter. The plague of company light upon thee! I will fear to catch it, and give way.
When I know not what else to do, I'll see thee again.

Timon.

When there is nothing living but thee, thou shalt be welcome. I had rather be a beggar's dog than Apemantus.

Apemantus.
Thou art the cap of all the fools alive.
Timon.
Would thou wert clean enough to spit upon!
Apemantus.
A plague on thee! thou art too bad to curse.
Timon.
All villains that do stand, by thee, are pure.
Apemantus.
There is no leprosy but what thou speak'st.
Timon.
If I name thee.
I'll beat thee, but I should infect my hands.
Apemantus.
I would my tongue could rot them off!
Timon.
Away, thou issue of a mangy dog!
Choler does kill me that thou art alive;
I swoon to see thee.
Apemantus.
       Would thou wouldst burst!
Timon.

                Away,

Thou tedious rogue! I am sorry I shall lose
A stone by thee. (*Throws a stone at him.*)
Apemantus.
Beast!
Timon.
Slave!
Apemantus.
Toad!
Timon.
Rogue, rogue, rogue!
I am sick of this false world, and will love naught
But even the mere necessities upon't.
Then, Timon, presently prepare thy grave.
Lie where the light foam of the sea may beat
Thy gravestone daily. Make thine epitaph,
That death in me at others' lives may laugh.
(*To the gold.*) O thou sweet king-killer, and dear divorce
'Twixt natural son and sire; thou bright defiler
Of Hymen's purest bed; thou valiant Mars;

Thou ever young, fresh, loved, and delicate wooer,
Whose blush doth thaw the consecrated snow
That lies on Dian's lap; thou visible god,
That sold'rest close impossibilities
And mak'st them kiss; that speak'st with every tongue
To every purpose! O thou touch of hearts!
Think thy slave man rebels; and by thy virtue
Set them into confounding odds; that beasts
May have the world in empire!

Apemantus.

                    Would 'twere so,
But not till I am dead. I'll say thou'st gold.
Thou wilt be thronged to shortly.

Timon.

                    Thronged to?

Apemantus.

                              Ay.

Timon.

Thy back, I prithee.

Apemantus.

              Live, and love thy misery.

Timon.

Long live so, and so die. I am quit.

Apemantus.

(*Seeing others approach.*) Moe things like men! Eat,
Timon, and abhor them. (*Exit Apemantus.*)

from

ORESTES

by Euripides (translated by Kenneth Cavander)

HELEN, ELECTRA

What was Helen like afterward—when the Trojan War
was over and she had been returned, slightly used, no
longer quite so young, to Greece and her husband Menelaus? Myths retain their beauty and sublimity forever,
people do not; and that, in part at least, seems to be Euripides' point in the portrait of a rather matronly Helen
which he includes in his extraordinary and irreverent re-
telling of a final episode in the story of the house of Atreus.
(For introductory notes about the play, see p. 586.)

The woman whose beauty epitomized the brilliance and
the cause of the great war now hesitates to show her face
in the streets of Argos. At home in the palace, served by
a gaggle of bumbling Trojan slaves, she spends her days,
Electra says, counting the royal possessions, and waiting for
the time when Agamemnon's children will be gone and
the stuff will be hers. Though thoroughly self-righteous in
condemning the murder of her sister Clytemnestra, she is
quick to explain her own indiscretions as the work of fatal
powers quite beyond her control. But it is difficult to imagine this Helen as the object of Olympian passion or concern. She is apologetic, probably a bit plump, rather said,
clearly comic, and as her first remarks to Electra make
clear, inclined to be catty.

Helen's encounter with Electra occurs early in the play.
The scene is marked by subtleties of ironic characterization
that give a sharp, sometimes surprising, edge to lines that
taken hastily could seem quite straight.

Orestes, having killed Clytemnestra, has collapsed into

263

a trancelike sickness and seems ready (and not unwilling)
to die. He is nursed by a chorus of women and by his
sister Electra, a determined girl whose grip on life,
though she is discouraged at the moment, will clearly not
be broken easily. Helen comes upon them.

Helen.

  Electra, daughter of Clytemnestra and Agamemnon,
  You are a grown-up woman now, but still, I see,
  Without a husband . . . How could you find it in yourself
  To kill your mother? How could Orestes here . . .?
  Heaven help him!
  You can speak. I shall not be tainted by your guilt
  Because I believe the guilty one is really Apollo . . .
  Poor Clytemnestra—my own sister—murdered!
  It's too horrible to think of.
  The last time I saw her was the day I set sail for Troy—
  Some inhuman power took away my senses then,
  And decided my fate for me—and now I come back
  To find I have no sister. It hurts, it hurts, Electra.

Electra.

  Do you need me to tell you, Helen? Can't you see
  For yourself what has happened to Agamemnon's son?
  As for me, I live without sleep, and I nurse a corpse—
  Yes, that is all he is—one breath away from a corpse . . .
  Well, I blame no one for his suffering.
  So you and your husband, unscathed, untouched by sorrow,
  Find us here, in utter despair, broken in body and spirit.

Helen.

  How long has Orestes been lying on his bed?

Electra.

  Since he caused the living blood to flow from his mother's
  Body.

Helen.

  How terrible . . . But think of his mother . . . to die
  Like that.

Electra.

  Well, there it is. He can resist no more . . . The torment . . .

Helen.

  Will you do something, dear Electra, for my sake?

Electra.

I must take care of him . . . But if I can spare the time—
yes.

Helen.

Will you go to my sister's grave . . .?

Electra.

To my mother's . . .! You want me to do *that*?

Helen.

Just take some strands of my hair and an offering of wine.

Electra.

If you loved her, why not go there yourself?
Would it be wrong?

Helen.

I am ashamed to be seen here in Argos.

Electra.

Now you feel shame. What did you feel when you deserted
Your husband?

Helen.

You are right. But you are not kind.

Electra.

Why is it so hard for you to face the people here?

Helen.

Men who died at Troy have fathers still alive.
I am afraid of those fathers.

Electra.

So you should be. In Argos people spit out your name
Like a curse.

Helen.

Please, I am so afraid. Do this for me, and I shall feel
Much safer.

Electra.

I couldn't bear to set eyes on my mother's grave.

Helen.

But I can't ask a servant to go. That would be an insult
To the dead.

Electra.

Why not send your daughter Hermione?

Helen.

A young girl? She shouldn't have to walk through the
streets
Amongst all those people . . .

Electra.

But she ought to pay her respects to the departed,
To someone who was like a mother to her.

Helen.

That is true . . . Well, I'll do as you say, Electra.
I'll send my daughter. You're right.

from

THE MAN OF MODE, OR SIR FOPLING FLUTTER

by Sir George Etherege

Act II, scene 2
MRS. LOVEIT, BELLINDA, (PERT)

Written in 1676 by a courtier whose place in society was as secure as his place in the theater, *The Man of Mode* is a model of the elegantly worded, brittle, but often harshly cynical Restoration comedy of manners. Nearly all of the typical characters are there: the urbane wit, who, like Etherege himself and his apparent model the Earl of Rochester, is impeccable in dress and behavior, inevitably successful in a round of sexual encounters, and never, never betrayed by any awkward outbreak of his emotions; the country women who long to be town ladies but lack the wit for it; the town ladies who have the wit but not quite enough of it to prevent their falling in love (and into bed) with the hero; and that overblown imitation of the hero, the fop who gives his name to the play. It is sometimes difficult to accept that such characters and their plays are an accurate representation of an actual society, but beyond question they are. The carefully posed sentences and posturing actions contain a sharp, satiric realism which the actor must project at the same time that he plays the high comic style.

The scene reprinted here plays upon the tension between the manner and the actuality: while Bellinda appears to be doing one thing, she is with precise calculation doing something quite different, and at a third level her feelings give the scene still another interpretation.

Bellinda is a young lady of recognized wit and beauty. The most recent conquest of Mr. Dorimant, the play's

Rochester-like hero, she has been asked by him to help create a situation that will give him an excuse to break off with his former mistress, Mrs. Loveit. If, for example, Mrs. Loveit in a fit of jealousy should quarrel with Dorimant, he could bow to her anger, leave her, and never be criticized for having treated her badly—after all, *she* would have begun the quarrel and done the breaking-off. Mrs. Loveit is as elegantly pretty as Bellinda, but she is an easy victim of her rival's strategy; in the game of wit, which in large measure means outwitting, she is a loser from the start, for, unfortunate lady, she is afflicted (as her name suggests) with passion quite beyond her control. To set her off, Bellinda needs to do no more than remark that she has seen Dorimant at the playhouse with a lady in a mask (as London's theaters were the haunt of loose ladies of every social level, women who had successfully retained their reputations regularly went to the playhouse masked). While Bellinda maneuvers Mrs. Loveit with easy skill and delights in her success, she cannot help but feel some misgivings. At the end of the act, when Mrs. Loveit has broken off with Dorimant exactly according to plan, Bellinda will muse to herself:

> I wish I had not seen him use her so.
> I sigh to think that Dorimant may be
> One day as faithless, and unkind to me.

The setting is a room in Mrs. Loveit's house. Speaking with her maid, Pert, about her adoration of Dorimant and her distress at having heard nothing from him for two days, she is interrupted by the arrival of Bellinda.

Mrs. Loveit.
    ***—Bellinda! (*Running to her.*)
Bellinda.
    My dear!
Mrs. Loveit.
    You have been unkind of late.
Bellinda.
    Do not say unkind, say unhappy.
Mrs. Loveit.
    I could chide you. Where have you been these two days?

Bellinda.

Pity me rather, my dear, where I have been so tired with two or three country gentlemen, whose conversation has been more unsufferable than a country fiddle.

Mrs. Loveit.

Are they relations?

Bellinda.

No; Welsh acquaintance I made when I was last year at St. Winifred's. They have asked me a thousand questions of the modes and intrigues of the town, and I have told 'em almost as many things for news that hardly were so when their gowns were in fashion.

Mrs. Loveit.

Provoking creatures! How could you endure 'em?

Bellinda.

(*Aside.*) Now to carry on my plot. Nothing but love could make me capable of so much falsehood. 'Tis time to begin, lest Dorimant should come before her jealousy has stung her. (*Laughs, and then speaks on.*) I was yesterday at a play with 'em, where I was fain to show 'em the living, as the man at Westminster does the dead: "That is Mrs. Such-a-one, admired for her beauty; that is Mr. Such-a-one, cried up for a wit; that is sparkish Mr. Such-a-one, who keeps reverend Mrs. Such-a-one, and there sits fine Mrs. Such-a-one who was lately cast off by my Lord Such-a-one."

Mrs. Loveit.

Did you see Dorimant there?

Bellinda.

I did, and imagine you were with him and have no mind to own it.

Mrs. Loveit.

What should make you think so?

Bellinda.

A lady masked in a pretty dishabille, whom Dorimant entertained with more respect than the gallants do a common vizard.

Mrs. Loveit.

(*Aside.*) Dorimant at the play entertaining a mask! Oh, heavens!

Bellinda.

(*Aside.*) Good!

Mrs. Loveit.

Did he stay all the while?

Bellinda.

Til: the play was done and then led her out, which confirms me it was you.

Mrs. Loveit.

Traitor!

Pert.

Now you may believe he has business, and you may forgive him, too.

Mrs. Loveit.

Ingrateful, perjured man!

Bellinda.

You seem so much concerned, my dear, I fear I have told you unawares what I had better have concealed for your quiet.

Mrs. Loveit.

What manner of shape had she?

Bellinda.

Tall and slender. Her motions were very genteel; certainly she must be some person of condition.

Mrs. Loveit.

Shame and confusion be ever in her face when she shows it!

Bellinda.

I should blame your discretion for loving that wild man, my dear, but they say he has a way of bewitching that few can defend their hearts who know him.

Mrs. Loveit.

I will tear him out from mine or die i'the attempt.

Bellinda.

Be more moderate.

Mrs. Loveit.

Would I had daggers, darts, or poisoned arrows in my breast, so I could but remove the thoughts of him from thence!

Bellinda.

Fie, fie! your transports are too violent, my dear; this may be but an accidental gallantry, and 'tis likely ended at her coach.

Pert.

Should it proceed farther, let your comfort be, the conduct Mr. Dorimant affects will quickly make you know your rival, ten to one let you see her ruined, her reputation exposed to the town—a happiness none will envy her but yourself, madam.

Mrs. Loveit.

Who'er she be, all the harm I wish her is, may she love him as well as I do and may he give her as much cause to hate him.

Pert.

Never doubt the latter end of your course, madam.

Mrs. Loveit.

May all the passions that are raised by neglected love— jealousy, indignation, spite, and thirst of revenge—eternally rage in her soul as they do now in mine.

(*Walks up and down with a distracted air.*)

from

CANDIDA

by George Bernard Shaw

Act II
PROSERPINE, MARCHBANKS

To list the performers who have undertaken the parts of
Candida and Marchbanks is to catalogue the great ladies
and aspiring young actors of the theaters of London and
New York for the past seventy years. Shaw's comedy of the
infatuation of an idealistic young man for the understanding older woman misunderstood by her husband reappears
with welcome regularity, and somehow the casting almost
as regularly seems appropriate. What is less often noticed
is that this *is* a comedy of Shaw's and that, in his usual
quizzical way, he neatly toes the moral line while seeming
to give his audience something rather shocking: Candida
does, after all, choose to remain with her husband.

However, the excerpt reprinted here was chosen to encourage those ladies who have undertaken the too often un-
regarded part of Proserpine and to provide a look at
Marchbanks out of the glow of Candida's maternal brilliance or the dark glower of her husband. It is, in fact, a
very good scene that can get lost in the play as a whole.

The setting is the drawing room of St. Dominic's Par-
sonage, home of the Reverend James Morell, on Victoria
Park in the northeast quarter of London. The time is 1894,
a fine afternoon in October. The large table at which the
parson does his work is "littered with pamphlets, journals,
letters, nests of drawers, an office diary, postage scales
and the like." A spare chair for visitors stands in the middle of the room. The wall behind is fitted with bookshelves
(full). Facing the parson's end of the table is a door. There

is a fireplace, with a comfortable armchair and a flower-painted coal scuttle at one side, a miniature chair for children on the other, and above, a large autotype of the chief figure in Titian's *Assumption of the Virgin*. At the end of the table opposite the parson's chair stands a small table with a typewriter. This is the usual place of Miss Proserpine Garnett, Morell's typist, "a brisk little woman of about 30, of the lower middle class, neatly but cheaply dressed in a black merino skirt and a blouse, notably pert and quick of speech, and not very civil in her manner, but sensitive and affectionate." As an assistant to a clergyman of the Church of England, a man who is an active member of the Guild of St. Matthew and the Christian Socialist League, "a first-rate clergyman able to say what he likes to whom he likes," but "withal, a great baby, pardonably vain of his powers and unconsciously pleased with himself," she (the typist) takes her work and her employer with considerable seriousness. But she is not in the room at the moment. It is empty except for Eugene Marchbanks, "a strange, shy youth of 18, slight, effeminate, with a delicate childish voice, and a hunted tormented expression and shrinking manner that shew the painful sensitiveness of very swift and acute apprehensiveness in youth, before the character has grown to its full strength . . . He is so uncommon as to be almost unearthly, and to prosaic people there is something noxious in this unearthliness, just as to poetic people there is something angelic in it. His dress is anarchic. He wears an old blue serge jacket, unbuttoned, over a woollen lawn tennis shirt, with a silk handkerchief for a cravat, trousers matching the jacket, and brown canvas shoes. In these garments he has apparently lain in the heather and waded through the waters; and there is no evidence of his ever having brushed them." He is one of Morell's discoveries (the parson found him sleeping on the embankment beside the river). He was the donor of the Titian above the fireplace. This morning he announced that he is in love with Morell's wife, Candida, and with intense conviction set out to prove that he is the more appropriate man for her. This created some furor and he stayed for lunch. Now, left alone in the drawing room, he is trying to find out how the typewriter works.

Hearing someone at the door, he steals guiltily away to the window and pretends to be absorbed in the view. Miss Garnett, carrying the notebook in which she takes down Morell's letters in shorthand from his dictation, sits down at the typewriter and sets to work transcribing them, much too busy to notice Eugene. When she begins the second line she stops and stares at the machine. Something wrong evidently.

Proserpine.

Bother! Youve been meddling with my typewriter, Mr Marchbanks; and theres not the least use in your trying to look as if you hadnt.

Marchbanks.

(*Timidly.*) I'm very sorry, Miss Garnett. I only tried to make it write. (*Plaintively.*) But it wouldnt.

Proserpine.

Well, youve altered the spacing.

Marchbanks.

(*Earnestly.*) I assure you I didnt. I didnt indeed. I only turned a little wheel. It gave a sort of click.

Proserpine.

Oh, now I understand. (*She restores the spacing, talking volubly all the time.*) I suppose you thought it was a sort of barrel-organ. Nothing to do but turn the handle, and it would write a beautiful love letter for you straight off, eh?

Marchbanks.

(*Seriously.*) I suppose a machine could be made to write love letters. Theyre all the same, arnt they?

Proserpine.

(*Somewhat indignantly: any such discussion, except by way of pleasantry, being outside her code of manners.*) How do I know? Why do you ask me?

Marchbanks.

I beg your pardon. I thought clever people—people who can do business and write letters and that sort of thing— always had to have love affairs to keep them from going mad.

Proserpine.

(*Rising, outraged.*) Mr Marchbanks! (*She looks severely at him, and marches majestically to the bookcase.*)

Marchbanks.

(*Approaching her humbly.*) I hope I havnt offended you. Perhaps I shouldnt have alluded to your love affairs.

Proserpine.

(*Plucking a blue book from the shelf and turning sharply on him.*) I havnt any love affairs. How dare you say such a thing? The idea! (*She tucks the book under her arm, and is flouncing back to her machine when he addresses her with awakened interest and sympathy.*)

Marchbanks.

Really! Oh, then you are shy, like me.

Proserpine.

Certainly I am not shy. What do you mean?

Marchbanks.

(*Secretly.*) You must be: that is the reason there are so few love affairs in the world. We all go about longing for love: it is the first need of our natures, the first prayer of our hearts; but we dare not utter our longing: we are too shy. (*Very earnestly.*) Oh, Miss Garnett, what would you not give to be without fear, without shame—

Proserpine.

(*Scandalized.*) Well, upon my word!

Marchbanks.

(*With petulant impatience.*) Ah, dont say those stupid things to me: they dont deceive me: what use are they? Why are you afraid to be your real self with me? I am just like you.

Proserpine.

Like me! Pray are you flattering me or flattering yourself? I dont feel quite sure which. (*She again rises to get back to her work.*)

Marchbanks.

(*Stopping her mysteriously.*) Hush! I go about in search of love; and I find it in unmeasured stores in the bosoms of others. But when I try to ask for it, this horrible shyness strangles me; and I stand dumb, or worse than dumb, saying meaningless things: foolish lies. And I see the affection I am longing for given to dogs and cats and pet birds, because they come and ask for it. (*Almost whispering.*) It must be asked for: it is like a ghost: it cannot speak unless it is first spoken to. (*At his usual pitch, but with deep melancholy.*) All the love in the world is longing to speak; only it dare not, because it is shy! shy! shy! That is the world's tragedy. (*With a deep sigh he sits in the visitors' chair and buries his face in his hands.*)

Proserpine.

(*Amazed, but keeping her wits about her: her point of honor in encounters with strange young men.*) Wicked people get over that shyness occasionally, dont they?

Marchbanks.

(*Scrambling up almost fiercely.*) Wicked people means people who have no love: therefore they have no shame. They have the power to ask love because they dont need it: they have the power to offer it because they have none to give. (*He collapses into his seat, and adds, mournfully.*) But we, who have love, and long to mingle it with the love of others: we cannot utter a word. (*Timidly.*) You find that, dont you?

Proserpine.

Look here: if you dont stop talking like this, I'll leave the room, Mr. Marchbanks: I really will. It's not proper.

(*She resumes her seat at the typewriter, opening the blue book and preparing to copy a passage from it.*)

Marchbanks.

(*Hopelessly.*) Nothing thats worth saying is proper. (*He rises, and wanders about the room in his lost way.*) I cant understand you, Miss Garnett. What am I to talk about?

Proserpine.

(*Snubbing him.*) Talk about indifferent things. Talk about the weather.

Marchbanks.

Would you talk about indifferent things if a child were by, crying bitterly with hunger?

Proserpine.

I suppose not.

Marchbanks.

Well: *I* cant talk about different things with my heart crying out bitterly in its hunger.

Proserpine.

Then hold your tongue.

Marchbanks.

Yes: that is what it always comes to. We hold our tongues.

Does that stop the cry of your heart? for it does cry: doesnt it? It must, if you have a heart.

Proserpine.

(*Suddenly rising with her hand pressed on her heart.*) Oh, it's no use trying to work while you talk like that. (*She leaves her little table and sits on the sofa. Her feelings are keenly stirred.*) It's no business of yours whether my heart cries or not; but I have a mind to tell you, for all that.

Marchbanks.

You neednt. I know already that it must.

Proserpine.

But mind! if you ever say I said so, I'll deny it.

Marchbanks.

(*Compassionately.*) Yes, I know. And so you havent the courage to tell him?

Proserpine.

(*Bouncing up.*) Him! Who?

Marchbanks.

Whoever he is. The man you love. It might be anybody. The curate, Mr Mill, perhaps.

Proserpine.

(*With disdain.*) Mr Mill!!! A fine man to break my heart about, indeed! I'd rather have you than Mr Mill.

Marchbanks.

(*Recoiling.*) No, really: I'm very sorry; but you mustnt think of that. I—

Proserpine.

(*Testily, going to the fire-place and standing at it with her back to him.*) Oh, dont be frightened: it's not you. It's not any one particular person.

Marchbanks.

I know. You feel that you could love anybody that offered—

Proserpine.

(*Turning, exasperated.*) Anybody that offered! No, I do not. What do you take me for?

Marchbanks.

(*Discouraged.*) No use. You wont make me real answers: only those things that everybody says. (*He strays to the sofa and sits down disconsolately.*)

Proserpine.

(*Nettled at what she takes to be a disparagement of her manners by an aristocrat.*) Oh well, if you want original conversation, youd better go and talk to yourself.

Marchbanks.

That is what all poets do: they talk to themselves out loud; and the world overhears them. But it's horrible lonely not to hear someone else talk sometimes.

Proserpine.

Wait until Mr Morell comes. He'll talk to you. (*Marchbanks shudders.*) Oh, you neednt make wry faces over him: he can talk better than you. (*With temper.*) He'd talk your little head off. (*She is going back angrily to her place, when he, suddenly enlightened, springs up and stops her.*)

Marchbanks.

Ah! I understand now.

Proserpine.

(*Reddening.*) What do you understand?

Marchbanks.

Your secret. Tell me: is it really and truly possible for a woman to love him?

Proserpine.

(*As if this were beyond all bounds.*) Well!!

Marchbanks.

(*Passionately.*) No: answer me. I want to know: I must know. *I* cant understand it. I can see nothing in him but words, pious resolutions, what people call goodness. You cant love that.

Proserpine.

(*Attempting to snub him by an air of cool propriety.*) I simply dont know what youre talking about. I dont understand you.

Marchbanks.

(*Vehemently.*) You do. You lie.

Proserpine.

Oh!

Marchbanks.

You do understand; and you know. (*Determined to have an answer.*) Is it possible for a woman to love him?

Proserpine.

(*Looking him straight in the face.*) Yes. (*He covers his*

face with his hands.) Whatever is the matter with you!
(*He takes down his hands. Frightened at the tragic mask
presented to her, she hurries past him at the utmost possible distance, keeping her eyes on his face while he turns
from her and goes to the child's chair beside the hearth,
where he sits in the deepest dejection. As she approaches
the door, it opens and Burgess enters. Seeing him, she
ejaculates,* Praise heaven! here's somebody *and she feels
safe enough to resume her place at her table.*)

from

THE TAMING OF THE SHREW

by William Shakespeare

Act II, scene 1
KATHERINE, PETRUCHIO

From the Lunts to the Burtons, Shakespeare's Kate and her de-liberating spouse have kept the battle of the sexes center stage. Styles change; most recently *The Taming of the Shrew* has come on as a knockabout farce; but there have been more sophisticated interpretations, though none on record that have conceived of the conflict as purely a battle of minds. Cole Porter, of course, did it to music. Conflict there is, in whatever manner the director and actors choose to play it, and it begins in earnest in the scene reprinted here.

Kate is the angry-tempered daughter of a rich man who offers a comfortable inheritance to any man who will take her off his hands. Petruchio, though a man of considerable property, is an avowed fortune hunter who is willing to cope with the problems that come with the cash. First, however, he must bring the problem to the altar.

The place is Padua, Kate's home. A would-be suitor with a lute wrapped about his head has given us some evidence of Kate's manner of receiving suitors. For Petruchio this sight is simply a further inducement. "Now, by the world, it is a lusty wench," he says, "I love her ten times more than e'er I did. O how I long to have some chat with her!" And at his urging the father sends her out to meet him.

Petruchio.
  Good morrow, Kate; for that's your name, I hear.

Katherine.
Well have you heard, but something hard of hearing.
They call me Katherine that do talk of me.
Petruchio.
You lie, in faith! for you are call'd plain Kate,
And bonny Kate, and sometimes Kate the curst;
But, Kate, the prettiest Kate in Christendom,
Kate of Kate Hall. my super-dainty Kate,
For dainties are all Kates—and therefore, Kate,
Take this of me, Kate of my consolation:
Hearing thy mildness prais'd in every town,
Thy virtues spoke of, and thy beauty sounded,
Yet not so deeply as to thee belongs,
Myself am mov'd to woo thee for my wife.
Katherine.
Mov'd? In good time! Let him that mov'd you hither
Remove you hence. I knew you at the first
You were a moveable.
Petruchio.
                    Why, what's a moveable?
Katherine.
A join'd-stool.
Petruchio.
                    Thou hast hit it! Come sit on me.
Katherine.
Asses are made to bear, and so are you.
Petruchio.
Women are made to bear, and so are you.
Katherine.
No such jade as you, if me you mean.
Petruchio.
Alas, good Kate, I will not burden thee!
For, knowing thee to be but young and light—
Katherine.
Too light for such a swain as you to catch,
And yet as heavy as my weight should be.
Petruchio.
Should be! should—buzz!
Katherine.
                    Well ta'en, and like a buzzard.
Petruchio.
O slow-wing'd turtle! shall a buzzard take thee?

Katherine.

Ay, for a turtle, as he takes a buzzard.

Petruchio.

Come, come, you wasp! i' faith, you are too angry.

Katherine.

If I be waspish, best beware my sting.

Petruchio.

My remedy is then to pluck it out.

Katherine.

Ay, if the fool could find it where it lies.

Petruchio.

Who knows not where a wasp does wear his sting?
In his tail.

Katherine.

In his tongue.

Petruchio.

Whose tongue?

Katherine.

Yours, if you talk of tales. And so farewell.

Petruchio.

What, with my tongue in your tail? Nay, come again!
Good Kate, I am a gentleman.

Katherine.

That I'll try.
(*She strikes him.*)

Petruchio.

I swear I'll cuff you if you strike again.

Katherine.

So may you lose your arms.
If you strike me, you are no gentleman;
And if no gentleman, why then no arms.

Petruchio.

A herald, Kate? O, put me in thy books!

Katherine.

What is your crest? a coxcomb?

Petruchio.

A combless cock, so Kate will be my hen.

Katherine.

No cock of mine; you crow too like a craven.

Petruchio.

Nay, come, Kate, come! you must not look so sour.

Katherine.

It is my fashion when I see a crab.

Petruchio.

Why, here's no crab, and therefore look not sour.

Katherine.

There is, there is!

Petruchio.

Then show it me.

Katherine.

                    Had I a glass, I would.

Petruchio.

What, you mean my face?

Katherine.

Well aim'd of such a young one.

Petruchio.

Now, by Saint George, I am too young for you.

Katherine.

Yet you are wither'd.

Petruchio.

'Tis with cares.

Katherine.

I care not.

Petruchio.

Nay, hear you, Kate. In sooth you scape not so!

Katherine.

I chafe you if I tarry. Let me go.

Petruchio.

No, not a whit; I find you passing gentle.
'Twas told me you were rough and coy and sullen,
And now I find report a very liar;
For thou art pleasant, gamesome, passing courteous,
But slow in speech, yet sweet as springtime flowers.
Thou canst not frown, thou canst not look askance,
Nor bite the lip, as angry wenches will,
Nor hast thou pleasure to be cross in talk;
But thou with mildness entertain'st thy wooers,
With gentle conference, soft and affable.
Why does the world report that Kate doth limp?
O sland'rous world! Kate like the hazel twig
Is straight and slender, and as brown in hue
As hazelnuts, and sweeter than the kernels.
O, let me see thee walk: thou dost not halt.

Katherine.

Go, fool! and whom thou keep'st command.

Petruchio.

Did ever Dian so become a grove
As Kate this chamber with her princely gait?
O, be thou Dian, and let her be Kate;
And then let Kate be chaste, and Dian sportful!

Katherine.

Where did you study all this goodly speech?

Petruchio.

It is extempore, from my mother wit.

Katherine.

A witty mother! witless else her son.

Petruchio.

Am I not wise?

Katherine.

Yes; keep you warm.

Petruchio.

Marry, so I mean, sweet Katherine, in thy bed.
And therefore, setting all this chat aside,
Thus in plain terms: your father hath consented
That you shall be my wife, your dowry 'greed on;
And, will you, nill you, I will marry you.
Now, Kate, I am a husband for your turn;
For, by this light, whereby I see thy beauty,
Thy beauty, that doth make me like thee well,
Thou must be married to no man but me;
For I am he am born to tame you, Kate,
And bring you from a wild Kate to a Kate
Conformable as other household Kates.

* * *

Here comes your father. Never make denial.
I must and will have Katherine to my wife.

from

GHOSTS

by Henrik Ibsen (translated by Kai Jurgensen and
Robert Schenkkan)

Act II
MANDERS, MRS. ALVING

The social issues—divorce and venereal disease—whose
mention on the stage once horrified the majority of Ibsen's
audiences no longer seem daring or shocking. But *Ghosts*
remains compellingly strong to modern audiences who see
beyond the surface issues the deeper questions of individual
and social hypocrisy and the tortuous, ambiguous intercon-
nections of human responsibility. The play unfolds with
the inexorability of a classical tragedy; indeed, it has often
been compared to Sophocles' *Oedipus* as a search into the
past for the truth, which, when found, proves to be a trap
of guilt and destruction. As a play of ideas, it is shaped
to its theme, far from naturalistic, and at times mechanical;
but in realizing its ideas in subtle, fully dimensioned characterizations, it achieves the realism Ibsen admired and for
which he has so often been praised. Pastor Manders is a
triumph of ruthless satirical exposure in a realistic vein;
Mrs. Alving is simply one of the great characters of modern
drama.

Married by her family to a profligate man whose money
and position made him a good catch, Mrs. Alving has lived
a lie of respectability, hiding her husband's drunkenness
and sexual affairs, managing his estate, coping with his
public duties in order to preserve appearances. Determined
that her son Oswald should not be influenced by his father
and so grow to be like him, she has kept the boy in
schools far from home. Now Alving is dead. As a final

285

symbol of his respectability, an orphanage has been built in his name. For Mrs. Alving the project is a way of buying her freedom from the past and pretense: she has given for the orphanage all the money that came to her through her marriage. Oswald has come home from Paris, where he has been an art student. Mrs. Alving looks forward to a new life without subterfuge.

Pastor Manders has come from town to assist at the dedication of the orphanage. Early in her marriage Mrs. Alving had tried to leave her husband and fled to Manders, whom she loved. Manders, despite his affection for her, had persuaded her to return to Alving. Manders looks back on this as a triumph over his emotions. Mrs. Alving suggests that it was a kind of defeat. On every issue they hold similarly opposing views—on Oswald's bohemian life in Paris, on the "shocking" books Mrs. Alving reads and keeps on her parlor table, on the need to worry about "what people will say." Mrs. Alving, in a way that Manders condemns as "modern," asserts the necessity for honesty; Manders reiterates traditional "ideals" (though it is soon clear that his concern is primarily for appearances).

This disagreement runs through the play in a series of confrontations, one of which is reprinted here. But beyond the question of truth vs. hypocrisy is the problem of responsibility and the strength of the past. Mrs. Alving has labored to protect her son from the influence of his father. Yet at the end of the act which precedes this scene, she has overheard Oswald flirting with the maid, Regina—words and a situation that almost exactly match an incident in Oswald's father's life. And one of the truths Mrs. Alving discovers near the end of the play is the destruction of her son by syphilis inherited from his father.

The scene is a roomy sun parlor in Mrs. Alving's house in western Norway. There is a window downstage left and near it a small sofa with a sewing table before it. Center is a round table with books, magazines, and newspapers. The table is surrounded by chairs. Doors left and right lead to the dining room and other parts of the house. At the rear, the room continues into a narrower, glass-enclosed sun porch. A door in the right wall of the porch leads to the garden. Through the glass wall a somber fjord landscape can be made out; it is veiled by steady rain.

It is just after lunch. Manders and Mrs. Alving come out of the dining room.

Mrs. Alving.

(*Still in the doorway.*) I'm glad you enjoyed it, Mr. Manders. (*Speaking into the dining room.*) Aren't you coming, Oswald?

Oswald.

(*Offstage.*) No, thanks. I think I'll take a little walk.

Mrs. Alving.

Yes, do. The rain seems to have stopped for a while. (*She closes the dining-room door, goes to the hall door, and calls.*) Regina!

Regina.

(*Offstage.*) Yes, Mrs. Alving?

Mrs. Alving.

Go down to the laundry and help with the wreaths.

Regina.

All right, Mrs. Alving.

(*Mrs. Alving makes sure Regina has gone, then she closes the door.*)

Manders.

Are you sure he can't hear anything in there?

Mrs. Alving.

Not when the door is closed. And besides, he's going out.

Manders.

I'm still completely bewildered. I don't understand how I could eat a bite of that wonderful dinner.

Mrs. Alving.

(*Controlling her restlessness, walking up and down.*) I don't either. But what are we going to do?

Manders.

Yes, what? I certainly don't know. I am completely in-experienced in such matters.

Mrs. Alving.

I'm convinced that nothing serious has happened yet.

Manders.

No, heaven forbid! But it's an indecent state of affairs, just the same.

Mrs. Alving.

It's just an impulse of Oswald's, you can be sure.

Manders.

Well, as I say, I don't know anything about such things, but I do think that . . .

Mrs. Alving.

She's got to get out of my house. At once. That's clear. . . .

Manders.

Yes, of course.

Mrs. Alving.

But where? It wouldn't be right to . . .

Manders.

Where? Home to her father, of course.

Mrs. Alving.

To whom?

Manders.

To her . . . Oh, that's right. Engstrand isn't . . . Good God, Mrs. Alving, it isn't possible! You *must* be wrong.

Mrs. Alving.

Unfortunately, I'm not. Johanna had to admit it to me; and my husband couldn't deny it. So there wasn't anything to do but hush it up.

Manders.

No, I suppose not.

Mrs. Alving.

I sent the girl away at once, and gave her a fairly generous sum to keep quiet. The rest she took care of herself when she got to town. She picked up her old friendship with Engstrand. I suppose she hinted how much money she had, and told him some story about a foreigner who came by here in his yacht that summer. Then she and Engstrand were married in a great hurry. That's right, you married them yourself.

Manders.

But then how am I to understand . . . ? I remember very well Engstrand came to arrange for the wedding. He was completely crushed, and accused himself bitterly for the liberties he and his sweetheart had taken.

Mrs. Alving.

Yes, of course he had to take the blame.

Manders.

But such dishonesty! To *me!* I would never have thought it of Jacob Engstrand. I will certainly take him to task for it; let him prepare himself for that. . . . And the immorality of such a marriage! For money . . . ! How much did the girl have?

Mrs. Alving.

Three hundred crowns.

Manders.

Can you imagine such a thing . . . to let yourself be married to a fallen woman for three hundred miserable crowns!

Mrs. Alving.

Then what about me? Who married a fallen man.

Manders.

Good God . . . what are you saying? A fallen man!

Mrs. Alving.

Do you think he was purer when I went to the altar with him than Johanna was when Engstrand married her?

Manders.

But there's a tremendous difference . . .

Mrs. Alving.

Not so much. There's a great difference in the price, of course; a measly three hundred crowns and a whole fortune.

Manders.

How can you compare such things? After all, you had consulted your heart and your family.

Mrs. Alving.

(*Not looking at him.*) I thought you understood to whom I'd lost what you call my heart.

Manders.

(*Aloof.*) If I'd understood anything like that, I wouldn't have been a daily guest in your husband's house.

Mrs. Alving.

At any rate, it's a fact that I certainly didn't consult myself about.

Manders.

Well, your nearest relatives, then . . . as a young woman should . . . your mother and both your aunts.

Mrs. Alving.

Yes, that's true. The three of them added it all up for me. It's incredible how they got the sum to look as if it would be sheer stupidity to refuse such an offer. If mother could only look down now and see what all that splendor has led to.

Manders.

You can't hold anyone responsible for the outcome. This much is clear, anyway: your marriage had a firm foundation in law and order.

Mrs. Alving.

(*By the window.*) Oh, this blind acceptance of law and order! I often think that's the thing that causes all the unhappiness in the world.

Manders.

Mrs. Alving, it's sinful to talk like that.

Mrs. Alving.

Maybe so. But I don't agree with all these restraints and conditions any longer. I can't! I've got to struggle through to freedom.

Manders.

What do you mean?

Mrs. Alving.

(*Drumming with her fingers on the windowsill.*) I should never have hidden the truth about my husband's life. But I didn't dare do anything else then . . . not just for his sake but for my own. That's how cowardly I was.

Manders.

Cowardly?

Mrs. Alving.

If people had found out, they'd have said something like this: "Poor man, no wonder he carries on . . . with his wife deserting him."

Manders.

There would have been a certain amount of truth in it.

Mrs. Alving.

(*Looking steadily at him.*) If I were the person I ought to be, I'd call Oswald in and say, "Listen, my boy: your father was no good . . ."

Manders.

But great heavens . . . !

Mrs. Alving.

. . . And tell him everything I've told you, word for word.

Manders.

This is shocking, Mrs. Alving.

Mrs. Alving.

I know. I know very well. I'm shocked at the thought myself. (*She leaves the window.*) That's how cowardly I am.

Manders.

You call it cowardice to do your simple duty? Have you forgotten that a child is supposed to love and honor his father and mother?

Mrs. Alving.

Let's not be so trite. Let's ask: should Oswald love and honor *his* father?

Manders.

Isn't there a voice in your heart, a mother's heart, that tells you not to destroy your son's ideals?

Mrs. Alving.

But what about the truth?

Manders.

But what about the ideals?

Mrs. Alving.

Oh . . . ideals, ideals! If only I weren't such a coward!

Manders.

Don't despise ideals, Mrs. Alving; you'll have to pay for it later. Let's take Oswald's case; I'm afraid he doesn't have many as it is; but I have been able to see this much: he looks up to his father with great idealism.

Mrs. Alving.

You're right.

Manders.

And you, yourself, created and nourished this image by your letters.

Mrs. Alving.

Yes, I followed the precepts of duty and the conventions. That's why I lied to my son year after year. Oh . . . what a coward, what a coward I've been!

Manders.

You've built up a happy illusion in your son's mind, Mrs. Alving; and you certainly shouldn't underestimate that.

Mrs. Alving.

Hm, who knows whether it really is such a good thing . . . ? But I'm not going to stand for any foolishness with Regina. I'm not going to let him make the poor girl unhappy.

Manders.

Good heavens . . . no; that would be awful!

Mrs. Alving.

If I were sure that he's serious, and that it would be for his happiness . . .

Manders.

What? What then?

Mrs. Alving.

But I'm afraid it wouldn't; because Regina isn't the right kind of girl.

Manders.

Well? What do you mean?

Mrs. Alving.

If I weren't such a miserable coward, I would tell him this: "Marry her, or do anything you please, but don't lie about it."

Manders.

But good God! Would you let him marry her! Why, that's revolting . . . ! I never heard of such a thing . . . !

Mrs. Alving.

You haven't? Honestly now, Mr. Manders, don't you suppose there are plenty of married people all over the country just as closely related?

Manders.

I don't understand you at all.

Mrs. Alving.

Oh, yes, you do.

Manders.

Oh, you're thinking of cases where possibly . . . Yes, unfortunately, ordinary family life isn't always as pure as it ought to be. But in such cases as you're talking about, you don't always know . . . at least not with certainty. But in *this* case . . . how can you, the mother, be willing to let your . . . ?

Mrs. Alving.

But I'm not . . . I *don't* want it . . . not for anything in the world. That's just what I'm saying.

Manders.

No, but it's because you're a "coward," as you say. But supposing you weren't. . . . Good God, what a disgusting alliance!

Mrs. Alving.

For that matter, they say if you go back far enough, we

have all sprung from that kind of alliance. And who is
it that arranged the world like that, Mr. Manders?

Manders.

I'm not going to discuss such questions with you, Mrs.
Alving; you're far from having the right attitude for that.
But how dare you say that it's "cowardly" of you . . . !

Mrs. Alving.

I'll tell you exactly what I mean. I'm afraid because of
the ghosts inside me, the ghosts I can never quite free
myself from.

Manders.

The what?

Mrs. Alving.

The ghosts. When I heard Regina and Oswald in there, I
felt as if I were being haunted. But I almost think we are
all ghosts, Mr. Manders. It isn't what we've inherited from
our parents that walks again in us. It's all sorts of lifeless
old ideas and dead faiths and things like that. They're not
alive in us, but they cling to us all the same, and we can't
shake them off. Even just reading the paper, I can see
ghosts between the lines. The whole country must be full
of them, numberless, like grains of sand. And all of us
are so miserably afraid of the light.

Manders.

Aha . . . ! There we have the fruits of your reading. A
pretty harvest! Oh, these revolutionary, freethinking
books! Disgusting!

Mrs. Alving.

You're wrong, Mr. Manders. It was you, yourself, who set
me thinking; and I thank you for it.

Manders.

I?

Mrs. Alving.

When you forced me to obey these so-called laws of duty
and obligation; when you praised as right and proper what
my whole being rebelled against as something loathsome.
Then I began to check the seams of your wisdom. I just
wanted to pick a little at one knot; but when I had untied
that, the whole thing unraveled. And then I realized that
it was all factory-made.

Manders.

(*Quietly, shaken.*) And is this what I won by the hardest fight of my life?

Mrs. Alving.

You ought to call it your most pathetic defeat.

Manders.

It was the greatest victory I ever won, Helen . . . the victory over myself.

Mrs. Alving.

It was a crime against us both.

Manders.

When I commanded you, and said: "Woman, go home to your lawful husband." the time you came to me lost and crying, "Here I am; take me!" Was that a crime?

Mrs. Alving.

I think it was.

Manders.

You and I don't understand each other.

Mrs. Alving.

Not any longer, at least.

Manders.

Never . . . never even in my most secret thoughts, have I ever regarded you as anything but another man's wife.

Mrs. Alving.

Oh . . . is that so?

Manders.

Helen . . . !

Mrs. Alving.

It's so easy to forget what we were.

Manders.

Not for me. I'm the same as I always was.

Mrs. Alving.

(*Changing the subject.*) All right, let's forget the past. Today you're up to your ears in boards and committees, and I'm wrestling with old ghosts, inside and out.

Manders.

The ones on the outside . . . I'll be glad to help you get rid of them. After all the terrible things I've heard from you today, I can't let a young girl stay in your house.

Mrs. Alving.

Don't you think the best idea would be to provide for her . . . I mean, see to it she was married.

Manders.

Undoubtedly. I think that would be just the thing. Regina is at that age now when . . . well, of course, I don't know anything about it, but . . .

Mrs. Alving.

Regina matured early.

Manders.

Yes, didn't she? I seem to remember that she was remarkably well developed, physically, when I prepared her for confirmation. But temporarily, anyway, she must go home, so her father can keep an eye on her. . . . Oh, but that's right, Engstrand isn't . . . How could he . . . how could *he* hide the truth from me!

    (There is a knock at the hall door.)

Mrs. Alving.

Who could that be? Come in!

from

THE SILVER CORD

by Sidney Howard

Two Scenes from Act II, scene 1 and Act II, scene 2
ROBERT, HESTER; MRS. PHELPS, DAVID

This play is the modern theater's first serious, realistic presentation of Mom as the loving destroyer of the sons to whom she gave birth. Though the well-made mechanics of Howard's plotting are at times less persuasive than convenient, his scenes of confrontation—mother with sons, mother with rivals for those sons' affections—and his character portraits, especially of the mother herself, are as sharply effective now as they were in 1926, when the play first jarred Broadway audiences.

Mrs. Phelps has two sons: Robert, who has never left home, and David, who has been given two years of freedom to study architecture in Europe and returns with a wife. The play begins with the homecoming of Dave and his new wife, Christina; it ends as they leave (or rather, escape), taking with them Hester, the girl whom Robert was to have married. In the time between, less than twenty-four hours, Mrs. Phelps has conducted a ruthless campaign—subtly at first, but finally with panic-driven directness—to "save" her sons from the women whom she can see only as thieves come to take from her the affections of the "little boys" to whom, frustrated in her own marriage, she has given all of her life and love.

With Robert she is successful. Engineering a cozy conversation with him, she helps him to "discover" that Hester, his fiancée, shows no real affection for him and that he in turn is not at all certain he loves Hester. She then contrives that Robert have an opportunity to test this theory in a private chat with Hester. (For Mrs. Phelps's portrait of herself, see p. 206.)

The time is evening, after dinner; the place, Mrs. Phelps's living room, "decorated in the best manner of 1905, and cluttered with the souvenirs of maternal love, European travel, and an orthodox enthusiasm for the arts." There has been an uncomfortable half-hour of after-dinner coffee, and Chris and Dave have gone for a walk alone. Hester has angered Mrs. Phelps by her support of Chris, and, delighted when she learns that Chris is to have a baby, announces that she too is eager to have children. When Mrs. Phelps, with a knowing glance at Robert, suggests that this is the only reason Hester wants to marry her son, Hester, not sorry to shock Mrs. Phelps, replies that it is a very good reason "and that's that." As Robert rises to pick up the coffee tray (and to end the conversation), Mrs. Phelps quickly stands up and takes the tray out of his hands. "Her eyes meet Robert's and there is no mistaking the intention of the look she gives him. Then, without a word, she goes up center, and out of the room with the tray."

Robert.

(*Starting after her.*) Mother! . . . Hester didn't mean . . . Oh! . . . (*He turns back to Hester.*) Hester, how could you!

Hester.

I don't know . . . but I don't care if I did!

Robert.

(*R of sofa LC.*) It doesn't make things any easier for me.

Hester.

(*Moving towards him to the extreme R end of the sofa and looking up at him.*) Oh, Rob dear, I *am* sorry!

Robert.

(*Whose actions in moving the furniture betray the uneasiness of his mind.*) You've got Mother all ruffled and upset. (*He moves away from Hester, taking the chair from the top of the table back to the desk up stage RC.*) Now we'll have to smooth her down and have all kinds of explanations, and everything. (*He returns to C and carries the small table into the hall to the L and returns immediately.*) Really, it was too bad of you.

Hester.

I know. I lost my temper. . . . You understand, don't you?

Robert.

(*Up C.*) I understand that you're a guest in Mother's house.

Hester.

Is that *all* you understand? Oh, Rob! (*She turns away from him.*)

Robert.

(*At R end of the sofa.*) I'm sorry, Hester. But, for the moment, I'm thinking of Mother.

Hester.

(*Still turned from Robert.*) I see . . . I'll apologize.

Robert.

That's up to you. (*He turns on his R to the L end of the settee RC.*)

Hester.

I suppose she'll never forgive me. It isn't this, though.

Robert.

(*Standing at the settee with his back to Hester.*) This?

Hester.

The scene I made.

Robert.

What do you mean?

Hester.

I don't know. . . . Some mothers like the girls their sons marry.

Robert.

Doesn't that depend on the girls?

Hester.

Not entirely.

Robert.

You mustn't be unjust to Mother.

Hester.

Rob, I'm a little tired of hearing about your mother.
            (*Robert irritably turns up stage.*)
(*Suddenly penitent again, turning to face Robert.*) Oh, I didn't mean to say that! I didn't mean it a bit! (*She rises, standing by the sofa.*) I'm sorry, Rob. . . . Now I'm apologizing to you. Don't you hear me?

Robert.

(*Facing Hester up stage C.*) Yes, I hear you. What then?

Hester.

(*Moving to Robert.*) Oh, what difference does it make? I'm not marrying your mother. I'm marrying you. And I love you, Rob! I love you!

Robert.

(*About to embrace her, checks himself and drops his hands.*) Yes, my dear.

Hester.

I'll never be bad again.

Robert.

I'm willing to take your word for it.

Hester.

You'd better be. (*She puts her hand up to his shoulder and looks into his face, half playfully.*) Oh, you *are* angry with me, Rob!

Robert.

No, I'm not.

Hester.

(*Taking her hand from Robert's shoulder, and crossing in front of him, siting on the L end of the settee RC.*) You're a queer one.

Robert.

(*Moving down a little C.*) Think so? How?

Hester.

(*Without looking at him.*) As a lover. I've never seen another like you.

Robert.

Haven't you? (*A thought strikes him, but he keeps his position.*) Tell me something, Hester.

Hester.

What?

Robert.

Have you had many?

Hester.

(*Looking round at him.*) Many what?

Robert.

Lovers.

Hester.

(*Turning away again.*) Oh, Robert, what a thing to say to a lady!

Robert.

You know what I mean.

Hester.

(*A little seriously.*) I'm not quite sure I want to answer.

Robert.

I'm not asking for their names.

Hester.

Oh, I shouldn't mind that . . . the truth is . . . I don't know . . .

Robert.

You must.

Hester.

(*More easily.*) I don't really. I used to think . . . oh, quite often . . . that one of my young men was coming to the point . . . but . . .

Robert.

Yes?

Hester.

But none of them ever did.

Robert.

That surprises me. Why not?

Hester.

I don't think it was entirely lack of allure, Rob.

Robert.

Of course it wasn't!

Hester.

I think it was because I always laughed.

Robert.

You didn't laugh at me.

Hester.

You looked foolish enough, now that I think of it.

Robert.

Yes. I dare say . . . (*He turns up stage to the upper window. There is a pause, then he comes down R and stands at the R end of the settee.*) So I *was* the only one.

Hester.

Say the only one I didn't laugh at, please. You make me sound so undesirable. (*She picks up the cushion, punches it, puts it behind her and leans back.*)

Robert.

I didn't mean to. (*Sits on sofa beside her leaning forward, his arms on his knees.*) Tell me, Hester . . .

Hester.

Anything.

Robert.

Have you thought what it will mean to be my wife?

Hester.

A very pleasant life.

Robert.

For you?

Hester.

I certainly hope so.

(*A slight pause.*)

Robert.

I don't know that I quite share your enthusiasm for children.

Hester.

You will.

Robert.

They don't exactly help a career, you know.

Hester.

Have you got a career? (*She sits forward.*)

Robert.

I fully intend to have one.

Hester.

I'm glad to hear it.

Robert.

I've got just as much talent as Dave has.

Hester.

What kind of talent?

Robert.

I haven't decided. I can draw pretty well. I'm not a bad musician. I might decide to compose. I might even write. I've often thought of it. And children, you see . . .

Hester.

I don't know much about careers, but Lincoln had children and adored 'em, and if you can do half as well as he did . . .

Robert.

Then my preferences aren't to be considered?

Hester.

(*With a sudden firmness in her voice.*) You just leave things to me. If we're poor, I'll cook and scrub floors. I'll bring up our children. I'll take care of you whether we live in New York or Kamschatka. This business is up to me, Rob. Don't let it worry you.

Robert.

(*Defeated in the attitude he has assumed.*) I only wanted to make sure you understood my point of view.

Hester.

(*Rising and moving to the lower window, her manner a little ruffled.*) If I don't, I shall, so let's cut this short.

(*Robert, who has not altered his position, turns his head in her direction, watching her uneasily as she draws aside the curtain of the window.*)

Hallo!

Robert.

(*His chain of thought unbroken.*) What is it?

Hester.

There goes your mother down the road.

Robert.

(*Rising and joining her, putting one knee upon the seat at the window and bending forward below Hester.*) So it is! What can she be doing?

Hester.

(*Turning away from the window on her R hand, going up stage R and across to the piano.*) She's fetching her darling David in out of the cold. I knew she would.

Robert.

(*Getting off the seat, stepping back, and facing up towards Hester.*) Hester, would you mind not speaking that way of mother?

Hester.

(*Handling some sheets of music.*) Can't she leave them alone for a minute?

Robert.

She's the worrying kind.

Hester.

Oh, rot! (*She turns away from the piano and comes down L to the fireplace.*)

Robert.

(*Keeping his position R.*) Evidently you're bent on making things as difficult as possible for me.

Hester.

(*Looking at the fire.*) I'm sorry you feel that.

(*There is a long irritable pause.*)

Robert.

(*Irresolutely, moving to the front of the settee RC.*) Hester!

Hester.

Yes?

Robert.

(*Slowly going across to LC.*) Have you thought any more about our honeymoon?

Hester.

Didn't we decide to go abroad?

Robert.

Abroad's a pretty general term. You were to think *where* you wanted to be taken.

Hester.

I left that to you.

Robert.

You said you "didn't care."

Hester.

I don't.

Robert.

Nor where we live after . . . nor how.

Hester.

(*With a trace of tired emphasis.*) I don't . . . I don't . . . I want to live with *you*. (*Suddenly changing her tone, looking up at him in tender expostulation.*) What's the use of this, Rob?

Robert.

We've never talked seriously about our marriage before.

Hester.

(*Patiently.*) What is there to say about it?

Robert.

A great deal.

Hester.

(*Her endurance failing her a little, she turns to the L end of the sofa and gives the cushion a little nervous shake.*) I don't agree. Marriages are things of feeling. They'd better *not* be talked about.

Robert.

Real marriages can stand discussion!

Hester.

(*Looking quickly round at Robert.*) Rob!

Robert.

What?

Hester.

That wasn't nice.

Robert.

Wasn't it?

Hester.

(*Suddenly frightened she comes to a position a little above him on his L.*) What's the matter, Rob? I'll talk as seriously as you please. Do I love you? Yes. Am I going to make you a good wife? I hope so, though I may make mistakes. Are you going to be happy with me? I hope that, too, but you'll have to answer it for yourself. (*She moves towards the fire.*)

Robert.

I can't answer it.

Hester.

(*Stopping suddenly in her movement.*) Why can't you?

Robert.

Because I'm not sure of it.

Hester.

(*In a low, amazed voice.*) Aren't you, Rob?

Robert.

These things are better faced before than after.

Hester.

(*With a half-step towards him, her voice hardening.*) What is it you're trying to say?

Robert.

If only we could be sure!

Hester.

(*Stunned.*) So that's it!

Robert.

(*Moving close to her, his hands gripping her shoulders.*) Are you so sure you want to marry me?

Hester.

(*Drawing back from him, turning on her R up to the L side of the sofa LC, her back to him.*) How can I be— now?

Robert.

(*Moving to the L and standing below her.*) Marriage is such a serious thing. You don't realize how serious.

Hester.

Don't I?

Robert.

No . . . I hope you won't think harshly of me. . . . And, mind you, I haven't said I wanted to break things off . . . I only want . . .

Hester.

Please, Rob! (*She moves away and up to the side of the piano, her back still to him.*)

Robert.

(*Taking the place she has just left, facing up stage.*) No. You've got to hear me out.

Hester.

I've heard enough, thank you!

Robert.

I'm only trying to look at this thing . . .

Hester.

Seriously . . . I know . . .

Robert.

Because, after all, the happiness of three people is affected by it.

Hester.

(*Turning suddenly on her L hand.*) Three?

Robert.

As Mother said, before dinner.

Hester.

(*Coming close to the R of the sofa LC, slightly above it.*) So you talked this over with your mother?

(*During the following scene Hester, though shaken to her depths, keeps a control—her voice is quick, subdued and vibrant.*)

Robert.

Isn't that natural?

(*They are now standing at either end of the sofa. Robert has not moved his position, his back is to the fire, his L hand rests on the back of the sofa and he moves his palm upon it as he speaks, looking now and then, but only for a moment, at Hester. Hester keeps her eyes upon Robert searchingly.*)

Hester.

Is your mother the third?

Robert.

Wouldn't she be?

Hester.

Yes, I suppose she would . . . I think you might tell me what else she had to say.

Robert.

It was all wise and kind. You may be as hard as you like on me, but you mustn't be hard on poor, splendid, lonely Mother.

Hester.

(*Under her breath with an almost savage intensity.*) So she's lonely, too! What else did she say about us?

Robert.

Well, you haven't been very interested in planning our future. She notices such things.

Hester.

What else?

Robert.

She sees through people, you know.

Hester.

Through me?

(*There is a pause. Robert looks up at Hester. She is waiting for his answer. He is confused and draws back from his position at the end of the sofa, and then, as he speaks, paces across in front of it towards C.*)

Robert.

She thought, as I must say I do, that we didn't love each other quite enough to . . . (*He hesitates, stops in his walk and half turns to Hester.*) At least, she thought we ought to think very carefully before we . . .

(*Before he can finish his halting words Hester, with quick resolution, goes to him on his L, gripping both his arms almost fiercely, compelling him to face her; she still has control, but is near the breaking point.*)

Hester.

If you really want to be free . . . if you really want that, Rob, it's all right. It's perfectly all right . . . I'll set you free . . . Don't worry! . . . Only you've got to say so. You've *got* to! . . . Answer me, Rob. *Do* you want to be rid of me?

(*There is a pause. Robert cannot hold her gaze and his eyes fall. She takes the blow: releasing his arms.*)

I guess that's answer enough. (*She draws a little back from him and pulls the engagement ring from her finger.*) Here's your ring! (*She holds it towards him.*)

Robert.

Hester! Don't do anything we'll be sorry for afterwards! Don't, please! I can't take it! (*He turns away to the L arm of the settee RC, facing R.*)

Hester.

(*Without any sign of emotion, but speaking quickly.*) I shall have an easier time of it, if you keep away from me. I want to save my face . . . if I can. (*She has moved C to behind him, and again holds out the ring.*)

Robert.

Hester, please! (*Without turning.*)

Hester.

All right, if you won't go, I will. (*She draws back and is about to turn on her R towards the door C.*)

Robert.

(*Turning on his L hand to above her.*) I'm sorry. Of course I'll go.

Hester.

And take your ring with you.

(*A second's pause and Robert awkwardly holds out his hand for the ring; Hester drops it into it and quickly withdraws. He has just reached the door when she breaks into furious, hysterical sobbing. Her sobs rack her and seem, at the time, to strike Robert like the blows of a whip.*)

Robert.

(*Turning at the door.*) For God's sake, Hester . . .

(*She drops on to the sofa LC, her face in the cushion to the L, shaken by her hysterical sobs of wretchedness and humiliation. Robert, bewildered and distraught, irresolutely moves to her at the back of the sofa and then turns to the door and calls.*)

Mother! Christina! Come here! Hester . . .

(*Christina appears in the door. Mrs. Phelps follows her. Robert returns to the back of the sofa.*)

Can't you pull yourself together?

SECOND SCENE

Having succeeded in separating Robert from Hester, Mrs. Phelps turns her efforts to Dave, though it is late in the evening. For his homecoming Dave has been given his boyhood bedroom, still decorated with his prep school trophies and souvenirs, while Chris has been assigned a guest room in another part of the house. Mrs. Phelps has popped in several times and Robert, too, has come to call. Dave has let both of them know that he feels they have treated Hester badly. Robert has stood up for Mrs. Phelps, but neither that nor his mother's attempts to remind Dave of the happy old days, her sentimental claim to the special bond between mother and son, or her reference to her "heart condition" has seemed to sway Dave. Finally, in anger Mrs. Phelps has accused Dave of "treachery" and swept out of the room. Dave calls after her and tries the door that leads to her room; it is locked. "Manfully, he takes refuge in the sulks." He lights a cigarette "kicks off his slippers, throws his dressing-gown on to the stool, picks a book from the table, turns, and seeing the baby pillow [his own; Mrs. Phelps had carefully placed it on the bed] casts it over his shoulder so that it falls near the door, and flounces into bed."

Just as he is settled, reading, his mother opens the door again very slowly. She presents a tear-stained face to view and comes in.

Mrs. Phelps.

Smoking in bed, Dave boy!

David.

(*Starting and lowering his book.*) Eh?

Mrs. Phelps.

No, don't get up. (*She sees the pillow on the floor and picks it up.*) It's only Mother . . . (*She puts the pillow back in its place at the head of the bed, from the downstage side, moves a step back and sits on the edge of the bed facing David.*) Let me sit here as I used to do in the old days. (*She leans forward and takes the cigarette out of David's hand, rises and goes to the dressing-table, extinguishing it in an ash-tray.*)

David.

(*Sitting up.*) Mother, I didn't mean . . .

Mrs. Phelps.

(*Coming back to her place on the bed.*) Never mind. I was wrong to be hurt.

David.

But you had me all wrong. I mean . . . you and I . . . We're just the same as we always were . . . believe me, we are . . . Why, if anything came to spoil things between us . . .

Mrs. Phelps.

(*The first objective conquered.*) That's what I wanted you to say! (*She takes his hand, pulling him towards her and kissing him. With large indulgence.*) Now talk to me about Christina.

David.

(*Taken aback, without knowing why.*) Wha . . . ?

Mrs. Phelps.

Give me your hand in mine, and tell me all about her.

David.

(*Obeying rather reluctantly.*) What is there to tell?

Mrs. Phelps.

Well, for one thing, tell me you think she's going to like me!

David.

(*Warmly.*) She does already!

Mrs. Phelps.

(*With a note of playfulness.*) Doesn't think I'm an old-fashioned frump?

David.

I should say not! How could she?

Mrs. Phelps.

She's such a modern young lady. So lovely, but so very up-to-date. (*A little pause.*) Though I'm afraid of her, Dave.

David.

(*Laughingly.*) Afraid of Chris? Why?

Mrs. Phelps.

She's so much cleverer than I am. She makes me realize that I'm just a timid old lady of the old school.

David.

(*With correct indignation.*) You old!

Mrs. Phelps.

(*Archly, so brave about it.*) Yes, I am!

David.

Well, you and Chris are going to be the best friends ever.

Mrs. Phelps.

You *are* happy, aren't you?

David.

You bet I am!

Mrs. Phelps.

Really happy?

David.

Couldn't be happier!

Mrs. Phelps.

I'm so glad! Because anyone can see the difference between Christina and Hester. Of course, that's a little the difference between you and Rob. You know what I've always said. You are *my* son. Robert takes after his father. But you mustn't be impatient with Christina if she seems, at first, a little slow, a little resentful of our family. A little jealous . . .

David.

Not Chris!

Mrs. Phelps.

Oh, come now, Dave! I'm sure she's perfect, but you mustn't try to tell me she isn't human. Young wives are sure to be a little bit possessive and exacting and . . . selfish at first.

David.

(*With the trace of a frown.*) We needn't worry about that.

Mrs. Phelps.

No. . . . At first I thought Christina was going to be hard and cold. I didn't expect her to have our sense of humour, and I don't believe she has much of that. If only she will learn to care for me as I care for her, we can be so happy, all four of us together, can't we?

David.

You bet we can!

Mrs. Phelps.

(*Dreamily.*) Building our houses in Phelps Manor. . . . Deciding to put an Italian villa here and a little bungalow there . . .

(*As David grows a trifle restive.*)

But the important thing for you, Dave boy, is a sense of proportion about your marriage. I'm going to lecture you, now, for your own good. If, at first, Christina does seem a little exacting or unreasonable, particularly about us, re-

'member that she has to adjust herself to a whole new world here, a very different world from her friends in Omaha. And you must never be impatient with her. Because, if you are, I shall take her side against you.

David.

(*His mother's subtlety lost in his admiration.*) You *are* a great woman, Mother!

Mrs. Phelps.

You're the great one! How many boys of your age let their wives undermine all their old associations and loosen all their old ties!

David.

Chris wouldn't try that!

Mrs. Phelps.

She might not *want* to. But jealous girls think things that aren't so, and say things that aren't true. Morbid things.

David.

Morbid things? Chris?

Mrs. Phelps.

Only you won't pay too much attention or take her too seriously.

David.

But Chris wouldn't . . .

Mrs. Phelps.

As I said to Christina this afternoon: "Christina," I said "I cannot allow you to sacrifice David!"

David.

Chris sacrifice me! How?

Mrs. Phelps.

Why, by taking you away from your magnificent opportunity here.

David.

(*Rather dubiously.*) Oh!

Mrs. Phelps.

Be master in your own house. Meet her selfishness with firmness, her jealousy with fairness and her . . . her exaggerations with a grain of salt . . .

David.

What exaggerations?

Mrs. Phelps.

Well, you know . . . a girl . . . a young wife, like Christina . . . *might* possibly make the mistake of . . . well, of taking sides . . . in what happened downstairs, for instance . . . and without fully understanding. . . . You can see how fatal *that* would be. . . . But, if you face the facts always, Dave boy, and nothing *but* the facts, your marriage will be a happy one. And, when you want advice, come to your mother always.

David.

Thanks.

Mrs. Phelps.

Now, isn't your mother your best friend?

David.

You bet you are, Mummy!

Mrs. Phelps.

How long it is since you've called me that! Bless you, my dear boy! (*She leans over to seal her triumph with a kiss.*)

from

THE MELTING POT

by David Thomson

From Scene III
DAVID, ROGER

Mr. Thomson's unpublished play is an examination of the relationship of a boy and girl who have found their ways to New York City from widely different parts of the country and equally distant cultural backgrounds. They are the youth of the fifties who have come of age in the early sixties. Together they are trying to heal wounds, both real and imagined, through the relationship. From the beginning it is not a happy relationship. Elizabeth has had an abortion and is suffering the psychic scars of her operation. Roger worries about his provincial background, Tuba City, Iowa, and his lack of a college education. She is Jewish, he is not. He is from a rural home, she from a wealthy Boston family. They move together knowing that marriage for them must not happen until they have determined that "the relationship stands a chance."

The realism of the play encourages the audience to be more skeptical than the characters. The knowledge that they have made a break from the moral traditions they feel they have freed themselves from by living together permits us to remain interested through the knowledge of their alternatives. They have avoided making a commitment to marriage—a condition that carries with it, for them, a finality—a quality of forever. How long will it be, we wonder, before they realize the incompatible nature of their relationship?

Elizabeth's parents learn that she is involved with a boy and drive to New York on the day they receive the news.

313

They have been warned by the surgeon who performed Elizabeth's abortion that she may undertake an affair with someone she knows is undesirable just to strike back at her parents. They see the affair with Roger as the fulfillment of the doctor's prophesy. Roger is not Jewish. That is all they know—and that is enough. It is their duty, for Elizabeth's sake, to prevent the relationship from going any further. The visit has quite another effect and Elizabeth and Roger decide to marry.

The encounter between Elizabeth's father and lover, reprinted here, is the point at which the rational awareness of the circumstances of the play slip away. David attempts to determine the depth of the relationship and Roger responds by throwing up defenses to the obvious question of religion. In desperation David tells Roger about the abortion, "Elizabeth needs help, professional mental help." Roger no longer hears the older man—he feels that David is trying to protect himself by making it appear that Elizabeth is in trouble. There is no understanding reached. How could there be when the first question asked to Roger is understood as being about honorable intentions?

David.

I suppose you and Elizabeth are serious about one another . . . She's told me that you're deeply in love.

Roger.

Yes, we are. (*He turns and walks to the window.*)

David.

How serious?

Roger.

Very.

David.

(*After a pause.*) Just what does that mean?

Roger.

(*Turns to face David.*) It means that we're serious. Oh, I get it . . . you're asking me if my intentions toward your daughter are honorable.

David.

I don't think there is any reason for you to get so smart aleckly about this. I am concerned about my daughter.

Roger.

Then what precisely is it that you want to know? Ah, yes.

No, I am not Jewish. Right? That's what's bugging you.
I'm a goy.

David.

To be candid with you, yes, that does concern me. It concerns Elizabeth's mother as well.

Roger.

If it will make you feel any better, it's a concern of ours
as well. But if you're so concerned about your daughter,
don't you give her enough credit to work out her own
problems? (*He walks over to a bookcase.*) You see these
books? They're all about Judaism. Rabbi Samuels, you
may have heard of him, he recommended them to us.
We've met with him several times. We've read, studied,
it's called, all of them. You see Mr. Stein, in case you
didn't know, it is possible to become Jewish. But you,
you're concerned not with a Jewish son-in-law, but with
what I look like. A goy in your ermine ghetto.

David.

I never said . . .

Roger.

No, but your wife did.

David.

She . . .

Roger.

So get off our backs. If I decide to become Jewish, I'll
let you know, until then, forget it. It is, in short, none
of your business.

David.

Roger, let me speak. We came down here because we're
worried about Elizabeth. We wanted to meet you, the
boy she might be living with. We came with an open
mind. But damn it, son, you don't make it any easier for
us to like you. You're acting like a punk.

Roger.

I wondered when it was going to come to name calling . . .

David.

How much do you know about our daughter?

Roger.

What do you mean? How rich you are? How she's accustomed to living in style . . .

David.

No, that's not what I mean. Sit down. We really should be able to talk about these things. What I'm about to tell you is very hard for a father to talk about. (*Roger sits in the chair and David walks behind him and stands facing Roger's back.*) You see, I really am very deeply concerned about my daughter. Her happiness is my major concern. Yes, her mother's too, although it may not seem that way at times. It's been hard on Sarah—the whole thing. (*Pause as David moves over to the window.*) Roger, Elizabeth had an abortion just before she came to New York. No, don't interrupt me. God knows this is hard for a father. She got mixed up with a guy from the club. I've played golf with his father. Elizabeth swore it was the first and only time . . .

Roger.

(*Getting up and facing David.*) Mr. Stein, I've known about it for a long time. Save yourself the pain of re-calling it for my benefit.

David.

(*Surprised.*) You've known? She told you? (*Pause.*) Roger, I can't tell you how painful it was. You can't imagine the shock. Her mother, Sarah, well she's never fully re-covered.

Roger.

Yes, the memory of that night must be painful. You must have been pretty upset, almost crazy . . .

David.

I was . . .

Roger.

To call her a whore, your only child a whore when she needed you.

David.

She told you that?

Roger.

Yes, and she told me how you went around her bed-room throwing her clothes out the windows.

David.

Oh my God!

Roger.

She's told me about it a hundred times if she told me once.

David.

Roger, you've got to believe me, I never said or did any of that. Elizabeth needs help.

Roger.

Are you telling me that Elizabeth made up that nightmare? That you were a loving and understanding father . . .?

David.

(*The sarcasm has given him strength to collect himself.*) Listen son, let's not play this rough . . . I payed the best damn surgeon in Boston to perform that operation and I paid for the best hospital in Boston. D and C, that's what the record says, just a simple D and C. Cost me over a thousand for that D and C. So don't get smart with me.

Roger

Mr. Stein, I don't care what that operation cost you. How much did it cost Elizabeth, that's what I'm concerned with . . . I want to know why you felt so compelled to tell me about it in the first place? "My daughter had an abortion."

David.

Wait a minute.

Roger.

Wait, hell. I listened to you, now you listen to me. You come down here, drive down from Boston on the same day you find out that Elizabeth might have a boy friend, not a boy to your liking, not the boy next door. You come in here and put your arm around Elizabeth like she still belonged to you. Well man, let me tell you something, you don't give a damn about Elizabeth. All you care about is how you look to other people, and yes, to yourself. Well, I feel sorry for you, all your dreams shot to hell. Your wife has dogs that she calls children, and you don't have a son to take over his father's business . . .

David.

Roger!

Roger.

It doesn't work to come in here and tell me I'm not good enough. You can't scare me off by telling me that Elizabeth had an abortion. I think you stink.

David

(*Collapses into the chair.*) Roger, you've got to understand that wasn't my reason for telling you. You've got to listen to me.

Roger.

Why?

David.

Because Elizabeth needs help, professional mental help.

Roger.

Oh, hell.

David.

Elizabeth needs good competent help, not marriage. It's not just you . . . she can't marry anyone.

Roger.

Are you . . .

David.

It's true, Roger. After her operation the doctor warned me, said that Elizabeth may suffer some kind of nervous breakdown. It's fairly common. He said we should watch for certain signs—signs that she was in trouble. She might have an affair with someone, an older man, someone we could not approve of.

Roger.

You mean me . . .

David.

He went so far as to suggest that it might be someone, well a Negro.

Roger.

You must have been mighty glad when Tom told you I was white and young.

David.

Roger, I don't have to take this kind of abuse. I'm still Elizabeth's father. Elizabeth needs help. I think that between us we can see that she gets it. Her mother and I are willing to pay for it.

Roger.

Decent of you.

David.

I see that you are unwilling to listen to reason. Let me make myself clear. You have made it necessary for me to make a decision. If you and Elizabeth insist on getting married, we will cut you out of any and all monies that

Elizabeth might otherwise receive. You will not get a
penny from us, ever.

Roger.

I see. Is that your last word?

David

Yes, Roger, it is.

Roger.

I see.

David.

I knew you would.

Roger.

I understand what it is you're doing.

David.

You see Elizabeth . . .

Roger.

Is accustomed to a certain standard of living . . .

David.

I wasn't going to say that.

Roger.

You don't have to. Your wife already has.

David.

Style has nothing to do . . . (*Roger does not wait to hear
him out.*)

Roger.

Style. Style. That's just the word your wife used.

David.

So you . . .

Roger.

(*He explodes, as he speaks he crosses to the bathroom.*)
Style. Christ you two tell me about style, about Elizabeth's life style . . . (*He storms into the bathroom and
returns with his hands full of the contraceptive devices.*)
Here. Here's your daughter's life style. Diaphragm, diaphragm cream, jelly, foam, and rubbers, a douche . . .
(*He moves to a closed cabinet and jerks open the door,
pulling out books and pamphlets.*) And these, every damn
book ever written about birth control, about sex. Kraft-
Ebbing, Freud, The Salvation Army, you name it and it's
here. Style you say. Style. Mister, your daughter does
need help and it's your fault. You pimp for her at your
club, and when she gets laid you call her a whore. A
pimp calling his daughter a whore . . . Now you come in

here and threaten us with the only thing you understand—money . . . and you call it style. You're nothing but a goddamned pimp.

David.

Why you little . . . (*He lunges at Roger and then falls back in the chair clutching his chest. He takes some pills from his jacket and puts them in his mouth.*)

from

THE SCHOOL FOR SCANDAL

by Richard Brinsley Sheridan

Act II, scene 1
SIR PETER, LADY TEAZLE

Sheridan's comedy of manners, written to explode the
"sentiments" and sentimentalists that had given the eighteenth-century theater a preaching, "weeping sort of comedy," has held the stage for nearly two centuries. A part
of its persistent success is surely due to its gallery of superbly defined characters. Sir Peter and Lady Teazle are among
the favorites for actors and audiences.

Sir Peter Teazle is old enough to be his wife's father. The
essentials of the situation are thoroughly—indeed, painfully—summed up in that fact. One can fill out the story
with the details that Sir Peter found the girl wasting away
in the boredom of the country and brought her to the ex-
citements of London, that she took to the manners and
extravagances of fashionable society with a greater enthusiasm than Sir Peter could approve of or bear for long,
that she delighted in winning a place in a circle of posturing gossips whom Sir Peter abhors, that the members of
this circle spout "sentiments" of the highest moral tone
while pursuing amours of the most scandalous sort, that
they are encouraging the girl to follow their example, that
she is already on the brink of an affair, and that is
exactly what Sir Peter feared all along. One could add that
Sir Peter, for all his temper, is a good-humored man
among the straightforward men he likes and that he adores
his wife. One could remark further that Lady Teazle loves
her husband (or will discover she does in the course of the
play) and that she is not altogether comfortable when

321

flirting leads to rather more serious propositions. But when one has said that Sir Peter Teazle is old enough to be his wife's father, one has, really, said it all.

There is no prelude to the scene reprinted here. It begins an act, and it *is* an abrupt beginning. Sheridan brings his characters on—into a room in Sir Peter's house—talking, clearly at full voice.

A room in Sir Peter Teazle's house.
Enter Sir Peter and Lady Teazle.

Sir Peter.

Lady Teazle, Lady Teazle, I'll not bear it!

Lady Teazle.

Sir Peter, Sir Peter, you may bear it or not, as you please; but I ought to have my own way in everything—and what's more I will, too. What! though I was educated in the country I know very well that women of fashion in London are accountable to nobody after they are married.

Sir Peter.

Very well, ma'am, very well; so a husband is to have no influence, no authority?

Lady Teazle.

Authority! No, to be sure. If you wanted authority over me, you should have adopted me, and not married me; I am sure you were old enough.

Sir Peter.

Old enough!—aye, there it is. Well, well, Lady Teazle, though my life may be made unhappy by your temper; I'll not be ruined by your extravagance!

Lady Teazle.

My extravagance! I'm sure I'm not more extravagant than a woman of fashion ought to be.

Sir Peter.

No, no, madam, you shall throw away no more sums on such unmeaning luxury. 'Slife! to spend as much to furnish your dressing-room with flowers in winter as would suffice to turn the Pantheon into a greenhouse, and give a *fête champêtre* at Christmas.

Lady Teazle.

And am I to blame, Sir Peter, because flowers are dear in cold weather? You should find fault with the climate,

and not with me. For my part, I'm sure I wish it was
spring all the year round and that roses grew under our
feet.

Sir Peter.

Oons! madam—if you had been born to this, I shouldn't
wonder at your talking thus; but you forget what your
situation was when I married you.

Lady Teazle.

No, no, I don't; 'twas a very disagreeable one, or I should
never have married you.

Sir Peter.

Yes, yes, madam, you were then in somewhat a humbler
style—the daughter of a plain country squire. Recollect,
Lady Teazle, when I saw you first sitting at your tambour,
in a pretty figured linen gown, with a bunch of keys at
your side, your hair combed smooth over a roll, and your
apartment hung round with fruits in worsted of your own
working.

Lady Teazle.

Oh, yes! I remember it very well, and a curious life I led—
my daily occupation to inspect the dairy, superintend the
poultry, make extracts from the family receipt-book, and
comb my aunt Deborah's lapdog.

Sir Peter.

Yes, yes, ma'am, 'twas so indeed.

Lady Teazle.

And then, you know, my evening amusements!—to draw
patterns for ruffles, which I had not materials to make up;
to play Pope Joan with the curate; to read a sermon to my
aunt; or to be stuck down to an old spinet to strum my
father to sleep after a fox-chase.

Sir Peter.

I am glad you have so good a memory. Yes, madam,
these were the recreations I took you from; but now
you must have your coach—vis-à-vis—and three pow-
dered footmen before your chair; and, in the summer, a
pair of white cats to draw you to Kensington Gardens.
No recollection, I suppose, when you were content to ride
double, behind the butler, on a docked coach-horse.

Lady Teazle.

No—I swear I never did that. I deny the butler and the
coach-horse.

Sir Peter.

This, madam, was your situation; and what have I done for you? I have made you a woman of fashion, of fortune, of rank—in short, I have made you my wife.

Lady Teazle.

Well, then, and there is but one thing more you can make me to add to the obligation, and that is—

Sir Peter.

My widow, I suppose?

Lady Teazle.

Hem! hem!

Sir Peter.

I thank you madam—but don't flatter yourself: for though your ill conduct may disturb my peace, it shall never break my heart, I promise you: however, I am equally obliged to you for the hint.

Lady Teazle.

Then why will you endeavor to make yourself so disagreeable to me and thwart me in every little elegant expense?

Sir Peter.

'Slife, madam, I say, had you any of these little elegant expenses when you married me?

Lady Teazle.

Lud, Sir Peter! would you have me be out of the fashion?

Sir Peter.

The fashion, indeed! what had you to do with the fashion before you married me?

Lady Teazle.

For my part, I should think you would like to have your wife thought a woman of taste.

Sir Peter.

Aye—there again—taste! Zounds! madam, you had no taste when you married me!

Lady Teazle.

That's very true, indeed, Sir Peter; and, after having married you, I should never pretend to taste again, I allow. But now, Sir Peter, if we have finished our daily jangle, I presume I may go to my engagement at Lady Sneerwell's.

Sir Peter.

Aye, there's another precious circumstance—a charming set of acquaintance you have made there!

Lady Teazle.

Nay, Sir Peter, they are all people of rank and fortune, and remarkably tenacious of reputation.

Sir Peter.

Yes, egad, they are tenacious of reputation with a vengeance, for they don't choose anybody should have a character but themselves! Such a crew! Ah! many a wretch has rid on a hurdle who has done less mischief than these utterers of forged tales, coiners of scandal, and clippers of reputation.

Lady Teazle.

What, would you restrain the freedom of speech?

Sir Peter.

Ah! they have made you just as bad as any one of the society.

Lady Teazle.

Why, I believe I do bear a part with a tolerable grace. But I vow, I bear no malice against the people I abuse; when I say an ill-natured thing, 'tis out of pure good humor, and I take it for granted they deal exactly in the same manner with me. But Sir Peter, you know you promised to come to Lady Sneerwell's too.

Sir Peter.

Well, well, I'll call in, just to look after my own character.

Lady Teazle.

Then, indeed, you must make haste after me, or you'll be too late. So good-bye to ye.

(Exit Lady Teazle.)

Sir Peter.

So—I have gained much by my intended expostulation! Yet with what a charming air she contradicts everything I say, and how pleasingly she shows her contempt for my authority! Well, though I can't make her love me, there is great satisfaction in quarrelling with her, and I think she never appears to such advantage as when she is doing everything in her power to plague me.

(Exit.)

from

'TIS PITY SHE'S A WHORE

by John Ford

Act III, scene 6
ANNABELLA, FRIAR

Annabella, the daughter of a nobleman of Parma, is young
and beautiful. She is betrothed to a handsome nobleman,
as generous as he is rich, and to the world it seems a
perfect match. But the betrothal is based on a lie. Annabella
is marrying in order to acquire a father for the child she has
already conceived. The actual father, Annabella's lover, can
never be revealed; he is the girl's brother, Giovanni. (For
introductory notes about the play, see p. 440.)

Unwilling to go to the wedding Mass without first having
been absolved of her sins, Annabella confesses to an old
friar, her brother's tutor at the university. And in a scene
in which religious terror is realized with jarring power, the
friar labors to reclaim the girl's soul from the fires of
damnation.

The setting is Annabella's chamber in her father's palace
in Renaissance Parma.

*A table with wax lights; Annabella at confession before
the Friar; she weeps and wrings her hands.*
Friar.
I'm glad to see this penance; for, believe me,
You have unripped a soul so foul and guilty,
As, I must tell you true, I marvel how
The earth hath borne you up: but weep, weep on,
These tears may do you good; weep faster yet,
Whiles I do read a lecture.

326

Annabella.

                              Wretched creature!
Friar.

Ay, you are wretched, miserably wretched,
Almost condemned alive. There is a place,—
List, daughter!—in a black and hollow vault,
Where day is never seen; there shines no sun,
But flaming horror of consuming fires,
A lightless sulphur, choked with smoky fogs
Of an infected darkness: in this place
Dwell many thousand thousand sundry sorts
Of never-dying deaths: there damnèd souls
Roar without pity; there are gluttons fed
With toads and adders; there is burning oil
Poured down the drunkard's throat; the usurer
Is forced to sup whole draughts of molten gold;
There is the murderer for ever stabbed,
Yet can he never die; there lies the wanton
On racks of burning steel, whiles in his soul
He feels the torment of his raging lust.

Annabella.

Mercy! O mercy!

Friar.

                    There stand these wretched things
Who have dreamed out whole years in lawless sheets
And secret incests, cursing one another.
Then you will wish each kiss your brother gave
Had been a dagger's point; then you shall hear
How he will cry, "O, would my wicked sister
Had first been damned, when she did yield to lust!"—
But soft, methinks I see repentance work
New motions in your heart: say, how is't with you?

Annabella.

Is there no way left to redeem my miseries?

Friar.

There is, despair not; Heaven is merciful,
And offers grace even now. 'Tis thus agreed:
First, for your honour's safety, that you marry
My Lord Soranzo; next, to save your soul,
Leave off this life, and henceforth live to him.

Annabella.

Ay me!

Friar.

      Sigh not; I know the baits of sin
Are hard to leave; O, 'tis a death to do't:
Remember what must come. Are you content?

Annabella.

 I am.

Friar.

  I like it well; we take the time.—
Who's near us there?

from

JULIUS CAESAR

by William Shakespeare

Act IV, scene 3
CASSIUS, BRUTUS

The conspirators, led by Cassius and Brutus, have succeeded in their major aim: Caesar is dead. But other obstacles
are yet to be overcome—the forces of Mark Antony and
Caesar's nephew Octavius must be met in the field and defeated, and more important, it must be shown that men
who conspired to murder a tyrant can cooperate to win a
war and hold together a republic. If the leaders of the conspiracy quibble, bicker, and angrily fall out, what can be
expected of the lesser men who follow them?

Brutus and Cassius are unlike partners. The quick-
tempered Cassius, ambitious and too ready to resent the
acclaim awarded other men's achievements, seems a plot-
ter by nature. Brutus, sober and slow to commit himself to
action, a man for whom honor is a way of life, not simply
a word, can never be at ease with subterfuge. But moved by
much persuasion that the Roman Republic could not
survive the ambition of Caesar, Brutus has lent his strength
to the conspiracy and so linked himself irretrievably to the
fortunes—and the moods—of Cassius.

The scene is Brutus' tent in the midst of a military en-
campment. Cassius has burst into the camp and begun to
berate Brutus in front of a startled group of soldiers. Brutus, aware of the damage that can come from allowing
the men to see their commanders wrangling, has persuaded
Cassius to hold silent until they can speak in private. But
as they enter the tent, the anger of both men bursts out.

329

Cassius.

  That you have wrong'd me doth appear in this:
  You have condemn'd and noted Lucius Pella
  For taking bribes here of the Sardians;
  Wherein my letters, praying on his side,
  Because I knew the man, were slighted off.

Brutus.

  You wrong'd yourself to write in such a case.

Cassius.

  In such a time as this it is not meet
  That every nice offence should bear his comment.

Brutus.

  Let me tell you, Cassius, you yourself
  Are much condemn'd to have an itching palm;
  To sell and mart your offices for gold
  To undeservers.

Cassius.

                            I an itching palm!
  You know that you are Brutus that speaks this,
  Or, by the gods, this speech were else your last.

Brutus.

  The name of Cassius honours this corruption,
  And chastisement doth therefore hide his head.

Cassius.

  Chastisement!

Brutus.

  Remember March, the ides of March remember:
  Did not great Julius bleed for justice' sake?
  What villain touch'd his body, that did stab,
  And not for justice?   What! shall one of us,
  That struck the foremost man of all this world
  But for supporting robbers, shall we now
  Contaminate our fingers with base bribes,
  And sell the mighty space of our large honours
  For so much trash as may be grasped thus?
  I had rather be a dog, and bay the moon,
  Than such a Roman.

Cassius.

                            Brutus, bay not me;
  I'll not endure it: you forget yourself,
  To hedge me in.   I am a soldier, I,

Older in practice, abler than yourself
To make conditions.

Brutus.

                  Go to; you are not, Cassius.

Cassius.

I am.

Brutus.

I say you are not.

Cassius.

Urge me no more, I shall forget myself;
Have mind upon your health; tempt me no further.

Brutus.

Away, slight man!

Cassius.

Is 't possible?

Brutus.

                Hear me, for I will speak.
Must I give way and room to your rash choler?
Shall I be frighted when a madman stares?

Cassius.

O ye gods, ye gods!   Must I endure all this?

Brutus.

All this! ay, more: fret till your proud heart break;
Go show your slaves how choleric you are,
And make your bondmen tremble. Must I budge?
Must I observe you?   Must I stand and crouch
Under your testy humour?   By the gods,
You shall digest the venom of your spleen,
Though it do split you; for, from this day forth,
I'll use you for my mirth, yea, for my laughter,
When you are waspish.

Cassius.

                  Is it come to this?

Brutus.

You say you are a better soldier:
Let it appear so; make your vaunting true,
And it shall please me well. For mine own part,
I shall be glad to learn of noble men.

Cassius.

You wrong me every way; you wrong me, Brutus;
I said an elder soldier, not a better:
Did I say, 'better'?

Brutus.

               If you did, I care not.

Cassius.

  When Cæsar liv'd, he durst not thus have mov'd me.

Brutus.

  Peace, peace! you durst not so have tempted him.

Cassius.

  I durst not?

Brutus.

  No.

Cassius.

  What, durst not tempt him?

Brutus.

             For your life you durst not.

Cassius.

  Do not presume too much upon my love;

  I may do that I shall be sorry for.

Brutus.

  You have done that you should be sorry for.

  There is no terror, Cassius, in your threats;

  For I am arm'd so strong in honesty

  That they pass by me as the idle wind,

  Which I respect not. I did send to you

  For certain sums of gold, which you denied me;

  For I can raise no money by vile means:

  By heaven, I had rather coin my heart,

  And drop my blood for drachmas, than to wring

  From the hard hands of peasants their vile trash

  By any indirection.   I did send

  To you for gold to pay my legions,

  Which you denied me: was that done like Cassius?

  Should I have answer'd Caius Cassius so?

  When Marcus Brutus grows so covetous,

  To lock such rascal counters from his friends,

  Be ready, gods, with all your thunderbolts;

  Dash him to pieces!

Cassius.

             I denied you not.

Brutus.

  You did.

Cassius.

           I did not: he was but a fool

That brought my answer back. Brutus hath riv'd my heart.
A friend should bear his friend's infirmities,
But Brutus makes mine greater than they are.

Brutus.

I do not, till you practise them on me.

Cassius.

You love me not.

Brutus.

                    I do not like your faults.

Cassius.

A friendly eye could never see such faults.

Brutus.

A flatterer's would not, though they do appear
As huge as high Olympus.

Cassius.

Come, Antony, and young Octavius, come,
Revenge yourselves alone on Cassius,
For Cassius is aweary of the world;
Hated by one he loves; brav'd by his brother;
Check'd like a bondman; all his faults observ'd,
Set in a note-book, learn'd, and conn'd by rote,
To cast into my teeth.   O, I could weep
My spirit from mine eyes. There is my dagger,
And here my naked breast; within, a heart
Dearer than Pluto's mine, richer than gold:
If that thou be'st a Roman, take it forth;
I, that denied thee gold, will give my heart:
Strike, as thou didst at Cæsar; for, I know,
When thou didst hate him worst, thou lov'dst him better
Than ever thou lov'dst Cassius.

Brutus.

                    Sheathe your dagger:
Be angry when you will, it shall have scope;
Do what you will, dishonour shall be humour.
O Cassius, you are yoked with a lamb
That carries anger as the flint bears fire,
Who, much enforced, shows a hasty spark,
And straight is cold again.

Cassius.

                    Hath Cassius liv'd
To be but mirth and laughter to his Brutus,
When grief and blood ill-temper'd vexeth him?

Brutus.

When I spoke that I was ill-temper'd too.

Cassius.

Do you confess so much?   Give me your hand.

Brutus.

And my heart too.

Cassius.

O Brutus!

Brutus.

What's the matter?

Cassius.

Have not you love enough to bear with me,
When that rash humour which my mother gave me
Makes me forgetful?

Brutus.

Yes, Cassius; and from henceforth
When you are over-earnest with your Brutus,
He'll think your mother chides, and leave you so.

from

THE NIGHT OF THE IGUANA

by Tennessee Williams

Two Scenes from Act II and Act III
MAXINE, HANNAH; HANNAH, SHANNON

Maxine Faulk owns the Costa Verde, a rather casual hotel on a jungle hill above a beach in Mexico. "She is a stout, swarthy woman in her middle forties—affable and rapaciously lusty." Her husband has recently died, but there are still the boys who work for the hotel and there is Shannon, a sometime parson now tourist guide, alcoholic and haunted, whom Maxine hopes to install as a permanent guest of the Costa Verde. "I know the difference between loving someone and just sleeping with someone—even I know that," she tells Shannon when she proposes that he stay on indefinitely, "We've both reached a point where we've got to settle for something that works for us in our lives—even if it isn't on the highest kind of level."

Hannah Jelkes arrives at the hotel pushing her grandfather in a wheelchair. He is a New England poet, "97 years young," and they have traveled the world, he reciting his poetry and she selling water-colors and making character sketches of anyone who will pay. "Hannah is remarkable-looking—ethereal, almost ghostly. She suggests a Gothic cathedral image of a saint, but animated. She could be thirty, she could be forty; she is totally feminine and yet androgynous-looking—almost timeless." Her luck and her funds, like her grandfather's life, have almost run out; but like him she persists, unyielding. She has none of Maxine's sensuality or sexual experience, yet she can enter Shannon's loneliness, understand the "ghost" that tortures him, and free him from the cage of his self-condemnation. And she

335

is responsible for freeing the Iguana, the lizard that Maxine's boys have trapped and tied beneath the verandah until
they can kill and cook it.

Spotting Hannah as a sexual rival (which she is not),
Maxine attempts to get her out of the hotel, using Hannah's lack of money as an excuse. For Hannah the situation
has a very different meaning. To leave the hotel and go
down the hill to the "boarding house" that Maxine recom-
mends would be to acknowledge defeat for herself and her
grandfather. It would be a descent not simply to the town
but to anonymity, to poverty of spirit as well as of material
things; there would be no return.

It is sunset. The hotel verandah and the row of doors
to the cubicles that pass for rooms is "bathed in a deep
golden, almost coppery light; the heavy tropical foliage
gleams with wetness from a recent rain."

*Maxine comes around the turn of the verandah. To the
formalities of evening she had made the concession of
changing from levis to clean white cotton pants, and from
a blue work shirt to a pink one. She is about to set up the
folding cardtables for the evening meal which is served on
the verandah. All the while she is talking, she is setting up
tables, etc.*

Maxine.

Miss Jelkes?

*(Hannah lifts the mosquito net over the door of cubicle
number 3.)*

Hannah.

Yes, Mrs. Faulk?

Maxine.

Can I speak to you while I set up these tables for supper?

Hannah.

Of course, you may. I wanted to speak to you, too. *(She
comes out. She is now wearing her artist's smock.)*

Maxine.

Good.

Hannah.

I just wanted to ask you if there's a tub-bath Grandfather
could use. A shower is fine for me—I prefer a shower to
a tub—but for my grandfather there is some danger of

falling down in a shower and at his age, although he says
he is made out of India rubber, a broken hipbone would
be a very serious matter, so I. . . .

Maxine.

What I wanted to say is I called up the Casa de Huéspedes
about you and your Grampa, and I can get you in there.

Hannah.

Oh, but we don't want to *move!*

Maxine.

The Costa Verde isn't the right place for you. Y'see, we
cater to folks that like to rough it a little, and—well,
frankly, we cater to younger people.

     (*Hannah has started unfolding a cardtable.*)

Hannah.

Oh yes . . . uh . . . well . . . the, uh, Casa de Huéspedes,
that means a, uh, sort of a rooming house, Mrs. Faulk?

Maxine.

Boarding house. They feed you, they'll even feed you on
credit.

Hannah.

Where is it located?

Maxine.

It has a central location. You could get a doctor there
quick if the old man took sick on you. You got to think
about that.

Hannah.

Yes, I—(*She nods gravely, more to herself than Maxine.*)
—I *have* thought about that, but. . . .

Maxine.

What are you doing?

Hannah.

Making myself useful.

Maxine:

Don't do that. I don't accept help from guests here.

    (*Hannah hesitates, but goes on setting the tables.*)

Hannah.

Oh, please, let me. Knife and fork on one side, spoon on
the . . . ? (*Her voice dies out.*)

Maxine.

Just put the plates on the napkins so they don't blow
away.

Hannah.

Yes, it is getting breezy on the verandah. (*She continues setting the table.*)

Maxine.

Hurricane winds are already hitting up coast.

Hannah.

We've been through several typhoons in the Orient. Sometimes *outside* disturbances like that are an almost welcome distraction from *inside* disturbances, aren't they? (*This is said almost to herself. She finishes putting the plates on the paper napkins.*) When do you want us to leave here, Mrs. Faulk?

Maxine.

The boys'll move you in my station wagon tomorrow—no charge for the service.

Hannah.

That is very kind of you. (*Maxine starts away.*) Mrs. Faulk?

Maxine.

(*Turning back to her with obvious reluctance.*) Huh?

Hannah.

Do you know jade?

Maxine.

Jade?

Hannah.

Yes.

Maxine.

Why?

Hannah.

I have a small but interesting collection of jade pieces. I asked if you know jade because in jade it's the craftsmanship, the carving of the jade, that's most important about it. (*She has removed a jade ornament from her blouse.*) This one, for instance—a miracle of carving. Tiny as it is, it has two figures carved on it—the legendary Prince Ahk and Princess Angh, and a heron flying above them. The artist that carved it probably received for this miraculously delicate workmanship, well, I would say perhaps the price of a month's supply of rice for his family, but the merchant who employed him sold it, I would guess, for at least three hundred pounds sterling to an English lady who got tired of it and gave it to me, perhaps because I painted

her not as she was at that time but as I could see she must
have looked in her youth. Can you see the carving?

Maxine.

Yeah, honey, but I'm not operating a hock shop here, I'm
trying to run a hotel.

Hannah.

I know, but couldn't you just accept it as security for a
few days' stay here?

Maxine.

You're completely broke, are you?

Hannah.

Yes, we are—completely.

Maxine.

You say that like you're proud of it.

Hannah.

I'm not proud of it or ashamed of it either. It just happens
to be what's happened to us, which has never happened
before in all our travels.

Maxine.

(*Grudgingly.*) You're telling the truth, I reckon, but I told
you the truth, too, when I told you, when you came here,
that I had just lost my husband and he'd left me in such a
financial hole that if living didn't mean more to me than
money, I'd might as well have been dropped in the ocean
with him.

Hannah.

Ocean?

Maxine.

(*Peacefully philosophical about it.*) I carried out his burial
instructions exactly. Yep, my husband, Fred Faulk, was
the greatest game fisherman on the West Coast of Mexico
—he'd racked up unbeatable records in sailfish, tarpon,
kingfish, barracuda—and on his deathbed, last week, he
requested to be dropped in the sea, yeah, right out there
in that bay, not even sewed up in canvas, just in his fisherman outfit. So now old Freddie the Fisherman is feeding
the fish—fishes' revenge on old Freddie. How about that,
I ask you?

Hannah.

(*Regarding Maxine sharply.*) I doubt that he regrets it.

Maxine.

I do. It gives me the shivers.

SECOND SCENE

It is night. The electric power has been cut off during a rainstorm. The cubicles along the hotel verandah are lighted with oil lamps. The storm has passed and the moon "bathes the scene in an almost garish silver which is intensified by the wetness from the recent storm . . . At one side, a smudge-pot is burning to repel the mosquitoes."

The Reverend Shannon is tied into the hammock. Another guide has taken away his tourist ladies, and in an uncontrolled outburst of anger and guilt, he has wrenched at the cross suspended by a chain around his neck, insisting that it can be removed only by being torn off, and he has tried to run to the beach "to swim out to China." Maxine's boys have caught him and lashed him to the hammock. (For introductory notes about the character of Shannon, see p. 208.)

Hannah has watched the scene with horror, but Maxine insists that Shannon's struggle against the ropes is an act. "He likes it . . . so you keep out of it, honey."

When the others have left, Hannah stands silent, watching Shannon. She wears a kabuki robe and carries a gold-lacquered Japanese fan; at times her attitude has the style of a kabuki dancer's pose.

The first five lines reprinted here provide a useful beginning for the scene. In the play they are followed by a noisy interruption: a group of German tourists, clearly Nazis (the play is set in 1940), rush to see Shannon, to poke at him and make jokes about him, tormenting him like an animal in a trap. Then they leave.

The scene is interrupted a second time, as noted in the text, when Maxine tries to persuade Hannah to leave Shannon alone. But Maxine is called away to pour drinks for the German tourists, and Shannon and Hannah are left to themselves.

Shannon.
  Miss Jelkes?
Hannah.
  Yes.

Shannon.

Where are you?

Hannah.

I'm right here behind you. Can I do anything for you?

Shannon.

Sit here where I can see you. Don't stop talking. I have to fight this panic.

(*There is a pause. She moves a chair beside his hammock.* * * *)

(*The Germans troop around the verandah, laughing and capering gaily.*)

Shannon.

(*Suddenly, in a great shout.*) Regression to infantilism, ha ha, regression to infantilism . . . The infantile protest, ha, ha, ha, the infantile expression of rage at Mama and rage at God and rage at the goddam crib, and rage at the everything, rage at the . . . everything. . . . Regression to infantilism. . . .

(*Now all have left but Hannah and Shannon.*)

Shannon.

Untie me.

Hannah.

Not yet.

Shannon.

I can't stand being tied up.

Hannah.

You'll have to stand it a while.

Shannon.

It makes me panicky.

Hannah.

I know.

Shannon.

A man can die of panic.

Hannah.

Not if he enjoys it as much as you, Mr. Shannon.

(*She goes into her cubicle directly behind his hammock. The cubicle is lighted and we see her removing a small teapot and a tin of tea from her suitcase on the cot, then a little alcohol burner. She comes back out with these articles.*)

Shannon.

What did you mean by that insulting remark?

Hannah.

What remark, Mr. Shannon?

Shannon.

That I enjoy it.

Hannah.

Oh . . . that.

Shannon.

Yes. That.

Hannah.

That wasn't meant as an insult, just an observation. I don't judge people, I draw them. That's all I do, just draw them, but in order to draw them I have to observe them, don't I?

Shannon.

And you've observed, you think you've observed, that I like being tied in this hammock, trussed up in it like a hog being hauled off to the slaughterhouse, Miss Jelkes.

Hannah.

Who wouldn't like to suffer and atone for the sins of himself and the world if it could be done in a hammock with ropes instead of nails, on a hill that's so much lovelier than Golgotha, the Place of the Skull, Mr. Shannon? There's something almost voluptuous in the way that you twist and groan in that hammock—no nails, no blood, no death. Isn't that a comparatively comfortable, almost voluptuous kind of crucifixion to suffer for the guilt of the world, Mr. Shannon?

(She strikes a match to light the alcohol burner. A pure blue jet of flame springs up to cast a flickering, rather unearthly glow on their section of the verandah. The glow is delicately refracted by the subtle, faded colors of her robe—a robe given to her by a Kabuki actor who posed for her in Japan.)

Shannon.

Why have you turned against me all of a sudden, when I need you the most?

Hannah.

I haven't turned against you at all, Mr. Shannon. I'm just attempting to give you a character sketch of yourself, in words instead of pastel crayons or charcoal.

Shannon.

You're certainly suddenly very sure of some New England

spinsterish attitudes that I didn't know you had in you. I thought that you were an *emancipated* Puritan, Miss Jelkes.

Hannah.

Who is . . . ever . . . completely?

Shannon.

I thought you were sexless but you've suddenly turned into a woman. Know how I know that? Because you, not me—not me—are taking pleasure in my tied-up condition. All women, whether they face it or not, want to see a man in a tied-up situation. They work at it all their lives, to get a man in a tied-up situation. Their lives are fulfilled, they're satisfied at last, when they get a man, or as many men as they can, in the tied-up situation. (*Hannah leaves the alcohol burner and teapot and moves to the railing where she grips a verandah post and draws a few deep breaths.*) You don't like this observation of you? The shoe's too tight for comfort when it's on your own foot, Miss Jelkes? Some deep breaths again—feeling panic?

Hannah.

(*Recovering and returning to the burner.*) I'd like to untie you right now, but let me wait till you've passed through your present disturbance. You're still indulging yourself in your . . . your Passion Play performance. I can't help observing this self-indulgence in you.

Shannon.

What rotten indulgence?

Hannah.

Well, your busload of ladies from the Female College in Texas. I don't like those ladies any more than you do, but after all, they did save up all year to make this Mexican tour, to stay in stuffy hotels and eat the food they're used to. They want to be at home away from home, but you . . . you indulged yourself, Mr. Shannon. You did conduct the tour as if it was just for you, for your own pleasure.

Shannon.

Hell, what pleasure—going through hell all the way?

Hannah.

Yes, but comforted, now and then, weren't you, by the little musical prodigy under the wing of the college vocal instructor?

Shannon.

Funny, ha-ha funny! Nantucket spinsters have their wry humor, don't they?

Hannah.

Yes, they do. They have to.

Shannon.

(*Becoming progressively quieter under the cool influence of her voice behind him.*) I can't see what you're up to, Miss Jelkes honey, but I'd almost swear you're making a pot of tea over there.

Hannah.

That is just what I'm doing.

Shannon.

Does this strike you as the right time for a tea party?

Hannah.

This isn't plain tea, this is poppyseed tea.

Shannon.

Are you a slave to the poppy?

Hannah.

It's a mild, sedative drink that helps you get through nights that are hard for you to get through and I'm making it for my grandfather and myself as well as for you, Mr. Shannon. Because, for all three of us, this won't be an easy night to get through. Can't you hear him in his cell number 4, mumbling over and over the lines of his new poem? It's like a blind man climbing a staircase that goes to nowhere, that just falls off into space, and I hate to say what it is. . . . (*She draws a few deep breaths behind him.*)

Shannon.

Put some hemlock in his poppyseed tea tonight so he won't wake up tomorrow for the removal to the Casa de Huéspedes. Do that act of mercy. Put in the hemlock and I will consecrate it, turn it to God's blood. Hell, if you'll get me out of his hammock I'll serve it to him myself, I'll be your accomplice in this act of mercy. I'll say, "Take and drink this, the blood of our—"

Hannah.

Stop it! Stop being childishly cruel! I can't stand for a person that I respect to talk and behave like a small, cruel boy, Mr. Shannon.

Shannon.

What've you found to respect in me, Miss . . . Thin-Standing-Up-Female-Buddha?

Hannah.

I respect a person that has had to fight and howl for his decency and his—

Shannon.

What decency?

Hannah.

Yes, for his decency and his bit of goodness, much more than I respect the lucky ones that just had theirs handed out to them at birth and never afterwards snatched away from them by . . . unbearable . . . torments, I. . . .

Shannon.

You *respect* me?

Hannah.

I do.

Shannon.

But you just said that I'm taking pleasure in a . . . voluptuous crucifixion without nails. A . . . what? . . . painless atonement for the—

Hannah.

(*Cutting in.*) Yes, but I think—

Shannon.

Untie me!

Hannah.

Soon, soon. Be patient.

Shannon.

Now!

Hannah.

Not quite yet, Mr. Shannon. Not till I'm reasonably sure that you won't swim out to China, because, you see, I think of the . . . "the long swim to China" as another painless atonement. I mean I don't think you think you'd be intercepted by sharks and barracudas before you got far past the barrier reef. And I'm afraid you *would be*. It's as simple as that, if that is simple.

Shannon.

What's simple?

Hannah.

Nothing, except for simpletons, Mr. Shannon.

Shannon.

Do you believe in people being tied up?

Hannah.

Only when they might take the long swim to China.

Shannon.

All right Miss Thin-Standing-Up-Female-Buddha just light a Benson & Hedges cigarette for me and put it in my mouth and take it out when you hear me choking on it— if that doesn't seem to you like another bit of voluptuous self-crucifixion.

Hannah.

(*Looking about the verandah.*) I will, but . . . where did I put them?

Shannon.

I have a pack of my own in my pocket.

Hannah.

Which pocket?

Shannon.

I don't know which pocket, you'll have to frisk me for it. (*She pats his jacket pocket.*)

Hannah.

They're not in your coat pocket.

Shannon.

Then look for them in my pants' pockets.

(*She hesitates to put her hand in his pants' pockets, for a moment. Hannah has always had a sort of fastidiousness, a reluctance, toward intimate physical contact. But after the momentary fastidious hesitation, she puts her hands in his pants' pocket and draws out the cigarette pack.*)

Shannon.

Now light it for me and put it in my mouth.

(*She complies with these directions. Almost at once he chokes and the cigarette is expelled.*)

Hannah.

You've dropped it on you—where is it?

Shannon.

(*Twisting and lunging about in the hammock.*) It's under me, under me, burning. Untie me, for God's sake, will you—it's burning me through my pants!

Hannah.

Raise your hips so I can—

Shannon.

I can't, the ropes are too tight. Untie me, untieeeee meeeeee!

Hannah.

I've found it, I've got it! * * *

Shannon.

Now let me try a bit of your poppyseed tea, Miss Jelkes.

Hannah.

I ran out of sugar, but I had some ginger, some sugared ginger. (*She pours a cup of tea and sips it.*) Oh, it's not well brewed yet, but try to drink some now and the—(*She lights the burner again.*)—the second cup will be better. (*She crouches by the hammock and presses the cup to his lips. He raises his head to sip it, but he gags and chokes.*)

Shannon.

Caesar's ghost!—it could be chased by the witches' brew from Macbeth.

Hannah.

Yes, I know, it's still bitter.

(*The Germans appear on the wing of the verandah and go trooping down to the beach, for a beer festival and a moonlight swim. Even in the relative dark they have a luminous color, an almost phosphorescent pink and gold color of skin. They carry with them a case of Carta Blanca beer and the fantastically painted rubber horse. On their faces are smiles of euphoria as they move like a dream-image, starting to sing a marching song as they go.*)

Shannon.

Fiends out of hell with the . . . voices of . . . angels.

Hannah.

Yes, they call it "the logic of contradictions," Mr. Shannon.

Shannon.

(*Lunging suddenly forward and undoing the loosened rope.*) Out! Free! Unassisted!

Hannah.

Yes, I never doubted that you could get loose, Mr. Shannon.

Shannon.

Thanks for your help, anyhow.

Hannah.

Where are you going?

> (*He has crossed to the liquor cart.*)

Shannon.

Not far. To the liquor cart to make myself a rum-coco.

Hannah.

Oh. . . .

Shannon.

(*At the liquor cart.*) Coconut? Check. Machete? Check. Rum? Double check! Ice? The ice bucket's empty. O.K., it's a night for warm drinks. Miss Jelkes? Would you care to have your complimentary rum-coco?

Hannah.

No thank you, Mr. Shannon.

Shannon.

You don't mind me having mine?

Hannah.

Not at all, Mr. Shannon.

Shannon.

You don't disapprove of this weakness, this self-indulgence?

Hannah.

Liquor isn't your problem, Mr. Shannon.

Shannon.

What is my problem, Miss Jelkes?

Hannah.

The oldest one in the world—the need to believe in something or in someone—almost anyone—almost anything . . . something.

Shannon.

Your voice sounds hopeless about it.

Hannah.

No, I'm not hopeless about it. In fact, I've discovered something to believe in.

Shannon.

Something like . . . God?

Hannah.

No.

Shannon.

What?

Hannah.

Broken gates between people so they can reach each other, even if it's just for one night only.

Shannon.

One night stands, huh?

Hannah.

One night . . . communication between them on a verandah outside their . . . separate cubicles, Mr. Shannon.

Shannon.

You don't mean physically, do you?

Hannah.

No.

Shannon.

I didn't think so. Then what?

Hannah.

A little understanding exchanged between them, a wanting to help each other through nights like this.

Shannon.

Who was the someone you told the widow you'd helped long ago to get through a crack-up like this one I'm going through?

Hannah.

Oh . . . that. Myself.

Shannon.

You?

Hannah.

Yes. I can help you because I've been through what you are going through now. I had something like your spook—I just had a different name for him. I called him the blue devil, and . . . oh . . . we had quite a battle, quite a contest between us.

Shannon.

Which you obviously won.

Hannah.

I couldn't afford to lose.

Shannon.

How'd you beat your blue devil?

Hannah.

I showed him that I could endure him and I made him respect my endurance.

Shannon.

How?

Hannah.

Just by, just by . . . enduring. Endurance is something that spooks and blue devils respect. And they respect all the tricks that panicky people use to outlast and outwit their panic.

Shannon.

Like poppyseed tea?

Hannah.

Poppyseed tea or rum-cocos or just a few deep breaths. Anything, everything, that we take to give them the slip, and so to keep on going.

Shannon.

To where?

Hannah.

To somewhere like this, perhaps. This verandah over the rain forest and the still-water beach, after long, difficult travels. And I don't mean just travels about the world, the earth's surface. I mean . . . subterranean travels, the . . . the journeys that the spooked and bedeviled people are forced to take through the . . . the *unlighted* sides of their natures.

Shannon.

Don't tell me you have a dark side to your nature. (*He says this sardonically.*)

Hannah.

I'm sure I don't have to tell a man as experienced and knowledgeable as you, Mr. Shannon, that everything has its shadowy side?

(*She glances up at him and observes that she doesn't have his attention. He is gazing tensely at something off the verandah. It is the kind of abstraction, not vague but fiercely concentrated, that occurs in madness. She turns to look where he's looking. She closes her eyes for a moment and draws a deep breath, then goes on speaking in a voice like a hypnotist's, as if the words didn't matter, since he is not listening to her so much as to the tone and the cadence of her voice.*)

Hannah.

Everything in the whole solar system has a shadowy side to it except the sun itself—the sun is the single exception. You're not listening, are you?

Shannon.

(*As if replying to her.*) The spook is in the rain forest. (*He suddenly hurls his coconut shell with great violence off the verandah, creating a commotion among the jungle birds.*) Good shot—it caught him right on the kisser and his teeth flew out like popcorn from a popper.

Hannah.

Has he gone off—to the dentist?

Shannon.

He's retreated a little way away for a little while, but when I buzz for my breakfast tomorrow, he'll bring it in to me with a grin that'll curdle the milk in the coffee and he'll stink like a . . . a gringo drunk in a Mexican jail who's slept all night in his vomit.

Hannah.

If you wake up before I'm out, I'll bring your coffee in to you . . . if you call me.

Shannon.

(*His attention returns to her.*) No, you'll be gone, God help me.

Hannah.

Maybe and maybe not. I might think of something tomorrow to placate the widow.

Shannon.

The widow's implacable, honey.

Hannah.

I think I'll think of something because I have to. I can't let Nonno be moved to the Casa de Huéspedes, Mr. Shannon. Not any more than I could let you take the long swim out to China. You know that. Not if I can prevent it, and when I have to be resourceful, I can be very resourceful.

Shannon.

How'd you get over your crack-up?

Hannah.

I never cracked up, I couldn't afford to. Of course, I nearly did once. I was young once, Mr. Shannon, but I was one of those people who can be young without really having their youth, and not to have your youth when you are young is naturally very disturbing. But I was lucky. My work, this occupational therapy that I gave myself— painting and doing quick character sketches—made me

look out of myself, not in, and gradually, at the far end
of the tunnel that I was struggling out of I began to see
this faint, very faint gray light—the light of the world
outside me—and I kept climbing toward it. I had to.

Shannon.

Did it stay a gray light?

Hannah.

No, no, it turned white.

Shannon.

Only white, never gold?

Hannah.

No, it stayed only white, but white is a very good light to
see at the end of a long black tunnel you thought would
be never-ending, that only God or Death could put a stop
to, especially when you . . . since I was . . . far from sure
about God.

Shannon.

You're still unsure about him?

Hannah.

Not as unsure as I was. You see, in my profession I have
to look hard and close at human faces in order to catch
something in them before they get restless and call out,
"Waiter, the check, we're leaving." Of course sometimes,
a few times, I just see blobs of wet dough that pass for
human faces, with bits of jelly for eyes. Then I cue in
Nonno to give a recitation, because I can't draw such
faces. But those aren't the usual faces, I don't think they're
even real. Most times I *do* see something, and I can catch
it—I *can*, like I caught something in your face when I
sketched you this afternoon with your eyes open. Are you
still listening to me? (*He crouches beside her chair, looking up at her intently.*) In Shanghai, Shannon, there is a
place that's called the House for the Dying—the old and
penniless dying, whose younger, penniless living children
and grandchildren take them there for them to get through
with their dying on pallets, on straw mats. The first time
I went there it shocked me, I ran away from it. But I came
back later and I saw that their children and grandchildren
and the custodians of the place had put little comforts
beside their death-pallets, little flowers and opium candies
and religious emblems. That made me able to stay to draw
their dying faces. Sometimes only their eyes were still

alive, but Mr. Shannon, those eyes of the penniless dying
with those last little comforts beside them, I tell you, Mr.
Shannon, those eyes looked up with their last dim life
left in them as clear as the stars in the Southern Cross,
Mr. Shannon. And now . . . now I am going to say something to you that will sound like something that only the
spinster granddaughter of a minor romantic poet is likely
to say . . . Nothing I've ever seen has seemed as beautiful
to me, not even the view from this verandah between the
sky and the still-water beach, and lately . . . lately my
grandfather's eyes have looked up at me like that. . . .
(*She rises abruptly and crosses to the front of the verandah.*) Tell me, what is that sound I keep hearing down
there?

Shannon.

There's a marimba band at the cantina on the beach.

Hannah.

I don't mean that, I mean that scraping, scuffling sound
that I keep hearing under the verandah.

Shannon.

Oh, that. The Mexican boys that work here have caught
an iguana and tied it up under the verandah, hitched it to
a post, and naturally of course it's trying to scramble
away. But it's got to the end of its rope, and get any
further it cannot. Ha-ha—that's it. (*He quotes from Nonno's poem:* "And still the orange," *etc.*) Do you have any
life of your own—besides your water colors and sketches
and your travels with Grampa?

Hannah.

We make a home for each other, my grandfather and I.
Do you know what I mean by a home? I don't mean a
regular home. I mean I don't mean what other people
mean when they speak of a home, because I don't regard
a home as a . . . well, as a place, a building . . . a house
. . . of wood, bricks, stone. I think of a home as being a
thing that two people have between them in which each
can . . . well, nest—rest—live in, emotionally speaking.
Does that make any sense to you, Mr. Shannon?

Shannon.

Yeah, complete. But. . . .

Hannah.

Another incomplete sentence.

Shannon.

We better leave it that way. I might've said something to hurt you.

Hannah.

I'm not thin skinned, Mr. Shannon.

Shannon.

No, well, then, I'll say it. . . . (*He moves to the liquor cart.*) When a bird builds a nest to rest in and live in, it doesn't build it in a . . . a falling-down tree.

Hannah.

I'm not a bird, Mr. Shannon.

Shannon.

I was making an analogy, Miss Jelkes.

Hannah.

I thought you were making yourself another rum-coco, Mr. Shannon.

Shannon.

Both. When a bird builds a nest, it builds it with an eye for the . . . the relative permanence of the location, and also for the purpose of mating and propagating its species.

Hannah.

I still say that I'm not a bird, Mr. Shannon, I'm a human being and when a member of that fantastic species builds a nest in the heart of another, the question of permanence isn't the first or even the last thing that's considered . . . necessarily? . . . always? Nonno and I have been continually reminded of the impermanence of things lately. We go back to a hotel where we've been many times before and it isn't there any more. It's been demolished and there's one of those glassy, brassy new ones. Or if the old one's still there, the manager or the Maitre D who always welcomed us back so cordially before has been replaced by someone new who looks at us with suspicion.

Shannon.

Yeah, but you still had each other.

Hannah.

Yes. We did.

Shannon.

But when the old gentleman goes?

Hannah.

Yes?

Shannon.

What will you do? Stop?

Hannah.

Stop or go on . . . probably go on.

Shannon.

Alone? Checking into hotels alone, eating alone at tables for one in a corner, the tables waiters call aces.

Hannah.

Thank you for your sympathy, Mr. Shannon, but in my profession I'm obliged to make quick contacts with strangers who turn to friends very quickly.

Shannon.

Customers aren't friends.

Hannah.

They turn to friends, if they're friendly.

Shannon.

Yeah, but how will it seem to be traveling alone after so many years of traveling with. . . .

Hannah.

I will know how it feels when I feel it—and don't say alone as if nobody had ever gone on alone. For instance, you.

Shannon.

I've always traveled with trainloads, planeloads and busloads of tourists.

Hannah.

That doesn't mean you're still not really alone.

Shannon.

I never fail to make an intimate connection with someone in my parties.

Hannah.

Yes, the youngest young lady, and I was on the verandah this afternoon when the latest of these young ladies gave a demonstration of how lonely the intimate connection has always been for you. The episode in the cold, inhuman hotel room, Mr. Shannon, for which you despise the lady almost as much as you despise yourself. Afterwards you are so polite to the lady that I'm sure it must chill her to the bone, the scrupulous little attentions that you pay her in return for your little enjoyment of her. The gentleman-of-Virginia act that you put on for her, your noblesse oblige treatment of her . . . Oh no, Mr. Shannon, don't kid yourself that you ever travel with someone. You have always traveled alone except for your spook, as you call it. He's your traveling companion. Nothing, nobody else has traveled with you.

Shannon.

Thank you for your sympathy, Miss Jelkes.

Hannah.

You're welcome, Mr. Shannon. And now I think I had better warm up the poppyseed tea for Nonno. Only a good night's sleep could make it possible for him to go on from here tomorrow.

Shannon.

Yes, well, if the conversation is over—I think I'll go down for a swim now.

Hannah.

To China?

Shannon.

No, not to China, just to the little island out here with the sleepy bar on it . . . called the Cantina Serena.

Hannah.

Why?

Shannon.

Because I'm not a nice drunk and I was about to ask you a not nice question.

Hannah.

Ask it. There's no set limit on questions here tonight.

Shannon.

And no set limit on answers?

Hannah.

None I can think of between you and me, Mr. Shannon.

Shannon.

That I will take you up on.

Hannah.

Do.

Shannon.

It's a bargain.

Hannah.

Only do lie back down in the hammock and drink a full cup of the poppyseed tea this time. It's warmer now and the sugared ginger will make it easier to get down.

Shannon.

All right. The question is this: have you never had in your

life any kind of a lovelife? (*Hannah stiffens for a moment.*) I thought you said there was no limit set on questions.

Hannah.

We'll make a bargain—I will answer your question *after* you've had a full cup of the poppyseed tea so you'll be able to get the good night's sleep you need, too. It's fairly warm now and the sugared ginger's made it much more— (*She sips the cup.*)—palatable.

Shannon.

You think I'm going to drift into dreamland so you can welch on the bargain? (*He accepts the cup from her.*)

Hannah.

I'm not a welcher on bargains. Drink it all. All. *All!*

Shannon.

(*With a disgusted grimace as he drains the cup.*) *Great* Caesar's ghost. (*He tosses the cup off the verandah and falls into the hammock, chuckling.*) The oriental idea of a Mickey Finn, huh? Sit down where I can see you, Miss Jelkes honey. (*She sits down in a straight-back chair, some distance from the hammock.*) Where I can see you! I don't have an x-ray eye in the back of my head, Miss Jelkes. (*She moves the chair alongside the hammock.*) Further, further, up further. (*She complies.*) There now. Answer the question now, Miss Jelkes honey.

Hannah.

Would you mind repeating the question.

Shannon.

(*Slowly, with emphasis.*) Have you never had in all of your life and your travels any experience, any encounter, with what Larry-the-crackpot Shannon thinks of as a lovelife?

Hannah.

There are . . . worse things than chastity, Mr. Shannon.

Shannon.

Yeah, lunacy and death are both a little worse, *maybe!* But chastity isn't a thing that a beautiful woman or an attractive man falls into like a booby trap or an overgrown gopher hole, is it? (*There is a pause.*) I still think you are welching on the bargain and I. . . . (*He starts out of the hammock.*)

Hannah.

Mr. Shannon, this night is just as hard for me to get through as it is for you to get through. But it's you that are welching on the bargain, you're not staying in the hammock. Lie back down in the hammock. Now. Yes. Yes, I have had two experiences, well, encounters, with. . . .

Shannon.

Two, did you say?

Hannah.

Yes, I said two. And I wasn't exaggerating and don't you say "fantastic" before I've told you both stories. When I was sixteen, your favorite age, Mr. Shannon, each Saturday afternoon my grandfather Nonno would give me thirty cents, my allowance, my pay for my secretarial and housekeeping duties. Twenty-five cents for admission to the Saturday matinee at the Nantucket movie theatre and five cents extra for a bag of popcorn, Mr. Shannon. I'd sit at the almost empty back of the movie theatre so that the popcorn munching wouldn't disturb the other movie patrons. Well . . . one afternoon a young man sat down beside me and pushed his . . . knee against mine and . . . I moved over two seats but he moved over beside me and continued this . . . pressure! I jumped up and screamed, Mr. Shannon. He was arrested for molesting a minor.

Shannon.

Is he still in the Nantucket jail?

Hannah.

No. I got him out. I told the police that it was a Clara Bow picture—it *was* a Clara Bow picture—and I was just overexcited.

Shannon.

Fantastic.

Hannah.

Yes, very! The second experience is much more recent, only two years ago, when Nonno and I were operating at the Raffles Hotel in Singapore, and doing very well there, making expenses and more. One evening in the Palm Court of the Raffles we met this middle-aged, sort of nondescript Australian salesman. You know—plump, bald-spotted, with a bad attempt at speaking with an upper-class accent and terribly overfriendly. He was alone

and looked lonely. Grandfather said him a poem and I did
a quick character sketch that was shamelessly flattering of
him. He paid me more than my usual asking price and
gave grandfather five Malayan dollars, yes, and he even
purchased one of my water colors. Then it was Nonno's
bedtime. The Aussie salesman asked me out in a sampan
with him. Well, he'd been so generous . . . I accepted. I
did, I accepted. Grandfather went up to bed and I went
out in the sampan with this ladies' underwear salesman.
I noticed that he became more and more. . . .

Shannon.

What?

Hannah.

Well . . . *agitated* . . . as the afterglow of the sunset faded
out on the water. (*She laughs with a delicate sadness.*)
Well, finally, eventually, he leaned toward me . . . we
were vis-à-vis in the sampan . . . and he looked intensely,
passionately into my eyes. (*She laughs again.*) And he
said to me: "Miss Jelkes? Will you do me a favor? Will
you do something for me?" "What?" said I. "Well," said
he, "if I turn my back, if I look the other way, will you
take off some piece of your clothes and let me hold it, just
hold it?"

Shannon.

Fantastic!

Hannah.

Then he said, "It will just take a few seconds." "Just a
few seconds for what?" I asked him. (*She gives the same
laugh again.*) He didn't say for what, but. . . .

Shannon.

His satisfaction?

Hannah.

Yes.

Shannon.

What did you do—in a situation like that?

Hannah.

I . . . gratified his request, I did! And he kept his promise.
He did keep his back turned till I said ready and threw
him . . . the part of my clothes.

Shannon.

What did he do with it?

Hannah.

He didn't move, except to seize the article he'd requested. I looked the other way while his satisfaction took place.

Shannon.

Watch out for commercial travelers in the Far East. Is that the moral, Miss Jelkes honey?

Hannah.

Oh, no, the moral is oriental. Accept whatever situation you cannot improve.

Shannon.

"When it's inevitable, lean back and enjoy it"—is that it?

Hannah.

He'd bought a water color. The incident was embarrassing, not violent. I left and returned unmolested. Oh, and the funniest part of all is that when we got back to the Raffles Hotel, he took the piece of apparel out of his pocket like a bashful boy producing an apple for his schoolteacher and tried to slip it into my hand in the elevator. I wouldn't accept it. I whispered, "Oh, please keep it, Mr. Willoughby!" He'd paid the asking price of my water color and somehow the little experience had been rather touching, I mean it was so *lonely*, out there in the sampan with violet streaks in the sky and this little middle-aged Australian making sounds like he was dying of asthma! And the planet Venus coming serenely out of a fair-weather cloud, over the Straits of Malacca. . . .

Shannon.

And that experience . . . you call that a. . . .

Hannah.

A love experience? Yes. I do call it one.

(*He regards her with incredulity, peering into her face so closely that she is embarrassed and becomes defensive.*)

Shannon.

That, that . . . sad, dirty little episode, you call it a . . . ?

Hannah.

(*Cutting in sharply.*) Sad it certainly was—for the odd little man—but why do you call it "dirty"?

Shannon.

How did you feel when you went into your bedroom?

Hannah.

Confused, I . . . a little confused, I suppose. . . . I'd

known about loneliness—but not that degree or . . . depth of it.

Shannon.

You mean it didn't *disgust* you?

Hannah.

Nothing human disgusts me unless it's unkind, violent. And I told you how gentle he was—apologetic, shy, and really very, well, *delicate* about it. However, I do grant you it was on the rather fantastic level.

Shannon.

You're. . . .

Hannah.

I am *what?* "Fantastic?"

(While they have been talking, Nonno's voice has been heard now and then, mumbling, from his cubicle. Suddenly it becomes loud and clear.)

§**Nonno.**

    And finally the broken stem,
        The plummeting to earth and then. . . .§

(His voice subsides to its mumble. Shannon, standing behind Hannah, places his hand on her throat.)

Hannah.

What is that for? Are you about to strangle me, Mr. Shannon?

Shannon.

You can't stand to be touched?

Hannah.

Save it for the widow. It isn't for me.

Shannon.

Yes, you're right. *(He removes his hand.)* I could do it with Mrs. Faulk, the inconsolable widow, but I couldn't with you.

Hannah.

(Dryly and lightly.) Spinster's loss, widow's gain, Mr. Shannon.

Shannon.

Or widow's loss, spinster's gain. Anyhow it sounds like some old parlor game in a Virginia or Nantucket Island parlor. But . . . I wonder something. . . .

Hannah.

What do you wonder?

Shannon.

If we couldn't . . . *travel* together, I mean just *travel* together?

Hannah.

Could we? In your opinion?

Shannon.

Why not, I don't see why not.

Hannah.

I think the impracticality of the idea will appear much clearer to you in the morning, Mr. Shannon. (*She folds her dimly gold-lacquered fan and rises from her chair.*) Morning can always be counted on to bring us back to a more realistic level. . . . Good night, Mr. Shannon. I have to pack before I'm too tired to.

Shannon.

Don't leave me out here alone yet.

Hannah.

I have to pack now so I can get up at daybreak and try my luck in the plaza.

Shannon.

You won't sell a water color or sketch in that blazing hot plaza tomorrow. Miss Jelkes honey, I don't think you're operating on the realistic level.

Hannah.

Would I be if I thought we could travel together?

Shannon.

I still don't see why we couldn't.

Hannah.

Mr. Shannon, you're not well enough to travel anywhere with anybody right now. Does that sound cruel of me?

Shannon.

You mean that I'm stuck here for good? Winding up with the . . . inconsolable widow?

Hannah.

We all wind up with something or with someone, and if it's someone instead of just something, we're lucky, perhaps . . . unusually lucky. (*She starts to enter her cubicle, then turns to him again in the doorway.*) Oh, and tomorrow. . . . (*She touches her forehead as if a little confused as well as exhausted.*)

Shannon.

What about tomorrow?

Hannah.

(*With difficulty.*) I think it might be better, tomorrow, if we avoid showing any particular interest in each other, because Mrs. Faulk is a morbidly jealous woman.

Shannon.

Is she?

Hannah.

Yes, she seems to have misunderstood our . . . sympathetic interest in each other. So I think we'd better avoid any more long talks on the verandah. I mean till she's thoroughly reassured it might be better if we just say good morning or good night to each other.

Shannon.

We don't even have to say that.

Hannah.

I will, but you don't have to answer.

Shannon.

(*Savagely.*) How about wall-tappings between us by way of communication? You know, like convicts in separate cells communicate with each other by tappings on the walls of the cells? One tap: I'm here. Two taps: are you there? Three taps: yes, I am. Four taps: that's good, we're together. *Christl* . . . Here, take this. (*He snatches the gold cross from his pocket.*) Take my gold cross and hock it, it's 22-carat gold.

Hannah.

What do you, what are you . . . ?

Shannon.

There's a fine amethyst in it, it'll pay your travel expenses back to the States.

Hannah.

Mr. Shannon, you're making no sense at all now.

Shannon.

Neither are you Miss Jelkes, talking about tomorrow, and. . . .

Hannah.

All I was saying was. . . .

Shannon.

You won't *be* here tomorrow! Had you forgotten you won't be here tomorrow?

Hannah.

(*With a slight shocked laugh.*) Yes I *had*, I'd *forgotten!*

Shannon.

The widow wants you out and out you'll go, even if you sell your water colors like hotcakes to the pariah dogs in the plaza. (*He stares at her, shaking his head hopelessly.*)

Hannah.

I suppose you're right, Mr. Shannon. I must be too tired to think or I've contracted your fever. . . . It had actually slipped my mind for a moment that—

§Nonno.

(*Abruptly, from his cubicle.*) Hannah!§

from

THE DUCHESS OF MALFI

by John Webster

Act I, scene 1
DUCHESS, ANTONIO, (CARIOLA)

A scene of gentle comedy, light and warm, closes the first
act of a play of cruelty and increasing darkness. Webster's
tragedy, first published in 1623 but presented at the Globe
as early as 1612, has been called a melodrama; but when
well performed, the violence and inhumanness on which it
seems so often to focus are revealed as neither unlikely nor
unreal among characters inhabiting a universe that lacks the
God-enforced moral dimension it had always been thought
to have—not shallow playwriting but a disillusioned world.
Before the play is done, the Duchess, her husband Antonio,
even the maid Cariola have been murdered. All is dark; the
actions of men in life seem vicious and senseless, the hope
of light after death wan at best.

   In contrast to the blackness into which the play careens
stands this early wooing scene. But the gentle, hopeful
words often suggest a second, darker meaning: *Quietus est*
is an odd phrase with which to seal a betrothal.

   The Duchess Giovanna is a widow, rich, and the ruler
of a dukedom. She is also a woman, young and subject to
her feelings. Though warned against remarriage by her
brothers, one a cardinal and the other a powerful duke, she
falls in love with her steward (the manager of her treasury
and estates) and determines that if she cannot publicly
make him her consort, she will have him as her husband in
secret. The problem, once she has made up her mind, is to
contrive a proposal. As the lady, she cannot be so forward
as to make the proposal herself, and for Antonio, a com-

moner and her servant, to propose to her would be presumptuous. The scene and its comedy are built on the Duchess' maneuvers to get past this ticklish situation in which the feelings of both characters are in tension with the roles society has asked them to play.

The setting is a formal reception room in the Duchess' palace—her "audience chamber" where she receives visiting dignitaries and conducts the business of her dukedom. When Antonio enters, she is apparently alone. However, Cariola, to whom she has told her secret plans, is hidden behind a curtain and can overhear the conversation.

Duchess.
  * * * I sent for you: sit down;
  Take pen and ink and write. Are you ready?
Antonio.
  Yes.
Duchess.
  What did I say?
Antonio.
  That I should write somewhat.
Duchess.
  O I remember.
  After these triumphs and this large expense,
  It's fit, like thrifty husbands, we inquire
  What's laid up for tomorrow.
Antonio.
  So please your beauteous excellence.
Duchess.
  Beauteous?
  Indeed, I thank you: I look young for your sake;
  You have ta'en my cares upon you.
Antonio.
  I'll fetch your grace
  The particulars of your revenue and expense.
Duchess.
  O you are an upright treasurer: but you mistook;
  For when I said I meant to make inquiry
  What's laid up for tomorrow, I did mean
  What's laid up yonder for me.
Antonio.
  Where?

Duchess.

In heaven.
I am making my will (as 'tis fit princes should,
In perfect memory), and, I pray sir, tell me,
Were not one better make it smiling thus
Than in deep groans and terrible ghastly looks,
As if the gifts we parted with procured
That violent distraction?

Antonio.

O much better.

Duchess.

If I had a husband now, this care were quit:
But I intend to make you overseer.
What good deed shall we first remember? Say.

Antonio.

Begin with that first good deed began i' the world
After man's creation, the sacrament of marriage:
I'd have you first provide for a good husband;
Give him all.

Duchess.

All?

Antonio.

Yes, your excellent self.

Duchess.

In a winding sheet?

Antonio.

In a couple.

Duchess.

Saint Winfred, that were a strange will!

Antonio.

'Twere strange if there were no will in you
To marry again.

Duchess.

What do you think of marriage?

Antonio.

I take it, as those that deny purgatory:
It locally contains or heaven or hell,
There's no third place in it.

Duchess.

How do you affect it?

Antonio.

My banishment, feeding my melancholy,

Would often reason thus—
Duchess.
Pray, let's hear it.
Antonio.
Say a man never marry, nor have children,
What takes that from him? Only the bare name
Of being a father, or the weak delight
To see the little wanton ride-a-cockhorse
Upon a painted stick, or hear him chatter
Like a taught starling.
Duchess.
Fie, fie, what's all this?
One of your eyes is bloodshot: use my ring to it,
They say 'tis very sovereign. 'Twas my wedding ring,
And I did vow never to part with it
But to my second husband.
Antonio.
You have parted with it now.
Duchess.
Yes, to help your eyesight.
Antonio.
You have made me stark blind.
Duchess.
How?
Antonio.
There is a saucy and ambitious devil
Is dancing in this circle.
Duchess.
Remove him.
Antonio.
How?
Duchess.
There needs small conjuration when your finger
May do it. Thus (*Placing ring on his finger.*) is it fit?
                    (*He kneels.*)
Antonio.
What said you?
Duchess.
Sir,
This goodly roof of yours is too low built;
I cannot stand upright in it nor discourse,
Without I raise it higher. Raise yourself;

Or, if you please, my hand to help you: so.
(Raises him.)

Antonio.

Ambition, madam, is a great man's madness,
That is not kept in chains and close-pent rooms,
But in fair lightsome lodgings, and is girt
With the wild noise of prattling visitants,
Which makes it lunatic beyond all cure.
Conceive not I am so stupid but I am
Whereto your favors tend, but he's a fool
That, being a-cold, would thrust his hands i' the fire
To warm them.

Duchess.

So, now the ground's broke,
You may discover what a wealthy mine
I make you lord of.

Antonio.

O my unworthiness!

Duchess.

You were ill to sell yourself.
This darkening of your worth is not like that
Which tradesmen use i' the city; their false lights
Are to rid bad wares off. And I must tell you,
If you will know where breathes a complete man
(I speak it without flattery), turn your eyes,
And progress through yourself.

Antonio.

Were there nor heaven
Nor hell, I should be honest: I have long served virtue,
And ne'er ta'en wages of her.

Duchess.

Now she pays it.
The misery of us that are born great!
We are forced to woo, because none dare woo us;
And as a tyrant doubles with his words
And fearfully equivocates, so we
Are forced to express our violent passions
In riddles and in dreams, and leave the path
Of simple virtue, which was never made
To seem the thing it is not. Go, go brag
You have left me heartless; mine is in your bosom:
I hope 'twill multiply love there. You do tremble.

Make not your heart so dead a piece of flesh,
To fear more than to love me. Sir, be confident.
What is it distracts you? This is flesh and blood, sir;
'Tis not the figure cut in alabaster
Kneels at my husband's tomb. Awake, awake, man!
I do here put off all vain ceremony
And only do appear to you a young widow
That claims you for her husband; and, like a widow,
I use but half a blush in it.

Antonio.

Truth speak for me:
I will remain the constant sanctuary
Of your good name.

Duchess.

I thank you, gentle love.
And 'cause you shall not come to me in debt,
Being now my steward, here upon your lips
I sign your *Quietus est.* This you should have begged now:
I have seen children oft eat sweetmeats thus,
As fearful to devour them too soon.

Antonio.

But for your brothers?

Duchess.

Do not think of them.
All discord without this circumference
Is only to be pitied, and not feared;
Yet, should they know it, time will easily
Scatter the tempest.

Antonio.

These words should be mine,
And all the parts you have spoke, if some part of it
Would not have savored flattery.

Duchess.

Kneel.

(*Cariola comes from behind the arras.*)

Antonio.

Ha!

Duchess.

Be not amazed; this woman's of my counsel.
I have heard lawyers say, a contract in a chamber
Per verba de presenti is absolute marriage.

(*She and Antonio kneel.*)

Bless, heaven, this sacred gordian, which let violence
Never untwine!

Antonio.

And may our sweet affections, like the spheres,
Be still in motion!

Duchess.

Quickening, and make
The like soft music!

Antonio.

That we may imitate the loving palms,
Best emblem of a peaceful marriage, that ne'er
Bore fruit, divided!

Duchess.

What can the Church force more?

Antonio.

That fortune may not know an accident,
Either of joy or sorrow, to divide
Our fixed wishes!

Duchess.

How can the Church build faster?
We now are man and wife, and 'tis the Church
That must but echo this. Maid, stand apart:
I now am blind.

Antonio.

What's your conceit in this?

Duchess.

I would have you lead your Fortune by the hand
Unto your marriage bed
(You speak in me this, for we now are one);
We'll only lie, and talk together, and plot
To appease my humorous kindred; and if you please,
Like the old tale in "Alexander and Lodowick,"
Lay a naked sword between us, keep us chaste.
O let me shroud my blushes in your bosom,
Since 'tis the treasury of all my secrets!

(Exeunt Duchess and Antonio.)

from

HIPPOLYTUS

by Euripides (translated by Kenneth Cavander)

NURSE, PHAEDRA

The play is a study of the awful power of passion, of feelings that overwhelm the human creatures who bear them. At the center of the drama are Phaedra, wife of King Theseus but wracked with love for her stepson, and Hippolytus, Theseus' son, as perversely dedicated to an ostentatious purity as his stepmother is to her warped desire. Above stand the goddesses Aphrodite and Artemis, serenely absolute in the opposed demands they make on the men below, the heat of lust and the iciness of chastity. No compromise is possible at either level. The only action conceivable is the compulsive drive to the catastrophic collision of these opposites, which is the subject of the drama; the only escape is death, which resolves the play.

Though the goddesses loom above the scene, the power of the play is not in them, for the focus is on the human characters and Euripides' genius is most evident in his development of the psychology of these passion-ridden beings. The playwright has often been praised for his modern insight into character and in particular for his portraits of women whom we would call neurotic and whom Aristophanes condemned simply as "bad women." Phaedra is one of the finest creations in this gallery.

The excerpt reprinted here comes early in the play. Phaedra has been struck down by some mysterious illness which her friends cannot identify. In fact, she is sick with desire for Hippolytus and with shame for that desire, and she can speak of this to no one. Her old nurse, however, is determined to find the cause, and she knows well how to

wheedle her way into Phaedra's confidence. Coming to
the room where Phaedra lies attended by the palace wom-
en, she begins her inquiries.

Nurse.

Life is ugly and disease revolts me.
Phaedra, what can I do? Have I done anything
Wrong? Look, here is the sunlight all brilliant
In your eyes, and the air is running to meet you. You can
  lie
Here on this couch, that has known your sickness
So long.
You could speak of nothing but coming out here, and now
You will be desperate to see your room again.
I know; nothing is right; even your own desires deceive
  you.
What you have, you do not like, and what you would like
You cannot have. . . .
Oh, I would rather lie ill myself than do the nursing.
Life is simple when one is sick, but nursing
Means the anguish of attention, and work always
Nudging at your hands.
Pain and worry—that is life, a long climb
In which you cannot pause for breath. Maybe
There is something beyond life, that we ought to love
More. Yes, but I cannot see through the clouds
And darkness what lies there. For here is life,
Twinkling about the earth before me, and I
Cannot lift my eyes from the toy—silly child.
We know nothing of another existence, cannot see
A world behind the one we know, for even
The words we use to tell of it, lead us from the truth.

Phaedra.

Lift me up, let me look. . . .
My body feels as slack as a broken doll.
Is that mine, that arm that tapers along the quilt?
Lift it for me, ladies. . . . Why is this coronet so heavy?
Take it away! Let my hair trespass where it likes
Along my shoulders.

Nurse.

Yes, my dear, you are safe, safe. Try not to toss yourself

About so cruelly; remember, you are a queen, and bear
Your sickness royally, calmly, gently.
Life is a struggle; but there is no escape.
Phaedra.
The water! There, coming coolly out of the well . . .
Oh, if only I could scoop up one mouthful of the innocent
    water,
And lie beneath the poplars in the meadow
Where the wind combs the grass, and sleep, and rest. . . .
Nurse.
Child, you must not let your words run wild
Like this; you can be heard here
And you are talking at a crazy gallop. . . .
Phaedra.
Let me go! Take me to the hills,
Up into the forest between the pines, where the hounds
Go roaring in the hunt, nearer, nearer to the running deer
That flashes and winks ahead.
Faster! Faster! Now, this is joy, to shout
And run at their heels, to send the spear rippling past
Your sun-struck hair, to feel the iron
Sharp and eager in your hand.
Nurse.
My little girl, you will break your heart!
Hunting is not for you; how could you go hunting?
And what could you want with streams and wells?
A hillside heavy with rivers comes down to your palace
    walls;
There is water there for you to drink.
Phaedra.
Artemis. She is queen in Limna, where the sea sleeps,
And hooves race and drum for her.
Oh, Artemis, let me come to your long beaches;
Give me a Venetian horse to ride and tame.
Nurse.
Nonsense, child, you're delirious!
First it was the hills, and you made me think
You wanted to hunt; and now you ask
For a horse, to ride over the long sands at Limna
That the waves have abandoned.
We need someone who sees far into the next world,
To tell us what power is riding your mind

And dragging you out of step with yourself.
Phaedra.

I have done wrong; I know that pain.
And my will is wicked, alone on its own path.
I was out of my mind. It was a power, whirling at me,
Driving me to . . . Oh, nurse, I am so unhappy!
Cover my head again; I cannot bear
To think what I have been saying. Cover my head.
I can feel a tear upon my cheek. You see,
My own eyes are putting me to shame.
I know what I ought to do, yet to think of it is agony.
That surrender thought. . . . No, that is wrong. . . .
Oh, I want to die, I want to forget!
Nurse.

Let me cover you. . . .
Who knows when death will do the same for my old
   bones?
A long life is a long lesson, and I
Have learnt that we should be careful how we let
Our affections draw us into others' lives.
We should always have an inner room in ourselves
Untenanted. The heart should not be tethered
Like a convict, but able either to free itself
Or to draw closer to the other heart.
It is a terrible strain to feel for another as I feel
For her, too much for one small soul. They say
A too intense and urgent life is dangerous;
It brings no happiness and blocks its own health.
That is why I think there is some point
In each of us, beyond which we must not pass,
For after that . . . I do not know what lies
After that, but all who have seen life
And learnt from it, will agree with me.
§Women of Troezen.

You are close to Queen Phaedra, nurse, she trusts you.
We can see she is woefully ill, but it is hard to know
What her sickness is. May we ask whether you can tell us?
Nurse.

I know nothing, nothing conclusive. She will not speak.
Women of Troezen.

But the unhappiness is there. How did it come?§

Nurse.

You cannot approach her. She stays alone in her silence.

§Women of Troezen.

How weak she is. Look, how her body is wasted.

Nurse.

What could we expect? It is three days since she ate.

Women of Troezen.

There is something inhuman about this hunger for death.
Does she really want to die?

Nurse.

To die? Well,§ she will not eat, and her life
Is like a rebel preparing to leave her.

§Women of Troezen.

It is strange. And does the king consent to this?

Nurse.

She hides the sickness and pretends to be well.

Women of Troezen.

But when he looks in her face the evidence is there.§

Nurse.

His majesty has gone to Delphi, to the oracle
Of Apollo.

§Women of Troezen.

But try to make her tell you what is wrong,
Why she is so distraught. Will nothing make her?§

Nurse.

I have tried everything, the truth is no nearer.
But I will not give up; I will not be discouraged.
Ladies, stay beside me, watch, and remember.
You will see how I serve her, slave for her, even in her
    sickness. . . .
(*To Phaedra.*) Listen, my darling, we'll forget all you said
Just now, shall we? Smile; unravel the frown
That tangles up your brow. Tell me what
You are thinking. I was wrong to let you lead me.
Now I've changed my mind; I mean to be sensible.
Look, if you are ill, and it is something hard to speak of,
There are women here to help you treat it. But if
You can explain to a man what is wrong, say so,
And we can tell a doctor. . . .
See! She refuses to speak.
Secrets, my dear, are sinful, Am I talking nonsense?
Well, prove that I am. Or am I right? Then admit it!

Look at me. Say something. . . . Oh, you frighten me!
Ladies, this is words wasted. I can do nothing—nothing
We are as far away from her as ever. She is hard.
Listen to me, Phaedra—and only the solemn
Ocean could hear this unmoved—if you die,
And leave your children alone in the world,
Perhaps to lose their inheritance . . . your children
Have an elder brother, a brother given them by the
    Amazon
(Blessed be her name and her power),
Not pure in blood, though he acts as if he were,
Your stepson, Hippolytus. . . .
(Phaedra gives a cry.) Ah, that is where it hurts.

Phaedra.

Nurse, that was cruel of you. I ask only silence.
I beg of you not to speak his name again.

Nurse.

You see, you have your sanity, and will not use it
To see what is best for your children, and your own life's
    sake.

Phaedra.

I do love my children. This raging winter
Has nothing to do with them.

Nurse.

Child, your hands have not dipped their innocence
In blood?

Phaedra.

My hands? No, they are clean. The stain
Lies in my soul

Nurse.

Someone hates you; it preys on your mind?

Phaedra.

He is dear to me. It is not his will, it is not mine;
Yet he destroys me.

Nurse.

Theseus has wronged you . . . ?

Phaedra.

May a sin of mine never come to his eyes.

Nurse.

But something evil is plucking at your life. What is it?

Phaedra.

Leave me to my wickedness; it does you no harm.

Nurse.

You mean no harm. But why do you keep yourself
Alone?

Phaedra.

Let me go! You don't know what you are forcing from
me.

Nurse.

I will know, I will, if I have to stay beside you
For ever.

Phaedra.

You silly woman, the truth is ugly.

Nurse.

Uglier than the pain of not hearing it from you?

Phaedra.

Do you want to kill me? . . . yet death would be an honest
End.

Nurse.

I only ask you because I want to help.
You can't hide it; you must not.

Phaedra.

It is a sick desire, I try all the time
To make it natural and good.

Nurse.

And all the more credit if you tell me what it is.

Phaedra.

Go away, for God's sake, and let go my hand!

Nurse.

No, you have a duty to me. I demand that duty!

Phaedra.

Oh, duty. If you insist on duty, I must yield.

Nurse.

I shall not say a word. . . . Tell the story as you will.

Phaedra.

It was my mother, poor woman, whose love was the first
tragedy.

Nurse.

You mean her love for the bull? Is it that?

Phaedra.

Then my sister, the wife of Dionysus,
Lived through her own horror.

Nurse.

Be careful, my dear. You call them unhappy,

But they were your family.
Phaedra.

And I am the third wretch to fall beneath the curse.
Nurse.

I am lost in your story, Phaedra, where are you leading
   me?
Phaedra.

The evil runs in my blood; it is nothing new.
Nurse.

I have not heard yet what I must know.
Phaedra.

Oh, nurse, you could not bear to say to me
What you are forcing me to say.
Nurse.

I have no second sight, my dear; I cannot read
Your hidden thoughts.
Phaedra.

Tell me, what is it like to be—what they call—in love?
Nurse.

Ah, sweet, my darling, as . . . and yet in the same
Sweetness there is a sting.
Phaedra.

Then I know only the second form.
Nurse.

Do you mean . . . are you in love, my dear? With whom?
Phaedra.

Someone who . . . his mother was an Amazon. . . .
Nurse.

Not Hippolytus?
Phaedra.

You spoke his name, not I.
Nurse.

No! You must not say these things to frighten me.
Oh, I have been fingered by death!
It is too horrible, this life is too horrible!
And the day, yes, you, the day,
And the sunlight I live through—I hate you, hate you
   both!
My body—waste! Nothing! Not mine! Get away!
Die, die! Lovely reason smiles

And kisses the beast it hates, and cannot help itself.
Love—you a goddess! Never!
You are a monster, a growth destroying
All of us—myself, Phaedra, the whole house!

CHAPTER IV

CHARACTER DEVELOPMENT IN TWO OR
MORE SCENES

Groups of scenes for the same characters.

from

A DAY BY THE SEA

by N. C. Hunter

Three Scenes from Act I; Act II, scene 2; and Act III
FRANCES, JULIAN

The play is a quiet drama of lost chances, the past revisited
but not remade, of a spring that brings beauty but no renewal. The lives of nine people cross at a seaside house;
they drift through a morning in the garden, picnic below
the cliffs in the afternoon; memories are raised, great plans
seem possible. The next morning some of the people leave
the house, others stay; nothing is changed, everything is
different, and except for the children, whose lives have yet
to begin, all have recognized their separate paths of no
return. It is a play of resignation, but far from somber, it
is illumined with humorous insight and sympathetic
comedy.

N. C. Hunter is a master of the tightly motivated, under-
stated scene. Perhaps it was this that attracted the finest
British actors of the 1950's to two of his plays. Sir John
Gielgud, who played Julian in *A Day by the Sea,* insisted,
despite a chorus of reviewers, that the play is not Chekhovian. But Chekhovian echoes certainly sounded in the
voices of Hunter's people for whom it is always too late.
And at his best, his meticulously calculated but seemingly
casual orchestration of trios and duets of characters can
bear comparison with Chekhov's plotting. In Hunter's third
acts everything seems to come together too neatly or not
at all. But for actors in search of scenes in which the development of subtext and subtle shading is truly rewarding
this is a playwright to know.

The shifting relationship of Julian and Frances is at the
center of *A Day by the Sea.* Frances, an attractive woman

383

in her late thirties, has come with her two children to have a holiday at Mrs. Anson's pleasant old house on the Dorset cliffs. Frances grew up here; when her parents died, Mrs. Anson simply moved her into the house and here she stayed until she married at nineteen. She has not been back for nearly twenty years, but she has come now, seeking escape from the publicity of a divorce that involved the attempted suicide of the very young man to whom she was briefly married after the death of her quiet rather elderly first husband. To the others, depending on their points of view, she is rather glamorous or unfortunately scandalous. Julian, Mrs. Anson's son, is among those who disapprove of Frances. At forty, Julian is a meticulous officer in the foreign service, as demanding of others as he is of himself, a man with no time for trivialities and no patience for his mother's insistence that international affairs would not go altogether awry if he allowed himself occasional moments for human affairs. At twenty-one Julian was an outstanding young man with a brilliant career ahead of him. At forty his triumphs seem somehow to have been delayed; he has a responsible post, but not yet a significant one. However, when he comes from Paris for a brief visit, he is as intensely (and exclusively) concerned as ever with great issues and great hopes for resolving the problems of the world. He cannot lie docilely in the sun in the chair his mother has specially set out for him, and Frances' presence in the house is an awkwardness he can barely excuse. She was the closest companion of his childhood, but now . . . "What has she turned into?" he asks his mother. "A Woman who takes some stupid youth as a second husband, leaves him after six months, gets involved in his attempted suicide, scandal, divorce . . . Really it's difficult to imagine that she has anything in common with the girl who used to run in this garden. We're simply strangers. What am I to say to her now? . . . It's embarrassing . . . How could she bear to come back here?"

In the sunny May morning, in Mrs. Anson's garden with its azaleas and the oak tree with a swing for the children, the garden table, some rustic chairs, and the one long deck chair with a sunshade for Julian, Frances and Julian find themselves alone. He has been listening impatiently to reports about drainage and a pigsty from the old man who looks after his mother's affairs. Frances comes from the

house with her work basket—"The last day of the holidays
there's always a pile of things to mend and mark." The
old man recalls the summers when Julian and Frances
climbed trees and swam in the sea below the house. Then
he leaves, saying, "I expect you've a great deal to talk
about." There is a silence.

Frances.

(*Darning a sock.*) Your mother put me back in the room
I always used to have, with the white furniture and the
little German prints of the four seasons by the bed. When
I woke this morning and looked round I felt, just for a
second or two, as if I'd never left here at all, but had
simply been dreaming. . . . It's a curious sensation to
come back to a house after twenty years, and see one's
own children playing where one once played oneself. It's
rather eerie—as though one were watching one's own
ghost. . . . What do you think of my children?

Julian.

They seem very nice.

Frances.

Their father was a very nice man.

Julian.

I never met him.

Frances.

Nor you did—I was forgetting. He hardly knew his children, they were so young when he was killed—they
weren't born till the war. . . . He was quiet, reserved. He
used to photograph birds. He could sit for hours in a
ditch or a hedge—just waiting. (*A laugh.*) Extraordinary
patience!

Julian.

I believe he was a good deal older than you.

Frances.

He was nearly twice my age.

Julian.

I should hardly have imagined that that was altogether
satisfactory.

Frances.

Not altogether. . . . On the other hand, he possessed what
was to me, at that time, an exceptional virtue.

Julian.

And what was that?

Frances.

He wanted to marry me.

Julian.

I see.

(*A pause.*)

Frances.

And you've been all over the world, I suppose. I heard of you from time to time. Weren't you Second Secretary in Rome when Michael French was there?

Julian.

Yes, I was.

Frances.

And you've enjoyed it all—the travelling, the life, the work? Has it all come up to expectations?

Julian.

I don't know whether "enjoyed" is the word. I've never regretted my choice of profession, if that's what you mean.

Frances.

Yes, that's what I mean. . . . And do you still paint?

Julian.

Paint? Oh, I gave that up years ago. I've really no time for that kind of thing.

Frances.

Ah, "no time"—it's the old story. As one grows older, so there seems to be less and less time. Do you remember how I used to play the piano? Well, do you know, I've not touched one since before the war. The other day I tried again, but, oh, how painful it was! My fingers were so stiff and clumsy, and I couldn't even read properly. It was depressing. . . . (*Pause.*) It's peaceful here. You must find it a pleasant change from Paris.

Julian.

I'm fond of Paris. One feels at the heart of things. To come back here is like stepping out of the world into a kind of never-never land. No doubt one would get used to it, but frankly I find the change almost too complete. People who live permanently in the country seem to inhabit a sort of vegetable world—it's another civilization.

Frances.

Everything's so slow and quiet. I like that.

Julian.

Evidently you like Paris too. I saw you there a few months ago.

Frances.

Oh? Where?

Julian.

Dining in a little restaurant near the Madeleine.

Frances.

And you never came to speak to me?

Julian.

You were not alone.

Frances.

Would you expect to find me dining alone in a Paris restaurant? (*A laugh.*) What an odd person you are!

Julian.

Well, to be perfectly candid, I didn't think it would be very profitable to either of us to renew a friendship after —after so many years.

Frances.

I see. . . . Then my coming here must have embarrassed you. When I accepted your mother's invitation, I didn't know you would be at home. But we're going to-morrow.

Julian.

I've no objection to your coming here, but surely you must understand that, under the circumstances, it is a little difficult—

Frances.

Yes, it was nearly tragedy. For a whole day they were doubtful whether he would live.

Julian.

You talk about it so calmly!

Frances.

I've lived with it so long.

Julian.

It's true, then—he attempted suicide?

Frances.

Quite true. He poisoned himself with sleeping tablets.

Julian.

Dreadful!

Frances.

For twenty-four hours he was on the Danger List.

Julian.

Such a young man!

Frances.

Yes, he was—very young.

Julian.

(*Moving towards her.*) I really cannot understand how you could possibly— (*Breaking off.*) However, no doubt you prefer not to discuss it.

Frances.

There's nothing to discuss. (*Almost defiantly.*) I was to blame—entirely.

SECOND SCENE

It is late afternoon. A blanket and picnic paraphernalia are spread out on the beach and a low breakwater near which a small fishingboat, now derelict, is drawn up. Behind are the beach, cliffs, and the country inland.

The picnic party has scattered—the children to hunt sea-shells, the elderly to go home to rest, the late-middle-aged to seek out a pub. Frances and Julian are again left alone. But Julian's mood has greatly changed. Earlier in the afternoon a senior officer in the foreign service has dropped in to let Julian know that his services are no longer required in the embassy in Paris. He is to have a London post and later something better. It is clear that Julian has been judged a man not appropriate for important jobs. He has worked, in fact, too hard, been too demanding, "not the kind who goes out of his way to make himself agreeable."

Julian's first response is anger, but as he considers his career his mood changes. "How I've worked!" he exclaims, "How I've worried! How important it has all seemed! Other people could idle and gossip in their offices, but not I . . . And suppose, instead, that I'd sat here for the last twenty years, building sand castles on the shore—would the world be much worse off, do you think? . . . People call me clever, but what have I to show for my forty years of life? Why, the first fool you stopped in the street with a home of his own and a wife and a dog would have more to boast of than I. Well, what have I? 'A lot of his work was greatly appreciated' . . . Think of the stupidity! Deliberately to shun all wonder, all pleasure, even love itself—isn't that to qualify for a madhouse?"

Now Julian sits on the beach, watches his mother help

his very old uncle climb back to the house, and turns to Frances.

Julian.

For many years my mother has been telling me that I work too hard and now, when she's proved to be perfectly right, she's indignant.

Frances.

Does that surprise you? You don't know much about human nature.

Julian.

No, perhaps not. . . . (*Thinking.*) Really, what does one know of other people's temperaments and motives and temptations? Nothing. To be censorious is simply stupid and impertinent. I had no business to speak to you as I did this morning. I hope you'll forgive me.

Frances.

Of course.

Julian.

Do you know how long it is since you and I were together on this beach? Nearly twenty years— (*He looks round.*) Nothing's changed. . . . People who think their lives important should look at rocks—rocks that have stood, say, for four hundred million years. . . . It's pathetic, isn't it, to think how long some of us continue to deceive ourselves. We build a legend round our little lives, put on a sort of permanent fancy-dress, and strut about without realizing quite how foolish we look. Imagine the conceit! . . . Of course, my leaving Paris will make not the slightest difference to anybody or anything. "Anson's gone," they'll say. "Well, he was a fussy, difficult devil. Good riddance." That's all. Suffering humanity will continue to suffer in the usual way, and nobody but a lunatic could possibly think otherwise.

Frances.

I always thought it was the wrong profession for you. You should have been a painter or a writer, and worked off all your romantic notions harmlessly on paper.

§(*Elinor comes in R, carrying a pail.*)

Elinor.

Look— (*Showing something in the pail to Frances.*) I found this in a pool.

Frances.

What is it, darling?

Elinor.

It's called ascidian, Matty says.

Frances.

Oh, yes. Ascidian.

Elinor.

Is Matty really leaving?

Frances.

Yes, darling. She's going to her sister.

Elinor.

When?

Frances.

To-morrow, when you go back to school.

Elinor.

Can she come back sometimes?

Frances.

Yes, I expect she can, if you'd like her to.

Elinor.

Yes, I should. . . . When can she come? Can she come next summer—next summer holidays?

Frances.

I daresay. You're losing a ribbon, dear. (*Re-ties ribbon in Elinor's hair.*) Yes, I daresay she could come for a week or so next summer.

Elinor.

Do you mind if I tell her that?

Frances.

No. You tell her, if you'd like to.

Elinor.

Thank you. (*She runs off R.*)

Frances.

(*Following her.*) Don't go too far away—we shall be leaving soon.

Elinor.

(*Off stage.*) Not yet! Not yet! Not yet! Matty!
(*They watch her go.*) §

Julian.

[Your daughter . . .] She's an attractive child.

Frances.

What will become of her? Has she a friendly star? I often wonder.

Julian.

We mustn't fear the future.

Frances.

No . . . no.

Julian.

(*After a pause.*) When I went to Washington you were still a schoolgirl. Hearing of your engagement came as quite a shock.

Frances.

I was nineteen.

Julian.

Yes, I know. . . . All the same, it seemed absurdly young. Nobody could be expected to know their own mind at that age.

Frances.

Oh, I did.

Julian.

I confess, it rather annoyed me at the time. What could you know of the world? How many men had you met? Why the hurry? Of course, it was none of my business, I realized that, and in any case, I could hardly interfere from the other side of the world.

Frances.

And suppose you had been here, how would you have interfered? I've always been obstinate, you know.

Julian.

At least we might have discussed it sensibly.

Frances.

Oh, "sensible discussion"—do you think that would have made any difference?

(*A short pause.*)

Julian.

You know how one day-dreams, imagining what might have happened had one made some different decision at some time? Well, I've wondered occasionally how you would have answered if I'd asked you, years ago, to marry me.

Frances.

Years ago?

Julian.

Say, before you met Miles Eddison—

Frances.

Oh, then! Why, then I'd have married you if you'd lifted your little finger.

Julian.

Is that true?

Frances.

True? (*Impatiently.*) Oh, don't be ridiculous! Surely you knew!

Julian.

Of course I didn't!

Frances.

And the trouble I took to please you! The dreadful books I waded through so I could talk about history and politics intelligently when you came home from Oxford. The way I walked when you wanted to walk, and bathed when you wanted to bathe, and dressed in the colours you liked, and played the music you chose, and listened while you talked and talked! . . . And you never knew! All wasted! (*Laughs.*) What did you think, I wonder? "Oh, she's a good sort, but rather tiresome the way she follows me about all the time, like a shadow—"

Julian.

(*Embarrassed.*) I wasn't thinking—

Frances.

Of course not. Why should you? There was so much else to excite and interest you in those days. . . . I remember the morning you had the notice of your appointment in Washington. How delighted you were! Washington! Everyone said it was splendid, splendid, and I joined in too— "How splendid, Julian!" and all I could think of was that it was three thousand miles away, and that I'd lost you.

Julian.

I didn't know!

Frances.

No, you didn't know. I remember we went to Southampton to see you off. You kissed your mother good-bye, and then, for some reason or other, you turned to me, gave my hair a little pull, and said, "Good-bye. Behave yourself." And that was as near as I ever got to a kiss from you. . . . And then the hooting of the ship as it sailed—that mournful trumpeting like the voice of doom—and you just a tiny figure, on the upper deck, waving. . . . There's something terrible about a ship sailing—it moves so slowly, slowly, that it drags your heart out with it . . .

(*A short pause.*)

Julian.

And a year later you married Eddison.

Frances.

A year? Was it only a year? It seemed so long!

Julian.

A year! Barely a year! If only you could have waited!

Frances.

Waited? For what? You could hardly find time to answer my letters. Just a perfunctory scribble to say how busy you were. Do you think I didn't turn those letters inside out to find one word that I could twist into a hope? What a year! I shall never forget it as long as I live. I didn't know what to do with myself, and the garden and the shore seemed so dull and desolate that I only longed to get away, anywhere, and never see the place again . . .

Julian.

Surely you knew I was fond of you!

Frances.

Fond? Were you fond? Oh, if only I'd been fond, and not lost, not damned, past saving in love! Perhaps I could have waited if I'd only been fond. As it was, I had somehow to be cured of you, or go out of my mind . . . I was very fond of Miles.

Julian.

What do you mean? You shouldn't have done it! To use marriage as a kind of opium—

Frances.

Why not? I made him happy, was loyal to him, gave him children—

Julian.

(*Sharply.*) You shouldn't have done it! It was wrong!

Frances.

(*Angry.*) Wrong? You find it very easy to make moral judgments! . . . (*A change of tone.*) Fancy exciting ourselves over such ancient history! How stupid! . . . Julian, do sit down.

Julian.

Our whole lives might have been entirely different, if only. . . .

Frances.

Ah, if, if, if—that's a silly game to play . . .

(*Doctor and Gregson can be heard talking off R.*)

Frances.

Here comes the doctor and Gregson.

Julian.

Those boring old men! Let's go.

Frances.

No, I think we'll stay.

Julian.

Why? Come for a walk with me—please! Please!

> (*She hesitates for a second.*)

Frances.

No, Julian . . . no.

Julian.

Why not? Why not?

> (*She doesn't answer. . . .*)

THIRD SCENE

The following morning, Frances and the children are preparing to leave. Julian has been up since dawn, walking in the garden and along the cliffs, and he is ebullient. He is chatting in the garden with the doctor who looks after his uncle when Frances enters. He gives the doctor a look —a signal—and the doctor goes quickly into the house.

Julian.

(*After a pause.*) . . . I have so wanted to speak to you. Twice yesterday evening I tried, but each time it seemed as if you were anxious to avoid it.

Frances.

We all talked so much yesterday—too much, perhaps. The children were very over-excited last night—Matty could do nothing with them. They were delighted to see you climb the cliff—(*A laugh.*) I couldn't help laughing. . . .

Julian.

(*Laughing.*) Yes, it was absurd.

Frances.

(*Looking at him.*) Really, you've changed so little. You're still a young man, just as I remember you years ago. Watching you climb that cliff you might have been twenty-five. . . . Do you know what it is that makes people grow older than their years? It's not hard work, it's not even failure. It's shame, disgust with oneself, living vul-

garly. . . . I didn't mean to talk seriously. . . . You were
out very early this morning.

Julian.

Yes, I went for a walk. In the wood I saw a tree that
was blown down in a gale some years ago. Although it
still lies on the ground, and most of its roots are broken,
its branches are covered with young leaves, and fresh
roots are growing in place of the old ones.

Frances.

(*After a short pause.*) Is that a parable?

Julian.

It might be. I can't help thinking that a life, like a tree,
might renew itself, put out fresh roots, as it were.

Frances.

Yes, but would it ever be quite straight again? Wouldn't
it always be twisted in some way? (*Lightly.*) We shall be
out of our depth in a minute. (*Moves towards house.*)
It's nearly time—

Julian.

(*Stopping her.*) Don't go. You keep evading me, and I
must talk to you.

Frances.

Then—let's talk of the past. Let's talk of what is pleasant.

Julian.

And the future? Couldn't that, perhaps, be pleasant too?
Last night, after you had gone to bed, my mother told me
something of what had happened between you and young
Farrar, and the more I thought of it the more I realized
the extent of my own responsibility.

Frances.

Oh, but that's nonsense!

Julian.

On the contrary, my thoughtless behaviour twenty years
ago drove you into an unsatisfactory marriage with Eddison, and all that followed was a direct consequence—that's
undeniable.

Frances.

Julian, you can't go through life feeling responsible for
the actions of a girl who happened, years ago, to fall in
love with you—without encouragement—

Julian.

No, but to enjoy affection and admiration as I enjoyed

yours, and then to leave, without a thought for your feelings—that seems to me sheer callousness.

Frances.

As if we aren't all callous when we're twenty! Put it out of your head, do—it's an old story. You can explain my behaviour in a hundred different ways, but nothing excuses it. (*She looks in her handbag.*) Oh, I meant to show you —rather an amusing photograph—

Julian.

(*Impatiently.*) Yes, but do you mind, please, not changing the subject? We've little enough time as it is, and before you go I must tell you— (*He breaks off.*) There, now I'm talking to you as if I were giving orders to a clerk, and what I want to tell you— (*Nervously.*) what I want to say, is simply to beg you to consider becoming my wife.

Frances.

Oh, Julian, no!

Julian.

Why "no"?

Frances.

You haven't thought. . . .

Julian.

I've thought all night and I'm sure! And the certainty, and the longing to speak to you, made me so impatient, and the hours till morning passed so slowly. . . . I walked because I couldn't stay still—I felt so exhilarated and the morning seemed to be shining entirely for my benefit!

Frances.

(*In distress.*) Oh, no!

Julian.

Surely it's simply providential that you and I should have met here again now, at this particular moment—

Frances.

Julian, it's not providential at all—it's only an accident. You're reading into our meeting some significance that isn't there. Don't think I'm not flattered and grateful, I am, but really it wouldn't do, Julian, it's not possible.

Julian.

I've been too awkward and abrupt. I understand that now —but in a year, say, when you've had time—

Frances.

No, it isn't that. It isn't time I need.

(*A short pause.*)

Julian.

Then you can only mean that it's not possible for you to love me, or to think of living as my wife . . . is that it?

(*A short pause.*)

Frances.

You think we would be happy, but we wouldn't. You think we can go back to the beginning and start again, but it's not possible, Julian—you're making a mistake.

Julian.

You say that with such appalling certainty! I know what you feel. Because you've had so much unhappiness, you can't believe in a new life—

Frances.

Oh, "a new life"! How like you that is! And do you know how it would end? I should disappoint you, Julian. . . . You believe so much, and I so little! You've such faith, such enthusiasm; you would be always with your head in the stars, and how could I follow? I should continually be lagging behind. . . . You think of me as the girl you used to know, grown older; but I'm not. I'm different, I'm changed. Some sort of flame seems to have burned out, and now I'm just cold and old and empty-hearted.

Julian.

(*Energetically.*) I don't believe it! And if you are I'll change all that! You shall be young again, and all the ugly wasted years shall be forgotten! Oh, for God's sake believe it! . . . Do you know that the only times that I remember with pleasure are the days when you and I spent our summers together here, in this house, on the beach, before I went away. It was always fine then—or so it seems now. . . . Oh, those days are gone, I know, and we've changed, but surely there's something left of them still alive, that might grow into a new kind of happiness. . . . No? . . . Is it so impossible? . . . Say something . . .

Frances.

(*In distress.*) I shouldn't have come here. This should never have happened. If I hadn't come back, you'd never have thought of me, never have wanted to see me again, and that would have been so much better. . . . Julian, dear, listen—take your mother's advice, and find someone young in heart.

Julian.

I'm not fit to share your unhappiness, is that it? Have

I really so little understanding? (*Pleading.*) Stay with me, Frances, please—

Frances.

(*Near tears.*) It's too late, Julian. It's too late.

(*A pause.*)

Julian.

Yes. And it's all my fault.

Frances.

Oh, don't talk like that. We have lived as we have because we are the people we are, that's all. . . . (*She takes his hand.*) Don't be unhappy—don't! . . .

from
THE SHOW-OFF
by George Kelly

Two Scenes from Act I and Act III
CLARA, MRS. FISHER

George Kelly called his play "a transcript of life in three
acts," and the precision with which, in 1924, he recreated
on his stage the sounds, sights, and feelings of middle-class
America has even now a remarkable authenticity. Of
course, his play's continuing years of success are due in
large measure to Kelly's having chosen in particular to
transcribe the comedy of life. Kelly's hero, an egotistical
bluffer who survives despite himself, stands at the center
of the comedy, but he is set off by a group of sensitively
drawn "ordinary" characters caught up in the everyday
concerns of life (and death), who give the play a truth and
warmth beyond the range of broad comedy. (For other
introductory notes about *The Show-Off*, see p. 153.
Another scene is printed on p. 231.)

Kelly's opening scene focuses on two such comic but
instantly recognizable and ultimately serious characters.
Mrs. Fisher—played by Helen Hayes in a recent production—is the mother of a girl, Amy, who has chosen as a
possible husband a man her parents can't abide. Clara Hyland, the girl's sister, is already married; her husband,
as she doesn't mind saying, is a "good provider" to whom
nobody can object.

The curtain rises on the central room—half dining room,
half sitting room—of the Fisher's house. For a moment
the room is empty.

*After a slight pause a door out at the left is heard to
close, and then Clara comes in carrying a fancy box of*

candy. She glances about the room and crosses to the kitchen-door at the right.

Clara.

Anybody out there? (*She crosses back again towards the left, laying the box of candy on the center-table as she passes. Upon reaching the parlor-doors, at the left, she opens them and calls into the parlor.*) You in there, Mom? (*Mrs. Fisher can be heard coming down the stairs. Clara turns, with a glance toward the hall-door, and moves over to the mirror above the mantelpiece. Mrs. Fisher appears in the hall-door and glances in at Clara.*)

Mrs. Fisher.

Oh, it's *you*, Clara. (*She peers out into the hall.*)

Clara.

Where is everybody?

Mrs. Fisher.

I thought I heard that front-door open.

Clara.

Where are they all?

Mrs. Fisher.

(*Moving towards the parlor-door.*) Your Pop's gone over to Gillespie's for some tobacco: I don't know where Joe is. (*She glances into the parlor, then turns and kisses Clara. Clara moves down to the chair at the left of the center-table and Mrs. Fisher moves over to the kitchen-door at the right.*) I don't know how you can stand that fur on you, Clara, a night like this.

Clara.

It's rather cool out.

Mrs. Fisher.

(*Calling out through the kitchen-door.*) You out there, Joe?

Clara.

(*Sitting down.*) He isn't out there.

Mrs. Fisher.

(*Turning around to the cellar-door at her left.*) He must be around here somewhere; he was here not two minutes ago, when I went upstairs. (*Opening the cellar-door and calling down.*) You down there, Joey?

Joe.

(*From the cellar.*) Yes.

Mrs. Fisher.

All right. (*Closes the cellar-door.*)

Joe.

What do you want?

Mrs. Fisher.

(*Turning to the cellar-door again.*) What?

(*Joe and Clara, speaking together.*)

Joe.

What do you want?

Clara.

He sez, "What do you want?"

Mrs. Fisher.

(*Opening the cellar-door again.*) I don't want anything; I was just wonderin' where you were. (*She closes the cellar-door and comes a step or two forward, fastening an old-fashioned brooch that she wears on the front of her dress.*) He spends half his time down in that cellar foolin' with that old radio thing. He sez he can make one himself, but I sez, "I'll believe it when I see it."

Clara.

There's some of that candy you like.

Mrs. Fisher.

(*Crossing to the center-table.*) Oh, did you bring me some more of that nice candy? (*Beginning to untie the ribbon around the candy.*) I never got a taste of that last you brought.

Clara.

Why not?

Mrs. Fisher.

Why,—Lady Jane took it away with her down to the office, and never brought it back. She sez the girls down there et it. I sez, "I guess you're the girl that et it." She sez she didn't, but I know she did.

Clara.

Well, I hope you'll keep that out of sight, and don't let her take that too.

Mrs. Fisher.

(*Opening the candy.*) Oh, she won't get her hands on this, I can promise you that. Let her buy her own candy if she's so fond of it.

Clara.

(*Opening the "Delineator".*) She won't *buy* much of *anything,* if she can get hold of it any *other* way.

Mrs. Fisher.

Oh, isn't that lovely! Look Clara—(*Tilting the box of candy towards Clara.*) Don't that look nice?

Clara.

Yes, they do their candy up nice.

Mrs. Fisher.

(*Gingerly picking up the cover of lace paper.*) That looks just like Irish point lace, don't it? (*Clara nods yes.*) I think I'll put that away somewhere,—in a book or something. My, look at all the colors—look Clara—did you ever see so many colors?

Clara.

It's pretty, isn't it?

Mrs. Fisher.

It's beautiful—seems a pity to spoil it. Do you want a bit of it, Clara?

Clara.

Not now, Mom.

Mrs. Fisher.

I think I'll take this pink one here. I *like* the pink ones. (*She picks up the box and the lid and moves around to the chair at the right of the table.*) Mind how they all have this little fancy paper around them. You'd wonder they'd bother, wouldn't you?—just for a bit of candy. (*She tastes the candy and chews, critically.*) That's nice candy, isn't it?

Clara.

Yes, *I* like bonbons.

Mrs. Fisher.

(*Sitting down.*) I do too—I think I like them better than most anything. (*Putting the box of candy down on the table.*) I'm sorry these are not all bonbons.

Clara.

(*Looking up from the "Delineator."*) They *are* all bonbons—(*Her mother looks at her.*) There's nothing else in there.

Mrs. Fisher.

Oh, are they!—I thought only the pink ones were the bonbons.

Clara.

No, they're all bonbons.

Mrs. Fisher.

Well, that's lovely. I can eat any one of them I like, then, can't I? (*She sits back in her chair and rocks and chews.*) How is it you're not home to-night, Clara?

Clara.

Frank had to go to a dinner of some kind at the Glenwood Club; so I thought I'd stay in town and get something. He said he might call for me here around eight o'clock. I was in anyway about my lamp.

Mrs. Fisher.

(*Rocking.*) Men are always going to dinners somewhere. Seems to me they can't talk about anything unless they've got a dinner in front of them. It's no wonder so many of them are fat.

Clara.

(*Turning a page of the "Delineator".*) Where's Amy,— upstairs?

Mrs. Fisher.

Yes, she's gettin' dressed. I was just hookin' her when you came in.

Clara.

Is she going out?

Mrs. Fisher.

I don't know whether she is or not,—I didn't hear her say. (*Leaning a bit towards Clara, and lowering her voice.*) But it's Wednesday night, you know.

Clara.

Is that fellow still coming here?

Mrs. Fisher.

Oh, right on the dot—such as he is. Sunday nights too now, as well as Wednesdays. It looks like a steady thing. And you never in your life heard anybody talk so much, Clara—I don't know how she stands him. Your Pop can hardly stay in the room where he is. I believe in my heart that's the reason he went over to Gillespie's to-night—so he wouldn't be listenin' to him.

Clara.

Doesn't she take him into the parlor?

Mrs. Fisher.

She does, yes; but she might just as well leave him out here; for he's not in there five minutes till he's out here again—talkin' about Socialism. That's all you hear,— Socialism—and capital and labor. You'd think he knew somethin' about it. And the Pennsylvania Railroad. He's always talkin' about that, too. That's where he works, you know. I don't know what he does down there. He sez himself he's head of the freight department; but as I sez to our Joe, I sez, "I don't know how *he* can be head of *anything*, from the talk of him. Joe sez he thinks he's a nut. And your Pop told him right to his face here last Sunday night—that he didn't know the meanin' of the *word* Socialism. (*She checks herself and gets up.*) I'd better not be talkin' so loud,—he's apt to walk in on us. (*She moves towards the hall-door and glances out.*) He's a great joker, you know—That's what he did last Sunday night. (*Coming forward again to a point above the center-table.*) I never got such a fright in my life. Your Pop and me was sittin' here talkin', just the way we are now, when, all of a sudden, I glanced up, and there he was,—standin' in the doorway there, doin' this (*She points her forefinger and thumb at Clara and wiggles her thumb. Clara laughs faintly.*)—as though he was a bandit, you know. Well,—I thought the breath'd leave my body. Then he sez, "Ha-ha!—that's the time I fooled you!" I don't know how long he'd been standin' there. But, as luck'd have it, we wasn't talkin' about him at the time: altho we *had* been talkin' about him five minutes before. I don't know whether he heard us or not, for I don't know how long he'd been standin' there. I hope he did: it'd just be the price of him, for bein' so smart. (*With a glance toward the hall-door, and speaking very confidentially.*) But, you know, what'd kill you, Clara, you can't say a *word* about him in front of her. (*Clara moves.*) Oh, not a word. No matter what he sez, she thinks it's lovely. When Joe told her here the other night he thought he was a nut, she just laughed, and said that Joe was jealous of him—because *he* could express himself and *he* couldn't. (*Clara smiles.*) You never *heard* such talk. And, you know, Clara, *I* think he wears a wig. (*Clara laughs.*) I do, honestly. And our Joe sez he thinks he does too. But when I asked *her* about it here one mornin', I thought she'd take the head right off me. You never *seen* anybody get themselves into such a temper. She sez, "It's a lie," she sez, "he *don't* wear a wig." She sez, "People always say somethin' like that about a fellow that makes a good appearance." But, *I* think he does, just the same; and the first chance I get I'm goin' to take a good look. (*She moves around to her chair again, at the right of the table.*) He often sits right here, you know, under this light, while he's talkin'; (*Selecting another piece of candy.*) and I'm goin' to look close the

very first chance I get. (*She sits down.*) *I* can tell a wig as
good as anybody. (*She rocks and looks straight out, chewing.*) She won't make a liar out of me.

Amy.

(*From the head of the stairs.*) Mom, did you see anything of that blue bar-pin of mine?

Mrs. Fisher.

(*Calling back to her.*) Which blue bar-pin?

Amy.

Well now, how many blue bar-pins have I got?

Mrs. Fisher.

I don't know how many you've got, and I don't care!
(*Turning back again and speaking rather to herself.*) So
don't be botherin' me about it. (*Calling up to Amy again.*)
If you can't find it, go look for it. (*She resumes her rocking and her chewing.*) She thinks all she's got to do is to
come to the head of them stairs and holler and everybody'll jump.—But she'll get sadly left.—I've got somethin' else to do besides waitin' on her. (*She takes another
bite of candy, and turns casually to Clara.*) Did you *get*
your lamp yet?

Clara.

No, that's what I was in town to-day about. The girl
sez they haven't been able to match the silk till yesterday.

Mrs. Fisher.

I wish I could get somethin' done to that one of mine there
in the parlor; the wire's right out through the silk in two
places.

Clara.

Why doesn't Amy take it in some day. (*Mrs. Fisher makes
a sound of amusement.*)—when she's going to work?

Mrs. Fisher.

Why don't she! It's all Amy can do to take *herself* into
work these days. I've almost got to *push* her out the door
every morning.

Clara.

Couldn't she take it over at lunch-time?

Mrs. Fisher.

She sez she hasn't time at lunch-time.

Clara.

Oh, she has so time.

Mrs. Fisher.

Of course she has.

Clara.

It's only at Ninth and Chestnut, and she's at Eighth.

Mrs. Fisher.

That's what I told her. I sez, "I bet if it was somethin' for yourself you'd have plenty of time." (*Leaning towards Clara.*) But, you know,—what *I* think, Clara—*I* think she's meetin' this fellow at lunch-time. Because in the mornin's here she stands fixin' herself there in front of that glass till it's a wonder to me she don't drop on the floor. And whenever you see them gettin' very particular that way all of a sudden—there's somethin' in the wind. I sez to her the other mornin', when she was settlin' herself there till I got tired lookin' at her, I sez, "You must be goin' to see him to-day, ain't you?" And she sez, "He must be on your mind, isn't he?" "No," I sez, "but by the looks of things, I think he's on yours. And," I sez, "maybe after you get him you won't think he was worth all the bother you went to." Because, you know, Clara, she don't know a *thing* about him; except that he works in the Pennsylvania freight office—I believe he *did* tell her that much. But *she* don't know whether he works there or not. He could tell her anything; and she'd believe it (*Taking another bite of candy and settling herself in her chair.*)— before she'd believe me.

Clara.

That's where he works (*Her mother looks at her sharply.*) —at the Pennsylvania freight office.

Mrs. Fisher.

How do you know?

Clara.

Frank knows him.

Mrs. Fisher.

Frank Hyland?

Clara.

Yes,—he sez he eats his lunch at the same place, there at Fifteenth and Arch.

Mrs. Fisher.

And, does he say he knows him?

Clara.

Yes. He sez he's seen him around there for a long time. I've often heard him speak of him, but I didn't know it

was the same fellow. Frank always called him Carnation
Charlie. He sez he's always got a big carnation in his buttonhole.

Mrs. Fisher.

(*Tapping the table conclusively.*) That's the one; he's always got it on when he comes here, too.

Clara.

Frank sez he's never seen him without it.

Mrs. Fisher.

I haven't either. And I believe in my heart, Clara, that's
what's turned her head. (*Clara smiles.*) You often see
things like that, you know. The worst fool of a man can
put a carnation in his coat or his hat over one eye, and
half a dozen sensible women'll be dyin' about him.

Clara.

Well, Frank sez this fellow's absolutely *crazy*.

Mrs. Fisher.

That's what your Father sez.

Clara.

He sez they kid the life out of him down around the restaurant there.

Mrs. Fisher.

Well, he don't know who Frank Hyland *is*, does he?

Clara.

No, Frank didn't tell him. He sez he just happened to get
talking to him the other day and he mentioned that he
was calling on a girl up this way named Fisher. So then
Frank found out what his right name was, and when he
came home he asked me about him.

Mrs. Fisher.

Well, is he sure it's the same fellow?

Clara.

He told him his name was Piper.

Mrs. Fisher.

(*With finality.*) That the name—Aubrey Piper. I don't
know where he got the Aubrey from; *I* never heard of
such a name before, did you?

Clara.

Yes, I've heard the name of Aubrey.

Mrs. Fisher.

(*Rocking.*) Well, I never did. Sounds to me more like a
place than a name. (*Amy can be heard coming down*

the stairs.) Here she comes. (*She snatches up the box of candy and puts it under her apron.*)

Clara.

Don't say anything, now.

Mrs. Fisher.

It'd be no use. (*Trying to be casual.*) What color are you havin' your lamp-shade made, Clara?

SECOND SCENE

Six months have passed. Amy has indeed married Aubrey Piper, who has lived up to everyone's worst expectations. Somehow, however, Amy seems happy. Mr. Fisher, Amy's father, has died, and the man from the insurance company has just called to give Mrs. Fisher a check for the life insurance. He has rather surprised Clara and Mrs. Fisher by telling them that Mr. Piper has inquired about a large accident policy for himself; Mr. Piper, as the ladies know, can't afford a policy of any size, much less an impressive one.

As Clara, having seen the insurance man out, closes the hall door, Mrs. Fisher turns, removing the glasses she needed to read the business papers, and moves toward the mantelpiece.

Mrs. Fisher.

* * * I'm glad you were here; I don't understand them insurance papers. (*She puts her glasses on the mantelpiece.*)

Clara.

(*Moving to the chair at the right of the center-table.*) What do you think you'll do with that money, Mom?

Mrs. Fisher.

Why, I think I'll just put it into a bank somewhere; everything is paid. And then I'll have something in my old days. (*She comes forward to the chair at the left of the center-table.*)

Clara.

Do you want me to put the check right into the bank?

Mrs. Fisher.

No,—I want to see the money first. (*She sits down.*) But, can you imagine that clown, Clara, takin' up that man's time talkin' about a fifty-thousand dollar policy; and him in debt to his eyes.

Clara.

(*Sitting down.*) What does it matter, Mom; you can
never change a man like Piper.

Mrs. Fisher.

No, but I hate to see him makin' such a fool of Amy; and
of all of us,—with his name in all the papers, and the
whole city laughin' at him.

Clara.

He doesn't mind that, he likes it.

Mrs. Fisher.

But, Amy's married to him, Clara,—that's the trouble.

Clara.

Amy doesn't mind it either, Mom, as long as its Aubrey.

Mrs. Fisher.

Well, she ought to mind it, if she's got any pride.

Clara.

(*Looking straight ahead, wistfully.*) She's in love with him,
Mom—she doesn't see him through the same eyes that
other people do.

Mrs. Fisher.

You're always talkin' about love; you give me a pain.

Clara.

Well, don't you think she is?

Mrs. Fisher.

How do *I* know whether she is or not? I don't know anything about when people are in love; except that they
act silly—most everybody that I ever knew that was. I'm
sure *she* acted silly enough when she took *him.*

Clara.

She might have taken worse, Mom. (*Mrs. Fisher looks at
her; and Clara meets the look.*) He does his best. He
works every day, and he gives her his money; and nobody
ever heard of him looking at another woman.

Mrs. Fisher.

But, he's such a rattle-brain, Clara.

Clara.

Oh, there are lots of things that are harder to put up with
in a man than that, Mom. I know he's terribly silly, and
has too much to say, and all that, but,—I don't know, I
feel kind of sorry for him sometimes. He'd so love to be
important; and, of course, he never will be.

Mrs. Fisher.

Well, I swear I don't know how Amy stands the everlastin' talk of his. He's been here now only a week, and I'm tellin' you, Clara, I'm nearly light-headed. I'll be glad when they go.

Clara.

I'd rather have a man that talked to much than one of those silent ones. Honestly, Mom, I think sometimes if Frank Hyland doesn't *say* something I'll go out of my mind.

Mrs. Fisher.

What do you want him to say?

Clara.

Anything; just so I'd know he had a voice.

Mrs. Fisher.

He's too sensible a man, Clara, to be talkin' when he has nothin' to say.

Clara.

I don't think it's so sensible, Mom, never to have anything to say.

Mrs. Fisher.

Well, lot's of men are that way in the house.

Clara.

But there are usually children there,—it isn't so bad.

Mrs. Fisher.

Well, if Amy ever has any children, and they have as much to say as their Father, I don't know what'll become of her.

Clara.

She'll get along some way; people always do.

Mrs. Fisher.

Leanin' on somebody else,—*that's* how they get along.

Clara.

There are always the Leaners and the Bearers, Mom. But, if she's in love with the man she's married to,—and he's in love with her,—and there are children——

Mrs. Fisher.

I never saw a married woman so full of love.

Clara.

I suppose that's because I never had any of it, Mom. (*Her mother looks over at her.*)

Mrs. Fisher.

Don't your man love you? (*Clara looks straight out, shaking her head slowly.*)

Clara.

He loved someone else before he met me.

Mrs. Fisher.

How do you know?

Clara.

The way he talks sometimes.

Mrs. Fisher.

Why didn't he marry her?

Clara.

I think he lost her. I remember he said to me one time—
"Always be kind, Clara, to anybody that loves you; for,"
he said, "a person always loses what he doesn't appreciate.
And," he said, "it's a *terrible* thing to lose love." He said,
"You never realize what it was worth until you've lost it."
I think that's the reason he gives Piper a hand once in a
while,—because he sees Amy's in love with him, and he
wants to make it easy for her; because I have an idea he
made it pretty hard for the woman that loved him. (*Mrs.
Fisher leans back and rocks slowly.*)

Mrs. Fisher.

Well, a body can't have everything in this world, Clara.

Copies of this play, in individual paper covered acting editions, are
available from Samuel French, Inc., 25 W. 45th St., New York,
N. Y. or 7623 Sunset Blvd., Hollywood, Calif. or in Canada Samuel
French (Canada) Ltd., 26 Grenville St., Toronto, Canada.

from

AFTER THE FALL

by Arthur Miller

Four Scenes from Act I and Act II
QUENTIN, MAGGIE

The action of the play takes place in the mind, thought,
and memory of its leading character. Though Miller had
originally imagined *Death of a Salesman* as a drama in
Willy Loman's head, *After the Fall* is more obviously set in
a landscape of the mind. The characters appear and fade
as they cross Quentin's thoughts, at times inserting a
single echoing word or idea into the pattern, at times overlapping as they do in Quentin's memory but did not in
actual time.

The play is Quentin's quest for a meaning, a search for
"a moment which he thinks he once had and which he
knows he must find again, the moment when his life, and
presumably life itself, cohered into form." It is a long
conversation with an invisible "Listener," for whom the
audience stands in. It takes place on a raked stage, almost
bare, though in the background stands "the blasted stone
tower of a German concentration camp." In the mental
background are other signs of inhumanity—friends betrayed by friends, lovers who no longer love, the complex
of infidelities, guilts, and demands of brothers, parents
and wives. There was a time—but no longer—"when there
were good people and bad people. And how easy it was to
tell! . . . Like some kind of paradise compared to this."
Yet the problem of placing responsibility remains, and in
the foreground a decision: dare Quentin, after two unsuccessful marriages, risk hurting another person, as he
knows he can, by marrying again? (For Quentin's opening
description of himself, see p. 97.)

Commissioned for the first production of the Lincoln

Center Repertory Company, the clearly autobiographical play won great interest, but the critics were cautious with their praise. The author's emotions and ideas are perhaps too close to the surface, too little shaped into a drama. But at times the play crystallizes into splendid, fully realized scenes, and the episodes recalling Quentin's meeting and marriage with his second wife, Maggie, are particularly strong.

The first sharp memory of Maggie is of an encounter on a park bench—on Fifth Avenue, perhaps, beside Central Park—with buses running along the avenue beyond. Angry with his wife, Louise, and facing problems in his law firm because he has agreed to represent an old friend who has been called to testify before a McCarthy-era congressional hearing, Quentin pauses on his way home to look at the people lounging and walking in the park. "Whatever made me think," he says to himself, "that at the end of the day I absolutely had to go home?" And he sits on the bench. Maggie appears, young and pretty, looking about for someone. "Now there's truth," Quentin thinks, "symmetrical, lovely skin, undeniable." Maggie turns to him and speaks.

Maggie.

'Scuse me, did you see a man with a big dog?

Quentin.

No. But I saw a woman with a little bird.

Maggie.

No, that's not him. Is this the bus stop?

Quentin.

Ya, the sign says—

Maggie.

(*Sitting beside him.*) I was standing over there and a man came with this big dog and just put the leash in my hand and walked away. So I started to go after him but the dog wouldn't move. And then this other man came and took the leash and went away. But I don't think it's really his dog. I think it's the first man's dog.

Quentin.

But he obviously doesn't want it.

Maggie.

But maybe he wanted for me to have it. I think the other man just saw it happening and figured he could get a free dog.

Quentin.

Well, you want the dog?

Maggie.

How could I keep a dog? I don't even think they allow dogs where I live. What bus is this?

Quentin.

Fifth Avenue. This is the downtown side. Where do you want to go?

Maggie.

(*After thinking.*) Well, I could go there.

Quentin.

Where?

Maggie.

Downtown.

Quentin.

Lot of funny things go on, don't they?

Maggie.

Well, he probably figured I would like a dog. Whereas I would if I had a way to keep it, but I don't even have a refrigerator.

Quentin.

Yes. That must be it. I guess he thought you had a refrigerator.

(*She shrugs. Pause. He looks at her as she watches for the bus. He has no more to say.*)

Louise.

(*Appearing.*) You don't talk to any woman—not like a *woman!* You think reading your brief is *talking* to me?

(*She exits. In tension Quentin leans forward, arms resting on his knees. He looks at Maggie again.*)

Quentin.

(*With an effort.*) What do you do?

Maggie.

(*As though he should know.*) On the switchboard. (*Laughs.*) Don't you remember me?

Quentin.

(*Surprised.*) Me?

Maggie.

I always sort of nod to you every morning through the window.

Quentin.

(*After an instant.*) Oh. In the reception room!

Maggie.

Sure! Maggie! (*Points to herself.*)

Quentin.

Of course! You get my numbers sometimes.

Maggie.

Did you think I just came up and started talking to you?

Quentin.

I had no idea.

Maggie.

(*Laughs.*) Well, what must you have thought! I guess it's that you never saw me altogether. I mean just my head through that little window.

Quentin.

Well, it's nice to meet all of you, finally.

Maggie.

(*Laughs.*) You go back to work again tonight?

Quentin.

No, I'm just resting for a few minutes.

Maggie.

(*With a sense of his loneliness.*) Oh. That's nice to do that. (*She looks idly about. He glances down her body as she rises.*) Is that my bus down there?

Quentin.

I'm not really sure where you want to go. . . .

(*A man apepars, eyes her, glances up toward the bus, back to her, staring.*)

Maggie.

I wanted to find one of those discount stores; I just bought a phonograph but I only have one record. I'll see you! (*She is half backing off toward the man.*)

Man.

There's one on Twenty-seventh and Sixth Avenue.

Maggie.

(*Turning, surprised.*) Oh, thanks!

Quentin.

(*Standing.*) There's a record store around the corner, you know.

Maggie.

But is it discount?

Quentin.

Well, they all discount—

Man.

(*Slipping his hand under her arm.*) What, ten per cent? Come on, honey, I'll get you an easy fifty per cent off.

Maggie.

(*To the man, starting to move off with him.*) Really? But a Perry Sullivan . . . ?

Man.

Look, I'll give it to you—I'll give you two Perry Sullivans. Come on!

Maggie.

(*She halts, suddenly aware, disengages her arm, backs.*) 'Scuse me, I—I—forgot something.

Man.

(*Reaching toward her.*) Look, I'll give you ten records. (*Calls off.*) Hold that door! (*Grabs her.*) Come on!

Quentin.

(*Moving toward him.*) Hey!

Man.

(*Letting her go, to Quentin.*) Ah, get lost! (*He rushes off.*) Hold it, hold the door!

(*Quentin watches the "bus" go by, then turns to her. She is absorbed in arranging her hair—but with a strangely doughy expression, removed.*)

Quentin.

I'm sorry, I thought you knew him.

Maggie.

No. I never saw him.

Quentin.

Well—what were you going with him for?

Maggie.

He said he knew a store. Where's the one you're talking about?

Quentin.

I'll have to think a minute. Let's see . . .

Maggie.

Could I sit with you? While you're thinking?

Quentin.

Sure!

(*They return to the bench. He waits till she is seated; she is aware of the politeness, glances at him as he sits. Then she looks at him fully, for some reason amazed.*)

That happen to you very often?

Maggie.

(*Factually.*) Pretty often.

Quentin.

It's because you talk to them.

Maggie.

But they talk to me, so I have to answer.

Quentin.

Not if they're rude. Just turn your back.

Maggie.

(*She thinks about that, and indecisively.*) Oh, okay. (*As though remotely aware of another world, his world.*) Thanks, though—for stopping it.

Quentin.

Well, anybody would.

Maggie.

No, they laugh. I'm a joke to them. You—going to rest here very long?

Quentin.

Just a few minutes. I'm on my way home—I never did this before.

Maggie.

Oh! You look like you always did. Like you could sit for hours under these trees, just thinking.

Quentin.

No. I usually go right home. (*Grinning.*) I've always gone right home.

Maggie.

See, I'm still paying for the phonograph, whereas they don't sell records on time, you know.

Quentin.

They're afraid they'll wear out, I guess.

Maggie.

Oh, that must be it! I always wondered. 'Cause you *can* get phonographs. How'd you know that?

Quentin.

I'm just guessing.

Maggie.

(*Laughing.*) I can never guess those things! I don't know why they do anything half the time! (*She laughs more deeply. He does.*) I had about ten or twenty records in Washington, but my friend got sick, and I had to leave. (*Pause. Thinks.*) His family lived right over there on Park Avenue.

Quentin.

Oh. Is he better?

Maggie.

He died. (*Tears come into her eyes quite suddenly.*)

Quentin.

(*Entirely perplexed.*) When was this?

Maggie.

Friday. Remember they closed the office for the day?

Quentin.

You mean—(*Astounded.*)—Judge Cruse?

Maggie.

Ya.

Quentin.

Oh, I didn't know that you—

Maggie.

Yeah.

Quentin.

He was a great lawyer. And a great judge too.

Maggie.

(*Rubbing tears away.*) He was very nice to me.

Quentin.

I was at the funeral; I didn't see you, though.

Maggie.

(*With difficulty against her tears.*) His wife wouldn't let me come. I got into the hospital before he died. But the family pushed me out and—I could hear him calling, "Maggie . . . Maggie!" (*Pause.*) They kept trying to offer me a thousand dollars. But I didn't want anything, I just wanted to say goodby to him! (*She opens her purse, takes out an office envelope, opens it.*) I have a little of the dirt. See? That's from his grave. His chauffeur drove me out— Alexander.

Quentin.

Did you love him very much?

Maggie.

No. In fact, a couple of times I really left him.

Quentin.

Why didn't you altogether?

Maggie.

He didn't want me to.

Quentin.

Oh. (*Pause.*) So what are you going to do now?

Maggie.

I'd love to get that record if I knew where they had a discount—

Quentin.

No, I mean in general.

Maggie.

Why, they going to fire me now?

Quentin.

Oh, I wouldn't know about that.

Maggie.

Although I'm not worried. Whereas I can always go back to hair.

Quentin.

To where?

Maggie.

I used to demonstrate hair preparations. (*Laughs, squirts her hair with an imaginary bottle.*) You know, in department stores? I was almost on TV once. (*Tilting her head under his chin.*) It's because I have very thick hair, you see? I have my mother's hair. And it's not broken. You notice I have no broken hair? Most women's hair is broken. Here, feel it, feel how—(*She has lifted his hand to her head and suddenly lets go of it.*) Oh, 'scuse me!

Quentin.

That's all right!

Maggie.

I just thought you might want to feel it.

Quentin.

Sure.

Maggie.

Go ahead. I mean if you want to. (*She leans her head to him again. He touches the top of her head.*)

Quentin.

It is, ya! Very soft.

Maggie.

(*Proudly.*) I once went from page boy to bouffant in less than ten minutes!

Quentin.

What made you quit?

(*A student sitting nearby looks at her.*)

Maggie.

They start sending me to conventions and all. You're supposed to entertain, you see.

Quentin.

Oh yes.

Maggie.

There were parts of it I didn't like—any more. (*She looks at the student, who turns away in embarrassment.*) Aren't they sweet when they look up from their books!

(The student walks off, mortified. She turns with a laugh to Quentin. He looks at her warmly, smiling. A clock strikes eight in a distant tower.)

Quentin.

Well, I've got to go now.

Maggie.

'Scuse me I put your hand on my head.

Quentin.

Oh, that's all right. I'm not *that* bad. *(He laughs softly, embarassed.)*

Maggie.

It's not bad to be shy.

> *(Pause. They look at each other.)*

Quentin.

You're very beautiful, Maggie.

> *(She smiles, straightens as though his words had entered her.)*

And I wish you knew how to take care of yourself.

Maggie.

Oh . . . *(Holding a ripped seam in her dress.)* I got this torn on the bus this morning. I'm going to sew it home.

Quentin.

I don't mean that.

> *(She meets his eyes again—she looks chastised.)*

Not that I'm criticizing you. I'm not at all. You understand?

> *(She nods, absorbed in his face.)*

Maggie.

I understand. I think I'll take a walk in the park.

Quentin.

You shouldn't. It's getting dark.

Maggie.

But it's beautiful at night. I slept there one night when it was hot in my room.

Quentin.

God, you don't want to do that. *(Glancing at the park loungers.)* Most of the animals around here are not in the zoo.

Maggie.

Okay. I'll get a record, then. 'Scuse me about my hair if I embarrassed you.

Quentin.

(Laughing.) You didn't.

Maggie.

(*Touching the top of her head as she backs away.*) It's just that it's not broken. (*He nods.*) I'm going to sew this home. (*He nods. She indicates the park, upstage.*) I didn't *mean* to sleep there. I just fell asleep.

     (*Several young men now rise, watching her.*)

Quentin.

I understand.

Maggie.

Well . . . see you! (*Laughs.*) If they don't fire me!

  (*She passes two men who walk step for step behind her, whispering in her ear together. She doesn't turn or answer. Now a group of men is beginning to surround her. Quentin, in anguish, goes and draws her away from them.*) Maggie! (*He takes a bill from his pocket, moving her across stage.*) Here, why don't you take a cab? It's on me. Go ahead, there's one right there! (*Points and whistles upstage and right.*) Go on, grab it!

Maggie.

Where—where will I tell him to go but?

Quentin.

Just cruise in the Forties—you've got enough there.

Maggie.

Okay, 'by! (*Backing out.*) You—you just going to rest more?

Quentin.

I don't know.

Maggie.

Golly, that's nice!

SECOND SCENE

Quentin has briefly recalled his brother, who sent him off to college, giving him his copy of Byron and his new argyle socks, and shouting after him as the train pulled out, "Wherever you are, this family's behind you. So buckle down, now, I'll send you a list of books."

The brother disappears, waving farewell. The lights shift and we are aware of Maggie, suddenly sitting up on her bed, addressing an empty space at the foot.

Maggie.

But could I read them?

Quentin.

(*Spinning about in quick surprise.*) Huh!

(*All the others have gone dark but him and Maggie.*)

Maggie.

I mean what kind of books? 'Cause, see—I never really graduated high school. Although I always liked poetry.

Quentin.

(*Breaks his stare at her and quickly comes down to the Listener.*) It's that I can't find myself in this vanity any more.

Maggie.

(*Enthralled, on bed.*) I can hardly believe you came! Can you stay five minutes? I'm a singer now, see? In fact— (*With a laugh at herself.*)—I'm in the top three. And for a long time I been wanting to tell you that . . . none of it would have happened to me if I hadn't met you that day.

Quentin.

Why do you speak of love? All I can see now is the power she offered me. All right. (*Turns to her in conflict, and unwillingly.*) I'll try. (*He approaches her.*)

Maggie.

I'm sorry if I sounded frightened on the phone but I didn't think you'd be in the office after midnight. (*Laughs at herself nervously.*) See, I only pretended to call you. Can you stay like five minutes?

Quentin.

(*Backing into the chair.*) Sure. Don't rush.

Maggie.

That's what I mean, you know I'm rushing! Would you like a drink? Or a steak? They have two freezers here. My agent went to Jamaica so I'm just staying here this week till I go to London Friday. It's the Palladium, like a big vaudeville house, and it's kind of an honor but I'm a little scared to go.

Quentin.

Why? I've heard you; you're marvelous. Especially . . . (*He can't remember a title.*)

Maggie.

No, I'm just flapping my wings yet. But did you read what that *News* fellow wrote? He keeps my records in the 'frigerator, case they melt!

Quentin.

(*Laughs with her, then recalls.*) "Little Girl Blue"! It's very moving, the way you do that.

Maggie.

Really? 'Cause, see, it's not I say to myself, "I'm going to

sound sexy," I just try to come *through*—like in love or
. . . (*Laughs.*) I really can't believe you're here!

Quentin.

Why? I'm glad you called; I've often thought about you
the last couple of years. All the great things happening
to you gave me a secret satisfaction for some reason.

Maggie.

Maybe 'cause you did it.

Quentin.

Why do you say that?

Maggie.

I don't know, just the way you looked at me. I didn't
even have the nerve to go see an agent before that day.

Quentin.

How did I look at you?

Maggie.

(*Squinching up her shoulders, a mystery.*) Like . . . out
of your *self*. Most people, they . . . just look *at* you. I
can't explain it. And the way you talked to me . . .

Louise.

(*Who has been sitting right, playing solitaire.*) You think
reading your brief is talking to me?

Maggie.

What did you mean—it gave you a secret satisfaction?

Quentin.

Just that—like in the office, I'd hear people laughing that
Maggie had the world at her feet—

Maggie.

(*Hurt, mystified.*) They laughed!

Quentin.

In a way.

Maggie.

(*In pain.*) That's what I mean; I'm a joke to most people.

Quentin.

No, it's that you say what you mean, Maggie. You don't
seem to be upholding anything, you're not—ashamed of
what you are.

Maggie.

W—what do you mean, of what I am?

        (*Louise looks up. She is playing solitaire.*)

Quentin.

(*Suddenly aware he has touched a nerve.*) Well . . . that
you love life, and . . . It's hard to define, I . . .

Louise.

The word is tart. But what did it matter as long as she praised you?

Quentin.

(*To Listener, standing, and moving within Maggie's area.*) There's truth in it—I hadn't had a woman's praise, even a girl I'd laughed at with the others—

Maggie.

But you didn't, did you?
                    (*He turns to her in agony.*)
Laugh at me?

Quentin.

No. (*He suddenly stands and cries out to Listener.*) Fraud! From the first five minutes! . . . Because! I should have agreed she *was* a joke, a beautiful piece, trying to take herself seriously! Why did I lie to her, play this cheap benefactor, this—(*Listens, and now unwillingly he turns back to her.*)

Maggie.

Like when you told me to fix where my dress was torn? You wanted me to be—proud of myself. Didn't you?

Quentin.

(*Surprised.*) I guess I did, yes. (*To Listener.*) By God I did!

Maggie.

(*Feeling she has budged him.*) Would you like a drink?

Quentin.

(*Relaxing.*) I wouldn't mind. (*Glancing around.*) What's all the flowers?

Maggie.

(*Pouring.*) Oh, that's that dopey prince or a king or whatever he is. He keeps sending me a contract—whereas I get a hundred thousand dollars if we ever divorce. I'd be like a queen or something, but I only met him in El Morocco once! (*She laughs, handing him his drink.*) I'm supposed to be his girl friend too! I don't know why they print those things.

Quentin.

Well, I guess everybody wants to touch you now.

Maggie.

Cheers! (*They drink; she makes a face.*) I hate the taste but I love the effect! Would you like to take off your shoes? I mean just to rest.

Quentin.

I'm okay. I thought you sounded on the phone like something frightened you.

Maggie.

Do you have to go home right away?

Quentin.

Are you all alone here?

Maggie.

It's okay. Oh hey! I cut your picture out of the paper last month. When you were defending that Reverend Harley Barnes in Washington? (*Taking a small framed photo from under her pillow.*) See? I framed it!

Quentin.

Is something frightening you, Maggie?

Maggie.

No, it's just you're here! It's odd how I found this—I went up to see my father—

Quentin.

He must be very proud of you now.

Maggie.

(*Laughing.*) Oh, no—he left when I was eighteen months, see—'cause he said I wasn't from him, although my mother always said I was. And they keep interviewing me now and I never know what to answer, when they ask where you were born, and all. So I thought if he would just see me, and you know, just—look at me . . . I can't explain it.

Quentin.

Maybe so you'll know who you are.

Maggie.

Yes! But he wouldn't even talk to me on the phone— just said, "See my lawyer," and hung up. But on the train back there was your picture, right on the seat looking up at me. And I said, "I know who I am! I'm Quentin's friend!" But don't worry about it—I mean you could just be somebody's friend, couldn't you?

Quentin.

(*After a slight pause.*) Yes, Maggie, I can be somebody's friend. It's just that you're so beautiful—and I don't only mean your body and your face.

Maggie.

You wouldn't even have to see me again. I would do anything for you, Quentin—you're like a god!

Quentin.

But anybody would have told you to mend your dress.

Maggie.

No, they'd have laughed or tried for a quick one. You know.

Quentin.

(*To Listener.*) Yes! It's all so clear—the honor! The first honor was that I hadn't tried to go to bed with her! She took it for a tribute to her "value," and I was only afraid! God, the hypocrisy! . . . But why do you speak of love?

Maggie.

Oh hey! You know what I did because of you? (*He turns back to her.*) I was christening a submarine in the Groton shipyard; 'cause I was voted the favorite of all the workers! And I made them bring about ten workers up on the platform, whereas they're the ones built it, right? And you know what the admiral said? I better watch out or I'll be a Communist. And suddenly I thought of you and I said, "I don't know what's so terrible; they're for the poor people." Isn't that what you believe?

Quentin.

I did, but it's a lot more complicated, honey.

Maggie.

Oh! I wish I knew something.

Quentin.

You know how to see it all with your own eyes, Maggie, that's more important than all the books.

Maggie.

But you know if it's true. What you see.

Quentin.

(*Puzzled.*) You frightened *now?* . . . You are, aren't you? (*Maggie stares at him in tension, a long moment passes.*) What is it, dear? You afraid to be alone here? (*Pause.*) Why don't you call somebody to stay with you?

Maggie.

I don't know anybody . . . like that.

Quentin.

(*After a slight pause.*) Can I do anything? . . . Don't be afraid to ask me.

Maggie.

(*In a struggle, finally.*) Would you . . . open that closet door?

Quentin.

(*Looks off, then back to her.*) Just open it?

Maggie.

Yes.

(*He walks into the dark periphery; she sits up warily, watching. He opens a "door." He returns. And she lies back.*)

Quentin.

Do you want to tell me something? I'm not going to laugh. (*Sits.*) What is it?

Maggie.

(*With great difficulty.*) When I start to go to sleep before. And suddenly I saw smoke coming out of that closet under the door. Kept coming and coming. It start to fill the whole room!

(*She breaks off, near weeping. He reaches and takes her hand.*)

Quentin.

Oh, kid—you've often dreamed such things, haven't you?

Maggie.

But I was awake!

Quentin.

Well it was a waking dream. It just couldn't stay down till you went to sleep. These things can be explained if you trace them back.

Maggie.

I know. I go to an analyst.

Quentin.

Then tell him about it, you'll figure it out.

Maggie.

It's when I start to call you before. (*She is now absorbed in her own connections.*) See, my mother—she used to get dressed in the closet. She was very—like moral, you know? But sometimes she'd smoke in there. And she'd come out—you know? with a whole cloud of smoke around her.

Quentin.

Well—possibly you felt she didn't want you to call me.

Maggie.

(*Astounded.*) How'd you know that?

Quentin.

You said she was so moral. And here you're calling a married man.

Maggie.

Yes! She tried to kill me once with a pillow on my face 'cause I would turn out bad because of—like her sin. And

I have her hair, and the same back. (*She turns half to him, showing a naked back.*) 'Cause I have a good back, see? Every masseur says.

Quentin.

Yes, it is. It's beautiful. But it's no sin to call me.

Maggie.

(*Shaking her head like a child with a relieved laugh at herself.*) Doesn't make me bad. Right?

Quentin.

You're a very moral girl, Maggie.

Maggie.

(*Delicately and afraid.*) W—what's moral?

Quentin.

You tell the truth, even against yourself. You're not pretending to be—(*Turns out to the Listener, with a dread joy.*)—innocent! Yes, that suddenly there was someone who—could not club you to death with their innocence! And now it's all laughable!

THIRD SCENE

Quentin recalls his marriage to Maggie and the gradual breakup. Her career is booming; more and more he gives his time not only to her legal work but to attending her rehearsals and acting as a buffer between her and the people with whom she works. Maggie is becoming temperamental about her work. When Quentin tries to calm her down, she says he has turned cold, that he loves her less than he did. In the background the lights come up briefly on Louise, looking as she did when she said similar things to Quentin. Maggie moves into the darkness and Quentin, alone, says, "I adore you, Maggie; I'm sorry; it won't ever happen again." Louise exits and Quentin continues, "Never! You need more love than I thought. But I've got it, and I'll make you see it, and when you do you're going to astound the world!"

A rose light floods the bed; Maggie emerges in a dressing gown.

Maggie.

(*Indicating out front.*) Surprise! You like it? See the material?

Quentin.

Oh, that's lovely! How'd you think of that?

Maggie.

All you gotta do is close them and the sun makes the bed all rose.

Quentin.

(*Striving for joy, embracing her on the bed.*) Yes, it's beautiful! You see? An argument doesn't mean disaster! Oh, Maggie, I never knew what love was!

Maggie.

(*Kissing him.*) Case during the day, like maybe you get the idea to come home and we make love again in daytime. (*She ends sitting in a weakness; nostalgically.*) Like last year, remember? In the winter afternoons? And once there was still snow on your hair. See, that's all I am, Quentin.

Quentin.

I'll come home tomorrow afternoon.

Maggie.

(*Half humorously.*) Well, don't *plan* it.

(*He laughs, but she looks at him strangely again, her stare piercing. His laugh dies.*)

Quentin.

What is it? I don't want to hide things any more, darling. Tell me, what's bothering you?

Maggie.

(*Shaking her head, seeing.*) I'm not a good wife. I take up so much of your work.

Quentin.

No, dear. I only said that because you—(*Striving to soften the incident.*)—you kind of implied that I didn't fight the network hard enough on that penalty, and I got it down to twenty thousand dollars. They had a right to a hundred when you didn't perform.

Maggie.

(*With rising indignation.*) But can't I be sick? I was sick!

Quentin.

I know, dear, but the doctor wouldn't sign the affidavit.

Maggie.

(*Furious at him.*) I had a pain in my side, for Christ's sake, I couldn't stand straight! You don't believe me, do you!

Quentin.

Maggie, I'm only telling you the legal situation.

Maggie.

Ask Ludwig what you should do! You should've gone in

there roaring! 'Stead of a polite liberal and affidavits—
I shouldn't have had to pay anything!

Quentin.

Maggie, you have a great analyst, and Ludwig is a phenomenal teacher, and every stranger you meet has all the
answers, but I'm putting in forty per cent of my time on
your problems, not just some hot air.

Maggie.

You're not putting forty per cent of—

Quentin.

Maggie, I keep a log, I know what I spend my time on!

(*She looks at him, mortally wounded, goes upstage to
a secretary, who enters with an invisible drink. Maid joins
them with black dress, and Maggie changes.*)

I'm sorry, darling, but when you talk like that I feel a
little like a fool. Don't start drinking, please.

Maggie.

Should never have gotten married; every man I ever
knew they hate their wives. I think I should have a
separate lawyer.

Quentin.

(*Alone on forestage.*) Darling, I'm happy to spend my
time on you; my greatest pleasure is to know I've helped
your work to grow!

Maggie.

(*As a group of executives surrounds her.*) But the only
reason I went to Ludwig was so I could make myself an
artist you'd be proud of! You're the first one that believed
in me!

Quentin.

Then what are we arguing about? We want the same
thing, you see? (*Suddenly to Listener.*) Yes, power! To
transform somebody, to save!

Maggie.

(*Emerging from the group, wearing reading glasses.*) He's
a very good lawyer; he deals for a lot of stars. He'll call
you to give him my files.

Quentin.

(*After a slight pause; hurt.*) Okay.

Maggie.

It's nothing against you; but like that girl in the orchestra,
that cellist—I mean Andy took too much but he'd have
gone in there and got rid of her. I mean you don't laugh
when a singer goes off key.

Quentin.

But she said she coughed.

Maggie.

(*Furiously.*) She didn't cough, she laughed!

Quentin.

Now, Maggie.

Maggie.

I'm not finishing this tape if she's in that band tomorrow! I'm entitled to my conditions, Quentin—and I shouldn't have to plead with my husband for my rights. I want her out!

(*The executives are gone.*)

Quentin.

I don't know what the pleading's about. I've fired three others in three different bands.

Maggie.

Well, so what? You're my husband. You're supposed to do that. Aren't you?

Quentin.

But I can't pretend to enjoy demanding people be fired—

Maggie.

But if it was your daughter you'd get angry, wouldn't you? Instead of apologizing for her?

Quentin.

(*Envisioning it.*) I guess I would, yes. I'm sorry. I'll do it in the morning.

Maggie.

(*With desperate warmth, joining him, sitting center.*) That's all I mean. If I want something you should ask yourself why, why does she want it, not why she shouldn't have it. . . . That's why I don't smile, I feel I'm fighting all the time to make you *see*. You're like a little boy, you don't see the knives people hide.

Quentin.

Darling, life is not all that dangerous. You've got a husband now who loves you.

(*Pause. She seems to fear greatly.*)

Maggie.

When your mother tells me I'm getting fat, I know where I am. And when you don't do anything about it.

Quentin.

But what can I do?

Maggie.

Slap her down, that's what you do!

(*Secretary enters with imaginary drink, which Maggie takes.*)

Quentin.

But she says anything comes into her head, dear—

Maggie

She insulted me! She's jealous of me!

Quentin.

Maggie, she adores you. She's proud of you.

Maggie.

(*A distance away now.*) What are you trying to make me think, I'm crazy? (*Quentin approaches her, groping for reassurance.*) I'm not crazy!

Quentin.

(*Carefully.*) The thought never entered my mind, darling. I'll . . . talk to her.

Maggie.

Look, I don't want to see her any more. If she ever comes into this house, I'm walking out!

Quentin.

Well, I'll tell her to apologize.

(*Secretary exits.*)

Maggie.

I'm not going to work tomorrow. (*She lies down on the bed as though crushed.*)

Quentin.

Okay.

Maggie.

(*Half springing up.*) You know it's not "okay"! You're scared to death they'll sue me, why don't you say it?

Quentin.

I'm not scared to death; it's just that you're so wonderful in this show and it's a pity to—

Maggie.

(*Sitting up furiously.*) All you care about is money! Don't shit me!

Quentin.

(*Quelling a fury, his voice very level.*) Maggie, don't use that language with me, will you?

Maggie.

Call me vulgar, that I talk like a truck driver! Well, that's where I come from. I'm for Negroes and Puerto Ricans and truck drivers!

Quentin.

Then why do you fire people so easily?

Maggie.

(*Her eyes narrowing—she is seeing him anew.*) Look. You don't want me. What the hell are you doing here?
            (*Father and Dan enter, above them.*)

Quentin.

I live here, and you do too, but you don't know it yet. But you're going to. I—

Father.

Where's he going? I need him! What are you?

Quentin.

(*Not turning to Father.*) I'm here, and I stick it, that's what I am. And one day you're going to catch on. Now go to sleep. I'll be back in ten minutes, I'd like to take a walk.
            (*He starts out and she comes to attention.*)

Maggie.

Where you going to walk?

Quentin.

Just around the block. (*She watches him carefully.*) There's nobody else, kid; I just want to walk.

Maggie.

(*With great suspicion.*) 'Kay.

FOURTH SCENE

A montage of overlapping memories, separate but all involving betrayal, briefly fills the stage. In particular there is the sound of a subway train and a pantomime of the men who saw Quentin's friend throw himself under the train when another friend had exposed him to the congressional committee and he thought there was no one left who wanted him as a friend. "In whose name," Quentin asks, "do you look into a face you loved, and say, Now you have been found wanting, and now in your extremity you die!"

The others disappear. "A tremendous crash of surf spins Quentin about . . . and the light of the moon is rising on the pier."

Alone, Quentin speaks: "By the ocean. That cottage. That night. The last night."

Maggie in a rumpled wrapper, a bottle in her hand, her hair in snags over her face, staggers out to the edge of the pier and stands in the sound of the surf. Now she starts to

topple over the edge of the pier, and he rushes to her and holds her in his hands. Maggie turns around and they embrace. Now the sound of jazz from within is heard, softly.
Maggie.

You were loved, Quentin; no man was ever loved like you.
Quentin.

(*Releasing her.*) Carrie tell you I called? My plane couldn't take off all day—
Maggie.

(*Drunk, but aware.*) I was going to kill myself just now. (*He is silent.*) Or don't you believe that either?
Quentin.

(*With an absolute calm, a distance, but without hostility.*) I saved you twice, why shouldn't I believe it? (*Going toward her.*) This dampness is bad for your throat, you oughtn't be out here.
Maggie.

(*She defiantly sits, her legs dangling.*) Where've *you* been?
Quentin.

(*Going upstage, removing his jacket.*) I've been in Chicago. I told you. The Hathaway estate.
Maggie.

(*With a sneer.*) Estates!
Quentin.

Well, I have to pay some of our debts before I save the world. (*He removes his jacket and puts it on bureau box; sits and removes a shoe.*)
Maggie.

(*From the pier.*) Didn't you hear what I told you?
Quentin.

I heard it. I'm not coming out there, Maggie, it's too wet.
(*She looks toward him, gets up, unsteadily enters
the room.*)
Maggie.

I didn't go to rehearsal today.
Quentin.

I didn't think you did.
Maggie.

And I called the network that I'm not finishing that stupid show. I'm an artist! And I don't have to do stupid shows, no matter what contract you made!
Quentin.

I'm very tired, Maggie. I'll sleep in the living room. Good night. (*He stands and starts out upstage.*)

Maggie.

What *is* this?

> (*Pause. He turns back to her from the exit.*)

Quentin.

I've been fired.

Maggie.

You're not fired.

Quentin.

I didn't expect you to take it seriously, but it is to me; I can't make a decision any more without something sits up inside me and busts out laughing.

Maggie.

That my fault, huh?

> (*Slight pause. Then he resolves.*)

Quentin.

Look, dear, it's gone way past blame or justifying ourselves, I . . . talked to your doctor this afternoon.

Maggie.

(*Stiffening with fear and suspicion.*) About what?

Quentin.

You want to die, Maggie, and I really don't know how to prevent it. But it struck me that I have been playing with your life out of some idiotic hope of some kind that you'd come out of this endless spell. But there's only one hope, dear—you've got to start to look at what *you're* doing.

Maggie.

You going to put me away somewhere. Is that it?

Quentin.

Your doctor's trying to get a plane up here tonight; you settle it with him.

Maggie.

You're not going to put *me* anywhere, mister. (*She opens the pill bottle.*)

Quentin.

You have to be supervised, Maggie. (*She swallows pills.*) Now listen to me while you can still hear. If you start going under tonight I'm calling the ambulance. I haven't the strength to go through that alone again. I'm not protecting you from the newspapers any more, Maggie, and the hospital means a headline. (*She raises the whisky bottle to drink.*) You've got to start facing the consequences of your actions, Maggie. (*She drinks whisky.*) Okay. I'll tell Carrie to call the ambulance as soon as she sees the signs. I'm going to sleep at the inn. (*He gets his jacket.*)

Maggie.

Don't sleep at the inn!

Quentin.

Then put that stuff away and go to sleep.

Maggie.

(*Afraid he is leaving, she tries to smooth her tangled hair.*) Could you . . . stay five minutes?

Quentin.

Yes. (*He returns.*)

Maggie.

You can even have the bottle if you want. I won't take any more. (*She puts the pill bottle on the bed before him.*)

Quentin.

(*Against his wish to take it.*) I don't want the bottle.

Maggie.

'Member how used talk to me till I fell asleep?

Quentin.

Maggie, I've sat beside you in darkened rooms for days and weeks at a time, and my office looking high and low for me—

Maggie.

No, you lost patience with me.

Quentin.

(*After a slight pause.*) That's right, yes.

Maggie.

So you lied, right?

Quentin.

Yes, I lied. Every day. We are all separate people. I tried not to be, but finally one is—a separate person. I have to survive too, honey.

Maggie.

So where you going to put me?

Quentin.

(*Trying not to break.*) You discuss that with your doctor.

Maggie.

But if you loved me . . .

Quentin.

But how would you know, Maggie? Do you know any more who I am? Aside from my name? I'm all the evil in the world, aren't I? All the betrayal, the broken hopes, the murderous revenge? (*She pours pills into her hand, and he stands. Now fear is in his voice.*) A suicide kills two people, Maggie, that's what it's for! So I'm removing myself, and perhaps it will lose its point. (*He resolutely starts out. She falls back on the bed. Her breathing is suddenly deep. He starts toward Carrie who sits in semi-darkness, praying.*) Carrie!

Maggie.

Quentin, what's Lazarus?

(*He halts: She looks about for him, not knowing he has left.*)

Quentin?

(*Not seeing him, she starts up off the bed; a certain alarm*) . . .

Quen?

(*He comes halfway back.*)

Quentin.

Jesus raised him from the dead. In the Bible. Go to sleep now.

Maggie.

Wha's 'at suppose to prove?

Quentin.

The power of faith.

Maggie.

What about those who have no faith?

Quentin.

They only have the will.

Maggie.

But how you get the will?

Quentin.

You have faith.

Maggie.

Some apples. (*She lies back. A pause.*) I want more cream puffs. And my birthday dress? If I'm good? Mama? I want my mother! (*She sits up, looks about as in a dream, turns and sees him.*) Why are you standing there? (*She gets out of bed, squinting, and comes up to him, peers into his face; her expression comes alive.*) You—you want music?

Quentin.

All right, you lie down, and I'll put a little music on.

Maggie.

No, you; you, sit down. And take off your shoes. I mean just to rest. You don't have to do anything. (*She staggers to the machine, turns it on; jazz. She tries to sing, but suddenly comes totally awake.*) Was I sleeping?

Quentin.

For a moment, I think.

Maggie.

(*Coming toward him in terror.*) Was—was my—was anybody else here?

Quentin.

No. Just me.

Maggie.

Is there smoke? (*With a cry she clings to him; he holds
her close.*)

Quentin.

Your mother's dead and gone, dear, she can't hurt you any
more, don't be afraid.

Maggie.

(*In the helpless voice of a child as he returns her to the
bed.*) Where you going to put me?

Quentin.

(*His chest threatening a sob.*) Nowhere, dear—the doctor'll decide with you.

Maggie.

See? I'll lay down. (*She lies down.*) See? (*She takes a
strange, deep breath.*) You—you could have the pills if
you want.

Quentin.

(*Stands and, after a hesitation, starts away.*) I'll have Carrie come in and take them.

Maggie.

(*Sliding off the bed, holding the pill bottle out to him.*) No.
I won't give them to Carrie. Only you. You take them.

Quentin.

Why do you want me to have them?

Maggie.

(*Extending them.*) Here.

Quentin.

(*After a pause.*) Do you see it, Maggie? Right now?
You're trying to make me the one who does it to you? I
grab them; and then we fight, and then I give them up,
and you take your death from me. Something in you has
been setting me up for a murder. Do you see it? (*He
moves backward.*) But now I'm going away; so you're not
my victim any more. It's just you, and your hand.

Maggie.

But Jesus must have loved her.

Quentin.

Who?

Maggie.

Lazarus?

(*Pause. He sees, he gropes toward his vision.*)

Quentin.

That's right, yes! He . . . loved her enough to raise her from the dead. But He's God, see . . . and God's power is love without limit. But when a man dares reach for that . . . he is only reaching for the power. Whoever goes to save another person with the lie of limitless love throws a shadow on the face of God. And God is what happened, God is what is; and whoever stands between another person and her truth is not a lover, he is . . . (*He breaks off, lost, peering, and turns back to Maggie for his clue.*) And then she said. (*He goes back to Maggie, crying out to invoke her.*) And then she said!

from

'TIS PITY SHE'S A WHORE

by John Ford

Three Scenes from Act I, scene 3; Act II, scene 1; and
Act V, scene 5
ANNABELLA, GIOVANNI, (PUTANA)

> Love is the tyrant of the heart; it darkens
> Reason, confounds discretion; deaf to counsel
> It runs a headlong course to desperate madness.
>
> John Ford, *The Lover's Melancholy*

"Pity" was meant to be the significant word in John Ford's
title, though modern audiences find it difficult not to give
undue attention to the final word, and *The New York
Times* once refused to accept advertisements that included
the full name of the play. Ford's concern was the dynamic
force of love, which neither the good intentions of individuals nor the strict injunctions of society or law could resist. Writing of men and women driven by consuming love
—by sexual frustration, adultery, incest—he portrayed
them not with revulsion but with pity, an understanding
that lent depth and intensity to situations that, viewed on
the surface, seemed merely sensational. And his dark, romantic tragedies move onto a modern stage with surprising
effectiveness and truth, for we too are aware of emotions
stronger than moral laws.

'*Tis Pity*, first presented in 1633, is set in Renaissance
Parma. Giovanni has returned from the university at
Bologna, a handsome and brilliant youth, once "esteemed
a wonder of [his] age," a serious young man not given to
the wild immorality characteristic of other young noblemen of Parma. He loves Annabella, who is as beautiful as
he is brilliant, as admired, as unspoiled, as promising. She is
his sister. Their story, as at least one critic has noticed, is
reminiscent of *Romeo and Juliet*, with the lovers divided

by moral law rather than a family feud. Played out to its
inevitable tragic conclusion against a background of blatant
sexual immorality, intrigue, and guile, it achieves, by contrast to the world around it, a simple poignancy.

Giovanni, when he first senses the nature of his love for
his sister, turns for help to a friar, his tutor at the university, who warns him that death is the certain reward of
such lust and begs him to pray to be cured of this infection rotting his soul. Giovanni accepts this counsel, but,
haunted still by his passion, grows increasingly silent and
morose.

Annabella is courted by several suitors, at least one of
them young, handsome, personable, and rich. But none
seems to match the qualities she sees in her brother.

That is the situation when Annabella, walking with her
tutor-guardian Putana, comes upon Giovanni standing
silent and in tears in one of the great rooms in their father's
house.

Giovanni.
  Lost! I am lost! my fears have doomed my death:
  The more I strive, I love; the more I love,
  The less I hope: I see my ruin certain.
  What judgment or endeavours could apply
  To my incurable and restless wounds,
  I throughly have examined, but in vain.
  O, that it were not in religion sin
  To make our love a god, and worship it!
  I have even wearied Heaven with prayers, dried up
  The spring of my continual tears, even starved
  My veins with daily fasts: what wit or art
  Could counsel, I have practised; but, alas,
  I find all these but dreams, and old men's tales,
  To fright unsteady youth; I'm still the same:
  Or I must speak, or burst. 'Tis not, I know,
  My lust, but 'tis my fate that leads me on.
  Keep fear and low faint-hearted shame with slaves!
  I'll tell her that I love her, though my heart
  Were rated at the price of that attempt.—
  O me! she comes.
                (*Enter Annabella and Putana.*)
Annabella.
          Brother!

Giovanni.

(*Aside.*)   If such a thing
As courage dwell in men, ye heavenly powers,
Now double all that virtue in my tongue!

Annabella.

Why, brother,
Will you not speak to me?

Giovanni.

                    Yes: how d'ye sister?

Annabella.

Howe'er I am, methinks you are not well.

Putana.

Bless us! Why are you so sad, sir?

Giovanni.

Let me entreat you, leave us a while, Putana.—
Sister, I would be private with you.

Annabella.

Withdraw, Putana.

Putana.

I will.—If this were any other company for her,
I should think my absence an office of some credit; but
I will leave them together. (*Aside, and exit.*)

Giovanni.

Come, sister, lend your hand: let's walk together!
I hope you need not blush to walk with me;
Here's none but you and I.

Annabella.

                    How's this?

Giovanni.

                              I'faith,
I mean no harm.
          —   Harm?

Annabella.

                    No, good faith.

Giovanni.

How is't with ye?

Annabella.

(*Aside.*) I trust he be not frantic.—
I am very well, brother.

Giovanni.

Trust me, but I am sick; I fear so sick
'Twill cost my life.

Annabella. -

Mercy forbid it! 'tis not so, I hope.

Giovanni.

I think you love me, sister.

Annabella.

                      Yes, you know

I do.

Giovanni.

I know't, indeed.—You're very fair.

Annabella.

Nay, then I see you have a merry sickness.

Giovanni.

That's as it proves. The poets feign, I read,
That Juno for her forehead did exceed
All other goddesses; but I durst swear
Your forehead exceeds hers, as hers did theirs.

Annabella.

'Troth, this is pretty!

Giovanni.

                      Such a pair of stars
As are thine eyes would, like Promethean fire,
If gently glanced, give life to senseless stones.

Annabella.

Fie upon ye!

Giovanni.

The lily and the rose, most sweetly strange,
Upon your dimpled cheeks do strive for change:
Such lips would tempt a saint; such hands as those
Would make an anchorite lascivious.

Annabella.

D'ye mock me or flatter me?

Giovanni.

If you would see a beauty more exact
Than art can counterfeit or nature frame,
Look in your glass, and there behold your own.

Annabella.

O, you are a trim youth!

Giovanni.

Here! (*Offers his dagger to her.*)

Annabella.

      What to do?

Giovanni.

                   And here's my breast; strike home!
Rip up my bosom; there thou shalt behold
A heart in which is writ the truth I speak.
Why stand ye?

Annabella.

        Are you earnest?

Giovanni.

                      Yes, most earnest.

You cannot love?

Annabella.

           Whom?

Giovanni.

                 Me. My tortured soul
Hath felt affliction in the heat of death.
O, Annabella, I am quite undone!
The love of thee, my sister, and the view
Of thy immortal beauty have untuned
All harmony both of my rest and life.
Why d'ye not strike?

Annabella.

           Forbid it, my just fears!
If this be true, 'twere fitter I were dead.

Giovanni.

True, Annabella! 'tis no time to jest.
I have too long suppressed the hidden flames
That almost have consumed me: I have spent
Many a silent night in sighs and groans;
Ran over all my thoughts, despised my fate,
Reasoned against the reasons of my love,
Done all that smoothed-cheeked virtue could advise;
But found all bootless: 'tis my destiny
That you must either love, or I must die.

Annabella.

Comes this in sadness from you?

Giovanni.

                   Let some mischief
Befall me soon, if I dissemble aught.

Annabella.

You are my brother Giovanni.

Giovanni.

             You
My sister Annabella; I know this,
And could afford you instance why to love
So much the more for this; to which intent
Wise nature first in your creation meant
To make you mine; else't had been sin and foul

To share one beauty to a double soul.
Nearness in birth and blood doth but persuade
A nearer nearness in affection.
I have asked counsel of the holy church,
Who tells me I may love you; and 'tis just
That, since I may, I should; and will, yes, will.
Must I now live or die?
Annabella.

                            Live; thou hast won
The field, and never fought: what thou hast urged
My captive heart had long ago resolved.
I blush to tell thee,—but I'll tell thee now,—
For every sigh that thou hast spent for me
I have sighed ten; for every tear shed twenty:
And not so much for that I loved, as that
I durst not say I loved, nor scarcely think it.
Giovanni.

Let not this music be a dream, ye gods,
For pity's sake, I beg ye!
Annabella.

                      On my knees, (*She kneels.*)
Brother, even by our mother's dust, I charge you,
Do not betray me to your mirth or hate:
Love me or kill me, brother.
Giovanni.

                       On my knees, (*He kneels.*)
Sister, even by my mother's dust, I charge you,
Do not betray me to your mirth or hate:
Love me or kill me, sister.
Annabella.

You mean good sooth, then?
Giovanni.

                              In good troth, I do;
And so do you, I hope: say, I'm in earnest.
Annabella.

I'll swear it, I.
Giovanni.

                      And I; and by this kiss,—
                            (*Kisses her.*)
Once more, yet once more: now let's rise (*They rise.*),—
  by this,
I would not change this minute for Elysium.
What must we now do?

446 Character Development

Annabella.

What you will.

Giovanni.

Come then;
After so many tears as we have wept,
Let's learn to court in smiles, to kiss, and sleep.

SECOND SCENE

A smaller room in the house. Giovanni and Annabella
enter.

Giovanni.

Come, Annabella,—no more sister now,
But love, a name more gracious,—do not blush,
Beauty's sweet wonder, but be proud to know
That yielding thou hast conquered, and inflamed
A heart whose tribute is thy brother's life.

Annabella.

And mine is his. O, how these stol'n contents
Would print a modest crimson on my cheeks,
Had any but my heart's delight prevailed!

Giovanni.

I marvel why the chaster of your sex
Should think this pretty toy called maidenhead
So strange a loss, when, being lost, 'tis nothing,
And you are still the same.

Annabella.

'Tis well for you;

Now you can talk.

Giovanni.

Music as well consists

In the ear as in the playing.

Annabella.

O, you're wanton!

Tell on't, you're best; do.

Giovanni.

Thou wilt chide me, then.

Kiss me:—so! Thus hung Jove on Leda's neck,
And sucked divine ambrosia from her lips.
I envy not the mightiest man alive;
But hold myself in being king of thee,
More great than were I king of all the world.

But I shall lose you, sweetheart.
Annabella.

                      But you shall not.
Giovanni.

You must be married, mistress.
Annabella.

                      Yes! to whom?
Giovanni.

Some one must have you.
Annabella.

                You must.
Giovanni.

                      Nay, some other.
Annabella.

Now, prithee do not speak so: without jesting
You'll make me weep in earnest.
Giovanni.

                      What, you will not!
But tell me, sweet, canst thou be dared to swear
That thou wilt live to me, and to no other?
Annabella.

By both our loves I dare; for didst thou know,
My Giovanni, how all suitors seem
To my eyes hateful, thou wouldst trust me then.
Giovanni.

Enough, I take thy word: sweet, we must part:
Remember what thou vow'st; keep well my heart.
Annabella.

Will you be gone?
Giovanni.

I must.
Annabella.

When to return?
Giovanni.

          Soon.
Annabella.

          Look you do.
Giovanni.

                Farewell.
Annabella.

Go where thou wilt, in mind I'll keep thee here.
And where thou art, I know I shall be there.

                              (*Exit Giovanni.*)

THIRD SCENE

Annabella has had to marry—she is with child. She has chosen Soranzo, the most admirable of her suitors. She has confessed to the friar and, under the lashing of his threats of damnation, has repented of her love for Giovanni. (The scene is reprinted on p. 326.) Giovanni regrets only the loss of Annabella.

Soranzo discovers Annabella's condition and, enraged that she has married him for honor, not for love, he threatens to kill her if she does not name his rival. She refuses, but Soranzo's servant pries the information from Putana, and Soranzo plots a spectacular vengeance to be brought to completion at a banquet to which he invites all the noblemen of the city. Annabella contrives to warn Giovanni, but he comes to the banquet, determined to save himself and his sister from the ruin her husband intends for them. As the guests gather at Soranzo's house, Giovanni secretly comes to Annabella's bedchamber.

Later Giovanni will appear before the horrified guests bearing Annabella's heart on his dagger, and he will die on Soranzo's sword.

Annabella richly dressed and Giovanni discovered lying on a bed.

Giovanni.
What, changed so soon! hath your new sprightly lord
Found out a trick in night-games more than we
Could know in our simplicity? Ha! is't so?
Or does the fit come on you, to prove treacherous
To your past vows and oaths?

Annabella.
                                        Why should you jest
At my calamity, without all sense
Of the approaching dangers you are in?

Giovanni.
What danger's half so great as thy revolt?
Thou art a faithless sister, else thou know'st,
Malice, or any treachery beside,
Would stoop to my bent brows: why, I hold fate
Clasped in my fist, and could command the course
Of time's eternal motion, hadst thou been
One thought more steady than an ebbing sea.

And what? you'll now be honest, that's resolved?

Annabella.

Brother, dear brother, know what I have been,
And know that now there's but a dining-time
'Twixt us and our confusion: let's not waste
These precious hours in vain and useless speech.
Alas, these gay attires were not put on
But to some end; this sudden solemn feast
Was not ordained to riot in expense;
I, that have now been chambered here alone,
Barred of my guardian or of any else,
Am not for nothing at an instant freed
To fresh access. Be not deceived, my brother;
This banquet is an harbinger of death
To you and me; resolve yourself it is,
And be prepared to welcome it.

Giovanni.

                            Well, then;
The schoolmen teach that all this globe of earth
Shall be consumed to ashes in a minute.

Annabella.

So I have read too.

Giovanni.

                      But 'twere somewhat strange
To see the waters burn: could I believe
This might be true, I could believe as well
There might be hell or Heaven.

Annabella.

                            That's most certain.

Giovanni.

A dream, a dream! else in this other world
We should know one another.

Annabella.

                            So we shall.

Giovanni.

Have you heard so?

Annabella.

                For certain.

Giovanni.

                            But d'ye think
That I shall see you there?—You look on me.—
May we kiss one another, prate or laugh,
Or do as we do here?

Annabella.

I know not that.

But, brother, for the present, what d'ye mean
To free yourself from danger? some way think
How to escape: I'm sure the guests are come.

Giovanni.

Look up, look here; what see you in my face?

Annabella.

Distraction and a troubled conscience.

Giovanni.

Death, and a swift repining wrath:—yet look;
What see you in mine eyes?

Annabella.

Methinks you weep.

Giovanni.

I do indeed: these are the funeral tears
Shed on your grave; these furrowed-up my cheeks
When first I loved and knew not how to woo.
Fair Annabella, should I here repeat
The story of my life, we might lose time.
Be record all the spirits of the air,
And all things else that are, that day and night,
Early and late, the tribute which my heart
Hath paid to Annabella's sacred love
Hath been these tears, which are her mourners now!
Never till now did Nature do her best
To show a matchless beauty to the world,
Which in an instant, ere it scarce was seen,
The jealous Destinies required again.
Pray, Annabella, pray! Since we must part,
Go thou, white in thy soul, to fill a throne
Of innocence and sanctity in Heaven.
Pray, pray, my sister!

Annabella.

Then I see your drift.—
Ye blessed angels, guard me!

Giovanni.

So say I.
Kiss me. If ever after-times should hear
Of our fast-knit affections, though perhaps
The laws of conscience and of civil use
May justly blame us, yet when they but know
Our loves, that love will wipe away that rigour

Which would in other incests be abhorred.
Give me your hand: how sweetly life doth run
In these well-coloured veins! how constantly
These palms do promise health! but I could chide
With Nature for this cunning flattery.
Kiss me again:—forgive me.

Annabella.

                    With my heart.

Giovanni.

Farewell!

Annabella.

        Will you be gone?

Giovanni.

                 Be dark, bright sun,
And make this mid-day night, that thy gilt rays
May not behold a deed will turn their splendour
More sooty than the poets feign their Styx!—
One other kiss, my sister.

Annabella.

                What means this?

Giovanni.

To save thy fame, and kill thee in a kiss.

                         (Stabs her.)

Thus die, and die by me, and by my hand!
Revenge is mine; honour doth love command.

Annabella.

O, brother, by your hand!

Giovanni.

               When thou art dead
I'll give my reasons for't; for to dispute
With thy—even in thy death—most lovely beauty,
Would make me stagger to perform this act,
Which I most glory in.

Annabella.

Forgive him, Heaven—and me my sins! Farewell,
Brother unkind, unkind—Mercy, great Heaven!
O, O! *(Dies.)*

Giovanni.

She's dead, alas, good soul! The hapless fruit
That in her womb received its life from me
Hath had from me a cradle and a grave.
I must not dally. This sad marriage-bed,
In all her best, bore her alive and dead.
Soranzo, thou hast missed thy aim in this:

I have prevented now thy reaching plots,
And killed a love, for whose each drop of blood
I would have pawned my heart.—Fair Annabella,
How over-glorious art thou in thy wounds,
Triumphing over infamy and hate!—
Shrink not, courageous hand, stand up, my heart,
And boldly act my last and greater part!

from

MEASURE FOR MEASURE

by William Shakespeare

Two Scenes from Act II, scene 2, and Act II, scene 4
ANGELO, ISABELLA, (LUCIO, PROVOST)

Shakespeare's remarkably serious comedy has provided a
wealth of problems for literary critics. For performers,
however, it has offered the challenge of two characters
whose shifts of character are the key to the play's significance and its excitement in the theater.

Angelo is the judge absolute for whom all crimes have
equal weight and none, if discovered, can go unpunished.
Named regent of Vienna during the absence of the city's
duke, he undertakes a thoroughgoing campaign of law en-
forcement designed to reform a thoroughly immoral popu-
lace. Among the first cases brought before him is that of
Claudio, a young man whose fiancée is pregnant though
their marriage has yet to be formalized. In fact, the marriage lacks only a technicality, the signing of the marriage
contract; according to the customs of the times, the couple
is married already. But Angelo insists that the letter of the
law be held to, and he condemns Claudio to death—an
example for other young men in the city. When other
officials suggest that Claudio's "criminal immorality" is
no more than a very human weakness, something that
could happen to anyone, Angelo rejects the appeals. What
he requires of Claudio, he says, is no more than he requires
of himself, and should he prove similarly weak, he would
expect to be similarly punished. Human weakness, of
course, is something Angelo has never experienced.

To Angelo's chambers comes Isabella, Claudio's sister, a
novice in a religious order particularly known for the

strictness of the rules by which it removes its members from contact with the world. As a novice, Isabella can be allowed to leave the nunnery for a time, and at the urging of Claudio's friends, particularly the dissolute Lucio, she has agreed to plead for her brother in Angelo's court. On the surface the confrontation (the scene reprinted below) can seem simple and direct: the figure of justice faced by the almost-nun who argues in terms of Christian mercy. But Shakespeare is subtler than that. The novice, pledged to an unworldly life, must plead mercy on behalf of immorality, of worldliness. And against cold law she must argue human warmth with passionate intensity. In herself, then, she is a contradiction; and in Angelo a contradiction—passion—wakes; the human feelings for which he condemned Claudio now stir in him.

Isabella's shift in approach is quite clearly marked; Lucio demands it and she complies. The subtext for Angelo is much more complex, and to a considerable extent left to the actor to determine. At what point, for example, do his emotions first respond to Isabella? At what point does he realize that this has happened? When does he decide that he must see her again?

The scene is preceded by a brief conversation in which Angelo curtly assures the Provost that he has had no second thoughts about ordering the execution of Claudio. The Provost tells him that Isabella has asked to speak with him. Angelo orders a servant to admit her. She enters with Lucio. The Provost turns to leave; Angelo asks him to remain, then speaks to Isabella.

Angelo.

Y' are welcome: what's your will?

Isabella.

I am a woeful suitor to your Honor,
Please but your Honor hear me.

Angelo.

                Well: what's your suit?

Isabella.

There is a vice that most I do abhor,
And most desire should meet the blow of justice,
For which I would not plead, but that I must;

For which I must not plead, but that I am
At war 'twixt will and will not.
Angelo.

                              Well: the matter?
Isabella.
I have a brother is condemn'd to die.
I do beseech you, let it be his fault,
And not my brother.
Provost.
(*Aside.*) Heaven give thee moving graces!
Angelo.
Condemn the fault, and not the actor of
  it?
Why, every fault's condemn'd ere it be done.
Mine were the very cipher of a function,
To fine the faults whose fine stands in record,
And let go by the actor.
Isabella.

                      O just, but severe law!
I had a brother then. Heaven keep your Honor!
Lucio.
(*Aside to Isabella.*) Give't not o'er so: to
  him again, entreat him,
Kneel down before him, hang upon his gown;
You are too cold. If you should need a pin,
You could not with more tame a tongue desire it.
To him, I say!
Isabella.
Must he needs die?
Angelo.

                      Maiden, no remedy.
Isabella.
Yes: I do think that you might pardon
  him,
And neither heaven nor man grieve at the mercy.
Angelo.
I will not do't.
Isabella.

                      But can you, if you would?
Angelo.
Look, what I will not, that I cannot do.

Isabella.

But might you do't, and do the world no
    wrong,
If so your heart were touch'd with that remorse
As mine is to him!

Angelo.

He's sentenc'd: 'tis too late.

Lucio.

(*Aside to Isabella.*)   You are too cold.

Isabella.

Too late? Why, no: I that do speak a
    word,
May call it back again. Well, believe this,
No ceremony that to great ones 'longs,
Not the king's crown, nor the deputed sword,
The marchal's truncheon, nor the judge's robe,
Become them with one half so good a grace
As mercy does.
If he had been as you, and you as he,
You would have slipp'd like him; but he, like you,
Would not have been so stern.

Angelo.

                          Pray you, be gone.

Isabella.

I would to heaven I had your potency,
And you were Isabel! Should it then be thus?
No: I would tell what 'twere to be a judge,
And what a prisoner.

Lucio.

(*Aside to Isabella.*) Ay, touch him! there's
    the vein.

Angelo.

Your brother is a forfeit of the law,
And you but waste your words.

Isabella.

                          Alas, alas.
Why, all the souls that were were forfeit once,
And He that might the vantage best have took,
Found out the remedy. How would you be,
If He, which is the top of judgment, should
But judge you as you are? O think on that!

And mercy then will breathe within your lips,
Like man new made.

Angelo.

               Be you content, fair maid.
It is the law, not I, condemn your brother.
Were he my kinsman, brother or my son,
It should be thus with him: he must die tomorrow.

Isabella.

Tomorrow? O, that's sudden,
Spare him, spare him!
He's not prepar'd for death. Even for our kitchens
We kill the fowl of season. Shall we serve heaven
With less respect than we do minister
To our gross selves? Good, good my lord, bethink
  you:
Who is it that hath died for this offence?
There's many have committed it.

Lucio.

        (*Aside to Isabella.*) Ay, well said.

Angelo.

The law hath not been dead, though it hath
  slept.
Those many had not dar'd to do that evil,
If the first that did th' edict infringe
Had answer'd for his deed. Now 'tis awake,
Takes note of what is done, and like a prophet
Looks in a glass that shows what future evils,
Either new, or by remissness new-conceiv'd,
And so in progress to be hatch'd and born,
Are now to have no successive degrees,
But, ere they live, to end.

Isabella.

               Yet show some pity

Angelo.

I show it most of all when I show justice,
For then I pity those I do not know,
Which a dismiss'd offense would after gall,
And do him right that, answering one foul wrong,
Lives not to act another. Be satisfied.
Your brother dies tomorrow. Be content.

Isabella.

So you must be the first that gives this
   sentence,
And he, that suffers. O, it is excellent
To have a giant's strength, but it is tyrannous
To use it like a giant!

Lucio.

(*Aside to Isabella.*) That's well said.

Isabella.

Could great men thunder
As Jove himself does, Jove would nere be quiet,
For every pelting, petty officer
Would use his heaven for thunder,
Nothing but thunder! Merciful heaven!
Thou rather with thy sharp and sulphurous bolt
Splits the unwedgeable and gnarled oak
Than the soft myrtle; but man, proud man,
Dress'd in a little brief authority,
Most ignorant of what he's most assur'd—
His glassy essence—like an angry ape,
Plays such fantastic tricks before high heaven
As makes the angels weep; who, with our spleens,
Would all themselves laugh mortal.

Lucio.

(*Aside to Isabella.*) O, to him, to him, wench!
   He will relent.
He's coming. I perceive't.

Provost.

(*Aside.*)   Pray heaven she win him!

Isabella.

We cannot weigh our brother with ourself:
Great men may jest with saints: 'tis wit in them,
But in the less foul profanation.

Lucio.

(*Aside to Isabella.*) Thou'rt i' th' right,
   girl: more o' that.

Isabella.

That in the captain's but a choleric word,
Which in the soldier is flat blasphemy.

Lucio.

(*Aside to Isabella.*) Art avis'd o' that? More
   on't.

Angelo.
Why do you put these sayings upon me?
Isabella.
Because Authority, though it err like
    others,
Hath yet a kind of medicine in itself,
That skins the vice o' th' top. Go to your bosom:
Knock there, and ask your heart what it doth know
That's like my brother's fault. If it confess
A natural guiltiness such as is his,
Let it not sound a thought upon your tongue
Against my brother's life.
Angelo.
  (*Aside.*)   She speaks, and 'tis
Such sense that my sense breeds with it. (*Aloud.*)
    Fare you well.
Isabella.
Gentle my lord, turn back.
Angelo.
I will bethink me. Come again tomorrow.
Isabella.
Hark how I'll bribe you. Good my lord,
    turn back.
Angelo.
How! Bribe me?
Isabella.
Ay, with such gifts that heaven shall share
    with you.
Lucio.
(*Aside to Isabella.*) You had marr'd all else.
Isabella.
Not with fond sickles of the tested gold,
Or stones whose rates are either rich or poor
As fancy values them; but with true prayers
That shall be up at heaven and enter there
Ere sunrise: prayers from preserved souls,
From fasting maids whose minds are dedicate
To nothing temporal.
Angelo.
                    Well: come to me tomorrow.
Lucio.
(*Aside to Isabella.*) Go to: 'tis well. Away!

Isabella.

Heaven keep your Honor safe!

Angelo.

(*Aside.*)   Amen.
For I am that way going to temptation,
Where prayers cross.

Isabella.

                    At what hour tomorrow
Shall I attend your lordship?

Angelo.

                         At any time 'fore noon.

Isabella.

'Save your Honor!
          (*Exeunt Isabella, Lucio, and Provost.*)

Angelo.

                              From thee: even from
  thy virtue.
What's this? What's this? Is this her fault or mine?
The tempter, or the tempted, who sins most?
Ha!
Not she; nor doth she tempt. But it is I
That, lying by the violet in the sun,
Do as the carrion does, not as the flower,
Corrupt with virtuous season. Can it be
That modesty may more betray our sense
Than woman's lightness? Having waste ground
  enough,
Shall we desire to raze the sanctuary,
And pitch our evils there? O, fie, fie, fie!
What dost thou? Or what art thou, Angelo?
Dost thou desire her foully for those things
That make her good? O, let her brother live!
Thieves for their robbery have authority
When judges steal themselves. What! do I love her,
That I desire to hear her speak again,
And feast upon her eyes? What is't I dream on?
O cunning enemy that, to catch a saint,
With saints dost bait thy hook! Most dangerous
Is that temptation that doth goad us on
To sin in loving virtue. Never could the strumpet,
With all her double vigor, art and nature,
Once stir my temper; but this virtuous maid

Subdues me quite. Ever till now,
When men were fond, I smil'd and wonder'd how.

(*Exit.*)

SECOND SCENE

In a sense this second confrontation is a reverse image
of the first. Now Angelo speaks on behalf of human feelings in passionate terms. Isabella, initially confused (or does
she merely pretend not to understand?), retreats until she
is as little in touch with the world, as icily absolute, as
Angelo was at the beginning of their first encounter. And
in the course of this transition, she must lose the sympathy
the audience felt for her at her entrance.

(The development of these characters does not stop with
this scene. The actress seriously interested in Isabella
should also study Act III, scene 1, in which Isabella
rejects Claudio's pleas that she save his life and the Duke
provides a way for her to adjust the strictures of her honor
to the needs of her brother; and Act V, scene 1, in which
her character undergoes a final series of transformations.
The conflicts in Angelo are also resolved in Act V, scene
1.)

Angelo.
When I would pray and think, I think and
   pray
To several subjects. Heaven hath my empty words,
Whilst my invention, hearing not my tongue,
Anchors on Isabel: heaven in my mouth,
As if I did but only chew his name,
And in my heart the strong and swelling evil
Of my conception. The state, whereon I studied,
Is like a good thing, being often read,
Grown sear'd and tedious; yea, my gravity,
Wherein, let no man hear me, I take pride,
Could I, with boot, change for an idle plume,
Which the air beats for vain. O place! O form!
How often dost thou with thy case, thy habit,
Wrench awe from fools, and tie the wiser souls
To thy false seeming! Blood, thou art blood:
Let's write 'good Angel' on the devil's horn,

Is't not the devil's crest? How now! who's there?
(*Enter Servant.*)

Servant.

One Isabel, a sister, desires access to you.

Angelo.

Teach her the way. (*Exit Servant.*) O
  heavens!
Why does my blood thus muster to my heart,
Making both it unable for itself,
And dispossessing all my other parts
Of necessary fitness?
So play the foolish throngs with one that swounds!
Come all to help him, and so stop the air
By which he should revive; and even so
The general, subject to a well-wish'd king,
Quit their own part, and in obsequious fondness
Crowd to his presence, where their untaught love
Must needs appear offense.
(*Enter Isabella.*)
                    How now, fair maid!

Isabella.

I am come to know your pleasure.

Angelo.

That you might know it, would much better
  please me
Than to demand what 'tis. Your brother cannot live.

Isabella.

Even so. Heaven keep your Honor!

Angelo.

Yet may he live a while; and, it may be,
As long as you or I. Yet he must die.

Isabella.

Under your sentence?

Angelo

Yea.

Isabella.

When, I beseech you? that in his reprieve,
Longer or shorter, he may be so fitted
That his soul sicken not.

Angelo.

Ha! fie, these filthy vices! It were as good
To pardon him that hath from nature stolen

A man already made, as to remit
Their saucy sweetness that do coin heaven's image
In stamps that are forbid: 'tis all as easy
Falsely to take away a life true made,
As to put metal in restrained meanes
To make a false one.

Isabella.
'Tis set down so in heaven, but not in
        earth.

Angelo.
Say you so? Then I shall pose you quickly.
Which had you rather, that the most just law
Now took your brother's life; or, to redeem him,
Give up your body to such sweet uncleanness
As she that he hath stain'd?

Isabella.
                        Sir, believe this,
I had rather give my body than my soul.

Angelo.
I talk not of your soul. Our compell'd sins
Stand more for number than for accompt.

Isabella.
                                How say
    you?

Angelo.
Nay, I'll not warrant that; for I can speak
Against the thing I say. Answer to this:
I, now the voice of the recorded law,
Pronounce a sentence on your brother's life.
Might there not be a charity in sin
To save this brother's life?

Isabella.
                        Please you to do't,
I'll take it as a peril to my soul.
It is no sin at all, but charity.

Angelo.
Pleas'd you to do't, at peril of your soul,
Were equal poise of sin and charity.

Isabella.
That I do beg his life, if it be sin,
Heaven let me bear it! You granting of my suit,
If that be sin, I'll make it my morn prayer

To have it added to the faults of mine
And nothing of your answer.
Angelo.

                            Nay, but hear me.
Your sense pursues not mine: either you are igno-
    rant,
Or seem so craftily; and that's not good.
Isabella.
Let me be ignorant, and in nothing good,
But graciously to know I am no better.
Angelo.
Thus wisdom wishes to appear most bright
When it doth tax itself, as these black masks
Proclaim an enshield beauty ten times louder
Than beauty could, display'd. But mark me.
To be received plain, I'll speak more gross:
Your brother is to die.
Isabella.
So.
Angelo.
And his offense is so, as it appears,
Accountant to the law upon that pain.
Isabella.
True.
Angelo.
Admit no other way to save his life—
As I subscribe not that, nor any other,
But in the loss of question—that you, his sister,
Finding yourself desir'd of such a person,
Whose credit with the judge, or own great place,
Could fetch your brother from the manacles
Of the all-building law; and that there were
No earthly mean to save him, but that either
You must lay down the treasures of your body
To this suppos'd, or else to let him suffer,
What would you do?
Isabella.
As much for my poor brother as myself:
That is, were I under the terms of death,
Th' impression of keen whips I'ld wear as rubies,
And strip myself to death, as to a bed

That longing have been sick for, ere I'ld yield
My body up to shame.

Angelo.

                    Then must your brother die.

Isabella.

And 'twere the cheaper way:
Better it were a brother died at once,
Than that a sister, by redeeming him,
Should die for ever.

Angelo

Were not you then as cruel as the sentence
That you have slander'd so?

Isabella.

Ignomy in ransom and free pardon
Are of two houses: lawful mercy
Is nothing kin to foul redemption.

Angelo.

You seem'd of late to make the law a ty-
   rant,
And rather prov'd the sliding of your brother
A merriment than a vice.

Isabella.

O, pardon me, my lord! It oft falls out,
To have what we would have, we speak not what
   we mean.
I something do excuse the thing I hate,
For his advantage that I dearly love.

Angelo.

We are all frail.

Isabella.

               Else let my brother die,
If not a fedary, but only he
Owe and succeed thy weakness.

Angelo.

Nay, women are frail too.

Isabella.

Ay, as the glasses where they view them-
   selves,
Which are as easy broke as they make forms.
Women! Help heaven! Men their creation mar
In profiting by them. Nay, call us ten times frail,
For we are soft as our complexions are,

And credulous to false prints.
Angelo.

                             I think it well:
And from this testimony of your own sex—
Since I suppose we are made to be stronger
Than faults may shake our frames—let me be bold.
I do arrest your words. Be that you are,
That is, a woman; if you be more, you're none.
If you be one, as you are well express'd
By all external warrants, show it now,
By putting on the destin'd livery.

Isabella.

I have no tongue but one. Gentle my lord,
Let me entreat you speak the former language.
Angelo..

Plainly conceive, I love you.
Isabella.

My brother did love Juliet.
And you tell me that he shall die for't.
Angelo.

He shall not, Isabel, if you give me love.
Isabella.

I know your virtue hath a licence in't,
Which seems a little fouler than it is,
To pluck on others.
Angelo.

                        Believe me, on mine honor,
My words express my purpose.
Isabella.

Ha! little honor to be much believ'd
And most pernicious purpose! Seeming, seeming!
I will proclaim thee, Angelo; look for't!
Sign me a present pardon for my brother,
Or with an outstretch'd throat I'll tell the world
  aloud
What man thou art.
Angelo.

                    Who will believe thee, Isabel?
My unsoil'd name, th' austereness of my life,
My vouch against you, and my place i' th' state,
Will so your accusation overweigh,
That you shall stifle in your own report

And smell of calumny. I have begun,
And now I give my sensual race the rein.
Fit thy consent to my sharp appetite;
Lay by all nicety and prolixious blushes,
That banish what they sue for: redeem thy brother
By yielding up thy body to my will,
Or else he must not only die the death,
But thy unkindness shall his death draw out
To ling'ring sufferance. Answer me tomorrow,
Or, by the affection that now guides me most,
I'll prove a tyrant to him. As for you,
Say what you can, my false oreweighs your true.

(*Exit.*)

Isabella.

To whom should I complain? Did I tell
  this,
Who would believe me? O perilous mouths!
That bear in them one and the selfsame tongue,
Either of condemnation or approof,
Bidding the law make curtsy to their will,
Hooking both right and wrong to th' appetite,
To follow as it draws. I'll to my brother.
Though he hath falne by prompture of the blood,
Yet hath he in him such a mind of honor,
That, had he twenty heads to tender down
On twenty bloody blocks, he'd yield them up,
Before his sister should her body stoop
To such abhorr'd pollution.
Then, Isabel, live chaste, and, brother, die:
More than our brother is our chastity.
I'll tell him yet of Angelo's request,
And fit his mind to death, for his soul's rest. (*Exit.*)

from
ENTERTAINING MR. SLOANE
by Joe Orton

Two Scenes from Act I and Act II
KATH, SLOANE, (KEMP)

Joe Orton's early death robbed the contemporary theater of its wittiest playwright since Oscar Wilde and its most audacious playwright since the very young days of Shaw. Not that Orton had Wilde's elegance (except in words) or Shaw's convictions (except, perhaps, in reverse). His style is a reaction to middle-class frumpiness and the mod-ish mumble of the 1950s; his beliefs are the disillusioned protest of the fed-up young against the hypocrisy of an overfed middle-aged society that says one thing and does quite another. Ultimately, he is a moralist, however un-likely that may seem while you are watching his play. But most of all his theater is funny, though your laughter chokes up—as Orton means it to do—at moments when you realize the horrendous things at which he has led you to laugh.

Orton's scenes are gifts to actors who can handle them, but his manner, like his plotting, is deceptively simple. His comedy, tumbling into slapstick, demands the seriousness, the truthfulness in persisting in the absurd, that real farce inevitably requires. And his lines work only with that seemingly tossed-off, actually calculated delivery that is the secret of acting with style.

Mr. Sloane, which won the London critics' *Variety* award as the best play of 1964, begins with a young man who needs a room and is invited to take up lodgings in the house of a middle-aged woman whose concern for his com-

468

fort can most politely be described as extensive. Mr. Sloane, the young man, is good-looking.

In his stage directions Orton calls only for "A room, evening." It is, the editor is certain, a dowdy room in an English suburb. There are a few fussy details: the lampshades may not actually have a fringe, but it seems as though they do.

(*Kath enters followed by Sloane.*)

Kath.

This is my lounge.

Sloane.

Would I be able to use this room? Is it included?

Kath.

Oh, yes. (*Pause.*) You mustn't imagine it's always like this. You ought to have rung up or something. And then I'd've been prepared.

Sloane.

The bedroom was perfect.

Kath.

I never showed you the toilet.

Sloane.

I'm sure it will be satisfactory.

(*He walks round the room examining the furniture. Stops by the window.*)

Kath.

I should change them curtains. Those are our winter ones. The summer ones are more of a chintz. (*Laughs.*) The walls need re-doing. The Dadda has trouble with his eyes. I can't ask him to do any work involving ladders. It stands to reason.

(*Pause.*)

Sloane.

I can't give you a decision right away.

Kath.

I don't want you to. (*Pause.*) What do you think? I'd be happy to have you.

(*Silence.*)

Sloane.

Are you married?

Kath.

(*Pause.*) I was. I had a boy . . . killed in very sad circum-

stances. It broke my heart at the time. I got over it
though. You do, don't you?

(*Pause.*)

Sloane.

A son?

Kath.

Yes.

Sloane.

You don't look old enough.

(*Pause.*)

Kath.

I don't let myself go like some of them you may have
noticed. I'm just over . . . As a matter of fact I'm forty-
one.

(*Pause.*)

Sloane.

(*Briskly.*) I'll take the room.

Kath.

Will you?

Sloane.

I'll bring my things over tonight. It'll be a change from my
previous.

Kath.

Was it bad?

Sloane.

Bad?

Kath.

As bad as that?

Sloane.

You've no idea.

Kath.

I don't suppose I have. I've led a sheltered life.

Sloane.

Have you been a widow long?

Kath.

Yes a long time. My husband was a mere boy. (*With a
half-laugh.*) That sounds awful doesn't it?

Sloane.

Not at all.

Kath.

I married out of school. I surprised everyone by the suddenness of it. (*Pause.*) Does that sound as if I had to get married?

Sloane.

I'm broadminded.

Kath.

I should've known better. You won't breathe a word?

Sloane.

You can trust me.

Kath.

My brother would be upset if he knew I told you. (*Pause.*) Nobody knows around here. The people in the nursing home imagined I *was* somebody. I didn't disillusion them.

Sloane.

You were never married then?

Kath.

No.

Sloane.

What about—I hope you don't think I'm prying?

Kath.

I wouldn't for a minute. What about—?

Sloane.

. . . the father?

Kath.

(*Pause.*) We always planned to marry. But there were difficulties. I was very young and he was even younger. I don't believe we would have been allowed.

Sloane.

What happened to the baby?

Kath.

Adopted.

Sloane.

By whom?

Kath.

That I could not say. My brother arranged it.

Sloane.

What about the kid's father?

Kath.

He couldn't do anything.

Sloane.

Why not?

Kath.

His family objected. They were very nice but he had a

duty you see. (*Pause.*) As I say, if it'd been left to him I'd be his widow today. (*Pause.*) I had a last letter. I'll show you some time. (*Silence.*) D'you like flock or foam rubber in you pillow?

Sloane.

Foam rubber.

Kath.

You need a bit of luxury, don't you? I bought the Dadda one but he can't stand them.

Sloane.

I can.

Kath.

You'll live with us then as one of the family?

Sloane.

I never had no family of my own.

Kath.

Didn't you?

Sloane.

No, I was brought up in an orphanage.

Kath.

You have the air of lost wealth.

Sloane.

That's remarkable. My parents, I believe, *were* extremely wealthy people.

Kath.

Did Dr. Barnardo give you a bad time?

Sloane.

No. It was the lack of privacy I found most trying. (*Pause.*) And the lack of real love.

Kath.

Did you never know your mamma?

Sloane.

Yes.

Kath.

When did they die?

Sloane.

I was eight. (*Pause.*) They passed away together.

Kath.

How shocking.

Sloane.

I've an idea that they had a suicide pact. Couldn't prove it of course.

Kath.

Of course not. (*Pause.*) With a nice lad like you to take care of you'd think they'd've postponed it. (*Pause.*) Criminals, were they?

Sloane.

From what I remember they were respected. You know, H.P. debts. Bridge. A little light gardening. The usual activities of a cultured community. (*Silence.*) I respect their memory.

Kath.

Do you? How nice.

Sloane.

Every year I pay a visit to their grave. I take sandwiches. Make a day of it. (*Pause.*) The graveyard is situated in pleasant surroundings so it's no hardship. (*Pause.*) Tomb an' all.

Kath.

Marble? (*Pause.*) Is there an inscription?

Sloane.

Perhaps you'd come with me this trip?

Kath.

We'll see.

Sloane.

I go in the autumn. I clean the leaves off the monument. As a tribute.

Kath.

Any relations?

Sloane.

None.

Kath.

Poor boy. Alone in the world. Like me.

Sloane.

You're not alone.

Kath.

I am. (*Pause.*) Almost alone. (*Pause.*) If I'd been allowed to keep my boy I'd not be. (*Pause.*) You're almost the same age as he would be. You've got the same refinement.

Sloane.

(*Slowly.*) I need . . . understanding.

Kath.

You do don't you. Here let me take your coat.

(*She helps him off with his coat.*)

You've got a delicate skin.

(*She touches his neck. His cheek. He shudders a little. Pause. She kisses his cheek.*)

Just a motherly kiss. A real mother's kiss.

(*Silence. She lifts his arms and folds them about her.*)

You'll find me very sentimental. I upset easy.

(*His arms are holding her.*)

When I hear of . . . tragedies happening to perfect strangers. There are so many ruined lives.

(*She puts her head on his shoulder.*)

You must treat me gently when I'm in one of my moods.

(*Silence.*)

Sloane.

(*Clearing his throat.*) How much are you charging? I mean—I've got to know.

(*He drops his arms. She moves away.*)

Kath.

We'll come to some arrangement. A cup of tea?

Sloane.

Yes I don't mind.

Kath.

I'll get you one.

Sloane.

Can I have a bath?

Kath.

Now?

Sloane.

Later would do.

Kath.

You must do as you think fit.

SECOND SCENE

It is some months later. Kath is preparing to tell Mr. Sloane the good news that she is going to have a baby— his. This situation, however it may strike Mr. Sloane, will infuriate Kath's brother, Ed, a fortyish boy scout with a keen interest in muscle-building, whose interest in Mr. Sloane's welfare rivals Kath's own. Indeed, Ed's interest in Kath's lodger is as nearly the same as hers as it can be, given the idiosyncrasies of gender. He has employed Mr.

Sloane as his chauffeur and done his best to inculcate him with the principles of clean living and body improvement.

There is reason for the audience to suspect that Mr. Sloane may have killed a man. At any rate, Kath's old father has evidence of this. The subject has not been made public, and like Ed's fury it is not important until later in the play, though already Mr. Sloane's rather sadistic treatment of the old man may well have tarnished his image in our eyes.

(*Morning. Sloane is lying on the settee. A newspaper covers his face. Kath enters. Looks at the settee.*)

Sloane.

Where you been?

Kath.

Shopping, dear. Did you want me?

Sloane.

I couldn't find you.

(*Kath goes to the window. Takes off her headscarf.*)

Kath.

What's Eddie doing?

Sloane.

A bit of servicing.

Kath.

But that's your job.

(*Sloane removes the newspaper.*)

He shouldn't do your work.

Sloane.

I was on the beer. My guts is playing up.

Kath.

Poor boy. (*Pause.*) Go and help him. For mamma's sake.

Sloane.

I may in a bit.

Kath.

He's a good employer. Studies your interests. You want to think of his position. He's proud of it. Now you're working for him his position is your position. (*Pause.*) Go and give him a hand.

Sloane.

No.

Kath.

Are you too tired?

Sloane.

Yes.

Kath.

We must make allowances for you. You're young.
(*Pause.*) You're not taking advantage are you?

Sloane.

No.

Kath.

I know you aren't. When you've had a drinkie go and help
him.

Sloane.

If you want.

(*Pause.*)

Kath.

Did mamma hear you were on the razzle?

Sloane.

Yes.

Kath.

Did you go up West? You were late coming home.
(*Pause.*) Very late.

Sloane.

Three of my mates and me had a night out.

Kath.

Are they nice boys?

Sloane.

We have interests in common.

Kath.

They aren't roughs are they? Mamma doesn't like you as-
sociating with them.

Sloane.

Not on your life. They're gentle. Refined youths. Thorpe,
Beck and Doolan. We toured the nighteries in the motor.

Kath.

Was Ed with you?

Sloane.

No.

Kath.

Did you ask him? He would have come.

Sloane.

He was tired. A hard day yesterday.

Kath.

Ask him next time.

(*Pause.*)

Sloane.

We ended up at a fabulous place. Soft music, pink shades, lovely atmosphere.

Kath.

I hope you behaved yourself.

Sloane.

One of the hostesses give me her number. Told me to ring her.

Kath.

Take no notice of her. She might not be nice.

Sloane.

Not nice?

Kath.

She might be a party girl.

(*Pause.*)

Sloane.

What exactly do you mean?

Kath.

Mamma worries for you.

Sloane.

You're attempting to run my life.

Kath.

Is baby cross?

Sloane.

You're developing distinctly possessive tendencies.

Kath.

You can get into trouble saying that.

Sloane.

A possessive woman.

Kath.

A mamma can't be possessive.

Sloane.

Can't she?

Kath.

You know she can't. You're being naughty.

Sloane.

Never heard of a possessive mum?

Kath.

Stop it. It's rude. Did she teach you to say that?

Sloane.

What?

Kath.

What you just said.

(*Sloane makes no reply.*)

You're spoiling yourself in my eyes, Mr. Sloane. You won't ring this girl will you?

Sloane.

I haven't decided.

Kath.

Decide now. To please me. I don't know what you see in these girls. You have your friends for company.

Sloane.

They're boys.

Kath.

What's wrong with them? You can talk freely. Not like with a lady.

Sloane.

I don't want to talk.

(*Pause.*)

Kath.

She might be after your money.

Sloane.

I haven't got any.

Kath.

But Eddie has. She might be after his.

Sloane.

Look, you're speaking of a very good class bird.

Kath.

I have to protect you, baby, because you're easily led.

Sloane.

I like being led. (*Pause.*) I need to be let out occasionally. Off the lead.

(*Pause.*)

Kath.

She'll make you ill.

Sloane.

Shut it. (*Pause.*) Make me ill!

Kath.

Girls do.

Sloane.

How dare you. Making filthy insinuations. I won't have it. You disgust me you do. Standing there without your teeth. Why don't you get smartened up? Get a new rig-out.

(*Pause.*)

Kath.

Do I disgust you?

Sloane.

Yes.

Kath.

Honest?

Sloane.

And truly. You horrify me. (*Pause.*) You think I'm kidding. I'll give up my room if you don't watch out.

Kath.

Oh, no!

Sloane.

Clear out.

Kath.

Don't think of such drastic action. I'd never forgive myself if I drove you away. (*Pause.*) I won't any more.

(*He attempts to rise. Kath takes his hand.*)

Don't go dear. Stay with me while I collect myself. I've been upset and I need comfort. (*Silence.*) Are you still disgusted?

Sloane.

A bit.

(*She takes his hand, presses it to her lips.*)

Kathy.

Sorry, baby. Better?

Sloane.

Mmmm.

(*Silence.*)

Kath.

How good you are to me.

Kemp.

(*Enters. He carries a stick. Taps his way to the sideboard.*) My teeth, since you mentioned the subject, Mr. Sloane, are in the kitchen in Stergene. Usually I allow a good soak overnight. But what with one thing and another I forgot. Otherwise I would never be in such a state. (*Pause.*) I hate people who are careless with their dentures.

from

THE CHANGELING

by Thomas Middleton and William Rowley

Two Scenes from Act II, scene 2; and Act III, scene 4
BEATRICE, DE FLORES

Beatrice-Joanna changes her mind. Engaged to a handsome
young nobleman, she discovers a few days before the wedding that she loves even more another handsome young
nobleman. To resolve this awkward situation, she coolly determines to make use of a third suitor, De Flores, a grotesquely ugly man whose person she loathes and whose
worshipful attentions she has persistently scorned. De
Flores is compliant; when Beatrice asks him to kill the unwanted bridegroom, he does so. But he is as coldly cal-
culating as the girl herself and in payment for the murder committed to order he claims license to make use of
Beatrice, once at least, as his lover.

The play, first acted in 1623, is an extraordinary and
powerful excursion into the dark reaches of intrigue and
desire. The complex plot is bloody and sensational, yet
the focus of the play is on the psychology of characters
trapped by situations and their own motivations—the wills,
limitations, and passions that define them as individuals.
The action is a series of interrelated "changes"—variations on the theme suggested by the title—among which the
transformation of Beatrice is the greatest and most shocking. At the outset a beautiful if self-centered virgin, she dies
a cruel, dishonest, whorish schemer, not inappropriately
mated with ugliness:

> What an opacous body hath that moon
> That last chang'd on us! here is beauty changed

480

To ugly whoredom; here servant-obedience
To a master sin, imperious murder.

The scenes reprinted below mark two significant stages
in the change of Beatrice. Together they also exemplify
that old, highly effective theatrical game, "changing places"
—in this case, the reversing of the master-servant relationship.

In a room in the castle of the governor of Alicante
(Beatrice's father), Beatrice and Alsemero, the nobleman
she loves, have met secretly and lamented the obstacles
—the fiancé and parents—that stand between them. Alsemero has offered to challenge the bridegroom, but Beatrice
will not allow him to risk his life. And killing, she says,
becomes a face less handsome than his. The remark brings
ugly De Flores to her mind, and though she says nothing
to Alsemero, a plan occurs to her. When Alsemero slips
away, De Flores, who has been spying on the lovers, appears.

De Flores.

(*Aside.*) I have watch'd this meeting, and do wonder
    much
What shall become of t'other; I'm sure both
Cannot be serv'd unless she transgress; happily
Then I'll put in for one: for if a woman
Fly from one point, from him she makes a husband,
She spreads and mounts then like arithmetic,
One, ten, a hundred, a thousand, ten thousand,
Proves in time sutler to an army royal.
Now do I look to be most richly rail'd at,
Yet I must see her.

Beatrice.

(*Aside.*)   Why, put case I loath'd him
As much as youth and beauty hates a sepulchre,
Must I needs show it? Cannot I keep that secret,
And serve my turn upon him?—See, he's here.
(*To him.*) De Flores.

De Flores.

(*Aside.*)   Ha, I shall run mad with joy;
She call'd me fairly by my name De Flores,
And neither rogue nor rascal!

Beatrice.

What ha' you done
To your face a-late? Y'have met with some good physician;
Y'have prun'd yourself, methinks, you were not wont
To look so amorously.

De Flores.

(*Aside.*)   Not I;
'Tis the same physnomy, to a hair and pimple,
Which she call'd scurvy scarce an hour ago:
How is this?

Beatrice.

Come hither; nearer, man!

De Flores.

(*Aside.*) I'm up to the chin in heaven.

Beatrice.

Turn, let me see;
Faugh, 'tis but the heat of the liver, I perceiv't.
I thought it had been worse.

De Flores.

(*Aside.*)   Her fingers touch'd me!
She smells all amber.

Beatrice.

I'll make a water for you shall cleanse this
Within a fortnight.

De Flores.

With your own hands, lady?

Beatrice.

Yes, mine own, sir; in a work of cure
I'll trust no other.

De Flores.

(*Aside.*)   'Tis half an act of pleasure
To hear her talk thus to me.

Beatrice.

When w'are us'd
To a hard face, 'tis not so unpleasing;
It mends still in opinion, hourly mends,
I see it by experience.

De Flores.

(*Aside.*)   I was blest
To light upon this minute; I'll make use on't.

Beatrice.

Hardness becomes the visage of a man well,
It argues service, resolution, manhood,
If cause were of employment.

De Flores.

                    'Twould be soon seen,
If e'er your ladyship had cause to use it.
I would but wish the honour of a service
So happy as that mounts to.

Beatrice.

                We shall try you—
Oh my De Flores!

De Flores.

(*Aside.*)   How's that?
She calls me hers already, *my* De Flores!
(*To Beatrice.*)—You were about to sigh out somewhat,
  madam.

Beatrice.

No, was I? I forgot,—Oh!

De Flores.

              There 'tis again,
The very fellow on't.

Beatrice.

           You are too quick, sir.

De Flores.

There's no excuse for't now, I heard it twice, madam;
That sigh would fain have utterance, take pity on't,
And lend it a free word; 'las, how it labours
For liberty! I hear the murmur yet
Beat at your bosom.

Beatrice.

          Would creation—

De Flores.

Ay, well said, that's it.

Beatrice.

           Had form'd me man.

De Flores.

Nay, that's not it.

Beatrice.

         Oh, 'tis the soul of freedom!
I should not then be forc'd to marry one

I hate beyond all depths, I should have power
Then to oppose my loathings, nay, remove 'em
For ever from my sight.

De Flores.

Oh blest occasion!—
Without change to your sex, you have your wishes.
Claim so much man in me.

Beatrice.

In thee, De Flores?
There's small cause for that.

De Flores.

Put it not from me,
It's a service that I kneel for to you.   (*Kneels.*)

Beatrice.

You are too violent to mean faithfully;
There's horror in my service, blood and danger,
Can those be things to sue for?

De Flores.

If you knew
How sweet it were to me to be employed
In any act of yours, you would say then
I fail'd, and us'd not reverence enough
When I receive the charge on't.

Beatrice.

(*Aside.*)   This is much, methinks;
Belike his wants are greedy, and to such
Gold tastes like angels' food (*To De Flores.*)—Rise.

De Flores.

I'll have the work first.

Beatrice.

(*Aside.*)   Possible his need
Is strong upon him; (*Gives him money.*)—there's to
  encourage thee:
As thou art forward and thy service dangerous,
Thy reward shall be precious.

De Flores.

That I have thought on;
I have assur'd myself of that beforehand,
And know it will be precious, the thought ravishes.

Beatrice.

Then take him to thy fury.

De Flores.
                        I thirst for him.
Beatrice.
  Alonzo de Piracquo.
De Flores.
                  His end's upon him;
  He shall be seen no more. (*Rises.*)
Beatrice.
                        How lovely now
  Dost thou appear to me! Never was man
  Dearlier rewarded.
De Flores.
                  I do think of that.
Beatrice.
  Be wondrous careful in the execution.
De Flores.
  Why, are not both our lives upon the cast?
Beatrice.
  Then I throw all my fears upon thy service.
De Flores.
  They ne'er shall rise to hurt you.
Beatrice.
                              When the deed's done,
  I'll furnish thee with all things for thy flight;
  Thou may'st live bravely in another country.
De Flores.
  Ay, ay, we'll talk of that hereafter.
Beatrice.
  (*Aside.*)   I shall rid myself
  Of two inveterate loathings at one time,
  Piracquo, and his dog-face.   (*Exit.*)
De Flores.
                  Oh my blood!
  Methinks I feel her in mine arms already,
  Her wanton fingers combing out this beard,
  And being pleased, praising this bad face.
  Hunger and pleasure, they'll commend sometimes
  Slovenly dishes, and feed heartily on 'em,
  Nay, which is stranger, refuse daintier for 'em.
  Some women are odd feeders.—I'm too loud.
  Here comes the man goes supperless to bed,
  Yet shall not rise to-morrow to his dinner.

SECOND SCENE

Beatrice's schemes move forward auspiciously. De Flores
has lured the bridegroom to a vault where he can kill
him secretly. Beatrice's father has met Alsemero and liked
the young man so much that he has said, "I wish I had
a daugher now for you." The father and lover walk off
together, leaving Beatrice alone to congratulate herself on
the successes she has achieved.

Beatrice.

                    So, here's one step
Into my father's favour; time will fix him.
I have got him now the liberty of the house:
So wisdom by degrees works out her freedom;
And if that eye be darkened that offends me
(I wait but that eclipse), this gentleman
Shall soon shine glorious in my father's liking,
Through the refulgent virtue of my love.

                  (*Enter De Flores.*)

De Flores.

(*Aside.*) My thoughts are at a banquet for the deed;
I feel no weight in't, 'tis but light and cheap
For the sweet recompense that I set down for't.

Beatrice.

De Flores.

De Flores.

        Lady?

Beatrice.

              Thy looks promise cheerfully.

De Flores.

All things are answerable, time, circumstance,
Your wishes, and my service.

Beatrice.

              Is it done then?

De Flores.

Piracquo is no more.

Beatrice.

My joys start at mine eyes; our sweet'st delights
Are evermore born weeping.

De Flores.

I've a token for you.

Beatrice.

For me?

De Flores.

But it was sent somewhat unwillingly,
I could not get the ring without the finger.

(Shows her the finger.)

Beatrice.

Bless me! What hast thou done?

De Flores.

Why, is that more
Than killing the whole man? I cut his heart-strings.
A greedy hand thrust in a dish at court,
In a mistake hath had as much as this.

Beatrice.

'Tis the first token my father made me send him.

De Flores.

And I made him send it back again
For his last token; I was loath to leave it,
And I'm sure dead men have no use of jewels.
He was as loath to part with't, for it stuck
As if the flesh and it were both one substance.

Beatrice.

At the stag's fall the keeper has his fees:
'Tis soon apply'd, all dead men's fees are yours, sir;
I pray, bury the finger, but the stone
You may make use on shortly; the true value,
Take't of my truth, is near three hundred ducats.

De Flores.

'Twill hardly buy a capcase for one's conscience, though,
To keep it from the worm, as fine as 'tis.
Well, being my fees I'll take it;
Great men have taught me that, or else my merit
Would scorn the way on't.

Beatrice.

It might justly, sir:
Why, thou mistak'st, De Flores, 'tis not given
In state of recompense.

De Flores.

No, I hope so, lady,
You should soon witness my contempt to't then!

Beatrice.

Prithee, thou look'st as if thou wert offended.

De Flores.

That were strange, lady; 'tis not possible
My service should draw such a cause from you.
Offended? Could you think so? That were much
For one of my performance, and so warm
Yet in my service.

Beatrice.

'Twere misery in me to give you cause, sir.

De Flores.

I know so much, it were so, misery
In her most sharp condition.

Beatrice.

                     'Tis resolv'd then;
Look you, sir, here's three thousand golden florins:
I have not meanly thought upon thy merit.

De Flores.

What, salary? Now you move me.

Beatrice.

                        How, De Flores?

De Flores.

Do you place me in the rank of verminous fellows,
To destroy things for wages? Offer gold?
The life blood of man! Is anything
Valued too precious for my recompense?

Beatrice.

I understand thee not.

De Flores.

                   I could ha' hir'd
A journeyman in murder at this rate,
And mine own conscience might have slept at ease,
And have had the work brought home.

Beatrice.

(Aside.)   I'm in a labyrinth;
What will content him? I would fain be rid of him.
(To De Flores.) I'll double the sum, sir.

De Flores.

                 You take a course
To double my vexation, that's the good you do.

Beatrice.

(Aside.) Bless me! I am now in worse plight than I was;

I know not what will please him. (*To De Flores.*)—For
  my fear's sake,
I prithee make away with all speed possible.
And if thou be'st so modest not to name
The sum that will content thee, paper blushes not;
Send thy demand in writing, it shall follow thee,
But prithee take thy flight.

De Flores.

                       You must fly too then.

Beatrice.

I?

De Flores.

I'll not stir a foot else.

Beatrice.

                What's your meaning?

De Flores.

Why, are not you as guilty, in (I'm sure)
As deep as I? And we should stick together.
Come, your fears counsel you but ill, my absence
Would draw suspect upon you instantly;
There were no rescue for you.

Beatrice.

(*Aside.*)   He speaks home.

De Flores.

Nor is it fit we two, engag'd so jointly,
Should part and live asunder.   (*Tries to kiss her.*)

Beatrice.

               How now, sir?
This shows not well.

De Flores.

            What makes your lip so strange?
This must not be betwixt us.

Beatrice.

(*Aside.*)   The man talks wildly.

De Flores.

Come, kiss me with a zeal now.

Beatrice

(*Aside.*)   Heaven, I doubt him!

De Flores.

I will not stand to beg 'em shortly.

Beatrice.

Take heed, De Flores, of forgetfulness,

'Twill soon betray us.
De Flores.

                    Take you heed first;
Faith, y'are grown much forgetful, y'are to blame in't.
Beatrice.

(*Aside.*) He's bold, and I am blam'd for't!
De Flores.

                                        I have eas'd you
Of your trouble, think on't, I'm in pain,
And must be eas'd of you; 'tis a charity,
Justice invites your blood to understand me.
Beatrice.

I dare not.
De Flores.

          Quickly!
Beatrice.

              Oh, I never shall!
Speak it yet further off that I may lose
What has been spoken, and no sound remain on't.
I would not hear so much offence again
For such another deed.
De Flores.

              Soft, lady, soft;
The last is not yet paid for! Oh, this act
Has put me into spirit; I was as greedy on't
As the parch'd earth of moisture, when the clouds weep.
Did you not mark, I wrought myself into't,
Nay, sued and kneel'd for"t: why was all that pains took?
You see I have thrown contempt upon your gold,
Not that I want it not, for I do piteously:
In order I will come unto't, and make use on't,
But 'twas not held so precious to begin with;
For I place wealth after the heels of pleasure,
And were I not resolv'd in my belief
That thy virginity were perfect in thee,
I should but take my recompense with grudging,
As if I had but half my hopes I agreed for.
Beatrice.

Why, 'tis impossible thou canst be so wicked,
Or shelter such a cunning cruelty,
To make his death the murderer of my honour!
Thy language is so bold and vicious,

I cannot see which way I can forgive it
With any modesty.

De Flores.

               Push, you forget yourself!
A woman dipp'd in blood, and talk of modesty?

Beatrice.

Oh misery of sin! Would I had been bound
Perpetually unto my living hate
In that Piracquo, than to hear these words.
Think but upon the distance that creation
Set 'twixt thy blood and mine, and keep thee there.

De Flores.

Look but into your conscience, read me there,
'Tis a true book, you'll find me there your equal:
Push, fly not to your birth, but settle you
In what the act has made you, y'are no more now;
You must forget your parentage to me:
Y'are the deed's creature; by that name
You lost your first condition, and I challenge you,
As peace and innocency has turn'd you out,
And made you one with me.

Beatrice.

               With thee, foul villain?

De Flores.

Yes, my fair murd'ress; do you urge me?
Though thou writ'st maid, thou whore in thy affection!
'Twas chang'd from thy first love, and that's a kind
Of whoredom in thy heart; and he's chang'd now,
To bring thy second on, thy Alsemero,
Whom (by all sweets that ever darkness tasted)
If I enjoy thee not, thou ne'er enjoy'st;
I'll blast the hopes and joys of marriage,
I'll confess all; my life I rate at nothing.

Beatrice.

De Flores!

De Flores.

I shall rest from all lovers' plagues then;
I live in pain now: that shooting eye
Will burn my heart to cinders.

Beatrice.

               Oh, sir, hear me.

De Flores.

  She that in life and love refuses me,

  In death and shame my partner she shall be.

Beatrice.

  Stay, hear me once for all; (*Kneels.*) I make thee master

  Of all the wealth I have in gold and jewels:

  Let me go poor unto my bed with honour,

  And I am rich in all things.

De Flores.

                    Let this silence thee;

  The wealth of all Valencia shall not buy

  My pleasure from me;

  Can you weep fate from its determin'd purpose?

  So soon may you weep me.

Beatrice.

                    Vengeance begins;

  Murder I see is followed by more sins.

  Was my creation in the womb so curs'd,

  It must engender with a viper first?

De Flores.

  Come rise, and shroud your blushes in my bosom;

                          (*Raises her.*)

  Silence is one of pleasure's best receipts:

  Thy peace is wrought for ever in this yielding.

  'Las, how the turtle pants! Thou'lt love anon

  What thou so fear'st and faint'st to venture on.   (*Exeunt.*)

from

THE BACCHAE

by Euripides (translated by Kenneth Cavander)

Three Scenes
PENTHEUS, DIONYSOS

Fascinating, enigmatic, frightening, *The Bacchae* seems to speak directly to a contemporary theater concerned to redefine the boundaries of dramatic experience and human feeling. Dionysos, its central figure and controlling spirit, is the contradictory god of ecstasy, joy, and peace, and of violence and slaughter; the god of irresistible rhythm and dance, of release into self-discovery and loss into self-oblivion.

There is no simple explanation of the play. It is clearly "about" ecstatic possession—by the god, by the frenzies of religious ritual, by the passions or instincts inherent in man that limit his civilizing of himself. Its major action is an extended confrontation between Dionysos and Pentheus, the rational, order-enforcing, moralizing (and inhibited) ruler of a city which the god claims as his own. At the beginning of the play, Dionysos identifies himself as the god he is; there is no disputing this truth despite his comic, effeminate appearance, his wig of long, blond curls, and (if the play is produced in a traditional way) the smiling mask he wears throughout. He is, as suits the god of theater, a god of many disguises. He is capable also of moving men to change their appearances, and before the play is done, he shows us a giggling, effeminate Pentheus, changed —or simply made more himself—by the power of Dionysos. In terms of appearance as of dominance, the two characters trade positions during the course of their drama —a transposition obvious enough by the third of the scenes

493

reprinted here, but one that comes about in a series of subtle adjustments that require careful defining by the actors playing the roles.

Thebes, Pentheus' city, is Dionysos' home. He was born here, the child of Zeus and a mortal maiden, Semele. Her grave stands at the back of the stage, still smoldering from the time Zeus appeared to her, as she demanded, in his own form and his fiery brilliance destroyed her. Now Semele's legend is in question; her sister, Pentheus' mother, has led the chorus of doubters who have dismissed the tale of Zeus's visits as a lie. In anger, Dionysos has returned to Thebes, taken possession of the women of the city, and led them in a frenzied dance to the mountain where his rituals are celebrated.

Young Pentheus is shocked and annoyed. Despite the advice of his grandfather, Cadmus, and the seer Tiresias, who scurry to pay their respects to the god ("If it isn't true, at least it's good for the family reputation"), Pentheus declares he will put an abrupt stop to the nonsense of this weird prophet who is disrupting order in his city. He orders that the prophet and the women be locked up. When his guards carry out his order, the prison locks open mysteriously and the women rush back to the mountain. Dionysos, however, is led to the palace in chains, and this is how Pentheus finds him when he comes out to view the prisoner. He is dressed in a fawn skin and carries a thyrsus (a twig of fennel tipped with ivy). The guard reports, Pentheus orders him to step back, and he and Dionysos face each other.

Pentheus.

Enough.
Let him go. He is inside the cage and he can't
Escape from us now. He doesn't move
So quick.
Well, stranger, you're not at all bad looking,
Are you? At least, to the women . . . Which is why
You have come to Thebes, I suppose . . . Long hair
Crinkling down your cheeks—you've never wrestled,
I presume—very desirable . . . White
Skin—you keep out of the sun, you cultivate
The shadows, where you hunt down love

With your handsome profile. Yes?
Who are you? Where do you come from?
Dionysos.
I am no one . . .
But I will give you an easier answer.
Have you ever heard of a river called Tmolos? It runs
Through fields of flowers . . .
Pentheus.
Yes, I know the river, it circles the town
Of Sardis.
Dionysos.
I come from there. My country is Lydia.
Pentheus.

                                    And these
Activities. How is it you bring them to Greece?
Dionysos.
Dionysos inspired me. Dionysos . . . He
Is the son of Zeus.
Pentheus.

                        So you have a Zeus
Over there, who fathers new powers
On the world.
Dionysos.

                        No. Zeus was united
With Semele in Thebes, and gave her the child
Here.
Pentheus.

                Did the irresistible urge
Come to you at night, or were you
"Inspired" in the daytime?
Dionysos.

                                    I saw him.

He saw me. And he gave me the secret
Means to summon his presence.
Pentheus.

                                And this secret—

What is it like? Can you tell me?
Dionysos.

                                    It must not

Be revealed to someone in whom Dionysos
Has not been born.

Pentheus.

                                        Those who share this secret—
Do they benefit—and how?

Dionysos.

                                        I am forbidden to tell.

But it is worth knowing.

Pentheus.

                                        You are clever, but
You're a fake! You want to make me curious.

Dionysos.

For a man who is so sure of what he knows
There are no powers, there is no other
Life. It simply escapes him.

Pentheus.

                                        You say you saw
Dionysos clearly . . . What did he look like?

Dionysos.

                                                What ever

He wished. I didn't arrange it.

Pentheus.

                                                Very good.

But once more you evade the issue,
Your statement was meaningless.

Dionysos.

The greatest truths often sound like babblings
Of madmen—till they are understood.

Pentheus.

                                                Are we

The first to be visited by you and your offer
Of supernatural aid?

Dionysos.

                                No. All
The people of the east are awake. They dance.
They live . . .

Pentheus.

                        They're out of their minds, we in Greece
Have more sense.

Dionysos.

                        No, in this case, less.
Their way is different, that is all.

Pentheus.

And these practices you claim are sacred

Do they take place at night, or in the day?
Dionysos.

Mostly at night. Darkness has dignity.
Pentheus.

For women the night hours are dangerous,
Lascivious hours . . .
Dionysos.

                People have been known
To sin during the day.
Pentheus.

                You play with words!
You'll be punished for that.
Dionysos.

                You soil mysteries
With your ignorant sneers. You'll be punished
For that.
Pentheus.

       He is so sure. The drunken dancer
Has been in training—for argument.
Dionysos.

                          Come,
Pronounce sentence. What terrible fate have you
In store for me?
Pentheus.

                First, I'll clip those flowing
Locks . . .
Dionysos.

            My hair must not be touched. I grow it
For Dionysos.
Pentheus.

            Next, you will hand over
Your wand, that branch you carry . . .
Dionysos.

                Take it from me
Yourself. I carry it for Dionysos.
Pentheus.

                Then
We shall lock you in prison, and you will never get out.
Dionysos.

Dionysos will free me, when I wish him to.

Pentheus.

Yes, when you get your followers around you and "summon

His presence."

Dionysos.

                    He sees. He is here. This minute he knows
What is being done to me.

Pentheus.

                              Where is he then?
I can't see him. Why doesn't he show himself?

Dionysos.

He's here, where I stand. You, being crass
And proud, see nothing.

Pentheus.

                    You're raving.

                                        He insults me.

He insults you all!

Dionysos.

                              I am sane. You

Are not. I say to you, set me free.

Pentheus.

And I say you go to prison, because
I am master here, I have the power.

Dionysos.

You don't know what your life is, what
You are doing, who you are . . .

Pentheus.

I am Pentheus
Son of Echion and Agave.

Dionysos.

                              Pentheus;
A very convenient name for a doomed man.

Pentheus.

Go away, go on! Go!
Lock him up somewhere near—in the stables.
Leave him to stare at the darkness,
Darkness all the time.
Dance in there!
And these creatures you have brought here, these
Accessories,
We'll either sell them, or we'll give their hands work

To do—not this banging, thumping on pieces of skin
But work. Spinning. Weaving. They'll belong to us.
Dionysos.
I leave you now. But I shall not suffer
What I have no need to suffer. Dionysos
Will punish you for your gross contempt. You
Say he does not exist. But when you send
Me to prison
It is you
Who commit the crime . . .
Against him.

SECOND SCENE

Dionysos has escaped. In the stable that was to be his prison the guards have found only a great bull. Again he confronts Pentheus, who rails at him, refusing to acknowledge that some supernatural power worked to free Dionysos. The god stands silent, smiling, as a messenger brings news of wild revels among the women and of a bloody foray into the countryside that ended with the tearing of beasts limb from limb. This, the messenger concludes, can only be the work of a great god.

Pentheus.
Now, I see . . . yes! Nearer . . . nearer!
This insufferable craze is like a fire, and it's spreading!
All Greece despises us. Now
Is the time we must take a firm stand.
Go to the gates of Electra, get every man
Under arms. I want all the cavalry, every
Spearman, every bowman, mobilized.
We attack the Bacchae at once . . .
This is too much. I have been too patient. I refuse
To be terrorized by a pack of women.
Dionysos.
I told you Pentheus, but you never listen.
You have not been good to me. All the same
I am going to warn you. You must not use force against
Dionysos.
End the war in yourself. He will not

Allow you to disturb his Bacchae. Leave them
In the mountains where they are happy.
Pentheus.

Don't preach
To me. You were in prison and you escaped.
Well, look after your freedom or I may remind
Myself that you have been judged and condemned.
Dionysos.

I
Would sacrifice to him . . . not rage and struggle
And kick. This is an eternal power—
You are a man.
Pentheus.

I'll sacrifice to him!
A blood sacrifice, a woman sacrifice—
That is all they are fit for. I will be lavish
There will be carnage in the glades of Kithairon.
Dionysos.

You'll lose. It will be an ignominious rout.
Your bronze shields won't hold off wooden sticks
And woman's hands.
Pentheus.

Will someone tell me how
To get rid of this man? Extricate me, someone!
Whatever I do to him, whatever he does
To me, it's the same. Talk, talk, talk!
Dionysos.

Excuse me—but you can settle all this,
No trouble, It is still possible.
Pentheus.

How? What
Do I do? Make myself lower than the lowest
In this country?
Dionysos.

I will bring the women
Here, without the use of force.
Pentheus.

Yes,
I see, thank you. This is the great master
Plan—the great deception.

Dionysos.

How can you call it
That? I want to keep you whole. I work
For nothing else.

Pentheus.

You arranged this with your friends.
License to dance, disorder in perpetuity.

Dionysos.

Certainly I arranged it, quite true—
With Dionysos.

Pentheus.

Bring out my armour . . .
You—
Keep quiet!

Dionysos.

Wait! Wait!! Do you want to see them . . .
In their nests up there in the hills, See
The women . . .?

Pentheus.

Yes, yes, I do, Yes,
I'll pay if I have to. Gold, How much? A thousand?
Ten thousand?

Dionysos.

You've fallen in love with my idea.
You can't wait. Why?

Pentheus.

I'll see them drunk,
Hoplessly drunk. It revolts me, but . . . I . . .

Dionysos.

But you really want to. That disgusting sight
Lures you there . . .?

Pentheus.

Yes, I told you, it does.
I won't say anything, I'll be quiet, I'll stay
Among the pine-trees.

Dionysos.

You can try to hide
But they'll pick up your scent.

Pentheus.

Good point. I'd forgotten.
I'll go openly.

Dionysos.

        I'll take you there. Would you like that?
The way is before you. Will you dare?

Pentheus.

                  Now!
Take me there now. I hate every minute
We lose.

Dionysos.

        Then you must be covered. Find yourself a chiffon
Dress to wear . . .

Pentheus.

              Wait, now what is
This? I'm a man, I don't change places
With any woman. Why should I?

Dionysos.

               In case
They kill you. Suppose you, a man, are discovered
There—you die.

Pentheus.

           Right again. I understand.
There is some intelligence in you. I should have seen it
Before.

Dionysos.

        Dionysos came alive in me.
All I know is him.

Pentheus.

           Yes, yes . . .
Now, this good advice of yours, how
Do we carry it out?

Dionysos.

          We go inside, and there
I prepare you for your journey.

Pentheus.

         How—prepare me?
Dress me up as a woman? Oh no, no,
I would be ashamed.

Dionysos.

        Have you lost heart? The sight
Of those possessed and demented women, it no longer
Interests you?

Pentheus.

> What kind of clothing did you say
> I have to wear?

Dionysos.

> Long hair to your shoulders.
> You must have a wig . . .

Pentheus.

> And then what else? Is there more
> To this costume?

Dionysos.

> A full-length robe.
> And for the head—a scarf.

Pentheus.

> Anything else
> You want to drape me in?

Dionysos.

> We'll give you a stick
> Covered with ivy to hold, and wrap a spotted
> Fawn skin round you . . .

Pentheus.

> No, I could never put on
> Women's clothing.

Dionysos.

> What will you do—fight them?
> It's a waste of your blood.

Pentheus.

> You're right. First we must go
> And watch. Nothing more yet.

Dionysos.

> That
> Makes better sense than hunting down evil
> With more evil.

Pentheus.

> How can I get through the streets
> Of Thebes and not be seen?

Dionysos.

> We'll find a secret
> Way. I'll lead you.

Pentheus.

> Anything—but I will not
> Be entertainment for that herd of females. Let's go
> Inside. I want to consider this plan.

Dionysos.

>   Decide,
> I'm ready for you. Nothing will be too much trouble . . .

Pentheus.

> No, inside . . . I may call out my army
> And march up there . . . Or I may follow
> Your advice. We shall see.

THIRD SCENE

Dionysos follows Pentheus into the palace, and while his
followers chant of the might of the gods and evoke the terror of Dionysos, he takes full possession of the man who
denied him. Pentheus will be led to the mountain and there,
like the animals, will be captured and torn apart; his
mother will bear his head into Thebes like a trophy of the
hunt. But before that he must expose himself to the ridi-
cule he threw at the god.

Dionysos comes from the palace, turns, and calls to Pentheus. When the young king appears, he wears a linen
dress over the fawn skin of a worshiper of Dionysos. A
wig of blond curls covers his head, and he carries a thyrsus.
He is rather dazed and sees double, like a man who has
drunk too much.

Dionysos.

> You! You with a white-hot wish for a peep
> At the forbidden. You, reaching out for the out-of-reach,
> You—I'm talking to you—Pentheus! Come
> Out here, in front of your palace, let me
> See you, dressed a woman of the wild wine
> Nights of Dionysos. Are you ready to spy?
> Your mother is there . . .
> All the women are there.
>   (*Enter Pentheus.*)
> Perfect! You are a daughter of Kadmos to the life.

Pentheus.

> No, listen. I think I see two suns,
> And two Thebes, the seven-gated city
> Has doubled . . . and you, you look
> Like a bull, leading me—horns sprout from your head . . .

All the time, were you that beast?
Are you the bull now . . .?
Dionysos.
Dionysos favors you. He is bound to us
For the wine-gifts we gave him. Before he was not
Pleased. But now he is. And you see
What you ought to see.
Pentheus.

              How do I look to you?
My aunt . . . isn't this how she walks? Or this . . . My
  mother
Agave,—isn't it? Isn't it Agave?
Dionysos.
It's them! When I look at you it's them I see . . .
Wait—a wisp of hair has come away.
It isn't lying where I set it, under the scarf.
Pentheus.
Inside, I went this way with my head,
That way—back, forward, back—I was being
A woman in a trance. And I made the hair
Come loose . . .
Dionysos.

          We must keep you groomed. I'll put it in place
Again. Here . . . lift your head up straight.
Pentheus.
Look . . . there . . . you do it. Make me pretty.
I am yours to play with. Take me.
Dionysos.

             Your sash is loose—
Look. And your dress is wrong. The pleats should hang
The same length round your ankles.
Pentheus.

             Yes,
I see . . . a little too long by the right foot.
But on this side it seems all right, touching
My heel just there . . .
Dionysos.

             Who is your best friend?
I am . . . You don't believe me? Wait 'til you see
Bacchae, how modest they are, how pure, how sane—
Astonishing.

Pentheus.

                    This branch with ivy—in my right
Hand—or my left? Which makes me
More like a genuine wild woman of the hills?

Dionysos.

Hold it in your right hand, and raise it
In time with your right foot . . . Very good.
I see a change, a new mind, in you . . .

Pentheus.

Now I could . . . I could hoist the whole of Kithairon
On my shoulder—valleys full of women
Dancing, madness and all! . . . Yes?

Dionysos.

                    Of course,
If you will it. Your mood was before most unhealthy
Now it is all it should be.

Pentheus.

Shall we bring iron bars, or shall I delve it
Up with my own bare hands, wedge
One shoulder or one arm under the hill-top . . .?

Dionysos.

And destroy the homes of the nymphs? No, no.
Pan lives there too. Let him go on playing
His pipes.

Pentheus.

                    You're right. One should not coerce women.
I shall hide myself in the boughs of a pine tree.

Dionysos.

                                        You find
The hiding place that suits you best. You're a spy
A secret witness of secret rites.

Pentheus.

                    Yes,
Imagine, they are nestling like birds in the thick leaves,
Locked in their lust, enjoying it . . .

Dionysos.

                            You must break in
And prevent them. Perhaps you will find them in the
    act . . .
Unless they find you first.

Pentheus.

                Take me through Thebes,
Right through the centre. I am the only man
Here who has any courage.

Dionysos.

                   Yes, you alone
Make sacrifices for your people, you alone,
And so—the test. It has always been there, waiting
For you. Follow me. I am your
Protector, your escort . . . as far as Kithairon—
Someone else will bring you back.

Pentheus.

Yes, my mother . . .

Dionysos.

In full view of everyone . . .

Pentheus.

That's why I'm going . . .

Dionysos.

You will be borne back on high.

Pentheus.

Yes, in triumph, you mean my great triumph!

Dionysos.

In the hands of your mother . . .

Pentheus.

You'll spoil me—all this pampering!

Dionysos.

Yes, I'll spoil you, I'll spoil you utterly.

Pentheus.

Still, I deserve it, and I shall have it!

Dionysos.

You, with your hell inside you, you go walking
To your hellish end—which will make you
Famous, far beyond this life, beyond
This time.
Agave, fling open your arms.
Prepare, you sisters, daughters of Kadmos,
I bring this young man to you—
Prepare for a great contest.
The victor shall be myself—and Dionysos.
As for the rest—wait, watch, and listen.

from

THE PRISONER

by Bridget Boland

Three Scenes from Act I, scene 1; Act II, scene 3;
and Act III, scene 2
PRISONER, INTERROGATOR, (WARDER)

Bridget Boland's play is a unique study in the interaction
of two characters, the dramatization, with documentary-like
precision, of that perfection of man's inhumanity that has
come to be called brainwashing. Except for brief interludes
with the rather comic prison Warder, the play focuses entirely on the contest of wills between the Prisoner and the
Interrogator. First presented in 1954 with Alec Guinness
and Jack Hawkins (and later filmed with the same actors),
The Prisoner provided an intense and exhausting evening
of theater. As an exercise in the communication of characters in conflict it is unmatched.

The three scenes reprinted here illustrate the range of
shifting characterization demanded by this play, each moment of which involves subtle adjustments of character and
character relationships. The Interrogator is openly determined to persuade the Prisoner to a change of mind, a confession of political and moral guilt, but the Prisoner, if he
is to remain true to himself, must be equally concerned to
work some change in his adversary. One, in short, must
break the other, and each exchange of words is both an
assertion of one man's strength and a test for a sign of
yielding in his opponent.

The characters are never given names nor is the country
named in which their drama takes place, though clearly it
has come under the control of a totalitarian government.
The time is not long after an international war, probably
World War II. During the war the Prisoner and the Inter-

rogator have worked underground against the same oppressor. Now they are of opposing factions.

The setting is a prison. At stage right is the interrogation room, which suggests a cell and is furnished only with essentials. There is a door up center and the impression of a barred window. Center is a desk with a swivel chair in front of it for the Prisoner and another chair behind. A telephone, typewriter, carafe of water and a glass stand on the table. There are one or two filing cabinets. At the beginning of the play, daylight streams through the window. However, the overhead light above the Prisoner's chair is soon turned on and, day or night, it is not switched off. A wall divides the stage, and to its left is the Prisoner's cell, entered by a winding stairway. At the foot of the stairs is a pillar with a circular seat around it. There is a high, barred window, a chair, a table, a bench with a blanket folded on it, no bed. The overhead light is always on.

As the play begins, the stage is empty. Through the door comes the Warder, "a man of uninteresting appearance, with one startling characteristic: a loud and unpleasant sniff, which punctuates the succeeding scenes at inappropriate intervals." He looks round the room, goes out again, and jerks his head beckoningly.

Interrogator.

  * * * (*To Prisoner.*) Cigarette?

Prisoner.

(*Laughing.*) Thank you—no.

Interrogator.

Given it up? I keep trying to.

Prisoner.

If I might smoke my own—while they last?

Interrogator.

Oh, now I do resent that. Drugged cigarettes already? You don't give me much credit for the art of conversation.

Prisoner.

On the contrary, I remember you as a young barrister conducting some of the most brilliant cross-examinations I've ever heard. When I was studying voice production for the pulpit, the ecclesiastical authorities thought the law courts less disedifying than the theatre. That was in the

days when cross-examinations were held in public, of
course. Nowadays I—smoke my own.

Interrogator.

Good-bye, Stephen. (*The Secretary goes out. The Interrogator lights both cigarettes.*) Now look here, Eminence,
stop treating me as a police inspector, and relax.

Prisoner.

You can hardly blame me, under the circumstances.

Interrogator.

I've told the Powers that Be that your arrest is the worst
gaffe they've made yet. You're a national monument.
"Please do not deface."

Prisoner.

Please, do not deface.

Interrogator.

I'm sorry. This is humiliating for you and it's shaming for
me. You're not just a national figure. Since the war, since
all your work for the Resistance under the Occupation,
you've been a man to every man of us. I have, if you'll
allow me to say so, a deep personal respect for you—
combined, of course, with a fanatical loathing of what,
for some reason, is always called your cloth! Come now—

Prisoner.

Well, I'm in your hands.

Interrogator.

Let's get down to it. (*He opens a file on the desk, and turns
pages.*) Official blather—higher official blather—"eyes
grey, hair thinning."

Prisoner.

I also have a tonsure.

Interrogator.

Born here in the capital—were you? I never knew that.

Prisoner.

Just off the fish market.

Interrogator.

Local boy makes good. I'd have said in a country town, a
lawyer's or a doctor's son.

Prisoner.

I could have told you more about yourself. We had that
acreage of your father's estate in your service dossier, in
the Resistance. Arable, pasture, and forest. Fishing too—
but a long way from fish markets. A noble inheritance.

Interrogator.

Heavens, don't tell the Government. You'll get me the sack. "War record—see separate file." A file to itself. There aren't many of us who'd need that.

Prisoner.

You did well enough, in your district.

Interrogator.

Do you ever regret those days?

Prisoner.

Among the wars, I prefer those in which one is on the same side as one's fellow countrymen.

Interrogator.

Ah, here it is. (*He looks over a paper in silence for a moment.*) I'm sorry. Do sit down. (*The Prisoner leans on the chair or on the table L, but remains standing. Still among the papers.*) I see you issued a statement to be published if you weren't back at the Cathedral within five hours, that any information you gave or confession you made would be the result of drugs or torture, and was not to be credited.

Prisoner.

"The result of human weakness," was what I said.

Interrogator.

Have you a human weakness? Well, I don't suppose you object to answering how many ordained priests there are in the country?

Prisoner.

Certainly not. Roughly four thousand odd.

Interrogator.

Granted most of the population was Catholic in the past, what about remaining members of recognized Catholic Societies and organizations?

Prisoner.

Why not look it up in the directory?

Interrogator.

Why not, indeed? (*The Interrogator sits casually on the edge of his desk to write the answers, leaning over with his back to the Prisoner.*)

Prisoner.

Counting the League of Decency and the Mothers' Unions?

Interrogator.

Oh, definitely, I should say.

Prisoner.

Divide the Catholic population by four, and then divide by three again, because they're all the same ladies wearing different hats, multiply by—call it eighteen thousand.

Interrogator.

Twenty?

Prisoner.

It's a rounder figure.

Interrogator.

Members of underground Catholic Societies and organizations. (*After a pause.*) That's what it says. (*They both laugh.*) Yes, they're a bit premature with that one. Members of the Christian Workers Trade Organizations?

Prisoner.

Offhand, a hundred and fifty-eight thousand. Disbanded. Suppressed—remember?

Interrogator.

So I'd heard. Propaganda centres, anti-government?

Prisoner.

None. No, wait—how many pulpits have we?

Interrogator.

(*Making a note.*) That seems to be that lot.

Prisoner.

Well, the last one was a gift, the booby prize. (*Not at all sorry.*) Forgive me, that was unkind.

Interrogator.

Your Eminence——

Prisoner.

I know. This is more awkward for you than it is for me.

Interrogator.

Hardly that, I suppose.

Prisoner.

Oh, I don't know, in spite of your political creed it's you who are the gentleman. Degrees as a lawyer and a Doctor, born a gentleman, of an ancient house. No titles nowadays, of course, but yours was a noble line.

Interrogator.

You're a Prince of the Church, aren't you?

Prisoner.

A temporal, practically a diplomatic appointment. We

think more highly of the Spiritual grades I have never achieved. Look, don't think I don't enjoy fencing with you, but your masters are in a hurry, I fancy. People who are going to make heaven on earth always are, so hadn't we better come to the point?

Interrogator.

A man attacking a fortress tries to get a plan of the defences.

Prisoner.

My dear sir, you should have asked for it! I am reasonably acute, my mind works fast, if not very deeply, I am tenacious, wary, proud, and have few of the finer feelings.

Interrogator.

Proud?

Prisoner.

Quite sinfully—of my record in dealings with your predecessors, the Gestapo. I am difficult to trap, impossible to persuade, and even more impossible to appeal to. Also, I've been here or hereabouts before, and I know the ropes. I am, besides, tolerably inured to physical pain. (*The Interrogator looks at him for a moment, and then goes to the house phone on the wall.*)

Interrogator.

Three one. . . . Stephen, bring me down the completed confession, will you? (*He hangs up and turns back.*)

Prisoner.

Already?

Interrogator.

You might care to hear it. I don't think it a very good one, myself, but it'll give us some sort of agenda to work from.

Prisoner.

The State isn't fussy about just what we say I've done?

Interrogator.

Cards on the table? No.

Prisoner.

There's no particular plot, counter revolution, or underground movement that they're anxious to unmask?

Interrogator.

Not unless you happen to know of one—in particular.

Prisoner.

They believe us harmless, but require us discredited. And the point of arresting me?

Interrogator.

To—deface the national monument. We can no longer afford you at home or abroad, for your own followers or foreign journalists to watch and quote.

Prisoner.

I am not, you know, beloved. I am not a likeable man.

Interrogator.

No. In an odd way, that's the point. It's not the personality of a demagogue we're up against, it's the record of a hero. That's what we have to destroy. You see, I take you at your own valuation, and show you my hand from the start.

Prisoner.

It might have been amusing, if we'd had time. What a pity you're on the wrong side.

Prisoner.

Tell me, you yourself, can you admit no possibility of good on—the other side?

Interrogator.

(*With complete honesty.*) No. Very little good on either, but on your side not even right. And we can't allow you the right to be wrong.

Prisoner.

Ah. That's the root of it.

Interrogator.

Don't tell me your side aren't the same in the parts of the world where they're on top. (*The door is opened by the Warder, and the Secretary brings in a thick sheet of typescript. Both he and the Warder stare with startled interest at the Prisoner.*) I expect this will have fluttered the dovecotes. You wouldn't care to sign it right away, and really shake them? You know, you might just as well.

Prisoner.

I'd love to read it first, if I may.

Interrogator.

Thank you, Stephen. (*He gestures to him to hand the typescript to the Prisoner and he does so, though clearly shocked by the break from routine.*) I know, I know, it's not even supposed to exist yet. We're just starting at the wrong end, that's all, in order to save time. (*The Interrogator sits down. The Secretary is about to remove the papers he placed earlier.*) No, no—I may need those. Run along. And, Stephen, I shall want you to stand by tonight. (*The Prisoner looks up quickly with a wry smile. The Warder, who has stood through this interchange, sniffs mournfully and holds the door open—for the Secretary to go out—closes it and moves the third chair against the wall by it on which he sits, composing himself for a long session.*) Sit down, your Eminence. (*At his tone, the Prisoner obeys with a little bow of formality. Their official relationship is established.*)

SECOND SCENE

It is difficult to tell how long the interrogation has continued—for hours or for days? The Prisoner's stamina and his skill in countering the Interrogator's strategies are remarkable. The easier methods—false documents, re-edited tape recordings, threats—have been dismissed now. The Prisoner has been shown the body of his mother—not dead, but anesthetized—and been told that unless he cooperates with the Interrogator, she will be put in the hands of the researchers at the Cancer Hospital. He is not persuaded: "Under the Occupation even people without religion or belief learned of duties above human relationships."

The Interrogator tries another approach. Like an analyst working to help a patient, he leads the Prisoner to talk of his childhood: the poverty he was determined to escape, the clothes that smelled of the fishmarket when he went to school, the labors to win a scholarship to the university, the decision to enter the priesthood rather than accept the scholarship. We learn also that the Interrogator, like the Prisoner, has moved beyond the world of his childhood: his family was aristocratic. There is a word, "heartless," posed by the Prisoner as he considers the relative ease with which he condemned his mother to the researcher. "Terrible to be without heart," he says. "For me, the hard decision would have been to sign the confession and destroy myself and my cause. But the cause was God's, not mine. I'd no choice—except to torment myself with it." And there is a confession of sorts: as a child the Prisoner stole—books and pencils and paper.

It is night. Is it the same night as the preceding scene or some later night? In the interrogation room the Prisoner, in shirt and trousers and looking disheveled, is struggling hysterically with the Warder. The Interrogator watches.

Prisoner.

I'll kill him—let me get at him. (*In obedience to the uplifted hand of the Interrogator, the Warder is careful only to restrain him. Eventually his struggles weaken and the Warder lowers him, exhausted, into the Interrogator's chair, where he lies shaking and gasping.*)

Interrogator.

Medical Officer, at once. (*The Warder glances in doubt at the Prisoner.*) No, that's all right. And remind him of the regulations about speaking before he comes in—with my compliments, of course, my compliments. (*The Warder goes. The Interrogator goes to the house phone into which he speaks quietly.*) Three one. . . . Stephen. . . . Well, blast it, go and wake him, and tell him forty-eight hours. I warned them to have everything standing by, and then I can only guarantee them twenty-four hours to play with. Is the relay of stenographers laid on . . . ? Right. (*He hangs up and goes to the Prisoner. He feels his pulse.*) Come now, pull yourself together. It's only that you've been talking for over fifteen hours. The prison doctor's coming.

Prisoner.

I can't keep watch any more.

Interrogator.

No need to be on guard any more. We're beyond that, aren't we? We're so close, you and I, you might as well try to be on guard against yourself.

Prisoner.

Feel friendship and talk, and something knows I mustn't. . . . Have I said anything?

Interrogator.

No. . . .

Prisoner.

About the Church?

Interrogator.

We're only talking about you. Forget the rest. Just about you—you and me. Now, here's the doctor, you've just been a little faint—(*The Warder shows in the Doctor who carries a small bag. The Interrogator, behind the Prisoner's back, lays a finger on his lips. The Doctor nods briskly and goes to the Prisoner, who submits limply. The Doctor feels his pulse, looks at his eyes.)* Just faintness, talking too long. The Doctor will give you something. That's it. *(The Doctor takes something from the case, the Warder gives him and fills a glass from carafe on table.)*

Prisoner.

Not faintness. I—lost control. Warder. I hope I didn't hurt you. Something I had to hold off . . .

Interrogator.

(To Doctor.) The last kick—poor brute. I know the signs. *(To Prisoner.)* That's right. It's all right. Drink this. *(The Doctor holds the glass to him.)*

Prisoner.

No, nothing in this room.

Interrogator.

Oh, come on, now! It's all right. Look—*(He drinks from the glass and gives it to the Prisoner.)* The things I have to drink for you. Filthy, isn't it? That's right. *(The Interrogator jerks his head quickly to the Doctor who makes the gesture of one writing a report. The Interrogator nods impatiently and—the Doctor goes. The Warder sits by the door. The Interrogator starts a gesture of dismissal and then turns it into one indicating absolute quiet.)* Better? You need someone to talk-to-yourself to, when yourself won't listen. Why do you hate yourself? I know you and I don't hate you.

Prisoner.

You must.

Interrogator.

I am supposed to, but I can't. You don't love your fellow men, do you?

Prisoner.

No.

Interrogator.

Is that it? Or something deeper? You've no delight in your God, have you? Nor ever had?

Prisoner.

No.

Interrogator.

Is that why you hate yourself? Your heroism in the Resistance was only to convince yourself, to prove yourself to yourself. Why should you need to? What must you keep proving?

Prisoner.

The flesh not weak——

Interrogator.

What were you ashamed of? Women?

Prisoner.

A priest.

Interrogator.

Even so?

Prisoner.

No.

Interrogator.

Well, before—before—

Prisoner.

Thank God, no.

Interrogator.

Not round the corners of your mind. Not alive, pulsing in the dark, not veiled, drowned, buried, waiting?

Prisoner.

No.

Interrogator.

You think all your life was a façade. What were you hiding? Why were you ashamed?

Prisoner.

Unclean flesh.

Interrogator.

Yes. Yes?

Prisoner.

My body of her flesh and blood.

Interrogator.

Your mother.

Prisoner.

Filth of her filth. I, me, at the root of it, her lust.

Interrogator.

Behind the Fish Market. A prostitute?

Prisoner.

Not even for money. A whore. Not even for money, for lust.

Interrogator.

Yes.

Prisoner.

Whelped in the kennel. Naked lust. Oh, I put a scholar's gown on it, wrapped it in a cassock, pride to cover it, and then success to justify the pride, something, always, to prove—what wasn't there.

Interrogator.

Not there. No love?

Prisoner.

Sentimental fools! There's no love in the kennel! Desire, seduction, and a quick satisfaction, and on to the next. There's no love in some of us! Don't you think I'd have found it if there were?

Interrogator.

Heredity. You were afraid——

Prisoner.

Oh, that cant phrase. Heredity. What else is my flesh but her flesh, where else did I get this crawling body that I'm buried in? All right, environment! The environment of a bed in the other room, listening to new feet blundering up the staircase, the whispering and the smothered laughter, and the bedsprings screeching beyond the stupid flowered paper on the wall! Remembering the smell of the woman who bent over you to try and kiss you good night. Where, before I was born or after it, would I find a heart?

Interrogator.

Surely you proved to yourself——

Prisoner.

Chastity, temperance, fortitude—but no love. I can serve men, or God, or my country, but I can't care. Open it up, tear it open, look for a heart—there's nothing there! (*He collapses, exhausted and fainting. The Interrogator stands looking down at him.*)

Interrogator.

(*Standing for a moment, steeling himself for the final stage—he does not move or touch the Prisoner. At last he takes the jug and dashes water over him.*) You fake, you empty husk of a man. Not so much alive in you as a maggot. (*The Prisoner rises, swaying.*) The National Monument! The hero of the Resistance who outwitted the Gestapo for his own vanity, the martyr for the Church who is only resisting for his own pride.

Prisoner.

Yes.

Interrogator.

His Eminence the Cardinal, the Papal Chaplain, who
flies to Rome on the high international business of the
Church, the diplomat, the wit, the cultivated man of the
world, is that you, Eminence? That's what you've shown
the world, that, and the great preacher with the voice of
fire and ice, who could fill your huge Cathedral to the
doors with intellectuals and society women and the sweep-
ings of the slums—Yes, you've lived a good life, haven't
you? For the greater glory of you, for the making of a
Prince of the Church, for the proving and perfecting of
the miserable little bastard of a backstreet drab who smelt
of fish.

Prisoner.

Forgiveness.

Interrogator.

Did you preach forgiveness, up there in your fine pulpit,
to those hungry faces with the eyes you didn't dare look
down into, forgiveness for those that stole?

Prisoner.

Of course—

Interrogator.

But with restitution. Didn't they have to give back what
they'd stolen? Mustn't they make amends and return what
they'd taken, poor devils, before they could be forgiven?
But not you. You could sin and wallow in the profit of it,
you could live on your sin and get fat on it. You could
steal—you could steal the estimation of the world, and
hug it to yourself to stuff the empty place where your
heart ought to be. You could feed your hungry vanity with
stolen honour and then confess your pride and be forgiven.
You never had to give back what you stole.

Prisoner.

Stolen honour—

Interrogator.

Yes, stolen honour! You know what you let men think of
you and you knew the cold, proud fake you were, without
the capacity for love of God or man! What right had you
to honour? What right?

Prisoner.

Restitution. How can you give back honour? (*This is the crucial moment for the Interrogator. He pauses for a moment, registering now.*)

Interrogator.

Give it back. Oh—difficult. Deface the National Monument, pull it down? No, that'd be suicide, there'd be nothing left.

Prisoner.

Nothing? Is there no more to me than that façade?

Interrogator.

Nothing. Pride. A prig who had to be respectable—a small man who had to be great and called it a vocation.

Prisoner.

Oh, God. What to do?

Interrogator.

(*With an effort.*) If you have the courage, tear down the façade, throw them back their dream opinion of you, rid yourself of it, be yourself at last.

Prisoner.

How?

Interrogator.

Tell them, as you've told me. But it'd take more than courage to do that.

Prisoner.

It would take humility.

Interrogator.

A majestic splendour of humility.

Prisoner.

(*Doubtfully.*) Splendour?

Interrogator.

(*Quickly.*) To end the splendour. Abasement.

Prisoner.

Smash it, shatter it, grind it in the dust! Oh, but I've loathed it so!

Interrogator.

You'll do it? (*The door opens quietly and the Secretary comes in, still disarrayed from a hasty call. The Interrogator grips something to control his emotion and signs to him to go. The Secretary, agitated but insistent, gives him a piece of paper, which the Interrogator shaking with tension, reads. The Prisoner suddenly kneels. Whispering.*)

Twenty-four hours. I warned them to have everything laid on. (*The Secretary whispers in his ear.*) They've got to be ready for the public hearing. Tell them that. It's in my grasp, and I shall be able to hold it for twenty-four hours. (*He indicates the Prisoner, who kneels, his hands over his ears, trying to concentrate his swimming thoughts. The Secretary whispers again. The Prisoner notices him and rises.*)

Prisoner.

Stephen. (*The Interrogator takes the Secretary by the arm and urges him out of the room, closing the door softly. The Prisoner is trying to get his bearings.*) That was Stephen. You have to be careful in here not to say——

Interrogator.

(*Pitching on the interrupted note.*) But you could hardly do that to your reputation, could you—to yourself?

Prisoner.

I mustn't sign the confession.

Interrogator.

No, not the confession.

Prisoner.

Not harm the Church or the people—

Interrogator.

We've given that up, remember? It's only you we're talking about now, nothing to do with politics, you and the honour of your soul. A different confession about nothing but you.

Prisoner.

A true confession?

Interrogator.

Yes, a true confession, that you could sign.

Prisoner.

That I must sign.

Interrogator.

(*Breathes a long sigh but still goes carefully.*) What must you say?

Prisoner.

All that I've told you. The mockery of a man.

Interrogator.

Will they ever believe it?

Prisoner.

There's no restitution if I can't make them believe it.

(The Interrogator signs behind the Prisoner's back to the Warder, who switches on the recording apparatus under desk.)

Interrogator.

What shall you say?

Prisoner.

That I am the son of my mother, and my whole life a fantasy to hide me. Write that I lied my way through school and stole my way to a scholarship. Write that I became a priest for my own glory and that all my service was to my own spiritual pride. Write that I never had any love—love of the heart—for God. I never had a heart. The only prayer I ever prayed from—almost from—a heart was "Lord, I believe; help Thou my unbelief."

Interrogator.

And the people? The faces below the pulpit?

Prisoner.

Write that I posed and postured for them. I ate when they were hungry. Tell them that when they called me in the night my first thought was anger. A woman dying in childbirth, uselessly, of a dead child, a man on the railway siding hanging mangled and screaming in the jaws of a crane, and my first thought when they woke me to go to them was anger, hatred of their stupidity and their suffering. I prayed for forgiveness, but I knew I had no heart.

Interrogator.

And in the war——

Prisoner.

Write that I betrayed them. *(The Interrogator is terrified of saying anything, but he needs more. He whispers.)*

Interrogator.

That you betrayed them. How?

Prisoner.

Write that, just that. Write that I betrayed them, and finish the mockery for ever. *(The Interrogator waits to see if any more will come, and then deliberately breaks up the atmosphere. He stretches and yawns.)*

Interrogator.

Oh, well, it's late. Soon be dawn. *(He laughs.)* It won't do, you know. Put like that, they'll never believe it.

Prisoner.

Why do you laugh? Why do you say that?

Interrogator.

Because you don't believe it, not one sanctimonious word of it.

Prisoner.

I spoke in all sincerity.

Interrogator.

"In all humility!" I know. Not you! You know if I wrote that down it would read like the death-bed of a saint. Still at it, my dear humbug. If we put that out, and shot you at dawn, you'd be canonized within a year; well, twenty-five years, or however long it takes.

Prisoner.

What can I do?

Interrogator.

Oh, use your wits man! There's only one line in all that weak rigmarole that would convey the truth.

Prisoner.

What was that?

Interrogator.

That in the war you betrayed them.

Prisoner.

Not true.

Interrogator.

Yes, that's why.

Prisoner.

No, no, that's madness!

Interrogator.

It's a mad world. Tell them the truth, and it only gleams like another false facet of virtue in your shining humility. Do you really want to start again as low as the gutter you came from? Tell them you betrayed them in the war. That they can understand.

Prisoner.

The men who worked under me—I betrayed them to the Gestapo. The links with the Allies, the chain that led out of the country. In the end I answered all they wanted to know. (*He looks at and feels his hands.*) Oh, God, am I doing right at last?

Interrogator.

Have you the courage to go through with this?

Prisoner.

To sign to this——

Interrogator.

Sign? They'll not believe it.

Prisoner.

My signature?

Interrogator.

Faked, they'll say.

Prisoner.

Recorded——

Interrogator.

You know what can be said yourself about recordings?

Prisoner.

In court.

Interrogator.

In the pubic court? Before the judge and jury, the people, and foreign journalists?

Prisoner.

Yes.

Interrogator.

Could you do that?

Prisoner.

I must.

Interrogator.

It couldn't be done.

Prisoner.

It must be done.

Interrogator.

(*Elaborately.*) The Government can hardly be expected to put on so elaborate a show as a State trial just to restore the honour of your immortal soul.

Prisoner.

Don't play with me, don't mock me. It must be done.

Interrogator.

You know, there is one way——

Prisoner.

What?

Interrogator.

Throw in enough politics to leaven the loaf, and they'll eat it.

Prisoner.

Politics? I mustn't confess, sign anything, I mustn't—I mustn't——

Interrogator.

The last shred of pride that spoils it all! You mustn't weaken, you mustn't fail, you, so certain of yourself when you arrived, with your wit and your sacred hands, and your insufferable conceit!

Prisoner.

(*Begins to laugh.*) That's it, isn't it? Let them see me in the weakness of the flesh and the meanness of the spirit. That will be degradation, that will be shame enough to burn the past and come through the flames, free.

Interrogator.

That is hysteria.

Prisoner.

No. No, calm. Forgive me a moment . . .

Interrogator.

No hysteria, and no hypnosis. I can't hypnotize you into saying anything you think wrong, remember that. It must be your will, not mine. Do you believe that this is what you must go through with?

Prisoner.

Only this way. Not drugged, nor hypnotized, nor hysterical. Sane, and whole, and with the courage—with the grace of God—to make restitution in my own way. Deface the monument. (*The Interrogator signs to the Warder, who brings the carafe and glass. The Interrogator pours water and drops into it the contents of a capsule which he takes from his pocket.*)

Interrogator.

You must rest now. It's a long time since you slept properly. You'll sleep well, and when you wake you'll walk straight into the court and shed the burden of your life. (*He gives the glass to the Prisoner, whose hand goes to his head in the effort to concentrate.*)

Prisoner.

You—you always taste it first. (*The Interrogator hesitates. The Warder makes a movement.*)

Interrogator.

Warder. Tell my secretary to carry on with the programme. The time factor remains as I said. Everything is in order for an hour or two.

Prisoner.

You must taste it.

Interrogator.

Of course. Here's to you, my friend. (*He toasts him and takes a long sip from the glass. The Prisoner drinks after him, thirstily. The Warder takes his arm and raises him, and with a small formal bow to the Interrogator, goes out on the Warder's arm. The Interrogator covers his face with his hands. After a moment he gets to his desk, lowers himself into his chair and with the abandonment of exhaustion, head on arms, falls asleep.*)

THIRD SCENE

The public confession has been made. The Prisoner, given some comforts now and a drug, has slept about a day and a half. He has dined well and heard, on the radio they have given him, a broadcast of his confession: "Did you betray . . .? . . . I did." When the Interrogator visits him in his cell, he threatens to kill him. "Now that I'm mad I can kill you . . . and I can kill you because I know where the chink in your armor is. It's near your heart." But the drugs hold his body immobile. Asked by the Warder why he came to bother the Prisoner now, the Interrogator replies, "Clinical interest . . . I wanted to see what I'd left of him." Clearly suffering from a great exhaustion, the Interrogator for a moment seems to lose control. "The mind of man," he says, "reasoning and creating, and beautiful. Do you know that that's what you mean by 'God'?" And he shouts, "Then if you smash it you must expect to feel guilty of blasphemy!"

In the morning the Prisoner, carefully dressed, awaits his execution. The Warder, who prides himself on his knowledge of human nature, has brought what he is certain is the final breakfast for his charge—kidneys, which the Prisoner, though he does not say so, cannot bear. There is a knock and the Interrogator is admitted to the room.

Interrogator.

Your instructions. Read them outside.
§**Warder.**

He's having his breakfast, sir. He's got to have time for a good breakfast. That's civilization, and always has been.§

Interrogator.

Yes, yes . . . outside. (*The Warder shrugs and goes.*) Well. (*There is no reaction.*)

Prisoner.

What more can you want of me, now?

Interrogator.

Nothing more.

Prisoner.

No. There would hardly be anything else. Must we talk? I haven't seen you in the week since the trial, and now that I hear your voice I find it hard to forgive my enemies, and I haven't long.

Interrogator.

Well. I've got to know this. Have you made peace with your conscience?

Prisoner.

Does it concern the Government?

Interrogator.

No.

Prisoner.

To complete the record scientifically, for the casebook?

Interrogator.

For my own personal satisfaction. It wouldn't interest you, but some—principles of mine are involved.

Prisoner.

Well, then: yes.

Interrogator.

You've forgiven yourself.

Prisoner.

Oh, no. But I believe I shall be forgiven. "He who will judge us is He who made us."

Interrogator.

So you've found here a peace you never really knew outside. Perhaps you should find it in your heart to thank me.

Prisoner.

The doctor who diagnosed the weakness? Perhaps I should. (*He speaks absolutely without interest, but the Interrogator misinterprets him.*) Shall I be allowed to see a priest before I die?

Interrogator.

You won't need one.

Prisoner.

I beg of you, let me see a priest.

Interrogator.

Still so much dignity.

Prisoner.

I—had the habit of it. As humbly as you like; a priest, before I die.

Interrogator.

You're not to die. (*The Prisoner is unable to believe he has heard aright.*) No.

Prisoner.

I was condemned. I am to be hanged. You were in court, you heard the sentence.

Interrogator.

It's been commuted.

Prisoner.

They couldn't commute it, after what I said.

Interrogator.

They have.

Prisoner.

I said I'd plotted madness—to set up a Council of State with myself at the head, I said—how could they let me live?

Interrogator.

It's policy.

Prisoner.

(*Frightened.*) To let me live? No!

Interrogator.

Listen. I asked to take over the business of telling you from the Prison Governor, I said it was my work to observe rare phenomena, like the sight of a man being reprieved from a revolting death.

Prisoner.

Oh! (*Relaxing with infinite relief. Almost laughing.*) I should have known by now. One last experiment, give the specimen a whiff of oxygen, and watch it wriggle on the slide under the microscope.

Interrogator.

I was playing at no clinical experiments. I thought I could help you to the idea. You are not to die. (*The Prisoner studies him and is convinced.*)

Prisoner.

I must. The poor, muddled, fools whose beliefs I've shattered—they must at least see that I can die.

Interrogator.

The sentence has been commuted.

Prisoner.

"Martyrdom." That's what you're afraid of. You needn't be. No one could make the world see me as a martyr now. Suicide. That's it, they think I'll take my own life, so that they can say that I committed the last cowardice of all. No . . . I shan't do that, you know.

Interrogator.

No. I didn't think you would.

Prisoner.

No. (*He turns away and there is a short pause while he faces the realization.*) I—had counted on execution. For me, this is the heavier sentence.

Interrogator.

There's more to come.

Prisoner.

What is it? Oh, man, you know me well enough by now to realize you've told me the worst of it. Well, what is it to be? Come on. What is it to be? Road gangs, oakum, or shall I drain you a fetid swamp? What'll you have?

Interrogator.

You're free to go. The gates will be opened. You've only to walk through.

Prisoner.

I was mad, at the trial, in a way. And then that insane fit of hysteria afterwards. Am I mad after all? Or asleep . . . ? They say you can't dream a taste. (*He takes something from the table and tries to eat it.*) Too dry, my mouth. They couldn't set me free.

Interrogator.

Can't you see? The harm's done, the object's achieved, but the effect mustn't be spoiled. Dead, you might be a martyr; imprisoned, you'd be an enigma; free, sane, whole, walking the world in the broad light of day, what harm can you do the Government?

Prisoner.

They'd be mad to risk it—what I might say——

Interrogator.

That you were talked into it?

Prisoner.

It's another of your tricks. It can't be true.

Interrogator.

Warder! (*The Interrogator goes to the door and raps on it, the Warder comes in. He grins cheerfully at the Prisoner.*)

Warder.

Think of that, eh?

Interrogator.

Give me the instructions.

Warder.

That's addressed to me—"Cell Warder number six."

Interrogator.

Idiot, the Governor and the Gate Warder and half a dozen other people have copies. Well, give it to the prisoner. (*The Warder gives the paper to the Prisoner who reads it while the Warder talks.*)

Warder.

Oh, want to see it in black and white, eh? Shook me, I don't mind telling you. (*The lack of reaction from the Prisoner penetrates. To Interrogator.*) Takes 'em different, you know, sir. Knew one once went out of his mind when the reprieve came. Straight jacket. You couldn't help laughing. "I'd sooner be hanged any day of the week," I said to my mate, "than look such a bloody damn fool as that, floundering about and squeaking like a bat, in a straightjacket." Couldn't help laughing. Sooner be hanged.

Interrogator.

Get out. Go on—outside.

Warder.

This here is my cell, sir. Number six.

Interrogator.

Get out.

Warder.

Amateurs. (*He goes, closing the door.*)

Prisoner.

How can they risk it? They won't for long.

Interrogator.

Don't fool yourself, there's no hope there. You're no danger to them. What could you say?

Prisoner.

My mother——! That you used my mother.

Interrogator.

Her own doctor sent her to the Cancer Hospital some time before you were arrested. You—hadn't kept in very close touch, had you?

Prisoner.

Is that true?

Interrogator.

Yes.

Prisoner.

Has she the disease?

Interrogator.

They think not.

Prisoner.

Thank God.

Interrogator.

For her sake, or yours?

Prisoner.

Always the expert. For hers. I have more sympathy than I had with human weakness.

Interrogator.

But—you see? Nothing you say can harm the Government, it's even to their advantage to have you set free.

Prisoner.

On what grounds?

Interrogator.

In recognition of your organizing the resistance in the early years of the war. They will say they believe you were only acting under your Church's orders, afterwards. They've drawn your sting. You can go.

Prisoner.

It's true, then.

Interrogator.

It's policy. There's nothing you can do.

Prisoner.

You devils. Out there, like Cain, branded; to live, to crawl on through life dragging out the scandal, trailing the offence. No!

Interrogator.

Listen——

Prisoner.

Death's easily come by, you mean, outside. I'll hang on every bush, it could fall out of any window, it'll be laid for me on every table, with the knife beside the plate. Death—death—just for the taking up. Always there, and not for me. I had so eased my mind with the certainty of it, I—can't see beyond it!

Interrogator.

You'll not take your life.

Prisoner.

My mother's an old woman. I could be twenty, thirty years. Yes, it's one thing I never thought of, it's more terrible than I could have thought of. Yes, I see. (*The Interrogator produces a revolver from an inner pocket.*)

Interrogator.

You flew at me once before. I can pretend to call to the warder for help as I fire. Do you want to pray? (*The Prisoner looks at him with eager gratitude.*)

Prisoner.

You'd do it? (*After a moment's struggle with himself, with a cry of pain.*) Oh, to tempt me to cheat with death!

Interrogator.

Do you want to pray?

Prisoner.

I—must not—ask you—to do murder. You're not offering me martyrdom. You're offering me escape. I've accepted the heavier sentence. (*The Interrogator slowly lowers the gun.*)

Interrogator.

I'd shoot a dog to put it out of such misery; and I couldn't kill you. You're entitled to your hell. What is it? Have I found a soul in you? What is it? When I saw you after the trial, trying to scream yourself mad, I was sick with loathing of what I'd done to you; I told myself it was reaction from the strain. But I was right; it shouldn't have been done. Not the lie itself—we needed the lie, it's done good—but the twisting and breaking of your spirit. We had no right—no cause however just can have the right to tamper with the mind of a man——Are you listening to me?

Prisoner.

Yes. Yes, talk. I need the time.

Interrogator.

I should console you, surely? You've shown me I've a power I daren't use again. What is it—your courage now, or your weakness then? Perhaps it's both, perhaps it's man —that anything so frail can be so brave. . . . You did find out my weakness, didn't you?

Prisoner.

(*Wearily.*) Humanity?

Interrogator.

Is that all?

Prisoner.

It's enough. (*The door opens and the Cell Warder appears, the Secretary with a sheaf of papers, and the Doctor are at his elbow.*)

Warder.

Sorry, sir; medical discharge certificate.

Interrogator.

Give it to me.

Warder.

It's the official one, sir. Copy to the Governor. The doctor, here——

Interrogator.

Give it to me. (*The Secretary gives him the papers. To Doctor.*) It's all right, I'll sign them. (*The Doctor nods and goes, leaving his stethoscope behind. The Interrogator jerks his head to the Secretary, to indicate to him to wait outside, and he and the Warder go out.*) There's something I can do, to lighten it for you. (*He clears a corner of the table, and begins to fill in the forms.*)

Prisoner.

How odd that he should think there could be anything about me you'd need to find out with a stethoscope.

Interrogator.

I've said that you're mentally incapable, not responsible for your actions; that you haven't been since a month before the trial, owing to the use of drugs—and torture. You can publish it—my name's nearly as well-known as yours, now, and they won't be able to disprove my signature or the prison seal. You've won. Go out and show it to them. You can undo some of what's been done, with that. (*The Prisoner tears the paper slowly across.*)

Prisoner.

Don't tempt me any more. Don't. (*He puts the paper on the table and crosses below the table to down R.*) That was dangerous. You took a risk with that.

Interrogator.

It was treachery. It was a betrayal of my cause. Do you realize what you've done to me? You've stirred me to pity enough to offer you death just now, against my orders—pity you didn't even need.

Prisoner.

God knows I welcomed it.

Interrogator.

And rejected it. And the courage of that drove me on to offer you another way to escape even more fatal to my cause.

Prisoner.

You're no convert.

Interrogator.

No. You haven't sold me your faith. You've only led me to fail in the absolute duty that I owe my own. Well, I can at least have the courage of my convictions. (*He goes up to the door and calls.*) Stephen! (*He returns at once to the table and stands between it and the chair. The door opens and the Cell Warder lets in the Secretary who goes to the foot of the stairs.*) Stephen, get on to the Press, national and foreign, and tell them I'm holding a press conference at the Ministry of Justice in half an hour. And, Stephen, when you've done that, clear out, will you? Think up some excuse that will take you outside the Ministry—there's no reason for you to be mixed up in this. (*The Secretary, intrigued but discreet, goes out in silence.*) I'm resigning my post at the Ministry of Justice.

Prisoner.

Are you?

Interrogator.

And I'm telling the Press why. Mine's not a job that can be done with reservations. The service of the people is too great a cause to allow individual sentiment to override the common good.

Prisoner.

Your mind hasn't changed. Your heart, perhaps . . .

Interrogator.

Just long enough for me not to be able to trust it any more. To do my job, I had to get so close to you that we were like two sides of the same man talking to each other. And I came to love and pity the other side and hate what I made it do.

Prisoner.

What next—for you now?

Interrogator.

An end to me, pretty soon. There won't be room for long for a man who's too—fastidious to trust.

Prisoner.

That's your war. Every story's the story of one man's war —the setting, the battlefield is only incidental. I shall have the world on my side against me, now.

Interrogator.

You've your religion——?

Prisoner.

I was never a man to whom religion was a consolation. I want no consolation. I wanted the worst, and they've thought of it—they, or God, thank God. Well, I'm ready. (*The Interrogator goes toward the door. The Prisoner, passing by the table, pauses.*) No kippers for them; he thought I'd like the kidneys. Have you a piece of paper? (*The Interrogator gives him an envelope. The Prisoner puts the kidneys into it, and puts it into his pocket. The Interrogator knocks on the door. The Warder, waiting at it, comes in.*)

Warder.

Ready? You've got a reception committee and a half out there—mobs of 'em!

CHAPTER V

ADVANCED SCENES

from

UNCLE VANIA

by Anton Chekhov (translated by Elizaveta Fen)

Act II
YELIENA, SONIA

The place is the dining room of one of Chekhov's houses
in the country, those houses whose inhabitants dream of
going to the city, where, for them, life can be fulfilled,
not simply marked by the passing of the seasons, the
years, and the account books that document the sale and
purchase of the rudiments of existence. Sonia, who is
young, grew up in this, her mother's house, and she will
not get to the city; nor will she marry the doctor, the
rather dashing-seeming if clearly middle-aged and somewhat discouraged man whom she loves and whom she and
Yeliena discuss in this scene. Yeliena, the second wife of
Sonia's father, is nearly as young as Sonia—27—but she
is from the city. The doctor calls Yeliena a bird of prey
(he classifies himself as an all-too-vulnerable sparrow),
but she is less consciously predatory than that: she is
young, married to an old husband whose apparent glamor
she has long since discovered is sham; she has no occupation, nothing to justify her existence; and she is bored,
enough so that she tends to use people and their emotions,
more out of languor than by intention, to amuse herself.
Though she does not yet fully realize it, she is ready to
flirt with the doctor in this way.

Sonia and Yeliena are almost perfect opposites: the
one with days of work and, as she says of her Uncle
Vania, who shares her country existence, "no joy in [her]
life"; the other with many apparent joys but no work to fill
her time. They have had a falling-out, brought on by the

539

general excitement of the visit of the city people to the
country and the annoyances of coping with Yeliena's
husband (Sonia's father), who is ill and irascible. But
alone in the late evening, each with her own reasons to
need human contact, they turn to each other. Yeliena has
had an uncomfortable encounter with Vania, who adores
her and persists in saying so until she runs from the room.
Sonia, using the transparent stratagem of pretending to
discuss a hypothetical situation, has asked the doctor what
he would do if she told him "a girl friend, or a young sister"
loved him. He has answered, "Nothing. I should let her
know that I couldn't love her." But she thinks he has failed
to understand her true meaning, and when he has gone,
she is torn between happiness that there is still a chance and
despair that she is not pretty. "How dreadful!" she says, "I
know I'm plain, I know, I know! . . . Last Sunday as people
were coming out of church I heard them talking about me
and a woman said: 'She's kind and generous, but what a
pity she is so plain.' " "So plain," she repeats as Yeliena
enters, but Yeliena has not heard her.

Yeliena.

(*Opens the windows.*) The storm's over. What lovely
fresh air! (*A pause.*) Where's the doctor?

Sonia.

He's gone.

(*A pause.*)

Yeliena.

Sophie!

Sonia.

What!

Yeliena.

How long are you going to go on being sulky with me?
We haven't done each other any harm . . . so why should
we behave like enemies? Come, do let us stop it. . . .

Sonia.

I wanted to myself. . . . (*Embraces her.*) Yes, don't let us
be cross any more. . . .

Yeliena.

That's fine!

(*Both are moved.*)

Sonia.

Has papa gone to bed?

Yeliena.

No, he's sitting in the drawing-room. . . . We don't speak to each other for weeks on end, but Heaven alone knows why. . . . (*Seeing that the sideboard is open.*) What's this?

Sonia.

Mihail Lvovich has been having supper.

Yeliena.

There's wine too. . . . Let's drink to our friendship.

Sonia.

Yes, let's.

Yeliena.

Out of the same glass. . . . (*Fills it.*) It's better like that. Now we are real friends?

Sonia.

Friends. (*They drink and kiss each other.*) I've been want-ing to make it up for ever so long, but I felt so ashamed somehow. . . . (*Cries.*)

Yeliena.

But why are you crying?

Sonia.

Never mind . . . there's no reason.

Yeliena.

Come, there, there. . . . (*Cries.*) I'm a queer creature— I've started crying too. . . . (*A pause.*) You're cross with me because you think I married your father for ulterior motives. . . . If you are impressed by oaths, I'll vow to you that I married him for love. I was attracted by him as a learned man, a celebrity. It wasn't real love, it was all artificial, but you see at that time it seemed real to me. I'm not to blame. But from the day of our marriage you've been punishing me with those shrewd, suspicious eyes of yours.

Sonia.

Come, peace, peace! Let's forget about it!

Yeliena.

You mustn't look at people like that—it doesn't suit you. You should believe everyone—or else you just can't live.

(*A pause.*)

Sonia.

Tell me honestly, as a friend. . . . Are you happy?

Yeliena.

No.

Sonia.

I knew that. One more question. Tell me frankly—
wouldn't you have liked your husband to be young?

Yeliena.

What a little girl you are still! Of course I should.
(*Laughs.*) Well, ask me something else, do. . . . .

Sonia.

Do you like the doctor?

Yeliena.

Yes, very much.

Sonia.

(*Laughs.*) Have I got a stupid face? . . . Yes? He's gone,
but I can still hear his voice and his footsteps, and when
I glance at that dark window I can see his face in it. Do
let me tell you about it. . . . But I mustn't speak so
loudly, I feel ashamed. Come to my room, we'll talk there.
Do I seem stupid to you? Own up. . . . Tell me something
about him.

Yeliena.

Well, what shall I tell you?

Sonia.

He's so clever. . . . He knows how to do things, he can
do anything. . . . He treats the sick, and he plants forests,
too. . . .

Yeliena.

It isn't a question of forests or medicine. . . . My dear,
don't you understand? . . . he's got talent! And do you
know what that means? Courage, freedom of mind,
breadth of outlook. . . . He plants a tree and wonders
what will come of it in a thousand years' time, and specu-
lates on the future happiness of mankind. Such people are
rare, and we must love them. . . . He drinks, sometimes he
seems a little coarse—but what does it matter? A talented
man can't stay free from blemishes in Russia. Just think
what sort of life this doctor leads! Impassable mud on the
roads, frost, snow-storms, vast distances, crude, primitive
people, poverty and disease all around him—it's hard for
a man who works and struggles day after day in such
surroundings to keep pure and sober till he's forty. . . .
(*Kisses her.*) I wish you happiness with all my heart, you

deserve it. . . . (*Gets up.*) As for me, I'm just a tiresome person of no importance. In my music studies, in my home life in my husband's house, in all my romantic affairs—in fact in everything I've just been a person of no importance. Really, Sonia, when you come to think of it, I'm a very, very unfortunate woman. (*Walks about in agitation.*) There's no happiness for me on this earth. None! Why do you laugh?

Sonia.

(*Laughs, hiding her face.*) I am so happy . . . so happy! . . .

Yeliena.

I should like to play something. . . . I should like to play something now. . . .

Sonia.

Do play! (*Embraces her.*) I can't sleep. . . . Do play!

Yeliena.

In a minute. Your father isn't asleep. When he's unwell, music irritates him. Go and ask him. If he doesn't mind, I'll play. Go.

Sonia.

I'm going. (*Goes out.*)

(*Watchman taps in the garden.*)

Yeliena.

It's a long time since I played the piano. I shall play and cry . . . cry like a foolish girl. (*Calling through the window.*) Is it you tapping, Yefim?

§Watchman's voice.

Yes, me.§

Yeliena.

Don't tap, the master's not well.

§Watchman's voice.

I'm just going. (*Whistles.*) Hey there! Good dog! Come, boy! Good dog!§

(*A pause.*)

Sonia.

(*Returning.*) We mustn't!

from
QUALITY STREET
by Sir James M. Barrie

Act I
PHOEBE, MISS SUSAN, VALENTINE

The first act of Barrie's play is a small Victorian tragedy
—small, viewed somewhat wryly, but nonetheless tragic
for that. It is as well, then, to note that the play has a
thoroughly happy ending: Captain Brown (as he becomes)
does not go away forever and Miss Phoebe is not permanently consigned to a life of single blessedness. But at
the end of Act I, things look dark indeed, and it is to be
supposed that when the play opened at London's Vaudeville Theatre in 1901 (to run for 459 performances) many
handkerchiefs scented with violet were rather damp and
crumpled before the first intermission.

It is said today Barrie was sentimental, and he was. But
at its best that sentimentality took the form of great
affection for his characters, which audiences even now
find it difficult not to share. Moreover, a gentle wit, very
practical common sense, and considerable sharp insight
into the foibles of men and women are the true source of
the peculiar charm (and extraordinary long life) of Barrie's
seemingly delicate plays. His best characters can be played
for real, and must be. The intricacy of motivations and
responses, true and pretended, which must be made clear
by the actress playing the young lady who prepares herself
to accept a proposal she does not receive, calls for subtle,
well-thought-out performance. There is, in addition, the
problem of recreating a period and a manner, for Miss
Phoebe and Miss Susan are ladies of a time and of a

particular style. And, while in perspective they are comic characters, they must also project true charm.

Misses Phoebe and Susan Throssel are sisters. By her own analysis, Susan is an old maid. Miss Phoebe, who has ringlets, is not. Indeed, as Susan informs three unmarried lady friends, in a scene remarkable for its needlepoint cattiness, Phoebe's proposal is expected hourly. The man, whom the ladies dare refer to no more specifically than by his initials, V. B., is Valentine Brown, a "frank genial young man of 25 who honestly admires the ladies, though he is amused by their quaintness," and is esteemed by them (and them alone, as he knows) as a wit.

"The scene is the blue and white room in the house of the Misses . . . Throssel in Quality Street; and in this little country town there is a satisfaction about living in Quality Street which even religion cannot give. Through the bowed window at the back we have a glimpse of the street. It is pleasantly broad and grass-grown, and is linked to the outer world by one demure shop, whose door rings a bell every time it opens and shuts . . . Now and again ladies pass in their pattens, a maid perhaps protecting them with an umbrella, for flakes of snow are falling discreetly. Gentlemen in the street are an event; but, see, just as we raise the curtain, there goes the recruiting sergeant to remind us that we are in the period of the Napoleonic wars."

The ladies to whom Miss Susan, somewhat previous to the event, has disclosed Miss Phoebe's engagement have left, not in the best of good humor. After a moment, Phoebe herself appears, still in her bonnet and flushed with good news. (Note: the excerpt reprinted here may well be divided in half and the first section, up to Valentine's entrance, used alone as a scene for two women.)

Phoebe.

(*Pained.*) Susan, you have been talking to them about V. B.

Miss Susan.

I could not help it. (*Eagerly.*) Now, Phoebe, what is it you have to tell me?

Phoebe.

(*In a low voice.*) Dear, I think it is too holy to speak of.

Miss Susan.

To your sister?

Phoebe.

Susan, as you know, I was sitting with an unhappy woman whose husband has fallen in the war. When I came out of the cottage *he* was passing.

Miss Susan.

Yes?

Phoebe.

He offered me his escort. At first he was very silent—as he has often been of late.

Miss Susan.

We know why.

Phoebe.

Please not to say that I know why. Suddenly he stopped and swung his cane. You know how gallantly he swings his cane.

Miss Susan.

Yes, indeed.

Phoebe.

He said: 'I have something I am wishful to tell you, Miss Phoebe; perhaps you can guess what it is.'

Miss Susan.

Go on!

Phoebe.

To say I could guess, sister, would have been unladylike. I said: 'Please not to tell me in the public thoroughfare'; to which he instantly replied: 'Then I shall call and tell you this afternoon.'

Miss Susan.

Phoebe!

(*They are interrupted by the entrance of Patty with tea. They see that she has brought three cups, and know that this is her impertinent way of implying that mistresses, as well as maids, may have a 'follower.' When she has gone they smile at the daring of the woman, and sit down to tea.*)

Phoebe.

Susan, to think that it has all happened in a single year.

Miss Susan.

Such a genteel competency as he can offer; such a desirable establishment.

Phoebe.

I had no thought of that, dear. I was recalling our first meeting at Mrs. Fotheringay's quadrille party.

Miss Susan.

We had quite forgotten that our respected local physician was growing elderly.

Phoebe.

Until he said: 'Allow me to present my new partner, Mr. Valentine Brown.'

Miss Susan.

Phoebe, do you remember how at the tea-table he facetiously passed the cake-basket with nothing in it!

Phoebe.

He was so amusing from the first. I am thankful, Susan, that I too have a sense of humour. I am exceedingly funny at times; am I not, Susan?

Miss Susan.

Yes, indeed. But he sees humour in the most unexpected things. I say something so ordinary about loving, for instance, to have everything either blue or white in this room, and I know not why he laughs, but it makes me feel quite witty.

Phoebe.

(*A little anxiously.*) I hope he sees nothing odd or quaint about us.

Miss Susan.

My dear, I am sure he cannot.

Phoebe.

Susan, the picnics!

Miss Susan.

Phoebe, the day when he first drank tea in this house!

Phoebe.

He invited himself.

Miss Susan.

He merely laughed when I said it would cause such talk.

Phoebe.

He is absolutely fearless. Susan, he has smoked his pipe in this room.

(*They are both a little scared.*)

Miss Susan.

Smoking is indeed a dreadful habit.

Phoebe.

But there is something so dashing about it.

Miss Susan.

(*With melancholy.*) And now I am to be left alone.

Phoebe.

No.

Miss Susan.

My dear, I could not leave this room. My lovely blue and white room. It is my husband.

Phoebe.

(*Who has become agitated.*) Susan, you must make my house your home. I have something distressing to tell you.

Miss Susan.

You alarm me.

Phoebe.

You know Mr. Brown advised us how to invest half of our money.

Miss Susan.

I know it gives us eight per cent, though why it should do so I cannot understand, but very obliging, I am sure.

Phoebe.

Susan, all that money is lost; I had the letter several days ago.

Miss Susan.

Lost?

Phoebe.

Something burst, dear, and then they absconded.

Miss Susan.

But Mr. Brown——

Phoebe.

I have not advertised him of it yet, for he will think it was his fault. But I shall tell him to-day.

Miss Susan.

Phoebe, how much have we left?

Phoebe.

Only sixty pounds a year, so you see you must live with us, dearest.

Miss Susan.

But Mr. Brown—he——

Phoebe.

(*Grandly.*) He is a man of means, and if he is not proud

to have my Susan I shall say at once: 'Mr. Brown—the door.'

(*She presses her cheek to Miss Susan's.*)

Miss Susan.

(*Softly.*) Phoebe, I have a wedding gift for you.

Phoebe.

Not yet?

Miss Susan.

It has been ready for a long time. I began it when you were not ten years old and I was a young woman. I meant it for myself, Phoebe. I had hoped that he—his name was William—but I think I must have been too unattractive, my love.

Phoebe.

Sweetest—dearest——

Miss Susan.

I always associate it with a sprigged poplin I was wearing that summer, with a breadth of coloured silk in it, being a naval officer; but something happened, a Miss Cicely Pemberton, and they are quite big boys now. So long ago, Phoebe—he was very tall, with brown hair—it was most foolish of me, but I was always so fond of sewing—with long straight legs and such a pleasant expression.

Phoebe.

Susan, what was it?

Miss Susan.

It was a wedding-gown, my dear. Even plain women, Phoebe, we can't help it; when we are young we have romantic ideas just as if we were pretty. And so the wedding-gown was never used. Long before it was finished I knew he would not offer, but I finished it, and then I put it away. I have always hidden it from you, Phoebe, but of late I have brought it out again, and altered it.

(*She goes to ottoman and unlocks it.*)

Phoebe.

Susan, I could not wear it. (*Miss Susan brings the wedding gown.*) Oh! how sweet, how beautiful!

Miss Susan.

You will wear it, my love, won't you? And the tears it was sewn with long ago will all turn into smiles on my Phoebe's wedding-day.

(They are tearfully happy when a knock is heard on the street door.)

Phoebe.

That knock.

Miss Susan.

So dashing.

Phoebe.

So imperious. *(She is suddenly panic-stricken.)* Susan, I think he kissed me once.

Miss Susan.

(Startled.) You *think*?

Phoebe.

I know he did. That evening—a week ago, when he was squiring me home from the concert. It was raining, and my face was wet; he said that was why he did it.

Miss Susan.

Because your face was wet?

Phoebe.

It does not seem a sufficient excuse now.

Miss Susan.

(Appalled.) Oh Phoebe, before he had offered?

Phoebe.

(In distress.) I fear me it was most unladylike.

(Valentine Brown is shown in. He is a frank, genial young man of twenty-five who honestly admires the ladies, though he is amused by their quaintness. He is modestly aware that it is in the blue and white room alone that he is esteemed a wit.)

Brown.

Miss Susan, how do you do, ma'am? Nay, Miss Phoebe, though we have met to-day already I insist on shaking hands with you again.

Miss Susan.

Always so dashing.

(Valentine laughs and the ladies exchange delighted smiles.)

Valentine.

(To Miss Susan.) And my other friends, I hope I find them in health? The spinet, ma'am, seems quite herself to-day; I trust the ottoman passed a good night?

Miss Susan.

(Beaming.) We are all quite well, sir.

Valentine.

May I sit on this chair, Miss Phoebe? I know Miss Susan likes me to break her chairs.

Miss Susan.

Indeed, sir, I do not. Phoebe, how strange that he should think so.

Phoebe.

(*Instantly.*) The remark was humorous, was it not?

Valentine.

How you see through me, Miss Phoebe.

(*The sisters again exchange delighted smiles. Valentine is about to take a seat.*)

Miss Susan.

(*Thinking aloud.*) Oh dear, I feel sure he is going to roll the coverlet into a ball and then sit on it.

(*Valentine, who has been on the point of doing so, abstains and sits guiltily.*)

Valentine.

So I am dashing, Miss Susan? Am I dashing, Miss Phoebe?

Phoebe.

A—little, I think.

Valentine.

Well, but I have something to tell you to-day which I really think is rather dashing. (*Miss Susan gathers her knitting, looks at Phoebe, and is preparing to go.*) You are not going, ma'am, before you know what it is?

Miss Susan.

I—I—indeed—to be sure—I—I know, Mr. Brown.

Phoebe.

Susan!

Miss Susan.

I mean I do not know. I mean I can guess—I mean—— Phoebe, my love, explain. (*She goes out.*)

Valentine.

(*Rather disappointed.*) The explanation being, I suppose that you both know, and I had flattered myself 'twas such a secret. Am I then to understand that you had foreseen it all, Miss Phoebe?

Phoebe.

Nay, sir, you must not ask that.

Valentine.

I believe in any case 'twas you who first put it into my head.

Phoebe.

(*Aghast.*) Oh, I hope not.

Valentine.

Your demure eyes flashed so every time the war was mentioned; the little Quaker suddenly looked like a gallant boy in ringlets.

(*A dread comes over Phoebe, but it is in her heart alone; it shows neither in face nor voice.*)

Phoebe.

Mr. Brown, what is it you have to tell us?

Valentine.

That I have enlisted, Miss Phoebe. Did you surmise it was something else?

Phoebe.

You are going to the wars? Mr. Brown, is it a jest?

Valentine.

It would be a sorry jest, ma'am. I thought you knew. I concluded that the recruiting sergeant had talked.

Phoebe.

The recruiting sergeant? I see.

Valentine.

These stirring times, Miss Phoebe—he is but half a man who stays at home. I have chafed for months. I want to see whether I have any courage, and as to be an army surgeon does not appeal to me, it was enlist or remain behind. To-day I found that there were five waverers. I asked them would they take the shilling if I took it, and they assented. Miss Phoebe, it is not one man I give to the King, but six.

Phoebe.

(*Brightly.*) I think you have done bravely.

Valentine.

We leave shortly for the Petersburgh barracks, and I go to London to-morrow; so this is good-bye.

Phoebe.

I shall pray that you may be preserved in battle, Mr. Brown.

Valentine.

And you and Miss Susan will write to me when occasion offers?

Phoebe.

If you wish it.

Valentine.

(*Smiling.*) With all the stirring news of Quality Street.

Phoebe.

It seems stirring to us; it must have been merely laughable to you, who came here from a great city.

Valentine.

Dear Quality Street—that thought me dashing! But I made friends in it, Miss Phoebe, of two very sweet ladies.

Phoebe.

(*Timidly.*) Mr. Brown, I wonder why you have been so kind to my sister and me?

Valentine.

The kindness was yours. If at first Miss Susan amused me—(*Chuckling.*) To see her on her knees decorating the little legs of the couch with frills as if it were a child! But it was her sterling qualities that impressed me presently.

Phoebe.

And did—did I amuse you also?

Valentine.

Prodigiously, Miss Phoebe. Those other ladies, they were always scolding you, your youthfulness shocked them. I believe they thought you dashing.

Phoebe.

(*Nervously.*) I have sometimes feared that I was perhaps too dashing.

Valentine.

(*Laughing at this.*) You delicious Miss Phoebe. You were too quiet. I felt sorry that one so sweet and young should live so grey a life. I wondered whether I could put any little pleasures into it.

Phoebe.

The picnics? It was very good of you.

Valentine.

That was only how it began, for soon I knew that it was I who got the pleasures and you who gave them. You have been to me, Miss Phoebe, like a quiet, old-fashioned

garden full of the flowers that Englishmen love best because they have known them longest: the daisy, that
stands for innocence, and the hyacinth for constancy, and
the modest violet and the rose. When I am far away,
ma'am, I shall often think of Miss Phoebe's pretty soul,
which is her garden, and shut my eyes and walk in it.

(*She is smiling gallantly through her pain when Miss
Susan returns.*)

Miss Susan.

Have you—is it—you seem so calm, Phoebe.

Phoebe.

(*Pressing her sister's hand warningly and imploringly.*)
Susan, what Mr. Brown is so obliging as to inform us of
is not what we expected—not that at all. My dear, he is
the gentleman who has enlisted, and he came to tell us
that and to say good-bye.

Miss Susan.

Going away?

Phoebe.

Yes, dear.

Valentine.

Am I not the ideal recruit, ma'am: a man without a wife
or a mother or a sweetheart?

Miss Susan.

No sweetheart?

Valentine.

Have you one for me, Miss Susan?

Phoebe.

(*Hastily, lest her sister's face should betray the truth.*)
Susan, we shall have to tell him now. You dreadful man,
you will laugh and say it is just like Quality Street. But indeed since I met you to-day and you told me you had
something to communicate we have been puzzling what
it could be, and we concluded that you were going to be
married.

Valentine.

Ha! ha! ha! Was that it!

Phoebe.

So like women, you know. We thought we perhaps knew
her. (*Glancing at the wedding-gown.*) We were even dis-
cussing what we should wear at the wedding.

Valentine.

Ha! ha! I shall often think of this. I wonder who would have me, Miss Susan? (*Rising.*) But I must be off; and God bless you both.

Miss Susan.

(*Forlorn.*) You are going!

Valentine.

No more mud on your carpet, Miss Susan; no more cover-lets rolled into balls. A good riddance. Miss Phoebe, a last look at the garden.

> (*Taking her hand looking into her face.*)

Phoebe.

We shall miss you very much, Mr. Brown.

Valentine.

There is one little matter. That investment I advised you to make, I am happy it has turned out so well.

Phoebe.

(*Checking Miss Susan, who is about to tell of the loss of the money.*) It was good of you to take all that trouble, sir. Accept our grateful thanks.

Valentine.

Indeed I am glad that you are so comfortably left; I am your big brother. Good-bye again. (*Looks round.*) This little blue and white room and its dear inmates, may they be unchanged when I come back. Good-bye.

(*He goes. Miss Susan looks forlornly at Phoebe, who smiles pitifully.*)

Phoebe.

A misunderstanding; just a mistake. (*She shudders, lifts the wedding-gown and puts it back in the ottoman. Miss Susan sinks sobbing into a chair.*) Don't, dear, don't—we can live it down.

Miss Susan.

(*Fiercely.*) He is a fiend in human form.

Phoebe.

Nay, you hurt me, sister. He is a brave gentleman.

Miss Susan.

The money; why did you not let me tell him?

Phoebe.

(*Flushing.*) So that he might offer to me out of pity, Susan?

Miss Susan.

Phoebe, how are we to live, with the quartern loaf at one and tenpence?

Phoebe.

Brother James——

Miss Susan.

You know very well that brother James will do nothing for us.

Phoebe.

I think, Susan, we could keep a little school—for genteel children only, of course. I would do most of the teaching.

Miss Susan.

You a schoolmistress—Phoebe of the ringlets; every one would laugh.

Phoebe.

I shall hide the ringlets away in a cap like yours, Susan, and people will soon forget them. And I shall try to look staid and to grow old quickly. It will not be so hard to me as you think, dear.

Miss Susan.

There were other gentlemen who were attracted by you, Phoebe, and you turned from them.

Phoebe.

I did not want them.

Miss Susan.

They will come again, and others.

Phoebe.

No, dear; never speak of that to me any more. (*In woe.*) I let him kiss me.

Miss Susan.

You could not prevent him.

Phoebe.

Yes, I could. I know I could now. I wanted him to do it. Oh, never speak to me of others after that. Perhaps he saw I wanted it and did it to please me. But I meant—indeed I did—that I gave it to him with all my love. Sister, I could bear all the rest, but I have been unladylike.

(*The curtain falls and we do not see the sisters again for ten years.*)

from

LONDON ASSURANCE

by Dion Boucicault

Act III
YOUNG COURTLY, GRACE

Boucicault's play, first performed in 1841, has been called
the best comedy of manners between Sheridan and Oscar
Wilde. If it lacks the biting edge of the earlier high comedies
and the epigrammatic finesse of Wilde, it does have a certain mad humorousness of its own that as recently as 1969
kept London audiences gasping to breathe between laughs.

The plot is a complex wonder that can only be untangled
in a full reading of the play, but the central problem is
clear enough: Young Courtly has fallen in love with very
beautiful, very rich Grace Harkaway, his father's betrothed.
He does not at first know that *she* is his father's betrothed,
nor does she, for much of the play, know for certain that
he is the son of her elderly fiancé. Hounded by creditors,
Young Courtly has fled to London to hide as a guest in
Grace's father's house, where a mutual friend has introduced him as Mr. Augustus Hamilton. When his father
appears, marriage contract in hand, Young Courtly man-
ages to persuade him that he (Young Courtly) is not himself but someone strikingly like him. Unfortunately, the
father requests that his son come to the country to meet the
bride, and it is necessary to arrange for Mr. Hamilton to
disappear. Before that is done, however, Mr. Hamilton
must somehow make his overtures to Grace.

In the morning room, in a pause before dinner, Young
Courtly is left alone with Grace and decides to make the
most of the moment. He is not a skillful wooer, and though
his intentions are immense, his performance leaves much

557

to be desired. He is not helped by the fact that Grace is inclined to speak in an aphoristic, indeed momentous, way
which he feels he should emulate. Happily, the girl is determined that he should succeed in his endeavor and, while
carefully seeming not to, does all she can to see that he
does. These maneuvers, and the complexities of cautious
conversation contradicted by rather frantic actions and
asides, add up to one of the theater's funnier proposal
scenes.

Courtly.

(*Alone.*) Things are approaching to a climax; I must appear in *propriâ personâ*—and immediately—but I must
first ascertain what are the real sentiments of this riddle
of a woman. Does she love me? I flatter myself—By
Jove, here she comes—I shall never have such an opportunity again!

(*Enter Grace.*)

Grace.

I wish I had never seen Mr. Hamilton. Why does every
object appear robbed of the charm it once presented to
me? Why do I shudder at the contemplation of this marriage, which, till now, was to me a subject of indifference?
Am I in love? In love! if I am, my past life has been the
work of raising up a pedestal to place my own folly on
—I—the infidel—the railer!

Courtly.

Meditating upon matrimony, madam?

Grace.

(*Aside.*) He little thinks he was the subject of my medi-
tations! (*Aloud.*) No.

Courtly.

(*Aside.*) I must unmask my battery now.

Grace.

(*Aside.*) How foolish I am—he will perceive that I tremble—I must appear at ease. (*A pause.*)

Courtly.

Eh? ah! um!

Grace.

Ah! (*They sink into silence again. Aside.*) How very awkward!

Courtly.

(*Aside.*) It is a very difficult subject to begin. (*Aloud.*)
Madam—ahem—there was—is—I mean—I was about to
remark—a—(*Aside.*) Hang me if it is not a very slippery
subject. I must brush up my faculties; attack her in her
own way. (*Aloud.*) Sing! oh, muse! (*Aside.*) Why, I have
made love before to a hundred women!

Grace.

(*Aside.*) I wish I had something to do, for I have nothing
to say.

Courtly.

Madam—there is—a subject so fraught with fate to my
future life, that you must pardon my lack of delicacy,
should a too hasty expression mar the fervent courtesy
of its intent. To you, I feel aware, I must appear in the
light of a comparative stranger.

Grace.

(*Aside.*) I know what's coming.

Courtly.

Of you—I know perhaps too much for my own peace.

Grace.

(*Aside.*) He *is* in love.

Courtly.

I forget all that befell before I saw your beauteous self; I
seem born into another world—my nature changed—the
beams of that bright face falling on my soul, have, from
its chaos, warmed into life the flowrets of affection, whose
maiden odours now float toward the sun, pouring forth on
their pure tongue a mite of adoration, midst the voices
of a universe. (*Aside.*) That's something in her own style.

Grace.

Mr. Hamilton!

Courtly.

You cannot feel surprised—

Grace.

I am more than surprised. (*Aside.*) I am delighted.

Courtly.

Do not speak so coldly.

Grace.

You have offended me.

Courtly.

No, madam; no woman, whatever her state, can be offended by the adoration even of the meanest: it is myself whom I have offended and deceived—but still I ask your pardon.

Grace.

(*Aside.*) Oh! he thinks I am refusing him. (*Aloud.*) I am not exactly offended, but—

Courtly.

Consider my position—a few days—and an insurmountable barrier would have placed you beyond my wildest hopes—you would have been my mother.

Grace.

I should have been your mother! (*Aside.*) I thought so.

Courtly.

No—that is, I meant Sir Harcourt Courtly's bride.

Grace.

(*With great emphasis.*) Never!

Courtly.

How! never! may I then hope?—you turn away—you would not lacerate me by a refusal?

Grace.

(*Aside.*) How stupid he is!

Courtly.

Still silent! I thank you, Miss Grace—I ought to have expected this—fool that I have been—one course alone remains—farewell!

Grace.

(*Aside.*) Now he's going.

Courtly.

Farewell forever! (*Sits.*) Will you not speak one word? I shall leave this house immediately—I shall not see you again.

Grace.

Unhand me, sir, I insist.

Courtly.

(*Aside.*) Oh! what an ass I've been! (*Rushes up to her, and seizes her hand.*) Release this hand? Never! never! (*Kissing it.*) Never will I quit this hand! it shall be my companion in misery—in solitude—when you are far away.

Grace.

Oh! should any one come! (*Drops her handkerchief; he stoops to pick it up.*) For heaven's sake do not kneel.

Courtly.

(*Kneels.*) Forever thus prostrate, before my soul's saint, I will lead a pious life of eternal adoration.

Grace.

Should we be discovered thus—pray, Mr. Hamilton—pray —pray.

Courtly.

Pray! I am praying; what more can I do?

Grace.

Your conduct is shameful.

Courtly.

It is. (*Rises.*)

Grace.

And if I do not scream, it is not for your sake—that—but it might alarm the family.

Courtly.

It might—it would. Say, am I wholly indifferent to you? I entreat one word—I implore you—do not withdraw your hand—(*She snatches it away—he puts his round her waist.*) You smile.

Grace.

Leave me, dear Mr. Hamilton!

Courtly.

Dear! Then I am dear to you; that word once more; say— say you love me!

Grace.

Is this fair? (*He catches her in his arms, and kisses her.*)
(*Enter Lady Gay Spanker.*)

§Lady Gay.

Ha! oh!§

Grace.

Gay! destruction!

(*Exit.*)

from

THE RELAPSE: OR, VIRTUE IN DANGER

by Sir John Vanbrugh

Act II, scene 1
AMANDA, BERINTHIA

Berinthia is less than perfect. Widowed young—and to her
great relief—she has had one "intrigue" with a less than
perfect man and looks forward to another, though she
prays "it may end as the first did, that we may both grow
weary at a time." She is, in short, a city woman in whom
charm and brittle realism are evenly balanced and for
whom life is a game with the odds in favor of the pretty,
the witty, the rich, and those who know better than to play
with their hearts rather than their heads.

Berinthia's cousin, Amanda, was also widowed young,
but amorous intrigues are not for her. She prefers country
life to London adventures, and she has worked a miracle:
she has caught, married, and reformed a rake, demonstrat-
ing thereby the power of a good woman's love.

Vanbrugh's play, first produced in 1696, is in the man-
nered style of Restoration comedy, but the surface
of elegantly posed language and gestures is never allowed to hide completely the earthily real, candidly observed characters beneath—a double level of characterization that lends itself particularly well to situations in which
people say one thing but mean quite another. *The Relapse*
is a sequel to an earlier play whose subject—treated with
no lack of moral sentiment—was the startling transformation of the rake, Loveless, into the faithful husband of
Amanda. Vanbrugh raises the question as to whether the
new man, exposed again to the temptations of the town,
would not revert to his old ways. Berinthia provides the
test case, and the answer, so far as the rake is concerned, is
the obvious one. But the end of the game is a draw, for

562

while Loveless succumbs (or has little difficulty in persuading Berinthia to do so), Amanda, similarly pressed by a facile would-be lover, once again reduces a rake to morality and moralizing.

The scene reprinted here comes early in the play. Loveless has taken a house in town, determined, he says, to prove that his good conduct does not depend on country isolation. He has been once to the theater, eyed a lady in the audience, and hurried home to tell his wife how readily he resisted this temptation. The lady, naturally, is Berinthia, the cousin whom Amanda has invited to call and whom she intends to persuade to share the house in town. Amanda, too, has had a city encounter: a Mr. Worthy has made very clear his more than casual concern for her. She has yet to mention this to her husband.

The setting is a room in the house in London. Loveless has been introduced to Berinthia and delighted Amanda by indicating that he would not object to Berinthia's coming to live with them. As he leaves the room, Amanda turns to her cousin, eager for advice and information about the town.

Amanda.

***Now, dear Berinthia, let me inquire a little into your affairs: for I do assure you, I am enough your friend to interest myself in everything that concerns you.

Berinthia.

You formerly have given me such proofs on't, I should be very much to blame to doubt it. I am sorry I have no secrets to trust you with, that I might convince you how entire a confidence I durst repose in you.

Amanda.

Why, is it possible that one so young and beautiful as you should live and have no secrets?

Berinthia.

What secrets do you mean?

Amanda.

Lovers.

Berinthia.

Oh, twenty! but not one secret amongst 'em. Lovers in this age have too much honor to do anything underhand; they do all above board.

Amanda.

That now, methinks, would make me hate a man.

Berinthia.

But the women of the town are of another mind: for by this means a lady may (with the expense of a few coquette glances) lead twenty fools about in a string for two or three years together. Whereas, if she should allow 'em greater favors, and oblige 'em to secrecy, she would not keep one of 'em a fortnight.

Amanda.

There's something indeed in that to satisfy the vanity of a woman, but I can't comprehend how the men find their account in it.

Berinthia.

Their entertainment, I must confess, is a riddle to me. For there's very few of 'em ever get farther than a bow and an ogle. I have half a score for my share, who follow me all over the town; and at the play, the Park, and the church, do (with their eyes) say the violentest things to me.—But I never hear any more of 'em.

Amanda.

What can be the reason of that?

Berinthia.

One reason is, they don't know how to go farther. They have had so little practice, they don't understand the trade. But, besides their ignorance, you must know there is not one of my half score lovers but what follows half a score mistresses. Now, their affections being divided amongst so many, are not strong enough for any one to make 'em pursue her to the purpose. Like a young puppy in a warren, they have a flirt at all, and catch none.

Amanda.

Yet they seem to have a torrent of love to dispose of.

Berinthia.

They have so. But 'tis like the rivers of a modern philosopher, (whose works, though a woman, I have read,) it sets out with a violent stream, splits in a thousand branches, and is all lost in the sands.

Amanda.

But do you think this river of love runs all its course without doing any mischief? Do you think it overflows nothing?

Berinthia.

O yes; 'tis true, it never breaks into anybody's ground that has the least fence about it; but it overflows all the commons that lie in its way. And this is the utmost achievement of those dreadful champions in the field of love—the beaux.

Amanda.

But prithee, Berinthia, instruct me a little farther; for I'm so great a novice I am almost ashamed on't. My husband's leaving me whilst I was young and fond threw me into that depth of discontent, that ever since I have led so private and recluse a life, my ignorance is scarce conceivable. I therefore fain would be instructed. Not (heaven knows) that what you call intrigues have any charms for me; my love and principles are too well fixed. The practic part of all unlawful love is—

Berinthia.

Oh, 'tis abominable! But for the speculative; that we must all confess is entertaining. The conversation of all the virtuous women in the town turns upon that and new clothes.

Amanda.

Pray be so just then to me, to believe, 'tis with a world of innocency I would inquire, whether you think those women we call women of reputation, do so really 'scape all other men, as they do those shadows of 'em, the beaux.

Berinthia.

O no Amanda; there are a sort of men make dreadful work amongst 'em, men that may be called the beaux' antipathy; for they agree in nothing but walking upon two legs.—These have brains; the beau has none. These are in love with their mistress; the beau with himself. They take care of her reputation; he's industrious to destroy it. They are decent: he's a fop. They are sound; he's rotten. They are men; he's an ass.

Amanda.

If this be their character, I fancy we had here e'en now a pattern of 'em both.

Berinthia.

His lordship and Mr. Worthy?

Amanda.

The same.

Berinthia.

As for the lord, he's eminently so, and for the other, I can assure you, there's not a man in town who has a better interest with the women, that are worth having an interest with. But 'tis all private: he's like a back-stair minister at court, who, whilst the reputed favorites are sauntering in the bedchamber, is ruling the roost in the closet.

Amanda.

He answers then the opinion I had ever of him. Heavens! What a difference there is between a man like him, and that vain nauseous fop, Sir Novelty.—(*Taking her hand.*) I must acquaint you with a secret, cousin. 'Tis not that fool alone has talked to me of love. Worthy has been tampering, too. 'Tis true, he has done't in vain; not all his charms or art have power to shake me. My love, my duty, and my virtue, are such faithful guards, I need not fear my heart should e'er betray me. But what I wonder at is this: I find I did not start at his proposal, as when it came from one whom I contemned. I therefore mention his attempt, that I may learn from you whence it proceeds; that vice (which cannot change its nature) should so far change at least its shape, so that the selfsame crime proposed from one shall seem a monster gaping at your ruin; when from another it shall look so kind, as though it were your friend, and never meant to harm you. Whence, think you, can this difference proceed? For 'tis not love, heaven knows.

Berinthia.

O no; I would not for the world believe it were. But possibly, should there a dreadful sentence pass upon you, to undergo the rage of both their passions; the pain you apprehend from one might seem so trivial to the other, the danger would not quite so much alarm you.

Amanda.

Fie, fie, Berinthia! you would indeed alarm me, could you incline me to a thought, that all the merit of mankind combined could shake that tender love I bear my husband. No! he sits triumphant in my heart, and nothing can dethrone him.

Berinthia.

But should he abdicate again, do you think you should

preserve the vacant throne ten tedious winters more in hopes of his return?

Amanda.

Indeed, I think I should. Though I confess, after those obligations he has to me, should he abandon me once more, my heart would grow extremely urgent with me to root him thence, and cast him out forever.

Berinthia.

Were I that thing they call a slighted wife, somebody should run the risk of being that thing they call—a husband.

Amanda.

O fie, Berinthia! no revenge should ever be taken against a husband. But to wrong his bed is a vengeance, which of all vengeance—

Berinthia.

Is the sweetest, ha! ha! ha! Don't I talk madly?

Amanda.

Madly, indeed.

Berinthia.

Yet I'm very innocent.

Amanda.

That I dare swear you are. I know how to make allowances for your humor. You were always very entertaining company; but I find since marriage and widowhood have shown you the world a little, you are very much improved.

Berinthia.

(*Aside.*) Alack a-day, there has gone more than that to improve me, if she knew all!

Amanda.

For heaven's sake, Berinthia, tell me what way I shall take to persuade you to come and live with me?

Berinthia.

Why, one way in the world there is—and but one.

Amanda.

Pray which is that?

Berinthia.

It is, to assure me—I shall be very welcome.

Amanda.

If that be all, you shall e'en lie here to-night.

Berinthia.

To-night!

Amanda.

Yes, to-night.

Berinthia.

Why, the people where I lodge will think me mad.

Amanda.

Let 'em think what they please.

Berinthia.

Say you so, Amanda? Why, then they shall think what they please: for I'm a young widow, and I care not what anybody thinks. Ah, Amanda, it's a delicious thing to be a young widow!

Amanda.

You'll hardly make me think so.

Berinthia.

Puh! because you are in love with your husband: but that is not every woman's case.

Amanda.

I hope 'twas yours, at least.

Berinthia.

Mine, say ye? Now I have a great mind to tell you a lie, but I should do it so awkwardly you'd find me out.

Amanda.

Then e'en speak the truth.

Berinthia.

Shall I?—Then after all I did love him, Amanda—as a nun does penance.

Amanda.

Why did not you refuse to marry him, then?

Berinthia.

Because my mother would have whipped me.

Amanda.

How did you live together?

Berinthia.

Like man and wife, asunder. He loved the country, I the town. He hawks and hounds, I coaches and equipage. He eating and drinking, I carding and playing. He the sound of a horn, I the squeak of a fiddle. We were dull company at table, worse a-bed. Whenever we met, we gave one another the spleen; and never agreed but once, which was about lying alone.

Amanda.

But tell me one thing, truly and sincerely.

Berinthia.

What's that?

Amanda.

Notwithstanding all these jars, did not his death at least extremely trouble you?

Berinthia.

O yes. Not that my present pangs were so very violent, but the afterpains were intolerable. I was forced to wear a beastly widow's band a twelvemonth for't.

Amanda.

Women, I find, have different inclination[s].

Berinthia.

Women, I find, keep different company. When your husband ran away from you, if you had fallen into some of my acquaintance, 'twould have saved you many a tear. But you go and live with a grandmother, a bishop, and an old nurse; which was enough to make any woman break her heart for her husband. Pray, Amanda, if ever you are a widow again, keep yourself so, as I do.

Amanda.

Why! do you then resolve you'll never marry?

Berinthia.

O no; I resolve I will.

Amanda.

How so?

Berinthia.

That I never may.

Amanda.

You banter me.

Berinthia.

Indeed I don't. But I consider I'm a woman, and form my resolutions accordingly.

Amanda.

Well, my opinion is, form what resolution you will, matrimony will be the end on't.

Berinthia.

Faith it won't.

Amanda.

How do you know?

Berinthia.

I'm sure on't.

Amanda.

Why, do you think 'tis impossible for you to fall in love?

Berinthia.

No.

Amanda.

Nay, but to grow so passionately fond, that nothing but the man you love can give you rest.

Berinthia.

Well, what then?

Amanda.

Why, then you'll marry him.

Berinthia.

How do you know that?

Amanda.

Why, what can you do else?

Berinthia.

Nothing—but sit and cry.

Amanda.

Psha!

Berinthia.

Ah, poor Amanda! you have led a country life: but if you'll consult the widows of this town they'll tell you you should never take a lease of a house you can hire for a quarter's warning.

from

THE SCHOOL FOR WIVES

by Jean Baptiste Poquelin de Molière,
translated by Richard Wilbur

Two Scenes from Act II, scenes 4 and 5, and Act V, scene 4
ARNOLPHE, AGNÈS

Molière's comedy rings ecstatic changes on the old theme
of the outwitting of the cynic who chooses a wide-eyed
bride for safety's sake. Arnolphe has long and noisily enjoyed the distresses of his acquaintances whose too-clever
wives have played them false. But growing older and richer,
having purchased an estate and a grand new name, La
Souche, Arnolphe determines to marry. Determined also
never to be the butt of his wife's perfidy or his friends'
jokes, he has a plan: Agnès, his bride to be, has been his
ward since she was four and he has managed her education to ensure that she is not only innocent but ignorant.
No seed of an idea has been planted in her head, except,
of course, a sense of grateful duty to Arnolphe. Of men,
except Arnolphe, she knows nothing, and she is kept locked
in Arnolphe's house where his servants guard her night and
day. The plan is foolproof and based on perfect logic—a
witless wife can never outwit her husband.

The plan collapses, of course, and Arnolphe is proved
a fool. Returning from a trip, eager to set the date for his
wedding, he meets the handsome son of an old friend, one
unacquainted with Arnolphe's new name, and listens in horror as the boy tells of his schemes—already well in hand—
to steal the intended bride of some old idiot called "La
Zouche." Arnolphe dashes home, roars at his servants, and
calls for the girl to be brought to him. The ensuing conversation is reprinted below.

571

Like all great farces, the play is far from easy to perform. But Richard Wilbur's couplets nearly speak themselves and in his translation the old comedy rediscovers its original liveliness and insight into human folly. Taking New York by surprise in 1971, the play—and Brian Bedford's astounding Arnolphe—played to overflowing houses while newer, lesser comedies went begging.

The setting is Arnolphe's house. In the background the servants, Alain and Georgette, cower as their master confronts them with his discovery that they have failed to protect Agnès from the eyes—and worse?—of a conniving suitor. Calling for the girl to be brought to him, he makes a desperate effort to rein in his temper.

Scene IV.
Arnolphe.

> (*Aside.*)
> A certain Greek presumed once to advise
> The great Augustus, and his words were wise:
> When you are vexed, he said, do not forget,
> Before you act, to say the alphabet,
> So as to cool your temper, and prevent
> Rash moves which later on you might repent.
> In dealing with Agnès, I have applied
> That counsel, and I've bidden her come outside,
> Under the pretext of a morning stroll,
> So that I can relieve my jangled soul
> By seeking dulcetly to draw her out
> And learn the truth, and put an end to doubt.
> (*Calling.*)

Come out, Agnès.

> (*To Alain and Georgette.*)
> Go in.

Scene V.
Arnolphe.

> The weather's mild.

Agnès.

Oh, yes.

Arnolphe.

> Most pleasant.

Agnès.

Indeed!

Arnolphe.

What news, my child?

Agnès.

The kitten died.

Arnolphe.

Too bad, but what of that?
All men are mortal, my dear, and so's a cat.
While I was gone, no doubt it rained and poured?

Agnès.

No.

Arnolphe.

You were bored, perhaps?

Agnès.

I'm never bored.

Arnolphe.

During my ten days' absence, what did you do?

Agnès.

Six nightshirts, I believe; six nightcaps, too.

Arnolphe.

(After a pause.)
My dear Agnès, this world's a curious thing.
What wicked talk one hears, what gossiping!
While I was gone, or so the neighbors claim,
There was a certain strange young man who came
To call upon you here, and was received.
But such a slander's not to be believed,
And I would wager that their so-called news—

Agnès.

Heavens! Don't wager; you'd be sure to lose.

Arnolphe.

What! Is it true, then, that a man—

Agnès.

Oh, yes.

In fact, he all but lived at this address.

Arnolphe.

(Aside.)
That frank reply would seem to demonstrate
That she's still free of guile, at any rate.
(Aloud.)
But I gave orders, Agnès, as I recall,

That you were to see no one, no one at all.
Agnès.
I disobeyed you, but when I tell you why,
You'll say that you'd have done the same as I.
Arnolphe.
Perhaps; well, tell me how this thing occurred.
Agnès.
It's the most amazing story you ever heard.
I was sewing, out on the balcony, in the breeze,
When I noticed someone strolling under the trees.
It was a fine young man, who caught my eye
And made me a deep bow as he went by.
I, not to be convicted of a lack
Of manners, very quickly nodded back.
At once, the young man bowed to me again,
I bowed to him a second time, and then
It wasn't very long until he made
A third deep bow, which I of course repaid.
He left, but kept returning, and as he passed,
He'd bow, each time, more gracefully than the last,
While I, observing as he came and went,
Gave each new bow a fresh acknowledgement.
Indeed, had night not fallen, I declare
I think that I might still be sitting there,
And bowing back each time he bowed to me,
For fear he'd think me less polite than he.
Arnolphe.
Go on.
Agnès.
          Then an old woman came, next day,
And found me standing in the entryway.
She said to me, "May Heaven bless you, dear,
And keep you beautiful for many a year.
God, who bestowed on you such grace and charm,
Did not intend those gifts to do men harm,
And you should know that there's a heart which bears
A wound which you've inflicted unawares."
Arnolphe.

(Aside.)

Old witch! Old tool of Satan! Damn her hide!
Agnès.
"You say I've wounded somebody?" I cried.

"Indeed you have," she said. "The victim's he
Whom yesterday you saw from the balcony."
"But how could such a thing occur?" I said;
"Can I have dropped some object on his head?"
"No," she replied, "Your bright eyes dealt the blow;
Their glances are the cause of all his woe."
"Good heavens, Madam," said I in great surprise,
"Is there some dread contagion in my eyes?"
"Ah yes, my child," said she. "Your eyes dispense,
Unwittingly, a fatal influence:
The poor young man has dwindled to a shade;
And if you cruelly deny him aid,
I greatly fear," the kind old woman went on,
"That two days more will see him dead and gone."
"Heavens," I answered, "that would be sad indeed.
But what can I do for him? What help does he need?"
"My child," said he, "he only asks of you
The privilege of a little interview;
It is your eyes alone which now can save him,
And cure him of the malady they gave him."
"If that's the case," I said, "I can't refuse;
I'll gladly see him, whenever he may choose."
Arnolphe.

(*Aside.*)

O "kind old woman!" O vicious sorceress!
May Hell reward you for your cleverness!
Agnès.
And so I saw him, which brought about his cure.
You'll grant I did the proper thing, I'm sure.
How could I have the conscience to deny
The succor he required, and let him die—
I, who so pity anyone in pain,
And cannot bear to see a chicken slain?
Arnolphe.

(*Aside.*)

It's clear that she has meant no wrong, and I
Must blame that foolish trip I took, whereby
I left her unprotected from the lies
That rascally seducers can devise.
Oh, what if that young wretch, with one bold stroke,
Has compromised her? That would be no joke.

Agnès.

What's wrong? You seem a trifle irritated.
Was there some harm in what I just related?

Arnolphe.

No, but go on. I want to hear it all.
What happened when the young man came to call?

Agnès.

Oh, if you'd seen how happy he was, how gay,
And how his sickness vanished right away,
And the jewel-case he gave me—not to forget
The coins he gave to Alain and to Georgette,
You would have loved him also, and you too—

Arnolphe.

And when you were alone, what did he do?

Agnès.

He swore he loved me with a passion,
And said to me, in the most charming fashion,
Things which I found incomparably sweet,
And never tire of hearing him repeat,
So much do they delight my ear, and start
I know not what commotion in my heart.

Arnolphe.

(Aside.)

O strange interrogation, where each reply
Makes the interrogator wish to die!
                    (To Agnès.)
Besides these compliments, these sweet addresses,
Were there not also kisses, and caresses?

Agnès.

Oh, yes! He took my hands, and kissed and kissed
Them both, as if he never would desist.

Arnolphe.

And did he not take—something else as well?
            (HE notes that SHE is taken aback.)
Agh!

Agnès.

        Well, he—

Arnolphe.

                Yes?

Agnès.

                    Took—

Arnolphe.

What?

Agnès.

I dare not tell.

I fear that you'll be furious with me.

Arnolphe.

No.

Agnès.

Yes.

Arnolphe.

No, no.

Agnès.

Then promise not to be.

Arnolphe.

I promise.

Agnès.

He took my—Oh, you'll have a fit.

Arnolphe.

No.

Agnès.

Yes.

Arnolphe.

No, no. The devil! Out with it!
What did he take from you?

Agnès.

He took—

Arnolphe.

(Aside.)

God save me!

Agnès.

He took the pretty ribbon that you gave me.
Indeed, he begged so that I couldn't resist.

Arnolphe.

(Taking a deep breath.)

Forget the ribbon. Tell me: once he'd kissed
Your hands, what else did he do, as you recall?

Agnès.

Does one do other things?

Arnolphe.

No, not at all;
But didn't he ask some further medicine
For the sad state of health that he was in?

Agnès.

Why, no. But had he asked, you may be sure
I'd have done anything to speed his cure.

Arnolphe.

(*Aside.*)

I've got off cheap this once, thanks be to God;
If I slip again, let all men call me clod.

(*To Agnès.*)

Agnès, my dear, your innocence is vast;
I shan't reproach you; what is past is past.
But all that trifler wants to do—don't doubt it—
Is to deceive you, and then boast about it.

Agnès.

Oh, no. He's often assured me otherwise.

Arnolphe.

Ah, you don't know how that sort cheats and lies.
But do grasp this: to accept a jewel-case,
And let some coxcomb praise your pretty face,
And be complaisant when he takes a notion
To kiss your hands and fill you with "commotion"
Is a great sin, for which your soul could die.

Agnès.

A sin, you say! But please, Sir, tell me why.

Arnolphe.

Why? Why? Because, as all authority states,
It's just such deeds that Heaven abominates.

Agnès.

Abominates! But why should Heaven feel so?
It's all so charming and so sweet, you know!
I never knew about this sort of thing
Till now, or guessed what raptures it could bring.

Arnolphe.

Yes, all these promises of love undying,
These sighs, these kisses, are most gratifying;
But they must be enjoyed in the proper way;
One must be married first, that is to say.

Agnès.

And once you're married, there's no evil in it?

Arnolphe.

That's right.

Agnès.

Oh, let me marry then, this minute!

Arnolphe.

If that's what you desire, I feel the same;
It was to plan your marriage that I came.

Agnès.

What! Truly?

Arnolphe.

                    Yes.

Agnès.

                    How happy I shall be!

Arnolphe.

Yes, wedded life will please you, I foresee.

Agnès.

You really intend that we two—

Arnolphe.

                                        Yes, I do.

Agnès.

Oh, how I'll kiss you if that dream comes true!

Arnolphe.

And I'll return your kisses, every one.

Agnès.

I'm never sure when people are making fun.
Are you quite serious?

Arnolphe.

                        Yes, I'm serious. Quite.

Agnès.

We're to be married?

Arnolphe.

                    Yes.

Agnès.

                    But when?

Arnolphe.

                                        Tonight.

Agnès.

                    (*Laughing.*)

Tonight?

Arnolphe.

        Tonight. It seems you're moved to laughter.

Agnès.

Yes.

Arnolphe.

        Well, to see you happy is what I'm after.

Agnès.

Oh, Sir, I owe you more than I can express!
With him, my life will be pure happiness!

Arnolphe.

With whom?

Agnès.

With . . . him.

Arnolphe.

                                    With *him*! Well, think again.
You're rather hasty in your choice of men.
It's quite another husband I have in mind;
And as for "him," as you call him, be so kind,
Regardless of his pitiable disease,
As never again to see him, if you please.
When next he calls, girl, put him in his place
By slamming the door directly in his face;
Then, if he knocks, go up and drop a brick
From the second-floor window. That should do the trick.
Do you understand, Agnès? I shall be hidden
Nearby, to see that you do as you are bidden.

Agnès.

Oh dear, he's so good-looking, so—

Arnolphe.

                                                    Be still!

Agnès.

I just won't have the heart—

Arnolphe.

                                                    Enough; you will.

Now go upstairs.

Agnès.

                    How can you—

Arnolphe.

                                            Do as I say.

I'm master here; I've spoken; go, obey.

SECOND SCENE

Fortune's zigzag course and Molière's plotting have
whisked Agnès from the grasp of her guardian into the
arms of young Horace, her would-be lover, who promptly
returns her to Arnolphe. Horace has not discovered that
Arnolphe and La Souche are the same man; concerned to

protect the girl's reputation as well as her innocence until
he can obtain his father's permission to marry her, Horace
asks his father's friend—Arnolphe, of course—to conceal
the girl for him. Arnolphe, disguised in a cloak, eagerly
takes the girl in charge and hastily bids Horace godspeed
and begone.

Scene IV.
Arnolphe.
   (Hiding his face in his cloak, and disguising his voice.)
  Come, this is not where you're to stay, my child;
  It's elsewhere that you shall be domiciled.
  You're going to a safe, sequestered place.
     (Revealing himself, and using his normal voice.)
  Do you know me?
Agnès.

(Recognizing him.)

Aagh!

Arnolphe.

You wicked girl! My face

  Would seem, just now, to give you rather a fright.
  Oh, clearly I'm a most unwelcome sight:
  I interfere with your romantic plan.
     (Agnès turns and looks in vain for Horace.)
  No use to look for help from that young man;
  He couldn't hear you now; he's gone too far.
  Well, well! For one so young, how sly you are!
  You ask—most innocently, it would appear—
  If children are begotten through the ear,
  Yet you know all too well, I now discover,
  How to keep trysts—at midnight—with a lover!
  What honeyed words you spoke to him just now!
  Who taught you such beguilements? Tell me how,
  Within so short a time, you've learned so much!
  You used to be afraid of ghosts and such:
  Has your gallant taught you not to fear the night?
  You ingrate! To deceive me so, despite
  The loving care with which you have been blessed!
  Oh, I have warmed a serpent at my breast
  Until, reviving, it unkindly bit
  The very hand that was caressing it!

Agnès.
Why are you cross with me?
Arnolphe.

Oh! So I'm unfair?

Agnès.
I've done no wrong of which I am aware.
Arnolphe.
Was it right, then, to run off with that young beau?
Agnès.
He wants me for his wife; he's told me so.
I've only done as you advised; you said
That, so as not to sin, one ought to wed.
Arnolphe.
Yes, but I made it perfectly clear that I'd
Resolved, myself, to take you as my bride.
Agnès.
Yes; but if I may give my point of view,
He'd suit me, as a husband, better than you.
In all your talk of marriage, you depict
A state that's gloomy, burdensome, and strict;
But, ah, when *he* describes the married state,
It sounds so sweet that I can hardly wait.
Arnolphe.
Ah! So you love him, faithless girl!
Agnès.

Why, yes.

Arnolphe.
Have you the gall to tell me that, Agnès?
Agnès.
If it's the truth, what's wrong with telling it?
Arnolphe.
How dare you fall in love with him, you chit?
Agnès.
It was no fault of mine; he made me do it.
I was in love with him before I knew it.
Arnolphe.
You should have overcome your amorous feeling.
Agnès.
It's hard to overcome what's so appealing.
Arnolphe.
Didn't you know that I would be put out?

Agnès.
Why, no. What have you to complain about?
Arnolphe.
Nothing, of course! I'm wild with happiness!
You don't, I take it, love me.
Agnès.
                              Love you?
Arnolphe.
                                        Yes.
Agnès.
Alas, I don't.
Arnolphe.
                    You *don't?*
Agnès.
                         Would you have me lie?
Arnolphe.
Why don't you love me, hussy? Tell me why!
Agnès.
Good heavens, it's not I whom you should blame.
He made me love him; why didn't you do the same?
I didn't hinder you, as I recall.
Arnolphe.
I tried to make you love me; I gave my all;
Yet all my pains and strivings were in vain.
Agnès.
He has more aptitude than you, that's plain;
To win my heart, he scarcely had to try.
Arnolphe.
                    (*Aside.*)
This peasant girl can frame a neat reply!
What lady wit could answer with more art?
Either she's bright, or in what concerns the heart
A foolish girl can best the wisest man.
                    (*To Agnès.*)
Well, then, Miss Back-Talk, answer this if you can:
Did I raise you, all these years, at such expense,
For another's benefit? Does that make sense?
Agnès.
No. But he'll gladly pay you for your trouble.
Arnolphe.
                    (*Aside.*)
Such flippancy! It makes me rage redouble.

(*To Agnès.*)

You minx! How could he possibly discharge
Your obligations to me? They're too large.

Agnès.

Frankly, they don't seem very large to me.

Arnolphe.

Did I not nurture you from infancy?

Agnès.

Yes, that you did. I'm deeply obligated.
How wondrously you've had me educated!
Do you fancy that I'm blind to what you've done,
And cannot see that I'm a simpleton?
Oh, it humiliates me; I revolt
Against the shame of being such a dolt.

Arnolphe.

Do you think you'll gain the knowledge that you need
Through that young dandy's tutelage?

Agnès.

　　　　　　　　　　　　　　　Yes, indeed.

It's thanks to him I know what little I do;
I owe far more to him than I do to you.

Arnolphe.

What holds me back, I ask myself, from treating
So insolent a girl to a sound beating?
Your coldness irks me to the point of tears,
And it would ease my soul to box your ears.

Agnès.

Alas, then, beat me, if you so desire.

Arnolphe.

(*Aside.*)

Those words, and that sweet look, dissolve my ire,
Restoring to my heart such tender feeling
As makes me quite forget her double-dealing.
How strange love is! How strange that men, from such
Perfidious beings, will endure so much!
Women, as all men know, are frailly wrought:
They're foolish and illogical in thought,
Their souls are weak, their characters so bad,
There's nothing quite so silly, quite so mad,
So faithless; yet, despite these sorry features,
What won't we do to please the wretched creatures?

(*To Agnès.*)

Come, traitress, let us be at peace once more.
I'll pardon you, and love you as before.
Repay my magnanimity, and learn
From my great love to love me in return.

Agnès.

Truly, if I were able to, I would.
I'd gladly love you if I only could.

Arnolphe.

You can, my little beauty, if you'll but try.

(*HE sighs.*)

Just listen to that deep and yearning sigh!
Look at my haggard face! See how it suffers!
Reject that puppy, and the love he offers:
He must have cast a spell on you; with me,
You'll be far happier, I guarantee.
I know that clothes and jewels are your passion;
Don't worry: you shall always be in fashion.
I'll pet you night and day; you shall be showered
With kisses; you'll be hugged, caressed, devoured.
And you shall have your wish in every way.
I'll say no more; what further could I say?

(*Aside.*)

Lord, what extremes desire will drive us to!

(*To Agnès.*)

In short, no love could match my love for you.
Tell me, ungrateful girl, what proof do you need?
Shall I weep? Or beat myself until I bleed?
What if I tore my hair out—would that sway you?
Shall I kill myself? Command, and I'll obey you.
I'm ready, cruel one, for you to prove me.

Agnès.

Somehow, your lengthy speeches fail to move me.
Horace, in two words, could be more engaging.

Arnolphe.

Enough of this! Your impudence is enraging.
I have my plans for you, you stubborn dunce,
And I shall pack you out of town at once.
You've spurned my love, and baited me as well—
Which you'll repent of in a convent cell.

from

ORESTES

by Euripides (translated by Kenneth Cavander)

ELECTRA, ORESTES, PYLADES

This play is the most fascinating, least awe-struck presentation of the Orestes story produced by the Greek or any other theater. Its universe is absurd, its characters unheroic, its resolution a mind-jarring combination of wildly comic action and a deeply tragic point of view. And its paradoxes are worked out in totally theatrical terms.

Orestes, Electra, and Pylades, threatened with execution for the murder of Clytemnestra, beg and then demand that Menelaus, the king, grant them their lives. To force his hand, they determine to kill his wife Helen, to threaten to slit the throat of his little daughter (and to do the deed if need be), and moreover to burn down the house of Atreus. At the critical moment, as the three avengers stand atop the palace, firebrands in hand and knife at the throat of the little girl, Apollo stops the action, pairs everyone off (Orestes is to marry the child he was about to murder), and announces with bland good humor that everyone will live happily ever after. That this god-ordained resolution is incredible, given the characters concerned seems to be precisely Euripides' point: it *is* absurd, as is any myth if you try to be, not see, one. That character should be granted life when their sheer will to live has carried them to eliminate from themselves every human quality that can make life worth living, is a measure of the tragedy of man and the inanity or vicious irony of the gods.

In the scene reprinted here, Euripides details the transformation of three human beings into a trio of terrorists. It begins in a low key. Orestes' case has been heard by the

586

city assembly and they have voted for his execution. With
his friend Pylades he comes to tell Electra. Pylades has
still some spirit, but the brother and sister sense and accept
total defeat. From the beginning Orestes has been without
hope; only when Electra has revived him with her spirit has
he had the courage to face Menelaus and the others. Now
she, too, is overcome. When he tells her of the assembly's
decision, she can only stand and weep.

Electra.

(*Weeping.*) For you my brother . . . yes, these tears are
  for you.
I see you at the gates of death, close to the flames
That will eat up your body. Poor Orestes, this
Is the last time we shall be together—I could go mad
Thinking of it . . . !

Orestes.

Quiet, little sister . . . No more tears. The end
Is near, we cannot escape, so be content. Cruel
It may be, but you must . . .

Electra.

How can I be content? Never again to see the sun,
Never to see the dawn sky fill with light?

Orestes.

Don't! It's enough that I have to die once. Your words
Are like a second execution . . . Say no more.
We have known too much suffering . . .

Electra.

You're young, Orestes, it's not time for you
To die . . . You have a right to live and now
You're being denied that right.

Orestes.

In heaven's name, don't talk about it. You'll drain
All my courage away, and I'll start to weep like a woman.

Electra.

We're going to die! I must cry out against it!
Life is worth our tears, it's the most precious thing
There is.

Orestes.

But there's no way out. We have only one choice:
Either a rope knotted around our necks, or else
We pick up our swords and . . .

Electra.

Kill me now, Orestes! Don't let some Argive lay hands
On the child of Agamemnon and slaughter her
Like a dog.

Orestes.

No. I took my mother's life—let that be enough.
I refuse to touch you. Do it yourself . . . It doesn't matter
How, do it yourself.

Electra.

Very well. I'll show you how brave I am with cold steel.
First let me hold you in my arms . . .

Orestes.

Of course, if it makes you happy. Such a small thing
To ask for a few minutes away from death—to touch
Hands . . .

Electra.

My darling, I love you . . . your name is my name,
The sweetest name in the world to me . . .your soul
Is mine . . .

Orestes.

And I meant to be so strong . . . Here, let me kiss you . . .
And hold you . . . Why be ashamed? . . . It's foolish.
My dear sweet sister, we have no children, no life
Shared with another person, but we have this—
We can whisper to each other through our tears.

Electra.

(*Sighs.*) If only a single blow would kill us both,
And the same box of cedarwood enclose our bodies.

Orestes.

I know. I want that too—so much. You see how alone
We are? We have to share one grave for company.

Electra.

And Menelaus never said a word in your defense?
Never lifted a finger to save you . . . The coward!
He's betrayed my father!

Orestes.

Menelaus did not even show his face. Having set
His heart on the throne, he made sure he took
No risks for his friends . . . But look, Agamemnon
Was our father—let us act like the children of a king,
And die bravely. I'll prove to everyone that I am

My father's son when I sink this dagger in my heart.
Watch me, and do the same, and don't flinch.
Pylades, make sure we don't cheat death.
When it's over, lay the bodies out, and bury them
Side by side, near our father's tomb . . . Goodbye . . .
As you see, I go to do my duty . . .

Pylades.

Stop! . . . I am angry with you, Orestes—yes, angry:
You believed I would want to go on living
After you are dead.

Orestes.

But nothing obliges you to share my death.

Pylades.

Why not, since I cannot share your life?

Orestes.

You did not kill your mother, I did—god help me!

Pylades.

And I was your accomplice. I deserve the same punishment.

Orestes.

Go back home, and make your father happy. Don't throw away
Your life. You have a country of your own, and I
Have none. In your father's house, a rich inheritance
Awaits you. You have lost nothing—except my sister,
My unlucky sister, whom I betrothed to you because
I loved you, and you were my good friend. But you will find
Another wife for yourself, and get children with her.
All obligations are cancelled between us—no ties
Of blood or marriage remain . . .
But oh, I shall miss you, dear friend, dear companion.
Be happy . . . We are allowed to say those words to you,
Though you can never say them to us. Our lives are over
And so is our happiness.

Pylades.

How little you know me. May the earth, which gives us
All good things, and the clear bright air, shrink
From my living flesh, if ever I betray you,
And walk away to freedom leaving you trapped here.
I was one of the murderers, and I shall not try

To hide it. I helped you plan everything for which
You are now being punished. If you two are to die,
So must I. You said Electra was to be my wife . . .
Well, that is how I think of her now.
And if I were to go back to the land of Delphi
And the city of Phocians, what splendid story
Should I have to tell? . . . How I used to be your friend
Until things went badly for you? How I stopped
Being your friend when your good luck ran out?
No. We have always been inseparable, and we still are.
But since we are condemned to death, let us think
Of a way to hurt Menelaus as well.

Orestes.

If I could live to see that I would die happy.

Pylades.

Then keep your sword from doing its sharp work a while
And listen to me.

Orestes.

All right, provided I take revenge on the man I detest.

Pylades.

Lower your voice . . . I don't trust those women . . .

Orestes.

No, trust them. Everyone here is our friend.

Pylades.

Let us kill Helen, and break Menelaus' heart.

Orestes.

How? I'm ready, if there's any way it can be done.

Pylades.

With our swords. She's hiding in your palace now.

Orestes.

So she is . . . Taking stock of our possessions.

Pylades.

That will stop when Death claims her as his bride.

Orestes.

How shall we do this? She has a troop of foreigners
To protect her.

Pylades.

Those creatures? I'd never be afraid of a man
Who speaks in fractured Greek.

Orestes.

Yes, they'll fight to the death—for their hand mirrors

And perfume boxes!

Pylades.

Has she really brought all that rubbish back with her
From Troy?

Orestes.

Oh, Greece is much too cramped and austere for her!

Pylades.

Some races have a slave mentality; they cannot compete
With us.

Orestes.

If only this succeeds—I could bear to die twice over.

Pylades.

So could I. Just let me repay them for their cruelty
To you.

Orestes.

Tell me how you see your plan working.

Pylades.

We go inside. We pretend we're going to take our
lives . . .

Orestes.

So far I understand. What happens then?

Pylades.

We make a great parade of our grief and fear . . .

Orestes.

. . . bring tears to her eyes, while secretly
She will be laughing . . .

Pylades.

Her act will be no different from ours, then.

Orestes.

And how do we play this game out to its proper end?

Pylades.

We have these daggers hidden in our cloaks.

Orestes.

Can we make an end of her with all her guards around?

Pylades.

We'll lock them up in various rooms.

Orestes.

Yes, and if any of them makes a sound it will be
Our pleasant duty to cut his throat.

Pylades.

After that, the plan will work on its own.

Orestes.

"Death to Helen." I know the password by heart.

Pylades.

Good. Agreed. You see how well I advise you?
If we were to turn our weapons on a woman
Whose life was above reproach, we would be committing
A savage murder. As it is, this will be an execution
For all that Greece has suffered—for the fathers
Helen slaughtered, the sons she murdered, the brides
She widowed.
A wild cheer will go up to heaven, people will light
Bonfires to the gods, and shower us with thanks
For spilling the blood of this evil creature. No one
Will call you "matricide" for killing her. You'll never
Have to hear that word again. A new day will dawn for
     you.
You'll be known as the man who rid the world of Helen
The murderess. It is necessary, oh, so necessary,
That Menelaus should not triumph while your father,
You, and your sister die. As for your mother—
Well, there is nothing good to be said of that affair . . .
But think of your palace here. Menelaus would move in
And take possession, having won back his bride
Through Agamemnon's courage and daring. I would rath-
     er die
Than let Helen escape the edge of my sword. And if
We fail to settle accounts with her, let us burn
The house down, and throw ourselves in the flames.
That way, our honor will be safe whatever happens;
We shall preserve it either in the manner of our death,
Or in the means by which we save our lives.

Chorus.

The daughter of Tyndareus has earned the loathing
Of every woman in the world. She disgraced her sex.

Orestes.

(*Shouting with joy.*)
Now I know I have a friend! He's worth more
Than anything on earth—more than wealth, more than
     power!
I would barter the mindless worship of a whole army
For a single true and loyal friend. You were the one

Who devised a punishment for Aegisthus and now,
Once more, you deliver my enemies to my vengeance
And do not spare yourself. But I won't sing your praises
Any more. Even praise becomes tedious, I know.
Come what may, I am doomed. And so, before I die,
It would please me greatly to strike a blow
At my enemies. Somehow I must pay them back
For their treachery to me, and leave them with some hurt
To remind them of my own.
I am the true-born son of Agamemnon, who ruled
Greece without question. He was no tyrant, but still
His power was sanctioned by some divine decree.
I will not disgrace him by letting myself be butchered
Like a slave. I'll end my days as free men do—
And I'll make Menelaus *pay*!
And then, we might be lucky. Something might happen,
Some unexpected twist of fortune, that would save us . . .
To kill and not be killed—I pray it happens . . .
I pray . . .
This wish of mine, tasting sweet on the lips, costs
Nothing and the words, though made of air, lighten
The darkness in my heart.

Electra.
Orestes, I think I know a way to make your wish
Come true, a way to save all three of us.

Orestes.
What do you mean? Do you have second sight?
That quick brain of yours has thought of something—yes?

Electra.
Listen . . . And you too, come here . . . Listen carefully.

Orestes.
Tell us. A small hope will lift my spirits.

Electra.
You know Helen's daughter . . . ? Of course you do.

Orestes.
Hermione? Yes. My mother brought her up . . .

Electra.
She's gone to Clytemnestra's grave.

Orestes.
Why should she go there? How can that help us?

Electra.
She's gone to pour offerings of wine over the place

Where our mother lies.
Orestes.
You said this could save us . . . How?
Electra.
When she comes back, kidnap her and hold her hostage.
Orestes.
And this will bring the three of us back to life?
Electra.
Assume we have killed Helen. Then, if Menelaus
Should try to harm any of us, we threaten to kill
Hermione. You draw your sword and hold its blade
Against the girl's neck. If Menelaus, having seen
Helen lying in a pool of her own blood, decides
He does not want his daughter to die as well
And lets you go, release the girl, and let her father
Clasp his beloved baby in his arms. But if he can't control
His blazing temper, and attacks you, then slit
The girl's throat. But I think, however much Menelaus
Storms and blusters at first, he'll soon calm down
And be ready to make peace. His nature lacks
All resolution or strength. On this I base my hopes
Of coming out of this alive. I think it's a firm
Foundation.
Orestes.
Electra, you are wearing a disguise. You masquerade
As a woman, but inside you think and feel like a man!
You were born to live, not to die.
Pylades, this is the woman you are destined to lose,
You miserable wretch, or else—if you survive
To have as your wife in god-given happiness.
Pylades.
I pray I win her and bring her home with me,
Honored and praised as she deserves, to Phocis.
Orestes.
How long before Hermione gets back? It sounded
Excellent, what you said, provided we have time
For everything. First we have to snare the brat
This viper fathered.
Electra.
She must be close, judging by the length of time
She's been away.

Orestes.

Good. Now you, Electra, wait in front of the palace
And meet the girl when she returns. Keep a lookout
In case anyone comes who might help her, before
The execution is complete—or Menelaus gets back
Sooner than we expect. If he does, shout into the house,
Or knock on the door, but send a message in somehow.
Meanwhile we shall go inside and arm ourselves with
  swords
For this final engagement . . . Pylades, come.
You suffer through all my labors with me . . .
Oh, my father, now consigned to the dim mansions
Of the night, your son Orestes invokes your help
For those in need. Because I tried to help you,
I am persecuted. Though I did no wrong, your brother
Betrayed me. Now I plan to kill his wife. In this work
I ask you to become my accomplice.

Electra.

Yes, father, join us. Can you hear us there,
In the depths of the earth? Your children cry out
To you. For your sake we are hunted to death.

Pylades.

Close kinsman of my father, Agamemnon, hear
My prayers too . . . Protect your children.

Orestes.

I killed my mother . . .

Pylades.

. . . my hand was on the sword . . .

Electra.

. . . and I encouraged them, I gave them no excuse for
  delay.

Orestes.

This is for you, father, do not desert us.

Electra.

I remembered you.

Pylades.

They are testing you, will you not help your children?

Orestes.

My offering to you is my tears . . .

Electra.

My sobs . . .

Pylades.

Enough. Let us begin. There is work to be done.
If prayers can burrow their way through the earth
Yours have reached him.
O Zeus, first father of us all, the glory
Of incarnate justice, grant us success—all three.
Three friends we go into a great battle, but one
Decision awaits us all: either to come out alive,
Or suffer the penalty of death.

from

THE DANCE OF DEATH

by August Strindberg (translated by Elizabeth Sprigge)

Five Scenes from Part I: Act I, scene 1, and Act II,
scene 2; and Part II: Act I, scene 1; Act I, scene 2; and Act
II
THE CAPTAIN, ALICE, KURT

The recent production by Britain's National Theatre, with
a cast headed by Laurence Olivier and Geraldine McEwan,
made clear for modern audiences the dramatic force and
fascination of Strindberg's double-length drama of a marriage locked together by hate and of the man destroyed by
a husband and wife who use him in their deadly struggle.
In this extraordinary work, the playwright of early expres-
sionism kept meticulously within the bounds of naturalistic
theater, but at times the realistic action fired by his passionate involvement with his subject takes on the warped
shape of a nightmarish fantasy.

The Dance of Death is a stark dramatization of the duel
of the sexes, a clinical examination of a marriage in which
only one (if either) of the partners can survive. An aging,
unsuccessful captain of artillery and his wife live isolated
in the stone tower of an island fortress, once a prison.
Within the stone walls, words slice with a knife-edge and
silences speak antagonism. As husband and wife struggle
to make real their schemes to establish power over each
other—venomous plots conjured up by monomaniacal
imaginations—nightmare enters the waking world, reaches
out to poison those who brush near it, and drives on without relief to the grotesque tragedy of its conclusion.

One might more accurately say two conclusions. The long
drama involves shifting relationships and a competition for

power in which no character has the upper hand throughout. Indeed, the two parts of the play almost mirror each other: at the end of Part I, the wife nearly achieves victory, but the balance shifts to her husband; as Part II comes to its close, the husband is defeated in the midst of proclaiming his victory. Part I was written originally to be played on its own, but together the two parts form a unique, extended study in the interaction of characters. For that reason, so many scenes have been reprinted here, though each, of course, will stand on its own as a significant actors' exercise.

The play begins on a warm autumn evening in the 1890s. The glass doors in the archway that was the main entrance of the fortress have been swung open. Beyond is a beach with gun emplacements and the sea. The room inside—the setting for Part I, round, for it is a part of the old tower—is lit by the setting sun and a lamp suspended from the ceiling. There are flowers in a window at one side of the glass doors, a birdcage in a window at the other side. Doors in the side walls lead to other rooms and to the outside. There are a couch and two armchairs, a sewing table, sideboard, round porcelain stove, family portraits on a whatnot, a small piano, and a writing table with telegraphic apparatus on it (the Captain prefers the telegraph to the telephone). Swords and other military paraphernalia hang on a stand near the doorway, left. Above the piano, between two large, beribboned wreaths, is a portrait of a woman in theatrical costume.

The subject of the portrait, Alice, the Captain's wife, sits in the room. She is doing nothing. Her husband, wearing a rather worn-out undress uniform, riding boots and spurs, stands beside the writing table. He looks tired and bored. Not well, he has been told that drink will endanger his life, but he has had his grog this evening. There have been half-hearted attempts at a card game, the usual mutual recriminations, a brief argument with a maid about lighting the lamp. Alice's cousin, Kurt, has been discussed. It was he who brought the Captain and Alice together. He has come to the island as a civil servant, the Quarantine Officer, after fifteen years in America.

Occasionally sounds of music drift into the room; elsewhere on the island, the Doctor is having a party. The Captain and his wife have not been invited—the Captain does not mix with the Doctor, nor with anyone on the island ("Everyone is scum").

There is a knock at the door, left.

Alice.

Who can that be at this hour?

The Captain.

Jenny doesn't usually knock.

Alice.

Go and open it and don't call "come in"—that sounds like a workshop.

The Captain.

(*Going to the door.*) You don't like workshops.

(*The knocking is repeated.*)

Alice.

Open it, do!

(*The Captain opens it and takes the visiting card which is handed to him.*)

The Captain.

It's Kristin. . . . (*To the unseen Kristin.*) Has Jenny gone? (*Her reply is inaudible. To Alice.*) Jenny has gone.

Alice.

So I'm to be the maid again.

The Captain.

And I the man.

Alice.

Can't we have one of the garrison to help in the kitchen?

The Captain.

Not these days.

Alice.

But surely it wasn't Jenny who sent in that card?

(*The Captain puts on his glasses and looks at the card, then hands it to Alice.*)

The Captain.

You read it. I can't.

Alice.

(*Looking at the card.*) Kurt! It's Kurt. Go and bring him in.

The Captain.

(*Going out, left.*) Kurt! Well, that is nice! (*Alice arranges*

*her hair and seems to come to life. The Captain and Kurt
enter, left.*) Here he is, the blackguard! Welcome, old man!
(*Pats him on the back.*)

Alice.

Welcome to my home, Kurt!

Kurt.

Thank you. . . . It's a long time since we saw one another.

The Captain.

What is it? Fifteen years. And we've grown old.

Alice.

Oh, Kurt looks just as he was to me!

The Captain.

Sit down, sit down! Now first of all our programme. Any
engagement this evening?

Kurt.

I've been invited to the doctor's, but I haven't promised to
go.

Alice.

Then stay with your relatives.

Kurt.

That would be the natural thing to do, but on the other
hand, the doctor is my chief, and there'd be unpleasantness later.

The Captain.

Nonsense! I've never been afraid of my chiefs.

Kurt.

Afraid or not, there'd be unpleasantness just the same.

The Captain.

Here on the island, I'm master. Stick behind me and no
one will dare get at you.

Alice.

Be quiet Edgar! (*Takes Kurt's hand.*) Never mind about
masters and chiefs—you stay here with us. It's only
right and proper.

Kurt.

So be it. Specially as I find myself welcome here.

The Captain.

Why shouldn't you be welome? We haven't any quarrel with you.

(*Kurt cannot hide a certain embarrassment.*)

Why should we have? You were a bit reckless, but you
were young and I've forgotten it. I don't bear grudges.

(Alice looks vexed. All three sit at the sewing-table.)

Alice.

Well, have you been round the world?

Kurt.

Yes, and now I've landed up with you . . .

The Captain.

Whom you married off twenty-five years ago.

Kurt.

Hardly that . . . but let it go. It's nice to see that you've stuck together for twenty-five years.

The Captain.

Yes, we've rubbed along. Sometimes it's been a bit touch and go, but as you say, we've stuck it out. And Alice has had nothing to complain of. Plenty of everything, oodles of money . . . Perhaps you don't know I'm a famous writer—writer of textbooks.

Kurt.

Yes, I remember when our ways parted you had just brought out a shooting manual that was doing well. Is it still used in the military schools?

The Captain.

It is still there and still number one, although they've tried to throw it out for an inferior one . . . which of course is used now, though it's utterly worthless.

(Embarrassing silence.)

Kurt.

You've been abroad, I hear.

Alice.

Yes, just imagine. We've been to Copenhagen five times.

The Captain.

Yes. You see, when I took Alice away from the theatre . . .

Alice.

Took me?

The Captain.

Yes, I took you, as a wife should be taken . . .

Alice.

You're talking very big.

The Captain.

But afterwards I was always having it thrown at me that I'd ruined her brilliant career. . . . Hm! So I had to make amends by promising to take my wife to Copenhagen. And I've kept my promise faithfully. Five times we've been there. (*Holds up the fingers of his left hand.*) Five. Have you been to Copenhagen?

Kurt.

(*Smiling.*) No, I've been chiefly in America.

The Captain.

America? Pretty low place, what?

Kurt.

(*Taken aback.*) It's not Copenhagen.

Alice.

Have you . . . heard at all . . . from your children?

Kurt.

No.

Alice.

Forgive me, my dear, but it was rather heartless to leave them like that.

Kurt.

I didn't leave them. The Court gave their mother custody.

The Captain.

We won't talk about that now. Seems to me you were lucky to get out of that mess.

Kurt.

(*To Alice.*) Are your children well?

Alice.

Yes, thank you. They're at school in the town—they'll be grown up soon.

The Captain.

Yes, they're bright youngsters. The boy has a brilliant mind. Brilliant. He'll be on the General Staff.

Alice.

If they'll have him.

The Captain.

Have him? The makings of a Minister of War.

Kurt.

To change the subject . . . There's to be this Quarantine Station here—for plague, cholera, and so forth—and the doctor, as you know, will be my chief. What sort of man is he?

The Captain.

Man? He's not a man. He's a brainless scoundrel.

Kurt.

(*To Alice.*) How very unpleasant for me!

Alice.

It's not as bad as Edgar says, but I must admit he doesn't appeal to me.

The Captain.

He's a scoundrel. And so are the rest of them—the Customs Officer, the Postmaster, the telephone girl, the chemist, the pilot—the-what-do-they-call-him, the Alderman—scoundrels, the whole pack of them.

Kurt.

Are you on bad terms with the whole lot?

The Captain.

The whole lot.

Alice.

Yes, it's true, you can't have anything to do with those people.

The Captain.

It's as if all the tyrants in the country had been interned on this island.

Alice.

(*Ironically.*) How true!

The Captain.

(*Good-humouredly.*) Hm. Is that a dig at me? I'm no tyrant, not in my own home at any rate.

Alice.

You be careful!

The Captain.

(*To Kurt.*) You mustn't believe a word she says. I'm a very good husband and my old woman's the best wife in the world.

Alice.

Would you like a drink, Kurt?

Kurt.

No thanks, not at the moment.

The Captain.

You haven't become a . . . ?

Kurt.

Rather moderate, that's all.

The Captain.

American?

Kurt.

Yes.

The Captain.

I say be immoderate—or leave it alone. A man should be able to hold his liquor.

Kurt.

To return to our neighbours on the island—my position will bring me into contact with everyone. And it won't be plain sailing, because, however little one wants to, one's bound to become involved in other people's intrigues.

Alice.

Go on then, but you'll always come back to us, because your true friends are here.

Kurt.

Isn't it frightful to sit here alone surrounded by enemies?

Alice.

It's not pleasant.

The Captain.

It's not frightful at all. All my life I've had enemies and they've helped rather than harmed me. And when my time comes to die, I shall be able to say: "I owe nobody anything and I've never had anything as a gift. Everything I've got I've had to fight for."

Alice.

Yes, Edgar's path has not been strewn with roses.

The Captain.

With thorns and stones—flints. But there's your own strength. Do you know what I mean?

Kurt.

(*Simply.*) Yes, I learnt the limits of mine ten years ago.

The Captain.

Then you're a milksop.

Alice.

Edgar!

The Captain.

Well, he is a milksop if he can't rely on his own strength. True, when the mechanism's done for, nothing's left but a barrowful to tip out on a garden plot. But as long as the mechanism's intact, the thing is to kick and fight for all your worth, with both hands and both feet. That's my philosophy.

Kurt.

(*Smiling.*) You're amusing to listen to.

The Captain.

But don't you believe it?

Kurt.

No, I don't believe it.

The Captain.

Well, anyhow it's true.

(*During the above scene the wind has risen, and now one of the glass doors slams.*)

The Captain.

(*Rising.*) A gale's getting up. I felt it coming. (*He shuts the doors and taps the barometer.*)

Alice.

(*To Kurt.*) You'll stay to supper, won't you?

Kurt.

Thank you.

Alice.

It will be very simple. Our maid's just left.

Kurt.

I'm sure it will be fine.

Alice.

You're so easy to please, my dear Kurt.

The Captain.

(*At the barometer.*) You should just see how the barometer's falling. I felt it in my bones.

Alice.

(*Aside to Kurt.*) He's all on edge.

The Captain.

It's time we had supper.

Alice.

(*Rising.*) I'm just going to see to it. You two stay here and talk philosophy. (*To Kurt, aside.*) But don't contradict him or he'll lose his temper. And don't ask him why he isn't a Major. (*Kurt nods assent. Alice goes towards the door, right. The Captain sits down at the sewing-table with Kurt.*)

The Captain.

See we have something good, old girl!

Alice.

You would have if you gave me some money.

The Captain.

Always money!

(*Exit Alice.*)

(*To Kurt.*) Money, money, money! All day long I run round with a purse, till I begin to think I am a purse. Do you know what I mean?

Kurt.

Surely. With this difference . . . I thought I was a pocket-book.

The Captain.

Ha! So you know the type—those ladies! Ha! And you picked a proper one.

Kurt.

(*Evenly.*) All that can be forgotten now.

The Captain.

(*Ironically.*) A perfect jewel that one. Whereas I—in spite of everything—at least got myself a good woman. For she is honest, in spite of everything.

Kurt.

(*Smiling amiably.*) In spite of everything!

The Captain.

Don't laugh.

Kurt.

(*As before.*) In spite of everything!

The Captain.

Yes, she's been a faithful wife . . . a good mother, exceptionally good, but . . . (*Glances at the door, right*) . . . she has the devil of a temper. There have been times, you know, when I've cursed you for saddling me with her.

Kurt.

(*Affably.*) But I never did. Listen, my dear fellow . . .

The Captain.

Damn it, man! You talk a lot of rubbish and forget anything that's unpleasant to remember. . . . Don't get me wrong. You see, I'm used to commanding and blustering, but you know me and won't take offence.

Kurt.

Of course not. But I didn't saddle you with a wife. On the contrary . . .

The Captain.

(*Not allowing his flow to be interrupted.*) Don't you think life's an extraordinary business anyway?

Kurt.

It surely is.

The Captain.

As for growing old, it's not nice but it's interesting. Of course, I'm not old, but age is beginning to make itself felt. Your acquaintances die off and you grow lonely.

Kurt.

The man who has a wife to grow old with is fortunate.

The Captain.

Fortunate? Yes, that is fortunate, for one's children leave one too. You should never have left yours.

Kurt.

But I didn't. They were taken from me.

The Captain.

Now you mustn't take offence when I say that.

Kurt.

But it wasn't so.

The Captain.

Well, how it happened has been forgotten. But you *are* alone.

Kurt.

My dear fellow, one gets used to anything.

The Captain.

Could one . . . could one really get used to being entirely alone?

Kurt.

Just look at me.

The Captain.

What have you achieved these fifteen years?

Kurt.

What a question! These fifteen years.

The Captain.

They say you've come into some money and are rich.

Kurt.

I'm not rich . . .

The Captain.

I wasn't thinking of borrowing.

Kurt.

If you were, I'm ready . . .

The Captain.

Thank you so much, but I have my own debit and credit

account. You see . . . (*Glances at the door, right.*)
. . . in this household there must be no shortage of anything. The day I hadn't any money, off she'd go.

Kurt.

Oh no!

The Captain.

Oh yes! I know it. Believe it or not, she's always on the
look-out for the times when I do happen to be out of
funds, just for the pleasure of proving to me that I don't
support my family.

Kurt.

But I thought you said you had a big income.

The Captain.

Certainly I have a big income . . . but it isn't enough.

Kurt.

Then it's not big in the ordinary sense.

The Captain.

Life is extraordinary, and so are we.

> (*The telegraph begins tapping.*)

Kurt.

What's that?

The Captain.

Only the time signal.

Kurt.

Haven't you got a telephone?

The Captain.

Yes, in the kitchen. But we use the telegraph, because
the telephone girls repeat everything we say.

Kurt.

Social life out here must be grim.

The Captain.

Yes, it's perfectly abominable. The whole of life is abominable. And you, who believe in a sequel, do you think
there'll be peace afterwards?

Kurt.

There's bound to be storm and stress there too.

The Captain.

There too— if there is a there. Then rather annihilation.

Kurt.

How do you know annihilation would come without pain?

The Captain.

I shall drop down dead, without pain.

Kurt.

I see. You know that, do you?

The Captain.

Yes, I know it.

Kurt.

You aren't satisfied with your existence, are you?

The Captain.

(*Sighing.*) Satisfied? The day I die I shall be satisfied.

Kurt.

You can't know that. . . . Now, tell me, what are you two up to in this house? What's going on here? The very walls smell of poison—one feels sick the moment one comes in. I'd rather be off, if I hadn't promised Alice to stay. There's a corpse under the floor . . . and such hatred that one can scarcely breathe. (*The Captain collapses in his chair and stares vacantly.*) What's wrong with you? Edgar! (*The Captain does not move. Kurt slaps him on the back.*) Edgar!

The Captain.

(*Coming to.*) Did you say something? (*Looking round.*) Oh, it's you! I thought it was Alice. . . . Now . . . (*Relapses into apathy again.*)

Kurt.

This is terrible. (*Goes over and opens the door, right.*) Alice! (*Alice enters, wearing an apron.*)

Alice.

What's the matter?

Kurt.

I don't know. Look at him!

Alice.

(*Calmly.*) He does sometimes lose his senses like this. I'll play—that will bring him round. (*Goes towards the piano.*)

Kurt.

No, don't, don't! Let me try. Can he hear? Can he see?

Alice.

At this moment he can neither hear nor see.

Kurt.

Yet you can speak so calmly. Alice, what are you two up to in this house?

Alice.

Ask that man there.

Kurt.

That man! Why he's your husband!

Alice.

To me he's a stranger, as much of a stranger as twenty-five years ago. I know nothing about this man except that he . . .

Kurt.

Stop! He may hear you.

Alice.

He can hear nothing now.

(*A bugle call is heard.*)

(*The Captain springs to his feet and seizes his sword and cap.*)

The Captain.

Excuse me. I must just inspect the posts.

(*Exit The Captain through the centre doorway.*)

Kurt.

What's the matter with him?

Alice.

I don't know.

Kurt.

Is he out of his mind?

Alice.

I don't know.

Kurt.

Does he drink?

Alice.

There's more boasting about it than drinking.

Kurt.

Sit down and talk. Calmly and truthfully now.

Alice.

(*Sitting.*) What am I to say? That I've been in this tower a lifetime, imprisoned, guarded by a man I've always hated, and now hate so utterly that the day he died, I'd laugh aloud.

Kurt.

Why haven't you separated?

Alice.

Question! Twice we broke off our engagement, and since then not a day has passed in which we haven't tried to separate. But we are welded together—we can't escape.

Once we *did* separate—in our own home—for five years. Now only death can separate us. We know it, so we wait for him as the deliverer.

SECOND SCENE

Alice has won Kurt as an ally—or rather, the Captain has lost him. In a sudden change of character, the Captain has given up his grog, taken to wearing freshly cleaned uniforms, and clearly has some great project in mind. He has ordered Kurt's son, a cadet, to be transferred to his command on the island, though Kurt, who has not seen the boy since a separation from his wife years ago, wishes it otherwise. The Captain wants the boy as a hostage, Alice explains to Kurt, so that he can be your master; and he will try to isolate you from your son as he will try to isolate you from everyone on the island by ruining your reputation with stories of the divorce and other scandals.

The Captain announces that he himself has filed for divorce, that he intends to marry some younger, more suitable woman. Alice replies that she could not be more pleased, she will find a better husband.

"You are the first woman who has aroused my pity," Kurt says when the Captain has stormed out. "All the others seemed to me to deserve what they got."

Utterly against the Captain now because he wants to steal his son, Kurt declares, "He must die—he or I!"

Alice has a subtler plan. The Captain, she says, has embezzled. She knows, and certain men on the island know. She will expose him; in a few hours he will be arrested. "And I," she finishes, "will dance on his head!" Kurt calls her a devil, but he is as sensual as he is weak-willed, and when she moves toward him, declaring herself to be free, he rushes to embrace her.

Later, in the evening, the Captain has hurried into the room, clearly in a panic. He has lit the lamp and the candles on the tables, has overturned some of the furniture, and thrown the family pictures onto the floor. A sound from the telegraph strikes him with terror. He puts on his overcoat and leaves the room. After a moment, Alice enters. She is in outdoor clothes, with a hat and gloves.

She looks around, surprised to see so many lights. Kurt comes in through the doorway, left. He is obviously nervous.

Alice.

It looks like Christmas Eve in here!

Kurt.

Well?

Alice.

(*Holding out her hand for him to kiss.*) Thank me! (*Kurt reluctantly kisses her hand.*) Six witnesses, four of them firm as rock. The charge has been laid and the reply is coming here—by telegraph—right into the fortress.

Kurt.

I see.

Alice.

Say thank you, not "I see."

Kurt.

Why has he lighted so many candles?

Alice.

Because he's afraid of the dark, of course. . . . Look at that telegraph-key. It looks like the handle of a coffee-grinder, doesn't it? I grind, I grind, and the beans crack—like when teeth are drawn out.

Kurt.

What has he been doing to the room?

Alice.

It looks as if he means to move. And move he shall—down below!

Kurt.

Alice, don't talk like that! I find it revolting. He was the friend of my youth and did me many a kindness when I was in difficulties. . . . He is to be pitied.

Alice.

Then what about me, who have done nothing wrong and have had to sacrifice my career to this monster?

Kurt.

What about that career? Was it so brilliant?

Alice.

(*Furiously.*) What on earth do you mean? Don't you know who I am, what I was?

Kurt.

Now, now!

Alice.

Are you beginning too—already?

Kurt.

Already?

(*Alice flings her arms around Kurt's neck and kisses him. Kurt takes hold of her arms and bites her neck. She screams.*)

Alice.

You bit me!

Kurt.

(*Beside himself.*) Yes, I want to bite your throat and suck your blood like a lynx. You have roused the wild beast in me, which for years I've been trying to kill by self-denial and penance. I came here thinking myself rather better than you two, but now I am the vilest of the three. Now that I have seen you—in the full horror of your nakedness—now that passion has distorted my vision, I know the full force of evil. Ugliness has become beauty and goodness is growing ugly and feeble. . . . Come to me! I will suffocate you—with a kiss.

(*He embraces her.*)

Alice.

(*Showing him her ring finger.*) Look at the mark of the fetter you have broken! I was a slave and now am free.

Kurt.

But I shall bind you.

Alice.

You?

Kurt.

I!

Alice.

I thought at one moment you were . . .

Kurt.

Pious?

Alice.

Yes, you talked about the Fall.

Kurt.

Did I?

Alice.

And I thought you had come here to preach.

Kurt.

Did you? In an hour we shall be in town. Then you shall see what I am.

Alice.

We'll go to the theatre tonight and let everyone see us. The shame will be his if I run away. You realise that, don't you?

Kurt.

I'm beginning to realise it. Prison is not enough.

Alice.

No, it's not enough. There must be shame too.

Kurt.

A queer world! You commit a shameful act, and he has to bear the shame.

Alice.

As the world is so stupid.

Kurt.

It's as if these prison walls had soaked in all the evil of the criminals, and one only had to breathe here to catch it. You were thinking about the theatre and supper, I suppose. I was thinking about my son.

(Alice strikes him across the mouth with her glove.)

Alice.

Prig!

(Kurt raises his hand to box her ears. Alice shrinks back.)
Tout beau!

Kurt.

Forgive me!

Alice.

On your knees then!

(Kurt falls on his knees.)

On your face!

(Kurt touches the floor with his forehead.)

Kiss my foot!

(Kurt kisses her foot.)

And never do that again! Get up!

Kurt.

(Rising.) What have I come to? Where am I?

Alice.

You know where.

Kurt.

(Looking round in horror.) I almost think I'm . . .

(The Captain enters, right, leaning on a stick and look-ing wretched.)

The Captain.

May I talk to you, Kurt? Alone.

Alice.

About the safe-conduct?

The Captain.

(Sitting at the sewing-table.) Will you be so kind as to stay here with me for a moment, Kurt? And, Alice, will you grant us one moment's . . . peace?

Alice.

What is it now then? New signals. *(To Kurt.)* Do sit down.

> *(Kurt unwillingly sits at the sewing-table.)*

And listen to the words of age and wisdom. . . . If a tele-gram comes, let me know.

> *(Exit Alice, left.)*

The Captain.

(After a pause, with dignity.) Do you understand a human destiny like mine—like hers and mine?

Kurt.

No, as little as I understand my own.

The Captain.

Then what is the meaning of this mess?

Kurt.

In my better moments I have thought that the meaning was just that we should not understand, and yet submit.

The Captain.

Submit! Without some fixed point outside myself, I can't submit.

Kurt.

Obviously not. But as a mathematician, you should be able to find that unknown point from the data given you.

The Captain.

I have searched for it—but I haven't found it.

Kurt.

Then you've made some mistake in your calculations. Be-gin again.

The Captain.

I will begin again. Tell me, how did you come to be so resigned?

Kurt.

I'm not any longer. Don't overrate me.

The Captain.

You may have observed that my practice of the art of
living has been—elimination. That's to say, to cancel out
and pass on. Early in life I made myself a sack into which
I stuffed my humiliations, and when it was full I chucked
it into the sea. I don't believe any human being has suffered so many humiliations as I have. But when I cancelled them out and passed on, they ceased to exist.

Kurt.

I have noticed how you have created your own life in
your imagination, and created your own environment.

The Captain.

How could I have borne life if I hadn't? How could I have
endured?

(*Presses his hand to his heart.*)

Kurt.

How are you feeling?

The Captain.

Bad.

(*Pause, after which he speaks in an old man's quavering
voice, his lower jaw sagging.*)

But there comes a moment when the ability to create in
imagination, as you call it, fails. And then reality stands
out in all its nakedness. . . . That's terrible. You see, my
dear friend . . . (*Controls himself and speaks in his ordinary voice.*) Forgive me. When I was in town just now
and saw the doctor . . . (*His voice breaks again.*) . . . he
said that I was done for . . . (*In his ordinary voice.*) . . .
and that I couldn't live for long.

Kurt.

He said *that?*

The Captain.

Yes, he said that.

Kurt.

Then it wasn't true.

The Captain.

What wasn't? Oh, I see—no, it wasn't true.

(*Pause.*)

Kurt.

Wasn't the other thing true either?

The Captain.

What, my dear fellow?

Kurt.

About my son being sent here as a cadet.

The Captain.

I haven't heard a word about that.

Kurt.

You know your ability to cancel out your own misdeeds is unparalleled.

The Captain.

My dear fellow, I don't know what you're talking about.

Kurt.

Then you *are* done for.

The Captain.

Yes, there's not much of me left.

Kurt.

Look here, perhaps you didn't really file a petition for that divorce which would bring your wife into such disgrace.

The Captain.

Divorce? No, heard nothing of that.

Kurt.

(*Rising.*) Then you admit you were lying.

The Captain.

You use such strong language, my dear man. We all need to have allowances made for us.

Kurt.

You have found that out, have you?

The Captain.

(*Firmly, in a clear voice.*) Yes, I have found that out. . . . So, forgive me, Kurt! Forgive the whole business!

Kurt.

Well said. But I have nothing to forgive you. And I'm not now the man you believe me to be—and am quite unworthy to receive your confidences.

The Captain.

(*In a clear voice.*) Life has been so strange. So against me, so vindictive . . . and people were so vindictive that I became vindictive too. . . .

(*Kurt walks about uneasily and looks at the telegraph apparatus.*)

What are you looking at?

Kurt.

Can one switch off a telegraph receiver?

The Captain.

Hardly.

Kurt.

(*With increasing anxiety.*) Who is this Sergeant-Major Ostberg?

The Captain.

An honest enough fellow. Looks after his own interests, of course.

Kurt.

And what about the Quartermaster?

The Captain.

He's got his knife into me all right, but I've nothing against him.

(*Kurt looks out of the window and sees a moving lantern.*)

Kurt.

Why have they got a lantern out on the battery?

The Captain.

Is there a lantern there?

Kurt.

Yes, and people moving around.

The Captain.

It's probably what we call a fatigue-party.

Kurt.

What's that?

The Captain.

A few men and a bombardier. Probably some poor fellow's going to be locked up.

Kurt.

Oh!

(*Pause.*)

The Captain.

Now that you know Alice, what do you think of her?

Kurt.

I can't tell you . . . I don't understand people at all. She is as much an enigma to me as you are—as I am myself. The fact is, I'm getting to the age when wisdom admits: "I know nothing, I understand nothing . . ." But when I see an action, I want to know its motive. . . . Why did you push her into the water?

The Captain.

I don't know. It just seemed perfectly natural to me when I saw her on the jetty that she should go in.

Kurt.

Didn't you feel any remorse?

The Captain.

Never.

Kurt.

That's extraordinary.

The Captain.

Yes, it certainly is. So extraordinary that I can't believe it was I who behaved in such a caddish way.

Kurt.

Didn't it occur to you that she'd take her revenge?

The Captain.

She certainly has—fully—and I find that equally natural.

Kurt.

How have you arrived so quickly at this cynical resignation?

The Captain.

Since looking death in the eyes, life has presented itself from another angle. . . . Listen! If you had to judge between Alice and me, which of us would you say was in the right?

Kurt.

Neither. But I'm desperately sorry for you both, perhaps a little more for you.

The Captain.

Give me your hand, Kurt.

(*Kurt gives The Captain his hand and puts the other on his shoulder.*)

Kurt.

Old friend!

(*Alice enters left, carrying a parasol.*)

Alice.

Dear me, what intimacy! Ah, there's friendship for you! . . . Hasn't the telegram come?

Kurt.

(*Coldly.*) No.

Alice.

I have no patience with this delay. And when I've no pa-

tience I speed things up. . . . Watch now, Kurt, I'm going
to fire the last bullet at him—and then he'll fall. . . .
First, I load—I know the rifle-manual, you see—that
famous rifle-manual which never sold five thousand copies
. . . Then I take aim . . . (*Aims with her parasol.*) . . .
fire! How is the new wife? The young, the lovely, the unknown? You don't know. But I know how my lover is.

(*She throws her arms round Kurt's neck and kisses him.
He pushes her away.*)

He's quite well, but he's still shy. . . . (*To The Captain.*)
You poor wretch, whom I have never loved, you who were
too conceited to be jealous, you couldn't see how I've
been leading you by the nose.

(*The Captain draws his sword and rushes at her, but
only succeeds in striking the furniture.*)

Help! Help!

(*Kurt does not move. The Captain falls with the sword
in his hand.*)

The Captain.

Judith! Avenge me!

Alice.

Hurrah! He's dead.

(*Kurt moves toward the door, back.*)

The Captain.

(*Rising.*) Not yet.

(*He sheathes his sword and goes to sit in the armchair
by the sewing-table.*)

Judith! Judith!

Alice.

(*Going to Kurt.*) I'm coming now—with you.

(*Kurt pushes her away so that she falls to her knees.*)

Kurt.

Go to the hell from which you came! Goodbye for ever.

(*Turns towards the door.*)

The Captain.

Don't leave me, Kurt, she'll kill me!

Alice.

Kurt! Don't desert me! Don't desert us!

Kurt.

Goodbye.

(*Exit Kurt.*)

Alice.

(*With a complete change of mood.*) What a wretch! There's a friend for you!

The Captain.

(*Gently.*) Forgive me, Alice, and come over here. Come quickly!

Alice.

(*Going to him.*) I've never met such a wretch and such a hypocrite in all my life. . . . You are a man; I will say that for you.

The Captain.

Alice, listen . . . I can't live much longer.

Alice.

What?

The Captain.

The doctor said so.

Alice.

Then all that other talk wasn't true.

The Captain.

No.

Alice.

(*Distraught.*) Oh, what have I done?

The Captain.

It can all be put right.

Alice.

This can't be put right.

The Captain.

There's nothing that can't be put right, so long as one cancels it out and passes on.

Alice.

But the telegram! The telegram!

The Captain.

What telegram?

(*Alice falls on her knees beside The Captain.*)

Alice.

Are we doomed? Must this happen? I've destroyed myself, destroyed us both! Oh, why did you pretend to have done all that? And why did that man come and tempt me? . . . We are lost! Everything could have been put right; everything could have been forgiven in the bigness of your heart.

The Captain.

What is there that can't be forgiven? What haven't I forgiven you?

Alice.

That's true . . . but this can't be put right.

The Captain. -

I can't guess this one, although I know your devilish powers of invention.

Alice.

Oh, if I could only get out of this! If I could only get out of this, I'd take such care of you! Edgar, I would love you.

The Captain.

Just listen to that! Wherever am I?

Alice.

Do you realise no one can help us? No one on earth.

The Captain.

Who else then?

Alice.

(*Looking him in the eyes.*) I don't know. . . . Oh, what is to become of the children—with their name dishonoured?

The Captain.

Have you dishonoured their name?

Alice.

Not I! Not I! . . . Now they'll have to leave school. And when they go out into the world, they'll be as lonely as us, and as spiteful as us. . . . Then you didn't meet Judith either? I realise that now.

The Captain.

No. But cancel that out.

                    (*The telegraph taps. Alice jumps up.*)

Alice.

(*Screaming.*) Now we are done for! Don't listen to it!

The Captain.

(*Calmly.*) I won't listen to it, dear child. Calm yourself.

    (*Alice stands by the telegraph and gets on her toes so as to see out of the window.*)

Alice.

Don't listen! Don't listen!

The Captain.

(*Putting his hands over his ears.*) I'm stopping my ears, Lisa, my child.

(Alice kneels with her arms outstretched.)

Alice.

God help us—the fatigue-party is coming!

(She moves her lips as if in silent prayer.

The telegraph taps for a little longer, until a long strip of paper has appeared. Then there is silence again.

Alice rises, tears off the strip of paper and reads it to herself. Then she raises her eyes to heaven, goes over and kisses The Captain on the forehead.)

It is over. It was nothing.

(She sits down in the other chair, takes out her handkerchief, and bursts into tears.)

The Captain.

What are all these secrets?

Alice.

Don't ask me. It's over now.

The Captain.

Just as you please, my child.

Alice.

You wouldn't have said that three days ago. What's happened to you?

The Captain.

Well, my dear, when I had that first attack, I passed over for a while to the other side of the grave. What I saw I have forgotten, but the effect has lasted.

Alice.

What effect?

The Captain.

The hope of something better.

Alice.

Something better?

The Captain.

Yes. I never really have believed that this could be life itself. This is death—or worse.

Alice.

And we . . . ?

The Captain.

Were destined to torment one another, so it seems.

Alice.

Haven't we tormented one another enough?

The Captain.

I should think so. What havoc we have played too! (*Looks about.*) Shall we put the place in order? And clean up?

Alice.

(*Rising.*) Yes, if it's possible.

The Captain.

(*Rising and looking round the room.*) It can't be done in one day, that's certain.

Alice.

In two, then. Many days.

The Captain.

Let's hope so.

> (*Pause. The Captain sits down again.*)

So you didn't get free this time. But you didn't get me locked up either.

> (*Alice looks surprised.*)

Yes, I knew you wanted to put me in prison, but I cancel that out. . . . You have probably done worse things than that.

> (*Alice is speechless.*)

And I was not guilty of that embezzlement.

Alice.

And now I am to be your nurse?

The Captain.

If you will.

Alice.

What else is there for me to do?

The Captain.

I don't know.

> (*Alice slumps down in despair.*)

Alice.

These are surely the everlasting fires! Is there no end?

The Captain.

Yes, but we must have patience. Perhaps when death comes, life begins.

Alice.

Ah, if that were so . . . !

> (*Pause.*)

The Captain.

You think Kurt was a hypocrite, do you?

Alice.

Yes, I certainly do.

The Captain.

I don't. But everyone who comes near us grows evil and goes his way. . . . Kurt was weak and evil is strong.

(*Pause.*)

How insipid life is now! One used to fight; now one only shakes one's fists. . . . I feel pretty sure that in three months' time we shall be having our silver wedding—with Kurt as best man, and the doctor and Gerda among the guests. The Quartermaster will propose the toast and the Sergeant-Major lead the cheering. And if I know the Colonel, he will invite himself. . . .

(*Alice giggles.*)

Makes you laugh, eh? But do you remember Adolf's silver wedding—that fellow in the Rifles? The bride had to wear the ring on her right hand, because in a moment of tenderness the bridegroom had chopped off her left ring-finger with a bill-hook.

(*Alice holds her handkerchief to her face to stifle her laughter.*)

Are you crying? No, you're laughing, surely. Yes, child, that's how it is for us—part laughter and part tears. Which it should be, don't ask me! The other day I read in the paper that a man who had been divorced seven times and had married again seven times, finally eloped in his ninety-ninth year and remarried his first wife. There's love for you! Whether life is serious or just trivial, I haven't a clue. It can be its most painful when it's comic, and its most agreeable and peaceful when it's serious. . . . But if you finally decide to take yourself seriously, someone comes and makes a fool of you. Kurt, for example. . . . Do you want a silver wedding?

(*Alice is silent.*)

Do say yes. . . . They'll laugh at us, but what does that matter? We'll laugh with them—or else be serious—just as we choose.

Alice.

Yes—very well.

The Captain.

(*Seriously.*) So silver wedding it is. . . . (*Rises.*) Cancel out and pass on! So—let us pass on!

THIRD SCENE

The scene above ends Part I. For Part II the scene changes to the following summer and to an oval drawing room in white and gold, as light and hopeful as the fortress room was gloomy. French windows open onto a flowery terrace. There are a gilded sofa, table, and chairs, a grand piano, a writing table, and an easy chair imported from America. The house is Kurt's.

Kurt has talked with his son, Allan, who is in love (and miserable) with Judith, the daughter of Alice and the Captain. Father and son are on better terms now, and when Alice appears outside and Kurt asks Allan what he thinks of her, the boy answers simply, "I'd rather not say."

Alice enters in a light summer dress, carrying a parasol. Outside, the morning sunlight is cheerful.

Alice.

Good morning, Kurt. (*Her look indicates that Allan is to go.*)

Kurt.

(*To Allan.*) You had better go.

    (*Allan goes out, right. Alice sits on the sofa, left, with Kurt on a chair beside her.*)

Alice.

(*Confused.*) He's coming in a moment, so you needn't feel embarrassed.

Kurt.

Why should I?

Alice.

With your strict principles . . .

Kurt.

In regard to myself, yes.

Alice.

Yes . . . well . . . I forgot myself once, when I saw you as the liberator, but you kept your presence of mind . . . and so we have a right to forget—what never was.

Kurt.

Forget it then.

Alice.

However—I don't think *he* has forgotten.

Kurt.

Do you mean that night he fell down with a heart attack, and you rejoiced too soon, thinking he was dead?

Alice.

Yes. Since then he's been quite himself again, but when he stopped drinking he learnt to hold his tongue, and now he's terrifying. He's up to something I can't grasp.

Kurt.

Alice, your husband is a good-natured ass who does me endless favours.

Alice.

Beware of his favours! I know them.

Kurt.

Oh, really . . . !

Alice.

So he's hoodwinked you too. Don't you see the danger? Aren't you aware of the traps?

Kurt.

No.

Alice.

Then you're doomed to destruction.

Kurt.

Heaven preserve us!

Alice.

You see! Here am I, watching ruin creeping up on you like a cat. . . . I point it out, but you can't see it.

Kurt.

Allan, with his unbiased view, can't see it either. For that matter, he doesn't see anything but Judith, and surely that's a guarantee of good relations.

Alice.

Do you know Judith?

Kurt.

A coquettish little thing in pigtails and rather too short skirts.

Alice.

Quite. But I saw her in a long skirt the other day—and then she was a young lady—not so young either, with her hair up.

Kurt.

She is slightly precocious, I admit.

Alice.

And she's playing with Allan.

Kurt.

No harm in that, so long as it is play.

Alice.

I see—that's permitted. . . . Edgar will be here in a moment. He will sit in the easy chair—he has such a passion for it he could steal it.

Kurt.

He shall have it.

Alice.

Let him sit over there, and we'll stay here. And while he's talking about trivial matters, I'll interpret for you.

Kurt.

Oh, you're too cautions, too cautious, dear Alice! What could I have to fear, so long as I run the Quarantine Station efficiently and behave properly otherwise?

Alice.

You pin your faith in justice and honour and all that.

Kurt.

Yes—experience has taught me to. Once I pinned my faith in just the opposite. . . . That cost me dear.

Alice.

Here he comes!

Kurt.

I've never seen you frightened before.

Alice.

My courage was only unawareness of the danger.

Kurt.

The danger? You'll begin to frighten me soon.

Alice.

Oh, if only I could! . . . Here he is!

(*Enter The Captain, back, wearing a buttoned-up black morning coat and officer's cap, and carrying a silver-crooked cane. He greets them with a nod, crosses the room, and sits in the easy chair.*)

(*To Kurt.*) Let him speak first.

The Captain.

This is a superb chair you have, my dear Kurt. Really superb.

Kurt.

You shall have it as a present, if you will accept it.

The Captain.

I didn't mean that.

Kurt.

But that's what I mean. Just think of all I've had from you.

The Captain.

(*Volubly.*) What rot! . . . And sitting here, I get a view of the whole island, of all the walks—I can see all the people on their verandahs, all the ships at sea—coming in and going out . . . You certainly have hit on the best bit of this island, which is by no means one of the Isles of the Blest. Is it, Alice? . . . Yes, it's known as Little Hell, and here Kurt has built himself a Paradise. Without Eve, of course, for when she came that was the end of Paradise. By the way, did you know this was once a royal hunting lodge?

Kurt.

So I have heard.

The Captain.

You live royally, but shame to say, you have me to thank for it.

Alice.

(*To Kurt.*) You see? Now he wants to get you in his clutches.

Kurt.

I have so much to thank you for.

The Captain.

Oh nonsense! Listen, did you get those cases of wine?

Kurt.

Yes.

The Captain.

And you're satisfied?

Kurt.

More than satisfied. Please give your wine merchant my compliments and tell him so.

The Captain.

He always provides first-class stuff.

Alice.

(*To Kurt.*) At second-class prices—and you have to pay the difference.

The Captain.

What did you say, Alice?

Alice.

I? Nothing.

The Captain.

Yes. When this Quarantine Station was established, I thought of applying for the post, and to that end made a study of quarantine systems.

Alice.

(*To Kurt.*) That's a lie.

The Captain.

(*Boastfully.*) The archaic ideas of quarantine held by the authorities were not shared by me. I, in fact, was on the side of the Neptunists—as we called them, because they favoured the water method.

Kurt.

I beg your pardon! I remember very well that it was I who preached water on one occasion, and you, fire.

The Captain.

Did I? What rot!

Alice.

(*Loudly.*) Yes, I remember that too.

The Captain.

You do?

Kurt.

I remember it all the more clearly because . . .

The Captain.

(*Cutting him short.*) Well, that may be, but it makes no odds. (*Raising his voice.*) In any case . . . we have now reached the point when a new state of affairs . . .

       (*Kurt tries to break in.*)

don't interrupt! . . . a new state of affairs has arisen, and the quarantine system is about to take a giant step forward.

Kurt.

Apropos, do you know who it is who writes those silly articles in the newspaper?

The Captain.

(*Getting red.*) I don't know; but why do you call them silly?

Alice.

(*To Kurt.*) Take care! It was he who wrote them.

Kurt.

(*To Alice.*) He? (*To The Captain.*) Well, shall we say—
not very intelligent.

The Captain.

You're no judge of that.

Alice.

Do you mean to quarrel?

Kurt.

Oh no!

The Captain.

It's hard to keep the peace here on the island, but we
ought to set a good example.

Kurt.

Yes. Now can you explain this to me? When I came here
I made friends at once with all the officials and was on
confidential terms with the lawyer—as confidential, that's
to say, as one can be at our time of life. Well, after a time
—it was just after you got well again—one and then another began to cold-shoulder me, and yesterday the lawyer
cut me on the promenade. I can't tell you how hurt I was.
                    (*The Captain is silent.*)
Have you noticed any coldness towards yourself?

The Captain.

No, on the contrary.

Alice.

(*To Kurt.*) Don't you realise he has stolen your friends?

Kurt.

(*To The Captain.*) I wondered if it could be due to that
new issue of shares I refused to have anything to do with.

The Captain.

No, no. But can you tell me why you wouldn't subscribe?

Kurt.

Because I'd already put my small savings into your soda
factory. And also because a new issue means that the old
shares are doing badly.

The Captain.

(*Irrelevantly.*) That's a superb lamp you have. Where on
earth did you get it?

Kurt.

In the town, of course.

Alice.

(*To Kurt.*) Keep an eye on your lamp, Kurt.

Kurt.

(*To The Captain.*) You mustn't think I'm ungrateful or haven't confidence in you, Edgar.

The Captain.

Well, it doesn't show much confidence when you want to back out of a business you helped to start.

Kurt.

My dear fellow, common prudence requires one to save oneself and what one has, while there's still time.

The Captain.

Save? Is there danger pending? Do they mean to rob you?

Kurt.

Why put it so crudely?

The Captain.

Weren't you pleased when I helped you to invest your capital at six per cent?

Kurt.

Yes, I was grateful too.

The Captain.

You are *not* grateful. It's not in your nature to be, but you can't help that.

Alice.

(*To Kurt.*) *Listen* to him!

Kurt.

There are plenty of shortcomings in my nature and my fight against them is pretty unsuccessful, but I do recognise obligations. . . .

The Captain.

Show it then! (*Puts out his hand and picks up a newspaper.*) Look! What's this? . . . An announcement. (*Reads.*) Death of the Medical Superintendent.

Alice.

(*To Kurt.*) He's already speculating on the corpse.

The Captain.

(*As if to himself.*) This will bring about . . . certain changes.

Kurt.

In what respect?

The Captain.

(*Rising.*) We shall soon see.

Alice.

(*To The Captain.*) Where are you going?

The Captain.

I thing I'd better go into town.

(*He catches sight of an envelope on the writing-table, picks it up as if unconsciously, reads the address, and puts it back.*)

Excuse me for being so absent-minded.

Kurt.

No harm in that.

The Captain.

Here's Allan's geometry set. Where is the boy?

Kurt.

He's out playing with the girls.

The Captain.

That great boy? I don't like it. And Judith ought not to run about like that. . . . You keep an eye on your young gentleman, and I'll look after my young lady. (*Passing the piano, he strikes a few notes.*) Superb tone, this instrument. A Steinbech, eh?

Kurt.

Bechstein.

The Captain.

Yes, you're well off, Kurt. Thanks to me, who brought you here.

Alice.

(*To Kurt.*) That's a lie. He tried to prevent you coming.

The Captain.

Goodbye for the moment. I'll take the next boat.

(*On his way out, he examines the pictures on the walls.*
Exit.)

Alice.

Well?

Kurt.

Well?

Alice.

I don't understand yet what he's scheming. But—tell me one thing. That envelope he looked at . . . who was the letter from?

Kurt.

I'm sorry to say, it was my one secret.

Alice.

And he smelt it out. You see, he's a wizard, as I told you before. . . . Is anything printed on the envelope?

Kurt.

Yes, it says: "Electors' Association."

Alice.

Then he's guessed your secret. I understand—you want to get into Parliament. And now you'll have to watch *him* getting in instead.

Kurt.

Has he ever thought of that?

Alice.

No, but he's thinking of it now. I read it in his face while he was looking at the envelope.

Kurt.

Is that why he's going to town?

Alice.

No. He made that decision when he saw the obituary.

Kurt.

What has he to gain by the death of the Medical Officer?

Alice.

You may well ask. . . . Perhaps he was an enemy who got in the way of his schemes.

Kurt.

If he's as monstrous as you say, one has good reason to fear him.

Alice.

Didn't you see how he wanted to get you into his clutches and tie your hands, on the grounds of obligations which don't exist? For instance, he did not get you the post; on the contrary, he tried to prevent your getting it. He's a man-eater, an insect, a woodworm who will devour you internally, so that one day you're as hollow as a rotten pine tree. . . . He hates you, though he's bound to you by the memories of your early friendship.

Kurt.

How sharp-witted you become when you hate!

Alice.

How dull-witted one is when one loves! Blind and dull.

Kurt.

Oh no, don't say that!

Alice.

Do you know what's meant by a vampire? . . . Well, it's the soul of a dead person looking for a body to live in

as a parasite. Edgar has been dead ever since that fall of
his. He has no interests of his own, no personality, no in-
itiative. But if only he can get hold of somebody, he clings
to him, puts out his suckers, and begins to grow and
bloom. Now he's making a set at you.

Kurt.

If he comes too close, I'll shake him off.

Alice.

Shake off a burr—you'll see!

FOURTH SCENE

Among the Captain's schemes is a plan to marry his
daughter Judith to the Colonel, who controls the island.
But if the Captain has plans, so too has Alice. "Now I'll
try the art of war," she says, "I failed once . . . but now
I've learnt how it's done."

Later, Kurt enters the room to find Alice waiting for him.

Kurt.

Are you here already?

Alice.

Yes.

Kurt.

Has *he* come back?

Alice.

Yes.

Kurt.

What like?

Alice.

In dress uniform. So he has been at the Colonel's. Two
orders on his breast.

Kurt.

Two? I knew he was to get the Order of the Sword when
he retired. What's the other one?

Alice.

I don't know, but it's a white cross inside a red one.

Kurt.

Portuguese in that case. . . . Let's think. . . . Ah, didn't
his newspaper articles describe Quarantine Stations in
Portuguese harbours?

Alice.

Yes, so far as I remember.

Kurt.

And has he even been to Portugal?

Alice.

Never.

Kurt.

But I have been there.

Alice.

You shouldn't be so communicative. His hearing is very acute and he has an excellent memory.

Kurt.

Don't you think it was Judith who got him this decoration?

Alice.

No, really Kurt—there are limits! (*Rises.*) And you have overstepped them.

Kurt.

Are we going to bicker now?

Alice.

Depends on you. Don't interfere with my interests.

Kurt.

If they cross mine, I have to interfere with them, even if with a very cautious hand. . . . Here he comes!

Alice.

It's now that it will happen.

Kurt.

What will happen?

Alice.

You'll see.

Kurt.

May it be an attack then, for this state of siege has got on my nerves. I haven't a friend left on the whole island.

Alice.

Quick now! . . . You sit here on this side . . . he'll take the easy chair, of course, and I can prompt you.

(*Enter The Captain, back, in full dress uniform with the Order of the Sword and the Portuguese Order of Christ.*)

The Captain.

Good morning. So this is the rendezvous.

Alice.

You're tired. Sit down.

(The Captain, contrary to expectation, sits on the sofa, left.) Make yourself comfortable.

The Captain.

It's so nice here. You're very kind.

Alice.

(To Kurt.) Take care! He suspects us.

The Captain.

(Testily.) What's that you said?

Alice.

(To Kurt.) He's certainly been drinking.

The Captain.

(Bluntly.) No, he hasn't.

(Silence.)

Well? How have you been amusing yourselves?

Alice.

And you?

The Captain.

Haven't you noticed my Orders?

Alice.

No . . . o.

The Captain.

I thought not. You're jealous. It's usual to congratulate people when they're decorated.

Alice.

We have the honour to do so.

The Captain.

We get these things instead of the laurels actresses get.

Alice.

That refers to the wreaths on the wall at home in the tower . . .

The Captain.

Which you got from your brother . . .

Alice.

Oh, stop!

The Captain.

And which I've had to kotow to for twenty-five years . . . and which it has taken me twenty-five years to expose.

Alice.

Have you been seeing my brother?

The Captain.

From time to time.

(*Alice is taken aback.*
Silence.)

Well, Kurt? You're very silent.

Kurt.

I'm waiting.

The Captain.

Listen, I suppose you've heard the big news?

Kurt.

No.

The Captain.

Well, it's not very pleasant for me to have to be the one to . . .

Kurt.

Let's have it!

The Captain.

The soda factory has gone bust.

Kurt.

That's very bad news. How do you come out of it?

The Captain.

I'm all right. I sold out in time.

Kurt.

You did wisely.

The Captain.

But how do you come out of it?

Kurt.

Badly.

The Captain.

You've only yourself to blame. You should have sold out in time or have subscribed to the new shares.

Kurt.

Then I'd have lost them too.

The Captain.

Oh no! Because then the Company would have stayed on its feet.

Kurt.

Not the Company, but the Board. I regarded the new shares as a collection for the directors.

The Captain.

Can that point of view save you? That's the question now.

Kurt.

No, I shall have to give up everything.

The Captain.

Everything?

Kurt.

Even the house and furniture.

The Captain.

That's an appalling state of affairs.

Kurt.

I have been through worse.

(*Silence.*)

The Captain.

That's what happens when amateurs go in for speculation.

Kurt.

How can you say that? You know if I hadn't subscribed I'd have been boycotted. . . . "Further means of livelihood for coast-dwellers and sea-workers; unlimited capital, unlimited as the sea . . . philanthropy and national gain." That's what you wrote and had printed. And now you call it speculation.

The Captain.

(*Unmoved.*) What do you mean to do now?

Kurt.

I may have to have an auction.

The Captain.

You would do well to.

Kurt.

What do you mean?

The Captain.

What I said. (*Slowly.*) The fact is, there are going to be certain changes here.

Kurt.

Here on the island?

The Captain.

Yes. . . . For instance, your official residence will be exchanged for a simpler one.

Kurt.

Indeed?

The Captain.

Yes, it's intended to have the Quarantine Station on the far side of the island, by the water.

Kurt.

My original idea.

The Captain.

(*Drily.*) I know nothing of that. . . . I don't know your ideas on the subject. However, it's an excellent opportunity for you to get rid of your furniture—like that, it will scarcely be noticed—the scandal.

Kurt.

What?

The Captain.

The scandal. (*Working himself up.*) For it is a scandal to come to a new place and immediately get oneself into financial difficulties. And it's unpleasant for the relatives—most of all for the relatives.

Kurt.

Unpleasant most of all for me.

The Captain.

I'll tell you one thing, my dear Kurt. If you hadn't had me on your side in this affair, you would have lost your job.

Kurt.

That too!

The Captain.

You find it pretty difficult to be meticulous. There have been criticisms of you in the service.

Kurt.

Just criticisms?

The Captain.

Well, yes. For you are—in spite of your other admiral qualities—a slacker. Don't interrupt me! You're a terrible slacker.

Kurt.

That's marvellous!

The Captain.

However! The afore-mentioned charge is likely to happen pretty quickly. And I want to advise you to have the auction at once or try to sell privately.

Kurt.

Privately? Where could I find a buyer here?

The Captain.

Surely you don't mean I'm to come and settle myself in among your furniture? That would be a fine story. . . . (*Jerkily.*) Hm! Specially if one . . . considers what happened . . . at one time . . .

Kurt.

What's that? Do you mean what *didn't* happen?

The Captain.

(*Turning.*) You're very quiet, Alice. What's the matter, old girl? You're not in your usual form.

Alice.

I'm just thinking.

The Captain.

O Lord! Thinking, are you? But you have to think quickly, correctly, and clearly if it's to be of any use. . . . Well, think then! One, two three! . . . Aha, you can't do it! Well, then I'll have a shot. . . Where's Judith?

Alice.

She's somewhere about.

The Captain.

Where's Allan?

(*Alice is silent.*)

Where's the Lieutenant?

(*Alice is silent.*)

Well, Kurt, what do you mean to do with Allan now?

Kurt.

Do with him?

The Captain.

Well, you won't have the means to keep him in the Artillery, will you?

Kurt.

Perhaps not.

The Captain.

You must try to get him into some cheap Infantry regiment, up in Norrland or somewhere.

Kurt.

In Norrland?

The Captain.

Yes. Or else you must make him go in for something practical, right away. If I were in your shoes, I'd put him in an office. . . . Why not?

(*Kurt is silent.*)

In these enlightened times. Well? . . . Alice is so *unusually* silent. . . . Yes, my children, that's the way life's see-saw goes. Now one's on top, looking confidently around; then one's at the bottom, and then up one comes again. And so on. That's how it goes. Yes. . . . (*To Alice.*) Did you say something?

(*Alice shakes her head.*)

We may expect visitors here in a few days.

Alice.

Were you addressing me?

The Captain.

We may expect visitors in a few days. Distinguished visitors.

Alice.

Well, who?

The Captain.

You see! You're interested. . . . Now you can just sit there and guess who's coming. And while you're guessing, you can take this letter and read it once again.

(*Gives her an opened letter.*)

Alice.

My letter? Opened? Back from the post?

The Captain.

(*Rising.*) Yes. In my capacity as head of the family and your guardian, I watch over the family's most sacred interests, and cut with an iron hand every attempt to break family ties through a criminal correspondence. Yes.

(*Alice is beaten.*)

I am not dead, Alice, but don't be angry at this moment, when I am trying to lift us all out of an undeserved humiliation—undeserved on my part at least.

Alice.

Judith! Judith!

The Captain.

And Holofernes? Is that to be me? Pah!

(*Exit, back.*)

Kurt.

Who is this man?

Alice.

I don't know.

Kurt.

We are beaten.

Alice.

Yes . . . without any doubt.

Kurt.

He has stripped me to the bone, but so cunningly that I
can't accuse him of anything.

Alice.

Accuse? On the contrary, you're under an obligation to
him.

Kurt.

Does he know what he's doing?

Alice.

No, I don't believe he does. He obeys his nature and
his instincts, and now he seems to be in favour wherever
good and bad luck are meted out.

Kurt.

It must be the Colonel who is coming here.

Alice.

Probably. And so Allan must go away.

Kurt.

Do you really think so?

Alice.

Oh yes!

Kurt.

Then our ways divide.

Alice.

(*Preparing to go.*) For a little while. . . . But we shall
meet again.

Kurt.

Probably.

Alice.

And you know where?

Kurt.

Here.

Alice.

You realise that?

Kurt.

It's easy. *He's* going to take over the place and buy the
furniture.

Alice.

That's what I believe too. But don't desert me!

Kurt.

Not for so slight a cause.

Alice.

Goodbye.

Kurt.
(*As Alice goes.*) Goodbye.

FIFTH SCENE

Several weeks have passed. The Captain and Alice have taken up residence in the bright house with its gilded furniture. Judith's engagement to the Colonel has been confirmed, and with that important officer behind him, the Captain has become a power on the island.

Kurt, desperately needing the help the Captain offers toward the education of his son, has yielded his will entirely to the Captain's. Kurt's candidacy for Parliament seems still to hold good, but that is all the hope he has.

The Captain has arranged for Kurt's son to be transferred to a far distant post. There is no preventing it, but Judith finds she does not wish the boy to leave and rushes to the post office with some idea in mind.

It is a rainy afternoon. Kurt has been asked (commanded) to visit the Captain, and he waits in another room as Alice and her husband come into the drawing room. Though at the end of the play she will recall that Captain as he was at twenty and realize that she must have loved as well as hated him, her feelings now are not ambiguous: her opposition to her husband is as strong as before. For the moment, however, she lacks the means to attack.

The Captain sits in the easy chair imported from America and turns to Alice.

The Captain.
Call him in.
(*Alice goes to the door, left, and opens it. Then she sits on the sofa.*)
(*Enter Kurt, left.*)

Kurt.
You want to see me?

The Captain.
(*Amiably, but a trifle patronisingly.*) Yes, I have several matters of importance to tell you. Sit down.
(*Kurt takes the chair on the left.*)

Kurt.
I am all ears.

The Captain.

Well then . . . (*In a haranguing tone.*) You are aware that our quarantine system has been in a parlous state for close on a century . . . hm!

Alice.

(*To Kurt.*) That's the parliamentary candidate speaking.

The Captain.

But in accordance with today's unprecedented development in . . .

Alice.

(*To Kurt.*) Means of communication, naturally.

The Captain.

. . . in every possible respect, the Government has been considering a policy of expansion. To this end the Ministry of Health has appointed inspectors, and . . .

Alice.

(*To Kurt.*) He's dictating.

The Captain.

. . . you may as well know it sooner as later—I have been appointed a Quarantine Inspector.

(*Silence.*)

Kurt.

I congratulate you—and at the same time pay my respects.

The Captain.

Our personal relationship—due to our family connection —will remain unchanged. But now, to speak of another matter—your son Allan has, at my request, been transferred to an Infantry regiment in Norrland.

Kurt.

But I don't wish him to be.

The Captain.

Your wishes in this matter are subordinate to those of his mother . . . and since his mother has authorised me to act for her, I have made the afore-mentioned decision.

Kurt.

I admire you.

The Captain.

Is that your only reaction in this moment, when you are about to be parted from your son? Have you any really human feelings?

Kurt.

You mean I ought to be suffering?

The Captain.

Yes.

Kurt.

It would please you if I suffered. You want me to have to suffer.

The Captain.

Can you suffer? Once I was stricken with illness—you were there—and I can only remember an expression of unfeigned pleasure in your face.

Alice.

That's not true. Kurt sat at your bedside all night, and soothed you when your pangs of conscience became too sharp. But when you recovered, you were ungrateful.

The Captain.

(*Without appearing to hear Alice.*) Accordingly, Allan is to leave us.

Kurt.

Who's to provide the means?

The Captain.

I have already done so. That is to say, we have—a syndicate, which interests itself in the young man's future.

Kurt.

Syndicate?

The Captain.

Yes. And so that you may see that it's all in order, you can take a look at these lists.

(*He hands Kurt some papers.*)

Kurt.

Lists? (*Looks at the papers.*) Why, these are begging lists!

The Captain.

Call them that if you like.

Kurt.

Have you been begging for my son?

The Captain.

More ingratitude! An ungrateful person is the heaviest burden the earth has to bear.

Kurt.

Now I'm done for socially, and my candidature will come to nothing.

The Captain.

What candidature?

Kurt.

Why, for Parliament.

The Captain.

Surely you never dreamt of that? Particularly as you must have had a notion that I, as an older resident, intended to propose myself—whom you appear to have underrated.

Kurt.

Well, so that's finished, that too.

The Captain.

It doesn't seem to worry you much.

Kurt.

Now you've taken everything. Do you want anything else?

The Captain.

Have you anything else? And have you anything to reproach me with? Think hard now if you have anything with which to reproach me.

(Silence.)

Kurt.

In actual fact, nothing. Everything has been done correctly and lawfully, as between honest citizens in daily life. . . .

The Captain.

You say that in a tone of resignation I would call cynical. But your whole nature has a cynical bent, my dear Kurt, and therefore, at moments, I might be tempted to share Alice's opinion of you—that you are a hypocrite, a hypocrite of the first rank.

Kurt.

(Calmly.) Is that Alice's opinion?

Alice.

(To Kurt.) It was once. But it isn't any longer, for to bear what you have borne takes sheer heroism, or—something else.

The Captain.

I think the discussion may now be considered closed. Go and say goodbye to Allan, Kurt. He's taking the next boat.

Kurt.

(Rising.) So soon? . . . Ah, well, I've been through worse.

The Captain.

Yes, you say that so often that I begin to wonder what you were up to in America.

Kurt.

Up to? I was just dogged by misfortune. And it is the indisputable right of every human being to meet with misfortune.

The Captain.

(*Sharply.*) There are self-induced misfortunes. Was it that kind?

Kurt.

Isn't that a question of conscience?

The Captain.

(*Shortly.*) Have you got a conscience?

Kurt.

There are wolves and there are sheep. It's no honour to a man to be a sheep; but I'd rather be that than a wolf.

The Captain.

Don't you know the old truth that everyone shapes his own destiny?

Kurt.

Is it a truth?

The Captain.

And don't you know that it's one's own strength . . .

Kurt.

Yes, I do know that, since the night when your own strength betrayed you, so you were prostrate on the floor.

The Captain.

(*Raising his voice.*) A deserving man like yours truly— yes, look at me. I have striven for fifty years against a whole world; but I have in the end won the games through perseverance, attention to duty, energy, and—integrity.

Alice.

You should let others say that.

The Captain.

Others don't, because they're jealous. However! . . . We're expecting visitors here. . . . Today my daughter, Judith, is to meet her fiancé. . . . Where is Judith?

Alice.

She's out.

The Captain.

In the rain? Send for her!

Kurt.

Perhaps I might go now?

The Captain.

No, you stay! . . . Is Judith dressed? Respectably?

Alice.

Yes, she'll do. . . . Has the Colonel said for certain that he's coming?

The Captain.

(*Rising.*) Yes—that's to say, he's going to arrive and take us by surprise as it were. I'm expecting his telegram at any moment. (*Going, right.*) Back soon.

(*Exit The Captain.*)

Alice.

There you have the man. Is he human?

Kurt.

When you asked me that before, I said he wasn't. Now I believe him to be one of the commonest types that possess the earth. . . . Perhaps we're a bit like that ourselves. Profiting by other people, opportunists.

Alice.

He has eaten you and yours alive. . . . And you defend him?

Kurt.

I've been through worse. . . . But this man-eater has left my soul untouched—that he could not devour.

Alice.

What is this "worse" you've been through?

Kurt.

You ask that?

Alice.

Are you being rude?

Kurt.

No, I don't want to be—never ask that again.

(*Enter The Captain, right.*)

The Captain.

The telegram was there already. Read it please, Alice— my sight is so bad. (*Sits down heavily in the easy chair.*) Read it! You needn't go, Kurt.

(*Having read it quickly to herself, shows consternation.*)

Alice.

Well? Aren't you pleased?

(*Alice stares at The Captain.*)

(*Ironically.*) Who's it from?

Alice.

It's from the Colonel.

The Captain.

(*Delighted.*) You don't say so! . . . Well, what does he say?

Alice.

He says: "In view of Miss Judith's impertinent telephone message, I regard our relations as broken off—for good."
(*She stares at The Captain.*)

The Captain.

Once more if you please.

Alice.

(*Reading loudly.*) "In view of Miss Judith's impertinent telephone message, I regard our relations broken off—off for good."

The Captain.

(*Turning pale.*) This is Judith!

Alice.

And here is Holofernes.

The Captain.

What are you then?

Alice.

You will soon see.

The Captain.

This is your doing.

Alice.

No.

The Captain.

(*Furiously.*) This is your doing.

Alice.

No.

(*The Captain tries to rise and draw his sword, but has a stroke and falls back into his chair.*)

Now you've got what you deserve.

The Captain.

(*Whimpering senilely.*) Don't be angry with me. I'm very ill.

Alice.

Are you? I'm glad to hear it.

Kurt.

Let's carry him to bed.

Alice.

No, I won't touch him.

(*She rings the bell.*)

The Captain.

(*As before.*) Don't be angry with me. (*To Kurt.*) Look after my children!

Kurt.

That's rich. I'm to provide for his children, when he has stolen mine.

Alice.

What self-deception!

The Captain.

Look after my children!

(*He continues to babble incoherently.*)

Alice.

At last that tongue is stayed. It can brag no more, lie no more, wound no more. . . . You, Kurt, who believe in God, thank Him for me. Thank Him for freeing me from the tower, from the wolf, from the vampire.

Kurt.

Don't, Alice!

Alice.

(*In The Captain's face.*) Where's your own strength now. eh? And your energy?

(*The Captain, speechless, spits in her face.*)

If you can still spit venom, viper, I'll tear the tongue out of your throat.

(*She gives him a blow on the ear.*)

The head is off. . . . O Judith, glorious girl, whom I bore like vengeance beneath my heart, you, you have set us free—all of us! If you have any more heads, hydra, we'll take them too!

(*She pulls his beard.*)

So there is justice on earth after all! Sometimes I've dreamt of it, but I've never believed it. Kurt, ask God to forgive me for having misjudged Him. Oh, justice does exist! Now I'll become a sheep too. Tell Him that, Kurt. A little good fortune makes us better; it's misfortune that turns us into wolves.

(*Enter The Lieutenant, back.*)

The Captain has had a stroke. Please help us wheel the chair out.

§The Lieutenant.

Madam . . . §

Alice.

What is it?

§The Lieutenant.

Well, Miss Judith . . . §

Alice.

Help us here first. You can talk about Judith afterwards.

(*The Lieutenant wheels the chair out, right.*)

Out with the carcass! Out with it and throw everything open! The place must be aired.

(*She throws open the French windows. Outside it has cleared.*)

Ah!

Kurt.

Are you going to abandon him?

Alice.

A ship that has foundered is abandoned, and the crew saves itself. There's no need for me to lay out a decaying animal. Skinners or scavengers can look after him. A garden plot is too nice a place to receive that barrow-load of filth. . . . Now I'm going to bathe myself—to wash off all this dirt, if I can ever be clean again.

Scenes Classified by Number and Characters

(Letters in brackets indicate general classifications of types of plays: Drama [D], Comedy [C], Comedy-Drama [C-D].)

Scenes for One Man and One Woman—

After the Fall [D]; Quentin, Maggie—412, 421, 428, 433
Apple Cart, The [C]; Orinthia, Magnus—248
As You Like It [C]; Rosalind, Orlando—40
Candida [C]; Prosperine, Marchbanks—272
Changeling, The [D]; Beatrice, De Flores—480, 486
Dance of Death, The [D]; Judith, Allan—34
Day by the Sea, A [D] Matty, Doctor—240
Frances, Julian—383, 388, 394
Duchess of Malfi, The [D]; Duchess Antonio, Cariola—365
Entertaining Mr. Sloane [C]; Kath, Sloane—468, 474
Ghosts [D]; Manders, Mrs. Alving—285
Hatful of Rain, A [D]; Celia, Polo—75
London Assurance [C]; Young Courtly, Grace—557
Measure for Measure [C-D]; Angelo, Isabella, Lucio, Provost—453, 461
Night of the Iguana, The [D]; Hannah, Shannon—340
Petrified Forest, The [D]; Gabby, Squier—56
Resounding Tinkle, A [C]; Middie, Bro—145
Rose Tattoo, The [C-D]; Jack, Rosa—47, 50
School for Scandal, The [C]; Sir Peter, Lady Teazle—321
School for Wives, The [C]; Arnolphe, Agnes—571, 580

Show-Off, The [C-D] Clara, Aubrey—231
Silver Cord, The [D]; Robert, Hester—296
Mrs. Phelps, David—307
Taming of the Shrew, The [C]; Katherine, Petruchio—280
'Tis Pity She's a Whore [D]; Annabell, Friar—326
Annabella, Giovanni, Putana—440, 446, 448

Scenes for Two Women—

Conscious Lovers, The [C]; Isabella, Indiana—170
Hippolytus [D]; Nurse, Phaedra—372
Look Back in Anger [D]; Alison, Helena—162
Man of Mode, The, or Sir Fopling Flutter [C]; Mrs. Loveit, Bellinda, Pert—267
Night of the Iguana, The [D]; Maxine, Hannah—335
Orestes [D]; Helen, Electra—263
Relapse, The: Or, Virtue in Danger [C]; Amanda, Berinthia—562
Show-Off, The [C-D] Clara, Mrs. Fisher—399, 408
Two Gentlemen of Verona, The [C]; Julia, Lucetta—27
Uncle Vania [D]; Yeliena, Sonia—539
View from the Bridge, A [D]; Beatrice, Catherine—235
Walker, London [C]; Sarah, Mrs. Golightly—245

Scenes for Two Men—

Bacchae, The [D]; Pentheus, Dionysos—493, 499, 504

653

PLAYWRIGHTS AND PLAYS—a listing of the major plays by writers included in *Great Scenes from the World Theater*. (Note: The dates which follow the titles of the plays indicate the years of first performances.)

Jean Anouilh (1910–   )—The Traveler Without Baggage (1937), Thieves' Carnival (Bal de Voleurs, 1938), Antigone (1944), Euridice (Legend for Lovers), Ring Round the Moon (L'Invitation au Château, 1947), Mlle. Colombe (1950), Time Remembered (Léocadia, 1950), The Lark (1953), The Waltz of the Toreadors (1952).

Sir James M. Barrie (1860–1937)—Walker, London (1892) The Little Minister (1897), Quality Street (1901), The Admirable Crichton (1902), Peter Pan (1904), Alice Sit-by-the-Fire (1905), What Every Woman Knows (1908), The Twelve-Pound Look (1910), Dear Brutus (1917), Mary Rose (1920).

Bridget Boland (1913–   )—The Prisoner (1954).

Dion Boucicault (1820?–1890)—London Assurance (1841), The Corsican Brothers (1848), The Colleen Bawn (1860), Arrahna-Pogue (1864), The Shaughraun (1875).

Anton Chekhov (1860–1904)—Ivanov (1887), The Seagull (1896), Uncle Vanya (1897), The Three Sisters (1901), The Cherry Orchard (1904).

Mart Crowley (1935–   )—The Boys in the Band (1968).

Sir George Etherege (1634?–1692?)—The Comical Revenge (1664). She Would If She Could (1668), The Man of Mode, or Sir Fopling Flutter (1676).

Euripides (c. 480 B.C.–406? B.C.)—Alcestis (438), Medea (431), The Heracleidae (c. 428), Hippolytus (428), The Trojan Women (415), Electra (413), Helena (412), Iphigenia in Tauris (412), The Phoenician Women (c. 409), Orestes (408), The Bacchae (c. 405).

John Ford (1586?–c.1650,)—The Lover's Melancholy (1629), 'Tis Pity She's a Whore (1633), The Broken Heart (1633), Perkin Warbeck (1634).

Michael Gazzo (1923–   )—A Hatful of Rain (1955), The Night Circus (1958).

Oliver Goldsmith (1730?–1774)—The Good-natur'd Man (1768), She Stoops to Conquer (1773).

Christopher Hampton (1946–   )—When Did You Last See My Mother? (1967), Total Eclipse (1969), Etruscan Survival (1970).

Sidney Howard (1891–1939)—Swords (1921), They Knew What They Wanted (1924,) Pulitzer Prize (1925), Lucky Sam McCarver (1925), Ned McCobb's Daughter (1926), The Silver Cord (1926), Salvation (with Charles MacArthur, 1928), The Late Christopher Bean (1932), Alien Corn (1933), Yellow Jack (1934), Dodsworth (with Sinclair Lewis, 1934), Paths of Glory (with Humphrey Cobb, 1935), The Ghost of Yankee Doodle (1937).

N. C. Hunter (1908–   )—Waters of the Moon (1951), A Day by the Sea (1953), A Touch of the Sun (1958), The Tulip Tree (1963).

Henrik Ibsen (1828–1906)—Brand (1865), Peer Gynt (1867), The League

655

of Youth (1869), Emperor and Galilean (1873), Pillars of Society (1877), A Doll's House (1879), Ghosts (1881), An Enemy of the People (1882), The Wild Duck (1884), Rosmersholm (1886), The Lady from the Sea (1888), Hedda Gabler (1890), The Master Builder 1892), Little Eyolf (1894), John Gabriel Borkman (1896), When We Dead Awaken (1899).

George Kelly (1887–   )—Maggie the Magnificent (1920), The Torch-bearers (1922), The Show-Off (1924), Craig's Wife (1925), Daisy Mayme (1926), Behold the Bridegroom (1927), Philip Goes Forth (1931), The Deep Mrs. Sykes (1945), The Fatal Weakness (1946).

George Lillo (1693?–1739)—Sylvia, or The Country Burial (1730), The London Merchant (1731), Britannia and Batavia (1734), The Christian Hero (1735), Fatal Curiosity (1736), Marina (1738), Elmerick, or Justice Triumphant (1740).

Thomas Middleton (1580–1627)—Michaelmas Terme (1607), A Mad World, My Masters (1608), The Roaring Girle (with Thomas Dekker, 1611), A Fair Quarrel (with William Rowley, 1617), The Changeling (with William Rowley, 1623), A Game of Chesse (1624), A Chaste Maid in Cheapside (c.1613), Women Beware Women (c.1621).

Arthur Miller (1915–   )—All My Sons (N.Y. Critics' Circle Award, 1947), Death of a Salesman (Pulitzer Prize, N.Y. Critics' Circle Award, 1949), The Crucible (1953), A View From the Bridge (1955), After the Fall (1963).

Molière, pseudonym of Jean Baptiste Poquelin (1622–1673)—Les Précieuses ridicules (1659), L'École des femmes (1662), Le Tartuffe (1664), Le Misanthrope (1666), George Dandin (1668), L'Avare (1668), Le Malade imaginaire (1673).

Eugene O'Neill (1888–1953)—Beyond the Horizon (Pulitzer Prize, 1920), The Emperor Jones (1920), Anna Christie (Pulitzer Prize, 1922), Gold (1921), The Hairy Ape (1922), All God's Chillun Got Wings (1924), Desire Under the Elms (1924), The Great God Brown (1926), Lazarus Laughed (1928), Marco Millions (1928), Strange Interlude (Pulitzer Prize, 1928), Ah, Wilderness! (1933), Mourning Becomes Electra (1931), The Iceman Cometh (1946), Long Day's Journey into Night (Pulitzer Prize, N.Y. Critics' Circle Award, 1956), Touch of the Poet (1958).

Joe Orton (1933–1968)—Entertaining Mr. Sloane (1964), Crimes of Passion (1966), Loot (1966), What the Butler Saw (1968).

John Osborne (1929–   )—Look Back in Anger (1956), The Entertainer (1957), Epitaph for George Dillon (1958), The World of Paul Slickey (1959), Luther (1961), The Blood of the Bambergs (1962), Under Plain Cover (1962), Inadmissible Evidence (1964), A Patriot for Me (1965), A Bond Honoured (1966).

William Shakespeare (1564–1616)*—Comedy of Errors (1590), The Two Gentlemen of Verona (1591), Henry VI, parts 1, 2, and 3 (1592), Titus Andronicus (1593), Love's Labour's Lost (1593), Richard II (probably 1594), Midsummer Night's Dream (1595), Richard III (1595), Romeo and Juliet (1596), The Merchant of Venice (1596), King John (1596), Henry IV, parts 1 and 2 (1597), The Taming of the Shrew (1598), Much Ado About Nothing (1598), Henry V (1599), The Merry Wives of Windsor (1599), Julius Caesar (1599), As You Like It (1600), Twelfth Night (1600), Hamlet (1600), All's Well That Ends Well (1602), Troilus and Cressida (1602), Measure for Measure (1604), Othello (1604), King Lear (1605), Timon of Athens (1606), Macbeth

---

*The dating of first productions of Shakespeare's plays, a matter about which scholars sometimes differ, is here based on the chronology established by E. K. Chambers and amended by later editors.

(1606), Antony and Cleopatra (1607), Pericles, Prince of Tyre (1607), Coriolanus (1608), Cymbeline (1609), The Winter's Tale (1611), The Tempest (1611), Henry VIII (possibly not entirely Shakespeare's, 1611).

George Bernard Shaw (1856–1950)—Widowers' Houses (1892), Arms and the Man (1894), Candida (1898), Mrs. Warren's Profession (1902), Caesar and Cleopatra (1898), Man and Superman (1903), John Bull's Other Island (1904), Major Barbara (1905), Fanny's First Play (1911), Pygmalion (1914), Androcles and the Lion (1912), Heartbreak House (1917), Back to Methuselah (1921), Saint Joan (1923), The Apple Cart (1929), On the Rocks (1933), The Millionairess (1936), Geneva (1938).

Richard Brinsley Sheridan (1751–1816)—The Rivals (1775), St. Patrick's Day (1775), The Duenna (1775), A Trip to Scarborough (1777), The School for Scandal (1777), The Critics (1779).

Robert Emmet Sherwood (1896–1955)—The Road to Rome (1927), Reunion in Vienna (1931), The Petrified Forest (1935), Acropolis (1936), Idiot's Delight (1936), Abe Lincoln in Illinois (1938).

N. F. Simpson (1919–   )—The Hole (1958), A Resounding Tinkle (1958), The Cresta Run (1965).

Sir Richard Steele (1672–1729)—The Funeral (1701), The Lying Lover (1703), The Tender Husband (1705), The Conscious Lovers (1722).

John Steinbeck (1902–1968)—Of Mice and Men (1937), The Moon Is Down (1942).

August Strindberg (1849–1912)—The Father (1887), Creditors (1888), Miss Julie (1888), The Stronger (1890), There are Crimes and Crimes 1899), The Dance of Death (1901), Easter (1901), Swanwhite (1901), A Dream Play (1902), The Ghost Sonata (1907), The Great Highway (1909).

John Millington Synge (1871–1909)—In the Shadow of the Glen (1903), Riders to the Sea (1904), The Well of the Saints (1905), The Playboy of the Western World (1907), The Tinker's Wedding (1908), Deirdre of the Sorrows (1910).

David Thomson (1939–   )—The Melting Pot.

Sir John Vanbrugh (1664–1726)—The Relapse (1696), The Provoked Wife (1697), The Confederacy (1705), The Provoked Husband (completed by Colley Cibber, 1728).

John Webster (1580?–1634?)—Westward Ho (with Thomas Dekker, 1603–04), The White Devil (c. 1608), Appius and Virginia (c. 1609), The Duchess of Malfi (c. 1614).

Peter Weiss (1916–   )—Marat/Sade (1964), Die Ermittlung (1965).

Tennessee Williams (1914–   )—The Glass Menagerie (N.Y. Critics' Circle Award, 1945), A Streetcar Named Desire (Pulitzer Prize, N.Y. Critics' Circle Award, 1947), Summer and Smoke (1947), The Rose Tattoo (1950), Camino Real (1952), Cat on a Hot Tin Roof (Pulitzer Prize, N.Y. Critics' Circle Award, 1955), Garden District (1957), Sweet Bird of Youth (1959), The Night of the Iguana (1961), The Milk Train Doesn't Stop Here Any More (1962).

INDEX

659